ESSAYS ON MARX'S THEORY OF VALUE

ISAAK ILYICH RUBIN

Translated by Miloš Samardžija and Fredy Perlman
Text retrieved from marxists.org

Anti-copyright 1923 - 2020
No rights reserved. This book is encouraged to be reprinted and shared and made accessible by any means necessary.

Print ISBN: 978-3-0340-0472-5
A Radical Reprint

PATTERN BOOKS

Table of Contents

Preface and Introduction - 1
I: Marx's Theory of Commodity Fetishism - 57
Chapter 1: Objective Basis of Commodity Fetishism - 62
Chapter 2: The Production Process and its Social Form - 70
Chapter 3: Reification of Production Relations among People and Personification of Things - 79
Chapter 4: Thing and Social Function (Form) - 92
Chapter 5: Production Relations and Material Categories - 109
Chapter 6: Struve on the Theory of Commodity Fetishism - 113
Chapter 7: Marx's Development of the Theory of Fetishism - 120
II: Marx's Labor Theory of Value - 127
Chapter 8: Basic Characteristics of Marx's Theory of Value - 131
Chapter 9: Value as the Regulator of Production - 147
Chapter 10: Equality of Commodity Producers and Equality of Commodities - 155
 Chapter 11: Equality of Commodities and Equality of Labor - 169
Chapter 12: Content and Form of Value - 185
Chapter 13: Social Labor - 207
Chapter 14: Abstract Labor - 215
Chapter 15: Qualified Labor - 253
Chapter 16: Socially-Necessary Labor - 270
Chapter 17: Value and Demand - 286
> I: Value and Demand - 286
> II Value and Proportional Distribution of Labor - 299
> III: Value and Volume of Production - 314
> IV: Demand and Supply Equation - 322

Chapter 18: Value and Production Price - 332
> I: Distribution and Equilibrium of Capital - 334
> II: Distribution of Capital and Distribution of Labor - 331
> III: Production Price - 347
> IV: Labor-Value and Production Price - 366
> V: Historical Foundations of the Labor Theory of Value - 371

Chapter 19: Productive Labor - 377
Appendix - 399
Part 1 - 401
Part 2 - 417

PREFACE

Commodity Fetishism
Fredy Perlman, 1968

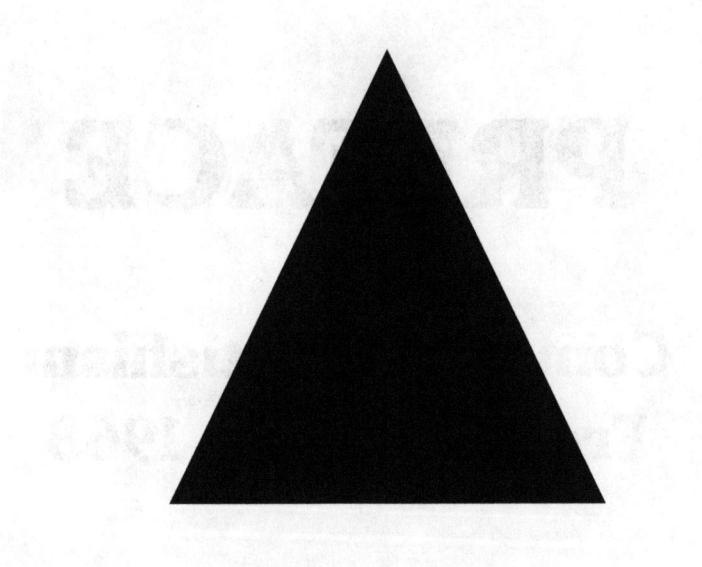

Preface ▲ 3

According to economists whose theories currently prevail in America, economics has replaced political economy, and economics deals with scarcity, prices, and resource allocation. In the definition of Paul Samuelson, "economics - or political economy, as it used to be called ... is the study of how men and society choose, with or without the use of money, to employ scarce productive resources, which could have alternative uses, to produce various commodities over time and distribute them for consumption, now and in the future, among various people and groups in society."[1] According to Robert Campbell, "One of the central preoccupations of economics has always been what determines price."[2] In the words of another expert, "Any community, the primers tell us, has to deal with a pervasive economic problem: how to determine the uses of available resources, including not only goods and services that can be employed productively but also other scarce supplies."[3]

---

[1] Paul A. Samuelson, Economics, An Introductory Analysis, New York: McGraw Hill, 1967, Seventh Edition, p. 1 and p. 5 (Italics by Samuelson). Samuelson's book is the prototype of the textbook currently used in American universities to teach students the principles of economics.

[2] Robert W. Campbell, "Marx, Kantorovich and Novozhilov: Stoimost versus Reality", Slavic Review, October, 1961, pp. 402- 418. Reprinted in Wayne A. Leeman, ed., Capitalism, Market Socialism and Central Planning, Boston: Houghton Mifflin, 1963, pp. 102-118, and also in Harry G. Shaffer, The Soviet Economy, New York: Appleton-Century-Crofts, 1963, pp. 350- 366. Campbell is currently an American Authority on Marxian Economics.

[3] Abram Bergson, The Economics of Soviet Planning, New Haven: Yale University Press, 1964, p. 3. Bergson is director of the Russian Research Center at Harvard University and, like Campbell, he is currently an Authority on Marxian Economics.

If economics is indeed merely a new name for political economy, and if the subject matter which was once covered under the heading of political economy is now covered by economics, then economics has replaced political economy. However, if the subject matter of political economy is not the same as that of economics, then the "replacement" of political economy is actually an omission of a field of knowledge. If economics answers different questions from those raised by political economy, and if the omitted questions refer to the form and the quality of human life within the dominant socialeconomic system, then this omission can be called a "great evasion".[4]

The Soviet economic theorist and historian I.I. Rubin suggested a definition of political economy which has nothing in common with the definitions of economics quoted above. According to Rubin, "Political economy deals with human working activity, not from the standpoint of its technical methods and instruments of labor, but from the standpoint of its social form. It deals with production relations which are established among people in the process of production."[5] In terms of this definition, political economy is not the study of prices or of scarce resources; it is a study of social relations, a study of culture. Political economy asks why the productive

---

[4] After the title of William Appleman Williams' The Great Evasion, Chicago: Quadrangle Books, 1964. Williams vividly describes some of the techniques of the evasion: "The tactics of escape employed in this headlong dash from reality would fill a manual of equivocation, a handbook of hairsplitting, and a guidebook to changing the subject." (p. 18).

[5] I. I. Rubin, Ocherki po teorii stoimosti Marksa, Moskva: Gosudarstvennoe Izdatel'stvo, 3rd edition, 1928, p. 41; present translation, p. 31. Rubin's book was not re-issued in the Soviet Union after 1928, and it has never before been translated. Future page citations in this preface refer to the 1973 Black Rose Books version

forces of society develop within a particular social form, why the machine process unfolds within the context of business enterprise, why industrialization takes the form of capitalist development. Political economy asks how the working activity of people is regulated in a specific, historical form of economy.

The contemporary American definitions of economics quoted earlier clearly deal with different problems, raise different questions, and refer to a different subject matter from that of political economy as defined by Rubin. This means one of two things: (a) either economics and political economy are two different branches of knowledge, in which case the "replacement" of political economy by economics simply means that the American practitioners of one branch have replaced the other branch, or (b) economics is indeed the new name for what "used to be called" political economy; in this case, by defining economics as a study of scarcity, prices, and resource allocation, American economists are saying that the production relations among people are not a legitimate subject for study. In this case the economists quoted above are setting themselves up as the legislators over what is, and what is not, a legitimate topic for intellectual concern; they are defining the limits of American knowledge. This type of intellectual legislation has led to predictable consequences in other societies and at other times: it has led to total ignorance in the excluded field of knowledge, and it has led to large gaps and blind spots in related fields of knowledge.

A justification for the omission of political economy from American knowledge has been given by Samuelson. In the balanced, objective language of an American professor, Samuelson says: "A billion people, one-third of the world's population, blindly regard Das Kapital as economic gospel. And yet, without the disciplined study of economic science, how can anyone form a reasoned opinion about the merits or lack of merits in the classical, traditional economics?[6] If "a billion people" regard Das Kapital "as economic gospel", it is clearly relevant to ask why only a few million Americans regard Samuelson's Economics "as economic gospel". Perhaps a balanced objective answer might be that "a billion people" find little that is relevant or meaningful in Samuelson's celebrations of American capitalism and his exercises in two-dimensional geometry, whereas the few million Americans have no choice but to learn the "merits in the classical, traditional economics". Samuelson's rhetorical question - "And yet, without the disciplined study of economic science, how can anyone form a reasoned opinion about the merits ...' - is clearly a two-edged sword, since it can be asked about any major economic theory, not merely Samuelson's; and it clearly behooves the student to draw his own conclusion and make his own choice after a "disciplined study" of all the major economic theories, not merely Samuelson's.

Although Samuelson, in his introductory textbook, devotes a great deal of attention to Marx, this essay will show that Samuelson's treatment hardly amounts to a "disciplined study" of Marx's political economy. The present essay will outline some of the central themes of Marx's political economy, particularly the themes which are treated in Rubin's Essays on Marx's Theory of Value. Rubin's book is a comprehensive, tightly argued exposition of the core of Marx's work, the theory of commodity fetishism and the theory of value. Rubin clarifies misconceptions which have resulted, and still result, from superficial readings and evasive treatments of Marx's work.

Marx's principal aim was not to study scarcity, or to explain price, or to allocate resources, but to analyze how the working activity of people is regulated in a capitalist economy. The subject of the analysis is a determined social structure, a particular culture, namely commodity-capitalism, a social form of economy in which

---

[6] Samuelson, op. cit., p. 1.

the relations among people are not regulated directly, but through things. Consequently, "the specific character of economic theory as a science which deals with the commodity capitalist economy ties precisely in the fact that it deals with production relations which acquire material forms." (Rubin, p.47).

Marx's central concern was human creative activity, particularly the determinants, the regulators which shape this activity in the capitalist form of economy. Rubin's thorough study makes it clear that this was not merely the central concern of the "young Marx" or of the "old Marx", but that it remained central to Marx in all his theoretical and historical works, which extend over half a century. Rubin shows that this theme gives the unity of a single work to fifty years of research and writing, that this theme is the content of the labor theory of value, and thus that Marx's economic theory can be understood only within the framework of this central theme. Marx's vast opusis not a series of disconnected episodes, each with specific problems which are later abandoned. Consequently, the frequently drawn contrast between an "idealistic young Marx" concerned with the philosophical problems of human existence, and a "realistic old Marx" concerned with technical economic problems,[7] is superficial and misses the essential unity of Marx's entire opus. Rubin shows that the central themes of the "young Marx" were being still further refined in the

---

[7] For example: "Curiously enough, it was the very young Marx (writing in the early 1840's) who developed ideas very much in the mood of other systems of thought that have such great appeal to the mentality of the 1950's and 1960's: psychoanalysis, existentialism, and Zen Buddhism. And contrariwise, the work of the mature Marx, which stressed economic and political analysis, has been less compelling to intellectuals of the advanced Western nations since the end of World War II." Robert Blauner, Alienation and Freedom: The Factory Worker and His Industry, Chicago: University of Chicago Press. 1964, p. 1.

final pages of Marx's last published work; Marx continually sharpened his concepts and frequently changed his terminology, but his concerns were not replaced. Rubin demonstrates this by tracing the central themes of works which Marx wrote in the early 1840's through the third volume of Capital, published by Engels in 1894. In the different periods of his productive life, Marx expressed his concern with human creativity through different, though related, concepts. In his early works, Marx unified his ideas around the concept of "alienation" or "estrangement". Later, when Marx refined his ideas of "reified" or "congealed" labor, the theory of commodity fetishism provided a focus, a unifying framework for his analysis. In Marx's later work, the theory of commodity fetishism, namely the theory of a society in which relations among people take the form of relations among things, the theory of a society in which production relations are reified, becomes Marx's "general theory of production relations of the commodity-capitalist economy". (Rubin, p. 3). Thus Marx's theory of value, the most frequently criticized part of his political economy, can only be understood within the context of the theory of commodity fetishism, or in Rubin's words, the "ground of Marx's theory of value can only be given on the basis of his theory of commodity fetishism, which analyzes the general structure of the commodity economy". (p. 61).

This essay will examine the relationship between the concept of alienation, the theory of commodity fetishism and the theory of value, and it will be shown that the three formulations are approaches to the same problem: the determination of the creative activity of people in the capitalist form of economy. This examination will show that Marx had no interest per se in defining a standard of value, in developing a theory of price isolated from a historically specific mode of production, or in the efficient allocation of resources. Marx's work is a critical analysis of how people are regulated in the capitalist economy; it is not a handbook on how to regulate people and things. The subtitle of

Marx's three volumes of Capital is "Critique of Political Economy", and not "Manual for Efficient Management". This does not mean that Marx did not consider problems of resource allocation important; it means that he did not consider them the central concern of political economy, a science of social relations.

Marx's first approach to the analysis of social relations in capitalist society was through the concept of alienation, or estrangement. Although he adopted the concept from Hegel, already in his earliest works Marx was critical of the content which Hegel gave to the concept. "For Hegel the essence of man - man - equals self-consciousness. All estrangement of the human essence is therefore nothing but estrangement of self-consciousness."[8] For Marx in 1844, Hegel's treatment of consciousness as man's essence is "a hidden and mystifying criticism", but Marx observes that "inasmuch as it grasps steadily man's estrangement, even though man appears only in the shape of mind, there lie concealed in it all the elements of criticism, already prepared and elaborated in a manner often rising far above the Hegelian standpoint."[9] Thus Marx adopts the concept of "estrangement" as a powerful tool for analysis, even though he does not agree with Hegel about what is estranged, namely he does not agree that thinking is the essence of man. For Marx in 1844, man's essence is larger than thought, larger than self-consciousness; it is man's creative activity, his labor, in all its aspects. Marx considers consciousness to be only one aspect of man's creative activity.

Thus, while he concedes that Hegel "grasps labor as the essence of man," he points out that "The only labor which Hegel knows and recognizes is abstractly mental

---

[8] Karl Marx, The Economic and Philosophic Manuscripts of 1844. New York: International Publishers, 1964, p. 178.

[9] Ibid., p. 176. (Italics in original.)

labor"[10] But Hegel does not only define self-consciousness as man's essence; he then proceeds to accommodate himself to alienated, externalized modes of consciousness, namely to religion, philosophy and state power; liege] "confirms this in its alienated shape and passes it off as his true mode of being - reestablishes it, and pretends to be at home in his other-being as such. Thus, for instance, after annulling and superseding religion, after recognizing religion to be a product of self-alienation, he yet finds confirmation of himself in religion as religion. Here is the root of Hegel's false positivism, or of his merely apparent criticism.'[11] However for Marx "There can therefore no longer be any question about an act of accommodation" and lie explains, "If I know religion as alienated human self- consciousness, then what I know in it as religion is not my self- consciousness, but my alienated self-consciousness. .."[12] In other words, even though Hegel formulated the concept of alienation, he was yet able to accommodate himself to religion and state power, namely to alienated forms of existence which negate man's essence even in Hegel's definition (as consciousness).

Thus Marx set himself two tasks: to reshape the concept of alienation, and to redefine man's essence. For this purpose Marx turned to Feuerbach, who completed the first task for him, and who went a long way in providing a provisional solution to the second. The solution to both tasks could be approached if practical, creative activity and the working relations of people with each other, were made the center, the focal point of theory. Only then would it be possible to see that religion, and philosophy as well, are not forms of realization but rather forms of alienation of man's essence. Marx acknowledged his debt: "Feuerbach's great achievement is: (1) The proof that philosophy is nothing else but

---

[10] Ibid., p. 177.

[11] Ibid., p. 184.

[12] Ibid., p. 185.

religion rendered into thought and expounded by thought, hence equally to be condemned as another form and manner of existence of the estrangement of the essence of man; (2) The establishment of true materialism and of real science, since Feuerbach also makes the social relationship 'of man to man' the basic principle of the theory ..."[13]

Marx acknowledged Feuerbach's role in reshaping the concept of alienation, namely in grasping religion and philosophy as alienations of the essence of man. However, a year later, in his Theses on Feuerbach of 1845, Marx expresses dissatisfaction with Feuerbach's grasp of the human essence. "Feuerbach resolves the essence of religion into the essence of man", but for Feuerbach the essence of man remains something isolated, unhistorical, and therefore abstract. For Marx, "the essence of man is not an abstraction inherent in each particular individual. The real nature of man is the totality of social relations."[14] Marx generalizes his dissatisfaction with Feuerbach: "The chief defect of all previous materialism (including that of Feuerbach) is that things, reality, the sensible world, are conceived only in the form of objects of observation, but not as human sense activity, not as practical activity ..."[15] Marx makes this charge more specific in a later work, where he says that Feuerbach "still remains in the realm of theory and conceives of men not in their given social connection, not under their existing conditions of life, which have made them what they are", and therefore "he never arrives at the really existing active men, but stops at the abstraction 'man' . . . he knows no other 'human relationships' 'of man to man' than love and friendship, and even then idealized ... Thus he never manages to

---

[13] Ibid., p. 172.

[14] Karl Marx, Theses on Feuerbach, in T.B. Bottomore and Maximillien Rubel, editors, Karl Marx, Selected Writings in Sociology and Social Philosophy, New York: McGraw Hill, 1964, p. 68.

[15] Ibid., p. 67.

conceive the sensuous world as the total living sensuous activity of the individuals composing it."[16]

Marx is able to reject Feuerbach's definition of man as an abstraction because, already in an early essay on "Free Human Production", Marx had started to view man in far more concrete terms, namely he had already started to view the world of objects as a world of practical human activity, creative activity. In this early essay, written in 1844, Marx's conception of man is still unhistorical; he did not explicitly reject this unhistorical view until he wrote The German Ideology with Engels in 1845-46, and the Poverty of Philosophy in 1847.

However, this early essay already brings human creative activity into focus, and thus it also points to the "essence" which is alienated in capitalist society. Marx asks the reader to imagine human beings outside of capitalist society, namely outside of history: "Suppose we had produced things as human beings: in his production each of us would have twice affirmed himself and the other. (1) In my production I would have objectified my individuality and its particularity, and in the course of the activity I would have enjoyed an individual life; in viewing the object I would have experienced the individual joy of knowing my personality as an objective, sensuously perceptible, and indubitable power. (2) In your satisfaction and your use of my product I would have had the direct and conscious satisfaction that my work satisfied a human need, that it objectified human nature, and that it created an object appropriate to the need of another human being ... Our productions would be so many mirrors reflecting our nature ... My labor would be a

---

[16] Karl Marx and Frederick Engels, The German Ideology, Moscow: Progress Publishers, 1964, pp. 58-59.

free manifestation of life and an enjoyment of life."[17] It is precisely this labor, this free production, this free manifestation and enjoyment of life, which is alienated in capitalist society: "Under the presupposition of private property my labor is an externalization of life because I work in order to live and provide for myself the means of living. Working is not living." At this point Marx vividly contrasts the idea of free, unalienated labor, with the alienated wage-labor he calls it forced labor - of capitalist society: "Under the presupposition of private property my individuality is externalized to the point where I hate this activity and where it is a torment for me. Rather it is then only the semblance of an activity, only a forced activity, imposed upon me only by external and accidental necessity and not by an internal and determined necessity ... My labor, therefore, is manifested as the objective, sensuous, perceptible, and indubitable expression of my self loss and my powerlessness."[18]

Thus Marx is led to a contrast between an unalienated, ideal, unhistorical man, and the alienated man of capitalist society. From here, we might follow Rubin and show the relationship of this contrast between the ideal and the actual to the later contrast between productive forces and relations of production. The later contrast becomes the basis for Marx's theory of commodity fetishism, and thus for his theory of value. However, before returning to Rubin's exposition, we will digress slightly to examine two types of interpretation which have recently been made of Marx's early works. One holds that Marx's theory of alienation can be accepted and applied without his critique of capitalism, and the other holds that the writings of 1844 contain the quintessence of Marx's thought and that the later works are merely reformulations of the same insights.

---

[17] From "Excerpt-Notes of 1844" in Writings of the Young Marx on Philosophy and Society, translated and edited by Loyd D. Easton and Kurt H. Guddat, Garden City: Anchor Books, 1967, p. 28 1. (italics in original)

[18] Ibid., p. 281-282.

The sociologist Robert Blauner reduces alienation to "a quality of personal experience which results from specific kinds of social arrangements."[19] On the basis of this reduction Blauner says that "Today, most social scientists would say that alienation is not a consequence of capitalism per se but of employment in the large-scale organizations and impersonal bureaucracies that pervade all industrial societies."[20] In other words, Blauner defines alienation as a psychological, personal experience, as something which the worker feels, and which is consequently in the mind of the worker and is not a structural feature of capitalist society. For Blauner to say that alienation so defined "is not a consequence of capitalism" is then a tautology. It is Blauner's very definition which makes it possible for him to treat alienation as a consequence of industry (namely the productive forces) and not as a consequence of capitalism (namely the social relations).

However, regardless of what "most social scientists would say," in Marx's work alienation is related to the structure of capitalist society, and not to the personal experience of the worker. It is the very nature of wage-labor, the basic social relation of capitalist society, which accounts for alienation: "The following elements are contained in wage-labor: (1) the chance relationship and alienation of labor from the laboring subject; (2) the chance relationship and alienation of labor from its object; (3) the determination of the laborer through social needs which are an alien compulsion to him, a compulsion to which he submits out of egoistic need and distress - these social needs are merely a source of providing the necessities of life for him, just as he is merely a slave for them; (4) the maintenance of his individual existence appears to the worker as the goal of his activity and his real action is only a means; he lives to

---

[19] Blauner, Alienation and Freedom: The Factory Worker and his Industry, p. 15.

[20] Ibid., p. 3

acquire the means of living."[21] In fact, Marx very explicitly located alienation at the very root of capitalist society: "To say that man alienates himself is the same as saying that the society of this alienated man is the caricature of his actual common life, of his true generic life. His activity, therefore, appears as torment, his own creation as a force alien to him, his wealth as poverty, the essential bond connecting him with other men as something unessential so that the separation from other men appears as his true existence." Marx adds that this capitalist society, this caricature of a human community, is the only form of society which capitalist economists are able to imagine: "Society, says Adam Smith, is a commercial enterprise. Each of its members is a merchant. It is evident that political economy establishes an alienated form of social intercourse as the essential, original, and definitive human form."[22]

In the Economic and Philosophic Manuscripts of 1844, Marx applies Feuerbach's concept of man's alienation of himself in religion, to man's alienation of himself in the product of his labor. The following passage comes very close to describing the world of commodities as a world of fetishes which regulate and dominate human life: "The more the worker expends himself in his work, the more powerful becomes the world of objects which he creates in face of himself, and the poorer he himself becomes in his inner life, the less he belongs to himself. It is just the same as in religion. The more of himself man attributes to God, the less he has left in himself. The worker puts his life into the object, and his life then belongs no longer to him but to the object. The greater his activity, therefore, the less he possesses ... The alienation of the worker in his product means not only that his labour becomes an object, takes on its own existence, but that it exists outside him, independently and alien to him,

---

[21] From "Excerpt-Notes of 1844," loc. cit., p. 275-276.

[22] Ibid., p. 272.

and that it stands opposed to him as an autonomous power.

The life which he has given to the object sets itself against him as an alien and hostile force."[23] In the same work, Marx comes very close to defining the product of labor as congealed labor, or reified labor, a formulation which is to reappear more than twenty years later in his theory of commodity fetishism: "The object produced by labour, its product, now stands opposed to it as an alien being, as a power independent of the producer. The product of labour is labour which has been embodied in an object, and turned into a physical thing; this product is an objectification of labour." The labor which is lost by the worker is appropriated by the capitalist: " ... the alienated character of work for the worker appears in the fact that it is not his work but work for someone else, that in work he does not belong to himself but to another person."[24] The result of this alienation of the worker's creative power is vividly described by Marx in a passage that summarizes the qualitative aspect of his theory of exploitation: "The less you are, the less you express your own life, the greater is your alienated life, the more you have, the greater is the store of your estranged being. Everything which the political economist takes from you in life and in humanity, he replaces for you in money and in wealth ..."[25] The producer alienates his creative power, in fact he sells it to the capitalist, and what he gets in exchange is different in kind from that creative power; in exchange for the creative power he gets things, and the less he is, as a creative human being, the more things he has.

---

[23] Bottomore and Rubel, eds., op. cit., p. 170.

[24] Ibid., p. 171 and 170.

[25] Karl Marx, Economic and Philosophic Manuscripts of 1844, New York: International Publishers, 1964, p. 150.

These formulations make it clear that, for Marx, alienation is inherent in the social relations of capitalist society, a society in which one class appropriates the labor which another class alienates; for Marx, wage-labor is, by definition, alienated labor. In terms of this definition of alienated labor, the statement that "alienation is not a consequence of capitalism" is meaningless.

The Yugoslav philosopher Veljko Korac has presented the theory of alienation formulated by Marx in 1844 as the final form of Marx's theory and Korac summarized this theory as follows: "Establishing through critical analysis man's alienation from man, from the product of his labor, even from his own human activity, Marx raised the question of abolishing all these forms of dehumanization, and the possibility of restoring human society."[26] In 1844 Marx did indeed speak of "rehabilitating" (if not exactly of "restoring") "human society": "Communism ... is hence the actual phase necessary for the next stage of historical development in the process of human emancipation and rehabilitation. Communism is the necessary pattern and the dynamic principle of the immediate future, but communism as such is not the goal of human development - which goal is the structure of human society."[27] In some passages of the Economic and Philosophic Manuscripts, Marx even spoke of communism as a return of human nature: "Communism is the positive abolition of private property, of human self-alienation, and thus, the real appropriation of human nature, through and for man. It is therefore the return of man himself as a social, that is, really human, being, a complete and conscious return which assimilates all the wealth of previous development. Communism as a complete naturalism is humanism, and as a complete humanism is naturalism ... The positive abolition of

---

[26] Veljko Korac, "In Search of Human Society," in Erich Fromm, editor, Socialist Humanism, Garden City: Anchor Books, 1966, p. 6. (Italics in original.)

[27] Marx, Economic and Philosophic Manuscripts of 1844, p. 146.

private property, as the appropriation of human life, is thus the positive abolition of all alienation, and thus the return of man from religion, the family, the State, etc., to his human, i.e., social life."[28] In 1844, Marx had also defined the agent, the social class, which would carry through this reappropriation of man's creative power, this return of man's human essence; it would be "a class with radical chains, a class in civil society that is not of civil society, a class that is the dissolution of all classes, a sphere of society having a universal character because of its universal suffering and claiming no particular right because no particular wrong but unqualified wrong is perpetrated on it; a sphere that can invoke no traditional title but only a human title ..."[29] Marx even described some of the social relations of an unalienated, human society: "Assume man to be man and his relationship to the world to be a human one: then you can exchange love only for love, trust for trust, etc. If you want to enjoy art, you must be an artistically cultivated person ..."[30]

Thus there is no doubt that in 1844, Marx spoke of a human society and a human essence which could be rehabilitated, returned, or restored. However, powerful and suggestive though these passages are, they cannot be viewed as the final formulation of Marx's social and economic theory, nor can Marx's later works be treated as mere re-statements of the same ideas. Erich Fromm is aware of this when he writes: "In his earlier writings Marx still called 'human nature in general' the 'essence of man.' He later gave up this term because he wanted to make it clear that 'the essence of man is no abstraction ... Marx also wanted to avoid giving the impression that he thought of the essence of man as an unhistorical

---

[28] Bottomore and Rubel, eds., op. cit., pp. 243-244

[29] Easton and Guddat, Writings of the Young Marx on Philosophy and Society, pp. 262-263.

[30] Marx, Economic and Philosophic Manuscripts, p. 169.

substance."[31] Fromm is also aware that Marx's concept of alienation, "although not the word, remains of central significance throughout his whole later main work, including The Capital."[32] Fromm does not, however, examine the stages which led from the concept of alienation to the theory of commodity fetishism, and in Fromm's own philosophical framework, the central problem is "to cease being asleep and

to become human". For Fromm this involves primarily changing one's ideas and one's methods of thinking: "I believe that one of the most disastrous mistakes in individual and social life consists in being caught in stereotyped alternatives of thinking

... I believe that man must get rid of illusions that enslave and paralyze him, that he must become aware of the reality inside and outside of him in order to create a world which needs no illusions. Freedom and independence can be achieved only when the chains of illusion are broken."[33]

In the Preface to The German Ideology, Marx ridicules would-be revolutionaries who want to free men from stereotyped alternatives of thinking, from the illusions that enslave and paralyze men. Marx has these revolutionaries announce: "Let us liberate them from the chimeras, the ideas, dogmas, imaginary beings under the yoke of which they are pining away. Let us revolt against the rule of thoughts. Let us teach men, says one, to exchange these imaginations for thoughts which correspond to the essence of man; says the second, to take up a critical attitude to them; says the third, to knock them out of their heads; and existing reality will collapse." Then Marx draws the ridicule to its conclusion: "Once

---

[31] Erich Fromm, Beyond the Chains of Illusion, New York: Pocket Books, Inc., 1962, p. 32.

[32] Ibid., p. 49.

[33] Ibid., pp. 196-197.

upon a time a valiant fellow had the idea that men were drowned in water only because they were possessed with the idea of gravity. If they were to knock this notion out of their heads, say by stating it to be a superstition, a religious concept, they would be sublimely proof against any danger from water."[34] In a letter written at the end of 1846, Marx turned the same critique against P.J. Proudhon: "... in place of the practical and violent action of the masses ... Monsieur Proudhon supplies the whimsical motion of his own head. So it is the men of learning that make history, the men who know how to purloin God's secret thoughts. The common people have only to apply their revelations. You will now understand why M. Proudhon is the declared enemy of every political movement. The solution of present problems does not lie for him in public action but in the dialectical rotations of his own mind."[35]

Between 1845 and 1847, Marx also abandons his earlier conception of a human essence or a human nature to which man can return: "As individuals express their life, so they are. What they are, therefore, coincides with their production, both with what they produce and with how they produce. The nature of individuals thus depends on the material conditions determining their production."[36] In fact, Marx goes on to say that man's ideas of his nature or his essence are themselves conditioned by the material conditions in which men find themselves, and therefore man's "essence" is not something to which he can return, or even something which he can conceive in thought, since it is constantly in a process of historical change. "Men are the producers of their conceptions, ideas, etc. - real, active men, as they are conditioned by a definite development of their

---

[34] Marx and Engels, The German Ideology, p. 23-24

[35] Letter of Marx to P.V. Annenkov. December 28, 1846, in Karl Marx, The Poverty of Philosophy, New York: International Publishers, 1963. p. 191.

[36] Marx and Engels, The German Ideology, p. 32.

productive forces and of the intercourse corresponding to these ... Consciousness can never be anything else than conscious existence, and the existence of men is their actual-life process." Consequently, "we do not set out from what men say, imagine, conceive, nor from men as narrated, thought of, imagined, conceived, in order to arrive at men in the flesh. We set out from real, active men, and on the basis of their real life-process we demonstrate the development of the ideological reflexes and echoes of this life-process."[37] Thus unlike the philosopher we quoted earlier, Marx no longer begins his analysis with "Marx's concept of Man"; he begins with man in a given cultural environment. Marx systematized the relationship between technology, social relations and ideas in The Poverty of Philosophy in 1847: "In acquiring new productive forces men change their mode of production, and in changing their mode of production ... they change all their social relations. The handmill gives you society with the feudal lord; the steammill, society with the industrial capitalist. The same men who establish their social relations in conformity with their material productivity, produce also principles, ideas and categories, in conformity with their social relations."[38] The next step is to pull man's "essence" into history, namely to say that man has no essence apart from his historical existence, and this is precisely what Marx does when he says that the "sum of productive forces, capital funds and social forms of intercourse, which every individual and generation finds in existence as something given, is the real basis of what the philosophers have conceived as 'substance' and 'essence of man' ..."[39]

Here Marx's contrast between an ideal, unalienated society, and the real capitalist society, has come to an end. Man creates the material conditions in which he lives, not in terms of an ideal society which he

---

[37] Ibid., p. 37.

[38] Marx, The Poverty of Philosophy, p. 109.

[39] Marx and Engels, The German Ideology, p. 50.

can "restore", but in terms of the possibilities and the limits of the productive forces which he inherits. Marx defines these historical limits and possibilities in the letter from which we quoted earlier: "... men are not free to choose their productive forces - which are the basis of all their history - for every productive force is an acquired force, the product of former activity. The productive forces are therefore the result of practical human energy; but this energy is itself conditioned by the circumstances in which men find themselves, by the productive forces already acquired, by the social form which exists before they do, which they do not create, which is the product of the preceding generation.

Because of this . . . a history of humanity takes shape which is all the more a history of humanity as the productive forces of man and therefore his social relations have been more developed."[40] "... People won freedom for themselves each time to the extent that was dictated and permitted not by their ideal of man, but by the existing productive forces."[41]

Marx has resolved man's essence into the historical conditions in which man exists, and thus he has been led to abandon the conflict between the alienated man of capitalist society and his unalienated human essence. However, Rubin points out that over a decade later, in 1859, the conflict reappears on a new plane, no longer in the form of a conflict between ideal and reality, but as a conflict between productive forces and social relations which are both parts of reality: "At a certain stage of their development, the material forces of production in society come into conflict with the existing relations of production ...

---

[40] Letter of Marx to Annenkov, loc. cit., p. 181.

[41] Marx and Engels, The German Ideology, p. 475.

From forms of development of the forces of production these relations turn into their fetters. Then comes the period of social revolution."⁴²

Having pointed to the relations of production, namely the social relations among people in the process of production, as the framework within which man's productive forces, his technology, develop, and as fetters which may obstruct the further development of technology, Marx now turns to a detailed characterization of the relations of production of capitalist society. And having abandoned the study of man's essence for the study of man's historical situation, Marx also abandons

---

⁴² Karl Marx, A Contribution to the Critique of Political Economy, Chicago: Charles H. Kerr & Co., 1904, p. 12. It is interesting to note that at this point, Marx begins to develop a general theory of cultural development and cultural change, or what the anthropologist Leslie White has called a "science of culture." (See Leslie A. White, The Science of Culture, New York: Grove Press, 1949.) The paragraph which contains the passage quoted above also contains the following formulation: "Just as our opinion of an individual is not based on what he thinks of himself, so can we not judge of such a period of transformation by its own consciousness; on the contrary, this consciousness must rather be explained from the contradictions of material life, from the existing conflict between the material forces of production and the relations of production. No social order ever disappears before all the productive forces, for which there is room in it, have been developed; and new higher relations of production never appear before the material conditions of their existence have matured in the womb of the old society. Therefore, mankind always takes up only such problems as it can solve; since, looking at the matter more closely, we will always find that the problem itself arises only when the material conditions necessary for its solution already exist or are at least in the process of formation." (pp. 12-13.)

the word "alienation", since the earlier use of the word has made it an abbreviated expression for "man's alienation from his essence". Already in The German Ideology, Marx had referred sarcastically to the word "estrangement" (or alienation) as "a term which will be comprehensible to the philosophers ",[43] implying that it was no longer an acceptable term to Marx. However, even though he abandons the word, Marx continues to develop the content which he had expressed with the word, and this further development takes Marx far beyond his early formulations, and just as far beyond the theorists who think the concept of alienation was fully developed and completed in the Economic and Philosophical Manuscripts of 1844. Rubin shows that this further development of the concept of alienation takes place precisely in the theory of commodity fetishism and the theory of value, and so I will now turn to Rubin's exposition of these theories and will attempt to make explicit their connections with the concept of alienation.[44]

Rubin outlines Marx's transition from the concept of alienation to the theory of commodity fetishism in the following terms: "In order to transform the theory of 'alienation' of human relations into a theory of 'reification' of social relations (i.e., into the theory of commodity fetishism), Marx had to create a path from utopian to scientific socialism, from negating reality in

---

[43] Marx and Engels, The German Ideology, p. 46.

[44] C. Wright Mills did not see the connection between the concept of alienation and Marx's later work, namely the three volumes of Capital, and consequently Mills reduced the question of alienation to "the question of the attitude of men toward the work they do." As a result, Mills was disappointed with Marx on this score: "to say the least, the condition in which Marx left the conception of alienation is quite incomplete, and brilliantly ambiguous." (C. Wright Mills, The Marxists, New York: Dell Publishing Co., 1962, p. 112.)

the name of an ideal to seeking within reality itself the forces for further development and motion." (Rubin, p. 57). The link between alienation and commodity fetishism is the concept of 'reification' (materialization or objectification) of social relations. Rubin traces certain stages in Marx's formulation of the concept of reification. In the Contribution to the Critique of Political Economy of 1859, Marx noted that in capitalist society, where labor creates commodities, "the social relations of men appear in the reversed form of a social relation of things."[45] In this work, social relations among people merely "appear" to take the form of things, they merely seem to be reified.

Consequently, Marx calls this reification a "mystification", and he attributes it to "the habit of everyday life".[46]

However, in Volume I of Capital, this reification of social relations is no longer merely an appearance in the mind of the individual commodity producer, and it is no longer a result of the commodity producer's thinking habits. Here, "the materialization of production relations does not arise from 'habits' but from the internal structure of the commodity economy. Fetishism is not only a phenomenon of social consciousness, but of social being." (Rubin, p. 59). The cause of the fetishism, namely the cause of the fact that relations among people lake the form of relations among things, is to be found in the characteristics of capitalist economy as a commodity economy: "The absence of direct regulation of the social process of production necessarily leads to the indirect regulation of the production process through the market, through the products of labor, through things." (Ibid.).

Consequently, the reification of social relations and the fetishism of commodities are not "chains of

---

[45] Marx, A Contribution to the Critique of Political Economy, p. 30.

[46] Ibid.

illusion" which can be "broken" within the context of capitalist society, because they do not arise from "stereotyped alternatives of thinking" (Erich Fromm). The capitalist form of social production "necessarily leads" to the reification of social relations; reification is not only a "consequence" of capitalism; it is an inseparable aspect of capitalism. Concrete, unalienated labor which is a creative expression of an individual's personality, cannot take place within the production process of capitalist society. The labor which produces commodities, namely things for sale on the market, is not concrete but abstract labor, "abstractly-general, social labor which arises from the complete alienation of individual labor" (Rubin, p. 147). In the commodity economy labor is not creative activity; it is the expenditure of labor-time, of labor-power, of homogeneous human labor, or labor in general. Nor is this the case at all times and in all places. "Only on the basis of commodity production, characterized by a wide development of exchange, a mass transfer of individuals from one activity to another, and indifference of individuals towards the concrete form of labor, is it possible to develop the homogeneous character of all working operations as forms of human labor in general" (Rubin, p. 138). In capitalist society, this labor-power which produces commodities is itself a commodity: it is a thing which is bought by the capitalist from the worker, or as Paul Samuelson puts it: "A man is much more than a commodity. Yet it is true that men do rent out their services for a price."[47] Thus labor in capitalist society is reified labor; it is labor turned into a thing.

The reified labor of capitalist society, the abstract, homogeneous labor-power which is bought by the capitalist for a price, is crystallized, congealed in commodities which are appropriated by the capitalist and sold on the market. The laborer literally alienates, estranges his creative power, he sells it. Since creative

---

[47] Samuelson, Economics, p. 542.

power refers to an individual's conscious participation in the shaping of his material environment, since the power to decide is at the root of creation, it would be more accurate to say that creative power simply does not exist for the hired worker in capitalist society. It is precisely the power to shape his circumstances that the laborer sells to the capitalist; it is precisely this power which is appropriated by the capitalist, not only in the form of the homogeneous labor-time which he buys for a price, but also in the form of the abstract labor which is congealed in commodities. This reified labor, this abstract labor which is crystallized, congealed in commodities, "acquires a given social form" in capitalist society, namely the form of value. Thus Marx "makes the 'form of value' the subject of his examination, namely value as the social form of the product of labor the form which the classical economists took for granted ..." (Rubin, p. 112). Thus, through the theory of commodity fetishism, the concept of reified labor becomes the link between the theory of alienation in the Economic and Philosophic Manuscripts of 1844 and the theory of value in Capital.

Marx's explanation of the phenomenon of reification, namely of the fact that abstract labor takes the "form of value", is no longer in terms of people's habits, but in terms of the characteristics of a commodity economy. In Capital, Marx points out that relations among people are realized through things, and that this is the only way they can be realized in a commodity economy: "The social connection between the working activity of individual commodity producers is realized only through the equalization of all concrete forms of labor, and this equalization is carried out in the form of an equalization of all the products of labor as values " (Rubin, p. 130). This is not only true of relations among capitalists as buyers and sellers of the products of labor, but also of relations between capitalists and workers as buyers and sellers of labor- power. It is to be noted that in the commodity economy, the laborer himself is a "free, independent" commodity producer.

The commodity he produces is his labor-power; he produces this commodity by eating, sleeping and procreating. In David Ricardo's language, the "natural price of labour" is that price which enables laborers "to subsist and perpetuate their race",[48] namely to reproduce their labor-power. The worker sells his commodity on the labor market in the form of value, and in exchange for a given amount of his commodity, labor- power, he receives a given sum of value, namely money, which he in turn exchanges for another sum of value, namely consumer goods.

It is to be noted that the laborer does not exchange creative power for creative power. When the worker sells his labor- power as abstract labor in the form of value, he totally alienates his creative power. When the capitalist buys a given quantity of the worker's labor-power, say eight hours of labor- power, he does not appropriate merely a part of that quantity, say four hours, in the form of surplus labor: the capitalist appropriates all eight hours of the worker's labor-lower. This labor-power then crystallizes, congeals in a given quantity of commodities which the capitalist sells on the market, which he exchanges as values for equivalent sums of money. And what the laborer gets back for his alienated labor-power is a sum of money which is "equivalent in value" to the labour-power. This relation of exchange of "equivalent values", namely the exchange of a given number of hours of labor-power for a given sum of money, conceals a quantitative as well as a qualitative aspect of exploitation. The quantitative aspect was treated by Marx in his theory of exploitation, developed in Volume I of Capital. The amount which the capitalist receives in exchange for the commodities he sells on the market is larger than the amount which he spends for the production of the commodities, which means that the capitalist appropriates a surplus in the form of profit. The

---

[48] David Ricardo, The Principles of Political Economy and Taxation, Homewood, Illinois: Richard D. Irwin. Inc., 1963, p. 45.

qualitative aspect was treated by Marx in his theory of alienation, and further developed in the theory of commodity fetishism. The two terms of the equivalence relation are not equivalent qualities; they are different in kind. What the worker receives in exchange for his alienated creative power is an "equivalent" only in a commodity economy, where man's creative power is reduced to a marketable commodity and sold as a value. In exchange for his creative power the worker receives a wage or a salary, namely a sum of money, and in exchange for this money he can purchase products of labor, but he cannot purchase creative power. In other words, in exchange for his creative power the laborer gets things. Thus When Marx speaks of the capitalist's appropriation of "surplus value" or "surplus labor", he refers to the quantitative aspect of exploitation, not the qualitative aspect. Qualitatively, the laborer alienates the entirety of his creative power, his power to participate consciously in shaping his material environment with the productive forces he inherits from previous technological development. This means that "it is true that men do rent out their services for a price" (Samuelson), and as a result, "The less you are, the less you express your own life, the greater is your alienated life, the more you have ..."[49]

In a commodity economy, people relate to each other only through, and by means of, the exchange of things: the relation of purchase and sale is "the basic relation of commodity society" (Rubin, p. 15). Production relations among people are established through the exchange of things because "permanent, direct relations between determined persons who are owners of different factors of productions, do not exist. The capitalist, the wage laborer, as well as the landowner, are commodity owners who are formally independent from each other. Direct production relations among them have yet to be established, and then in a form which is usual for commodity owners, namely in the form of purchase and

---

[49] Marx, Economic and Philosophic Manuscripts of 1844, p. 150.

sale" (Rubin, p. 18; italics in original). It is on the basis of these reified social relations, namely on the basis of production relations which are realized through the exchange of things, that the process of production is carried out in the capitalist society, because the "production relations which are established among the representatives of the different social classes (the capitalist, worker and landlord), result in a given combination of technical factors of production ..." (Rubin, p. 19). Thus it is through, and by means of, these reified social relations that productive forces, namely technology, are developed in capitalist society.

The capitalist's appropriation of the alienated creative power of society takes the form of an appropriation of things, the form of accumulation of capital. And it is precisely this accumulation of capital that defines the capitalist as a capitalist: "The capitalist's status in production is determined by his ownership of capital, of means of production, of things ..." (Rubin, p. 19).

Thus in Volume III of Capital, Marx says that "the capitalist is merely capital personified and functions in the process of production solely as the agent of capital"[50] and thus Rubin speaks of the "personification of things" (Rubin, Chapter 3). The capital gives the capitalist the power to buy equipment and raw materials, to buy labor-power, to engage the material and human agents in a productive activity which results in a given sum of commodities. In this process, the capital "pumps a definite quantity of surplus-labour out of the direct producers, or labourers; capital obtains this surplus-labour without an equivalent, and in essence it always remains forced labour - no matter how much it may seem

---

[50] Karl Marx, Capital: A Critique of Political Economy, Volume III, Moscow: Progress Publishers, 1966, p. 819.

to result from free contractual agreement."[51] In capitalist society a man without capital does not have the power to establish these relations. Thus, superficially, it seems that capital, a thing, possesses the power to hire labor, to buy equipment, to combine the labor and the equipment in a productive process, to yield profit and interest, "it seems that the thing itself possesses the ability, the virtue, to establish production relations." (Rubin, p. 21). In the words of the official American textbook, "Wages are the return to labor; interest the return to capital; rent the return to land."[52] Marx called this the Trinity Formula of capitalism: "In the formula: capital - interest, land - ground-rent, labour - wages, capital, land and labour appear respectively as sources of interest (instead of profit), ground-rent and wages, as their products, or fruits, the former are the basis, the latter the consequence, the former are the cause, the latter the effect; and indeed, in such a manner that each individual source is related to its product as to that which is ejected and produced by it."[53] Capital is a thing which has the power to yield interest, land is a thing which has the power to yield rent, labor is a thing which has the power to yield wages, and money "transforms fidelity into infidelity, love into hate, hate into love, virtue into vice, vice into virtue, servant into master, master into servant, idiocy into intelligence, and intelligence into idiocy",[54] or as American banks advertise, "money works for you." Rubin states that "vulgar economists ... assign the power to increase the productivity of labor which is inherent in The means of production and represents their technical function, to capital, i.e., a specific social form of production (theory of productivity of capital)" (Rubin, p. 28), and the economist who represents the post-World

---

[51] Marx, Capital, III, p. 819.

[52] Samuelson, Economics, p. 591.

[53] Marx, Capital, III, p. 816.

[54] Marx, Economic and Philosophic Manuscripts of 1844, p. 169.

War II consensus of the American economics profession writes in 1967 that "capital has a net productivity (or real interest yield) that can be expressed in the form of a percentage per annum..."[55]

A thing which possesses such powers is a fetish, and the fetish world "is an enchanted, perverted, topsy-turvy world, in which Mister Capital and Mistress Land carry on their goblin tricks as social characters and at the same time as mere things."[56] Marx had defined this phenomenon in the first volume of Capital: "... a definite social relation between men ... assumes, in their eyes, the fantastic form of a relation between things. In order, therefore, to find an analogy, we must have recourse to the mist-enveloped regions of the religious world. In that world the productions of the human brain appear as independent beings endowed with life, and entering into relation both with one another and the human race. So it is in the world of commodities with the products of men's hands. This I call the Fetishism which attaches itself to the products of labour, so soon as they are produced as commodities, and which is therefore inseparable from the production of commodities.

This Fetishism of commodities has its origin ... in the peculiar social character of the labour that produces them."[57] The fetishist, systematically attributing to things

---

[55] Samuelson, Economics, p. 572.

[56] Marx, Capital, III, p. 830, where the last part of this passage reads: "... in which Monsieur le Capital and Madame la Terre do their ghost-walking as social characters and at the same time directly as mere things." The version quoted above is from Marx on Economics, edited by Robert Freedman, New York: Harcourt, Brace & World, 1961, p. 65.

[57] Karl Marx, Capital, Volume 1, Moscow: Progress Publishers, 1965, p. 72; New York: Random Housc, 1906 edition, p. 83.

the outcomes of social relations, is led to bizarre conclusions: "What is profit the return to? ... the economist, after careful analysis, ends up relating the concept of profit to dynamic innovation and uncertainty, and to the problems of monopoly and incentives."[58] Rubin points out that, "Instead of considering technical and social phenomena as different aspects of human working activity, aspects which are closely related but different, vulgar economists put them on the same level, on the same scientific plane so to speak. ... This identification of the process of production with its social forms ... cruelly revenges itself" (Rubin, p. 28), and the economists are astonished to find that "what they have just thought to have defined with great difficulty as a thing suddenly appears as a social relation and then reappears to tease them again as a thing, before they have barely managed to define it as a social relation."[59]

The forces of production "alienated from labour and confronting it independently"[60] in the form of capital, give the capitalist power over the rest of society. "The capitalist glows with the reflected light of his capital" (Rubin, p. 25), and he is able to glow only because the productive power of the workers has been crystallized in productive forces and accumulated by the capitalist in the form of capital. The capitalist, as possessor of capital, now confronts the rest of society as the one at whose discretion production and consumption take place; he confronts society as its ruler. This process is celebrated in the official economics textbook: "Profits and high factor returns are the bait, the carrots dangled before us enterprising donkeys. Losses are our penalty kicks.

---

[58] Samuelson, Economics, p. 591.

[59] Marx, A Contribution to the Critique of Political Economy, p. 31.

[60] Marx, Capital, III, p. 824.

Profits go to those who have been efficient in the past - efficient in making things, in selling things, in foreseeing things.

Through profits, society is giving the command over new ventures to those who have piled up a record of success."[61]

It can now be shown that the preceding sequence is a detailed development, clarification, and concretization of the theory of alienation which Marx had presented in 1844. This can be seen by comparing the sequence with a passage cited earlier, written a quarter of a century before the publication of the theory of commodity fetishism in the first volume of Capital, and nearly half a century before the third volume: "The object produced by labour, its product, now stands opposed to it as an alien being, as a power independent of the producer. The product of labour which has been embodied in an object, and turned into a physical thing; this product is an objectification of labour....

The alienation of the worker in his product means not only that his labour becomes an object, takes on its own existence, but that it exists outside him, independently, and alien to him, and that it stands opposed to him as an autonomous power. The life which he has given to the object sets itself against him as an alien and hostile force."[62] This passage seems, in retrospect, like a summary of the theory of commodity fetishism. However, the definitions, the concepts, the detailed relationships which the passage seems to summarize were developed by Marx only decades later.

---

[61] Samuelson, Economics, p. 602.

[62] Marx, Economic and Philosophic Manuscripts of 1844, p. 108; the passage given above is quoted from Bottomore and Rubell, op. cit., p. 170-171.

The next task is to examine Marx's theory of value within the context of his theory of commodity fetishism, since, as Rubin points out, "The theory of fetishism is, per se, the basis of Marx's entire economic system, and in particular of his theory of value" (Rubin, p. 5). In this context, Rubin distinguishes three aspects of value: it is "(1) a social relation among people, (2) which assumes a material form and (3) is related to the process of production" (Rubin, p. 63). The subject of the theory of value is the working activity of people, or as Rubin defines it: "The subject matter of the theory of value is the interrelations of various forms of labor in the process of their distribution, which is established through the relation of exchange among things, i.e., products of labor" (Rubin, p. 67). In other words, the subject of the theory of value is labor as it is manifested in the commodity economy: here labor does not take the form of conscious, creative participation in the process of transforming the material rnvnonmcnt: it takes the form of abstract labor which is congealed in commodities and sold on the market as value. "The specific character of the commodity economy consists of the fact that the material-technical process of production is not directly regulated by society but is directed by individual commodity producers. . . . The private labor of separate commodity producers is connected with the labor of all other commodity producers and becomes social labor only if the product of one producer is equalized as a value with all other commodities" (Rubin, p. 70). Before analyzing how labor is allocated through the equalization of things, namely how human activity is regulated in capitalist society, Rubin points out that the form which labor takes in capitalist society is the form of value: "The reification of labor in value is the most important conclusion of the theory of fetishism, which explains the inevitability of 'reification' of production relations among people in a commodity economy" (Rubin, p. 72). Thus the theory of value is about the regulation of labor; it is the fact that most critics of the theory failed to grasp.

The question Marx raises is how the working activity of people is regulated in capitalist society. His theory of value is offered as an answer to this question. It will be shown that most critics do not offer a different answer to the question Marx raises, they object to the question. In other words, economists do not say that Marx gives erroneous answers to the question he raises, but that he gives erroneous answers to the questions they raise:

Marx asks: How is human working activity regulated in a capitalist economy?

Marx answers: Human working activity is alienated by one class, appropriated by another class, congealed in commodities, and sold on a market in the form of value.

The economists answer: Marx is wrong. Market price is not determined by labor; it is determined by the price of production and by demand. "The great Alfred Marshall" insisted that "market price - that is, economic value was determined by both supply and demand, which interact with one another in much the same way as Adam Smith described the operation of competitive markets."[63]

Marx was perfectly aware of the role of supply and demand in determining market price, as will be shown below. The point is that Marx did not ask what determines market price; he asked how working activity is regulated.

The shift of the question began already in the 1870's, before the publication of the second and third volumes of Marx's Capital. At that time capitalist economists revived the utility theory of value of Jean Baptiste Say and the supply-demand theory of price of

---

[63] Daniel R. Fusfeld, The Age of the Economist, Glenview, Illinois: Scott. Foresman & Co., 1966, p. 74.

Augustin Cournot,[64] both of which were developed in the early 19th century. The virtue of both approaches was that they told nothing about the regulation of human working activity in capitalist society, and this fact strongly recommended them to the professional economists of a business society. The revival of Say and Cournot was hailed as a new discovery, since the "new principle" drew a heavy curtain over the questions Marx had raised. "The new principle was a simple one: the value of a product or service is due not to the labor embodied in it but to the usefulness of the last unit purchased. That, in essence, was the principle of marginal utility", according to the historian Fusfeld.[65] In the eyes of the American economist Robert Campbell, the reappearance of the utility theory brought order into chaos: "The reconciliation of all these conflicting partial explanations into a unified general theory of value came only in the late nineteenth century with the concept of general equilibrium and the reduction of all explanations to the common denominator of utility by the writers of the utility school."[66] Fusfeld points out the main reason for the excitement: "One of the most important conclusions drawn front this line of thinking was that a system of free markets tended to maximize individual welfare."[67] It was once again possible to take for granted without questioning precisely what Marx had questioned. After hailing the reappearance of the utility

---

[64] Jean Baptiste Say, Traite d'Economie politique, first published in 1803. Augustin Cournot, Recherches sur les principes mathematiques de la theorie des richesses, 1838. The revival was carried out in the 1870's by Karl Menger, William Stanley Jevons, and Leon Walras, and the work was "synthesized" by Alfred Marshall in the 1890's.

[65] Op. cit., p. 73.

[66] Robert Campbell, "Marxian Analysis, Mathematical Methods, and Scientific Economic Planning", in Shaffer, op. cit., p. 352.

[67] Fusfeld, op. cit., p. 74.

theory, Campbell goes on to redefine economics in such a way as to exclude the very questions Marx had raised. Campbell does this explicitly: "One reflection of this new insight into the problem of value was the formulation of a new definition of economics, the one commonly used today, as the theory of allocation of scarce resources among competing ends."[68] Without mentioning that his own ideas about value were extant at the time of Ricardo, the scientific economist Campbell proceeds to dispose of Marx for retaining "ideas about value extant at the time of Ricardo". Campbell then uses the restrained, objective language of American social science to summarize Marx's life work: "Marx took the theory of value as it then existed, and compounded from some of its confusions a theory of the dynamics of the capitalist system. (It might be more accurate to describe the process the other way round: Marx had the conclusions and was trying to show how they flowed rigorously and inevitably from the theory of value then generally accepted. With the benefit of hindsight we may look back on his effort as a reductio ad absurdum technique for proving the deficiencies of Ricardian value theory.)" On the basis of this thorough analysis of Marx's work, Campbell dispassionately concludes: "Thus the bondage of a Marxist heritage in economic theory is not so much that the Marxist view is simply wrong in one particular (i.e., (fiat it assumes that value is created only by labor) as that it does not comprehend the basic problem of economic theory; it has not achieved a full understanding of what a valid economic theory must illuminate. That achievement came in the main-stream of world economic theorizing only after Marxism had already taken the turning to enter the blind alley mentioned above."[69] With economics thus redefined and Marx disposed of, it becomes possible, once again, to hold on to "a theory of value on the basis of analysis of the act of exchange as such, isolated from a determine social-economic context" (Rubin, pp.85-86).

---

[68] Campbell, loc. cit.

[69] Ibid.

Thus economists did not replace Marx's answers to his questions with more accurate answers; they threw out the questions, and replaced them with questions about scarcity and market price; thus economists "shifted the whole focus of economics away from the great issue of social classes and their economic interests, which has been emphasized by Ricardo and Marx, and centered economic theory upon the individual."[70] Fusfeld also explains why the economists shifted the focus: "The economists and their highly abstract theories were part of the same social and intellectual development that brought forth the legal theories of Stephen Field and the folklore of the self-made man",[71] i.e., the economists are ideologically at one with the ruling class, the capitalists, or as Samuelson put it, "Profits and high factor returns are the bait, the carrots dangled before us enterprising donkeys."[72]

Even theorists whose primary aim was not the celebration of capitalism have interpreted Marx's theory of value as a theory of resource allocation or a theory of price, and have underemphasized or even totally overlooked the sociological and historical context of the theory. This does not mean that problems of resource allocation or price have nothing to do with a historical and sociological analysis of capitalism, or that the elucidation of one aspect will necessarily add nothing to the understanding of the others. The point here is that a theory of resource allocation or a price theory need not explain why human working activity is regulated through things in the capitalist historical form of economy, since the theory of resource allocation or the price theory can begin its analysis by taking capitalism for granted. At the same time, a historical and sociological analysis of the capitalist economy need not explain the allocation of resources or the components of price in its attempt to

---

[70] Fusfeld, op. cit., p. 74.

[71] Ibid., p. 75.

[72] Economics, pp. 601-602; quoted earlier.

characterize the form which human working activity assumes in a given historical context. A price theorist may concern himself explicitly with the social form of the economy whose prices he examines, just as Marx did concern himself explicitly with problems of price and allocation. But this does not mean that all price theorists or resource allocators necessarily exhaust the sociological and historical problems, or even that they have the slightest awareness of capitalism as a specific historical form of economy, just as it does not mean that Marx necessarily exhausted the problems of price determination or resource allocation, even though he had far more profound awareness of these problems than most of his superficial critics, and even some of his superficial followers, give him credit for.

Oskar Lange pointed out that "leading writers of the Marxist school" looked to Marx for a price theory, and consequently "they saw and solved the problem only within the limits of the labor theory of value, being thus subject to all the limitations of the classical theory."[73] Yet Lange himself saw Marx's theory of value as an attempt to solve the problem of resource allocation. According to Lange, Marx "seems to have thought of labor as the only kind of scarce resource to be distributed between different uses and wanted to solve the problem by the labor theory of value."[74] It was rather Lange who devoted himself to developing a theory of resource allocation, not Marx, and "the unsatisfactory character of this solution"[75] is clearly due to the fact that Marx's theory was not presented as a solution to Lange's problems.

---

[73] Oskar Lange, On the Economic Theory of Socialism, New York: McGraw Hill, 1964 (published together with an essay by Fred M. Taylor), p. 141.

[74] Ibid., pp. 132-133.

[75] Ibid. p. 133.

Fred Gottheil, in a recent book on Marx, explicitly reduces Marx's theory of value to a theory of price. Unlike superficial critics of Marx, Gottheil points out that Marx was aware that in capitalist society prices are not determined by the "labor content" of commodities: "The concept of price which is incorporated in the analysis of the Marxian economic system is, without exception, the prices-of-production concept ..."[76] However, by reducing Marx's theory of value to a price theory, Gottheil pulls Marx's theory out of its sociological and historical context (Gottheil does not even mention Marx's theory of commodity fetishism). In this way Gottheil reduces Marx's historical and sociological analysis of the commodity capitalist economy to a mechanistic system from which Gottheil mechanically derives over 150 "predictions".

Joan Robinson knows that the construction of a theory of price was not the primary aim of Marx's analysis, and says that Marx "felt obliged to offer a theory of relative prices, but though he thought it essential we can see that it is irrelevant to the main point of his argument."[77] However, Robinson seems to be unaware of just what "the point of the argument" was: "The point of the argument was something quite different. Accepting the dogma that all things exchange at prices proportional to their values, Marx applies it to labour power. This is the clue that explains capitalism. The worker receives his value, his cost in terms of labour-time, and the employer makes use of him to produce more value than he costs."[78] Having reduced Marx's work to this "argument", Robinson is able to conclude: "On this plane the whole argument appears to be metaphysical, it provides a typical example of the way metaphysical ideas operate. Logically

---

[76] Fred M. Gottheil, Marx's Economic Predictions, Evanston: Northwestern University Press, 1966, p. 27.

[77] Joan Robinson, Economic Philosophy, Garden City: Anchor Books, 1964, p. 35.

[78] Ibid, p, 37, Italics in original.

it is a mere rigmarole of words but for Marx it was a flood of illumination and for latter-day Marxists, a source of inspiration."[79]

In an essay written more than half a century before Joan Robinson's Economic Philosophy, Thorstein Veblen came much closer than Robinson to "the point" of Marx's work: " ... within the domain of' unfolding human culture, which is the field of Marxian speculation at large, Marx has more particularly devoted his efforts to an analysis and theoretical formulation of the present situation - the current phase of the process, the capitalistic system.

And, since the prevailing mode of the production of goods determines the institutional, intellectual, and spiritual life of the epochs by determining the form and method of the current class struggle, the discussion necessarily begins with the theory of 'capitalistic production,' or production as carried on under the capitalistic system."[80] Veblen was also acutely aware of the irrelevance of critiques based on a reduction of Marx's theory of value to a price theory: "Marx's critics commonly identify the concept of 'value' with that of 'exchange value,' and show that the theory of 'value' does not square with the run of the facts of price under the existing system of distribution, piously hoping thereby to

---

[79] Ibid.

[80] Thorstein Veblen, "The Socialist Economics of Karl Marx", The Quarterly Journal of Economics. Vol: XX, Aug., 1906 , reprinted in The Portable Veblen, edited by Max Lerner, New York: Viking Press, 1948, p. 284. In a footnote, Veblen adds the explanation that "in Marxian usage 'capitalistic production' means production of goods for the market by hired labour under the direction of employers who own (or control) the means of production and are engaged in industry for the sake of a profit."

have refuted the Marxian doctrine; whereas. of course, they have for the most part not touched it."[81]

Marx's method, his approach to the problem he raised, was designed to cope with that problem, not with the problems raised by his critics, i.e., to answer how the distribution of labor is regulated, and not why people buy goods, or how resources are allocated, or what determines market price. Thus it was not in order to define what determines market price, but in order to focus on the problem of the regulation of labor, that Marx abstracted from the real capitalist economy, that he reduced it to its bare essentials, so to speak. Capitalism is a commodity economy; social relations are not established directly, but through the exchange of things. In order to learn how labor is regulated in an economy where this regulation takes place through the exchange of things, Marx constructs a model of a "simple commodity economy", namely an abstract economy in which social relations are established through the exchange of things, and in which the ratio around which commodities tend to exchange is determined by the labor-time expended on their production. The statement that commodities exchange in terms of the labor-tune expended on their production is then a tautology, since it is contained in the definition of Marx's model. The point of the abstraction is to focus on the regulation of labor in a commodity economy, not to answer what determines price in the actual capitalist society. In this context it is irrelevant to observe that there are "other factors of production" (such as land and capital) since, as Rubin points out, "the theory of value does not deal with labor as a technical factor of production, but with the working activity of people as the basis of the life of society, and with the social forms within which that labor is carried out" (Rubin, p. 82). It is also irrelevant to point out that "things other than labor" are exchanged, since "Marx does not analyze every exchange of things, but only the equalization of commodities through which the social equalization of labor is carried

---

[81] Ibid., pp. 287-288.

out in the commodity economy" (Rubin, p. 101). Marx's abstraction is not designed to explain everything; it is designed to explain the regulation of labor in a commodity economy.

In Chapter 2 of his economics textbook, Paul Samuelson finds Marx's method totally unacceptable. This academician, whose significance in American economics can probably he compared to Lysenko's in Soviet genetics, summarizes Marx's theory of value as follows: "The famous 'labor theory of valor' was adapted by Karl Marx from such classical writers as Adam Smith and David Ricardo. There is no better introduction to it than to quote from Adam Smith's Wealth of Nations. Smith employed the quaint notion of a Golden Age, a kind of Eden, wherein dwelt the noble savage before land and capital had become scarce and when human labor alone counted."[82] Having demonstrated his understanding of the theory, Samuelson then proceeds to a critical analysis of it, using the objective, restrained, non-ideological language of the American social sciences: "Karl Marx, a century ago in Das Kapital(1867), unfortunately clung more stubbornly than Smith to the oversimple labor theory. This provided him with a persuasive terminology for declaiming against 'exploitation of labor', but constituted bad scientific economics ..."[83] Before driving his demonstration to its conclusion, Samuelson offers his own theory of the origins of private property; property grows out of scarcity just as naturally as babies grown out of wombs: "But suppose that we have left Eden and Agricultural goods do require, along with labor, fertile land that has grown scarce enough to have become private property."[84] On the basis of this profound historical and sociological analysis of the economy in which he lives, the American Lysenko concludes: "Once factors other than

---

[82] Samuelson, Economics, p. 27.

[83] ibid, p. 29.

[84] Ibid, italics by Samuelson.

labor become scarce ... the labor theory of value fails. Q.E.D."[85]

However, in Chapter 34 of the same textbook, the same Samuelson explains the "Law of Comparative Advantage" with the same method of abstraction which Marx had used, namely he employs the same labor theory of value[86] in the same manner, and he refers to the same source, Ricardo. Samuelson even tells the reader that later on he "can give some of the needed qualifications when our simple assumptions arc relaxed."[87] In the introduction to his textbook, Samuelson even defends the method of abstraction: "Even if we had more and better data, it would still be necessary - as in every science - to simplify, to abstract, from the infinite mass of detail. No mind can comprehend a bundle of unrelated facts. All analysis involves abstraction. It is always necessary to idealize, to omit

detail, to set up simple hypotheses and patterns by which the facts can be related, to set up the right questions before going out to look at the world as it is."[88] Thus Samuelson cannot be opposed to Marx's method of analysis; what bothers him is the subject matter; what he opposes is analysis which asks why it is that "In our system individual capitalists earn interest, dividends, and profits, or rents and royalties on the capital goods that they supply. Every patch of land and every bit of equipment has a deed, or 'title of ownership,' that belongs to somebody directly - or it belongs to a corporation, then

---

[85] Ibid

[86] From Samuelson's explanation of the law of comparative advantage: "In America a unit of food costs 1 days' labor and a unit of clothing costs 2 days' labor. In Europe the cost is 3 days' labor for food and 4 days' labor for clothing," etc. Ibid., p. 649.

[87] Ibid., p. 648.

[88] Ibid., p. 8. Samuelson's italics.

indirectly it belongs to the individual stockholders who own the corporation."[89] Samuelson has already told his readers the answer: "Through profits, society is giving the command over new ventures to those who have piled up a record of success."[90]

Rubin points out that Marx's "simple commodity economy" cannot be treated as a historical stage that preceded capitalism: "This is a theoretical abstraction and not a picture of the historical transition from simple commodity economy to capitalist economy" (Rubin, p. 257). Consequently, the "labor theory of value is a theory of a simple commodity economy, not in the sense that it explains the type of economy that preceded the capitalist economy, but in the sense that it describes only one aspect of the capitalist economy, namely production relations among commodity producers which are characteristic for every commodity economy" (Rubin, p. 255). Marx was perfectly aware that he could not "construct the theory of the capitalist economy directly from the labor theory of value and ... avoid the intermediate links, average profit and production price. He characterized such attempts as 'attempts to force and directly fit concrete relations to the elementary relation of value', 'attempts which present as existing that which does not exist'" (Rubin, p. 255).

Rubin's book analyzes the connections between technology and social relations in a commodity economy where people do not relate to each other directly but through the products of their labor. In this economy, a technical improvement is not experienced directly by the producers as an enhancement of life, and is not accompanied by a conscious transformation of working activity. The working activity is transformed, not in response to the enhanced productive power of society, but in response to changes in the value of products. "The

---

[89] Ibid., p. 50.

[90] Ibid., p. 602.

moving force which transforms the entire system of value originates in the material-technical process of production. The increase of productivity of labor is expressed in a decrease of the quantity of concrete labor which is factually used up in production, on the average. As a result of this (because of the dual character of labor, as concrete and abstract), the quantity of this labor, which is considered 'social' or 'abstract,' i.e., as a share of the total, homogeneous labor of the society, decreases. The increase of productivity of labor changes the quantity of abstract labor necessary for production. It causes a change in the value of the product of labor. A change in the value of products in turn affects the distribution of social labor among the various branches of production ... this is the schema of a commodity economy in which value plays the role of regulator, establishing equilibrium in the distribution of social labor among the various branches..." (Rubin, p.66).

In the concrete conditions of the capitalist economy this process is more complex, but in spite of the added complexities the regulation of the productive activities of people is still carried out through the movement of things. In the capitalist economy "the distribution of capital leads to the distribution of social labor" (Rubin, p. 226). However, "our goal (as before) is to analyze the laws of distribution of social labor" (Rubin, p.228), and consequently "we must resort to a roundabout path and proceed to a preliminary analysis of the laws of distribution of capital". (Ibid.) The task becomes further complicated by the fact that, "if we assume that the distribution of labor is determined by the distribution of capital which acquires meaning as an intermediate link in the causal chain, then the formula of the distribution of labor depends on the formula of the distribution of capitals: unequal masses of labor which are activated by equal capitals are equalized with each other" (p.235). The gap between the distribution of capital and the distribution of labor is bridged through the concept of the organic composition of capital, which establishes a relation between the two processes (p. 237).

In his analysis, Rubin assumes "the existence of competition among capitalists engaged in different branches of production" and also "the possibility for the transfer of capital from one branch to another" (p. 230).[91] With these assumptions, "the rate of profit becomes the regulator of the distribution of capital" (p. 229). Rubin defines profit as "the surplus of the selling price of the commodity over the costs of its production" (p. 230). And a change in the cost of production is "in the last analysis caused by changes in the productivity of labor and in the labor-value of some goods" (p. 251). Schematically, the process can be summarized as follows. Technical change causes a change in the productivity of labor. This changes the amount of alienated, abstract labor which is congealed in certain commodities, and consequently changes the value of those commodities. This in turn affects the costs of production of branches which use the given commodities in their production process, and thus affects the profits of capitalists in those branches. The change in the profitability of the affected branches leads capitalists to move their capitals to other branches, and this movement of capitals in turn leads to a movement of workers to the other branches (although the movement of laborers is not necessarily proportional to the movement of capilals, since this depends on the organic composition of capital). Rubin's conclusion is that the regulation of labor in the capitalist society differs only in complexity, but not in kind, from the regulation of labor in a simple commodity economy: "Anarchy in social production; the absence of direct social relations among

---

[91] Rubin does not treat cases where the assumptions of perfect competition and perfect mobility of capital do not hold. Thus he does not extend his analysis to problems of imperialism, monopoly, militarism, domestic colonies (which today would come under the heading of racism). Rubin also does not treat changes in production relations caused by the increased scale and power of productive forces, some of which Marx had begun to explore in the third Volume of Capital, and does not treat its development or its transformations.

producers: mutual influence of their working activities through things which are the products of their labor, the connection between the movement of production relations among people and the movement of things in the process of material production: 'reification' of production relations, the transformation of their properties into the properties of 'things' - all of these phenomena of commodity fetishism are equally present in every commodity economy, simple as well as capitalist. They characterize labor-value and production price the same way" (p. 253, Rubin's italics). The first volume of Capital provides the context, the second volume describes the mechanism, and the third volume treats in detail the formidable process through which "the object produced by labour, its product, now stands opposed to it as an alien being, as a power independent of' the producer", the process through which "the life which he has given to the object sets itself against him as an alien and hostile force."

Fredy Perlman

Kalamazoo

1968

Introduction

There is a tight conceptual relationship between Marx's economic theory and his sociological theory, the theory of historical materialism. Years ago Hilferding pointed out that the theory of historical materialism and the labor theory of value have the same starting point, specifically labor as the basic element of human society, an element whose development ultimately determines the entire development of society.[92]

The working activity of people is constantly in a process of change, sometimes faster, sometimes slower, and in different historical periods it has a different character. The process of change and development of the working activity of people involves changes of two types: first, there are changes in means of production and technical methods by which man affects nature, in other words, there are changes in society's productive forces; secondly, corresponding to these changes there are changes in the entire pattern of production relations among people, the participants in the social process of production. Economic formations or types of economy (for example, ancient slave economy, feudal, or capitalist economy) differ according to the character of the production relations among people. Theoretical political economy deals with a definite social-economic formation, specifically with commodity-capitalist economy.

The capitalist economy represents a union of the material-technological process and its social forms, i.e. the totality of production relations among people. The concrete activities of people in the material-technical production process presuppose concrete production relations among them, and vice versa. The ultimate goal of science is to understand the capitalist economy as a whole, as a specific system of productive forces and production relations among people. But to approach this ultimate goal, science must first of all separate, by means

---

[92] Hilferding, R. "Böhm-Bawerks Marx-Kritik," Marx-Studien, Wien, 1904.

of abstraction, two different aspects of the capitalist economy: the technical and the social-economic, the material-technical process of production and its social form, the material productive forces and the social production relations. Each of these two aspects of the economic process is the subject of a separate science. The science of social engineering - still in embryonic state - must make the subject of its analysis the productive forces of society as they interact with the production relations. On the other hand, theoretical political economy deals with production relations specific to the capitalist economy as they interact with the productive forces of society. Each of these two sciences, dealing only with one aspect of the whole process of production, presupposes the presence of the other aspect of the production process in the form of an assumption which underlies its research. In other words, even though political economy deals with production relations, it always presupposes their unbreakable connection with the material-technical process of production, and in its research assumes a concrete stage and process of change of the material-productive forces.

Marx's theory of historical materialism and his economic theory revolve around one and the same basic problem: the relationship between productive forces and production relations. The subject of both sciences is the same: the changes of production relations which depend on the development of productive forces. The adjustment of production relations to changes of productive forces - a process which takes the form of increasing contradictions between the production relations and the productive forces, and the form of social cataclysms caused by these contradictions - is the basic theme of the theory of historical materialism.[93] By applying this general methodological approach to commodity-capitalist society we obtain Marx's economic theory. This theory

---

[93] Here we leave aside that part of the theory of historical materialism which deals with the laws of development of ideology.

analyzes the production relations of capitalist society, the process of their change as caused by changes of productive forces, and the growth of contradictions which are generally expressed in crises.

Political economy does not analyze the material-technical aspect of the capitalist process of production, but its social form, i.e., the totality of production relations which make up the "economic structure" of capitalism. Production technology (or productive forces) is included in the field of research of Marx's economic theory only as an assumption, as a starting point, which is taken into consideration only in so far as it is indispensable for the explanation of the genuine subject of our analysis, namely production relations. Marx's consistently applied distinction between the material-technical process of production and its social forms puts in our hands the key for understanding his economic system. This distinction at the same time defines the method of political economy as a social and historical science. In the variegated and diversified chaos of economic life which represents a combination of social relations and technical methods, this distinction also directs our attention precisely to those social relations among people in the process of production, to those production relations, for which the production technology serves as an assumption or basis. Political economy is not a science of the relations of things to things, as was thought by vulgar economists, nor of the relations of people to things, as was asserted by the theory of marginal utility, but of the relations of people to people in the process of production.

Political economy, which deals with the production relations among people in the commodity-capitalist society, presupposes a concrete social form of economy, a concrete economic formation of society. We cannot correctly understand a single statement in Marx's Capital if we overlook the fact that we are dealing with events which take place in a particular society. "In the study of economic categories, as in the case of every historical and social science, it must be borne in mind that as in reality so in our mind the subject, in this case modern bourgeois society, is given and that the categories are therefore but forms of expression, manifestations of existence, and frequently but one-sided aspects of this subject, this definite society." ". . .In the employment of the theoretical method [of Political Economy], the subject, society, must constantly be kept in mind as the premise from which we start."[94] Starting from a concrete sociological assumption, namely from the concrete social structure of an economy, Political Economy must first of all give us the characteristics of this social form of economy and the production relations which are specific to it. Marx gives us these general characteristics in his "theory of commodity fetishism," which could more accurately be called a general theory of production relations of the commodity capitalist economy.

---

[94] Marx, K., "Introduction to the Critique of Political Economy," in K. Marx, A Contribution to the Critique of Political Economy, Chicago,.Charles Kerr & Co., 1904, pp. 302 and 295.

I

Marx's Theory of Commodity Fetishism

Introduction

Marx's theory of commodity fetishism has not occupied the place which is proper to it in the Marxist economic system. The fact is that Marxists and opponents of Marxism have praised the theory, recognizing it as one of the most daring and ingenious of Marx's generalizations. Many opponents of Marx's theory of value have high regard for the theory of fetishism (Tugan-Baranovskii, Frank, and even Struve with qualifications[95]). Some writers do not accept the theory of fetishism in the context of political economy. They see it as a brilliant sociological generalization, a theory and critique of all contemporary culture based on the reification of human relations (Hammacher). But proponents as well as opponents of Marxism have dealt with the theory of fetishism mainly as an independent and separate entity, internally hardly related to Marx's economic theory. They present it as a supplement to the theory of value, as an interesting literary-cultural digression which accompanies Marx's basic text. One reason for such an interpretation is given by Marx himself, by the formal structure of the first chapter of Capital, where the theory of fetishism is given a

---

[95] Rykachev is an exception. He writes: "Marx's theory of commodity fetishism can be reduced to a few superficial, empty and essentially inaccurate analogies. It is not the strongest but almost the weakest section in Marx's system, this notorious disclosure of the secret of commodity fetishism, which through some kind of misunderstanding has preserved an aura of profundity even in the eyes of such moderate admirers of Marx as M. Tugan-Baranovskii and S. Frank." Rykachev, Dengi i denezhnaya vlast (Money and the Power of Money), 1910, p. 156.

separate heading.[96] This formal structure, however, does not correspond to the internal structure and the connections of Marx's ideas. The theory of fetishism is, per se, the basis of Marx's entire economic system, and in particular of his theory of value.

What does Marx's theory of fetishism consist of, according to generally accepted views? It consists of Marx's having seen human relations underneath relations between things, revealing the illusion in human consciousness which originated in the commodity economy and which assigned to things characteristics which have their source in the social relations among people in the process of production. "Unable to grasp that the association of working people in their battle with nature, i.e., the social relations among people, are expressed in exchange, commodity fetishism considers the exchangeability of commodities an internal, natural property of the commodities themselves. In other words, that which is in reality a relationship among people, appears as a relation among things within the context of commodity fetishism."[97] "Characteristics which had appeared mysterious because they were not explained on the basis of the relations of producers with each other were assigned to the natural essence of commodities. Just as the fetishist assigns characteristics to his fetish which do not grow out of its nature, so the bourgeois economist grasps the commodity as a sensual thing which possesses pretersensual properties."[98] The theory of fetishism

---

[96] In the first German edition of Capital, the entire first chapter, including the theory of commodity fetishism, appeared as one part with the general title "Commodities" (Kapital, I, 1867, pp. 1-44).

[97] Bogdanov, A., Kratkii kurs ekonomicheskoi nauki (Short Course of Economic Science), 1920, p. 105.

[98] Kautsky, K., The Economic Doctrines of Karl Marx, London: A. and C. Black, 1925, p. 11. (This translation of Kautsky's work contains misprints which are corrected in the citation given above.)

dispels from men's minds the illusion, the grandiose delusion brought about by the appearance of phenomena in the commodity economy, and by the acceptance of this appearance (the movement of things, of commodities and their market prices) as the essence of economic phenomena. However this interpretation, though generally accepted in Marxist literature, does not nearly exhaust the rich content of the theory of fetishism developed by Marx. Marx did not only show that human relations were veiled by relations between things, but rather that, in the commodity economy, social production relations inevitably took the form of things and could not be expressed except through things. The structure of the commodity economy causes things to play a particular and highly important social role and thus to acquire particular social properties. Marx discovered the objective economic bases which govern commodity fetishism. Illusion and error in men's minds transform reified economic categories into "objective forms" (of thought) of production relations of a given, historically determined mode of production-commodity production (C., I, p. 72).[99]

The theory of commodity fetishism is transformed into a general theory of production relations of the commodity economy, into a propaedeutic to political economy.

---

[99] The letter "C" stands for Capital, and the Roman numeral stands for the volume. The page numbers refer to the three volume edition of Karl Marx's Capital published by Progress Publishers, Moscow: Vol. I, 1965; Vol. II, 1967; Vol. 3, 1966

Chapter 1: Objective Basis of Commodity Fetishism

The distinctive characteristic of the commodity economy is that the managers and organizers of production are independent commodity producers (small proprietors or large entrepreneurs). Every separate, private firm is autonomous, i.e., its proprietor is independent, he is concerned only with his own interests, and he decides the kind and the quantity of goods he will produce. On the basis of private property, he has at his disposal the necessary productive tools and raw materials, and as the legally competent owner, he disposes of the products of his business. Production is managed directly by separate commodity producers and not by society. Society does not directly regulate the working activity of its members, it does not prescribe what is to be produced or how much.

On the other hand, every commodity producer makes commodities, i.e., products which are not for his own use, but for the market, for society. The social division of labor unites all commodity producers into a unified system which is called a national economy, into a "productive organism" whose parts are mutually related and conditioned. How is this connection created? By exchange, by the market, where the commodities of each individual producer appear in a depersonalized form as separate exemplars of a given type of commodity regardless of who produced them, or where, or in which specific conditions. Commodities, the products of individual commodity producers, circulate and are evaluated on the market. The real connections and interactions among the individual - one might say independent and autonomous - firms are brought about by comparing the value of goods and by exchanging them. On the market society regulates the products of labor, the commodities, i.e., things. In this way the community indirectly regulates the working activity of people, since the circulation of goods on the market, the rise and fall of their prices, lead to changes in the allocation of the working activity of the separate commodity producers, to their entry into certain branches of production or their exit from them, to the redistribution of the productive forces of society.

On the market, commodity producers do not appear as personalities with a determined place in the production process, but as proprietors and owners of things, of commodities. Every commodity producer influences the market only to the extent that he supplies goods to the market or takes goods from it, and only to this extent does he experience the influence and pressure of the market. The interaction and the mutual impact of the working activity of individual commodity producers take place exclusively through things, through the products of their labor which appear on the market. The expansion of farmland in remote Argentina or Canada can bring about a decrease of agricultural production in Europe only in one way: by lowering the price of agricultural products on the market. In the same way, the expansion of large-scale machine production ruins a craftsman, making it impossible for him to continue his previous production and driving him from the country to the city, to the factory.

Because of the atomistic structure of the commodity society, because of the absence of direct social regulation of the working activity of the members of society, the connections between individual, autonomous, private firms are realized and maintained through commodities, things, products of labor. "...The labor of the individual asserts itself as a part of the labor of society, only by means of the relations which the act of exchange establishes directly between the products, and indirectly, through them, between the producers" (C., I, p. 73). Due to the fact that individual commodity producers, who perform a part of society's total labor, work independently and separately, "the interconnection of social labor is manifested in the private exchange of the individual products of labor" (Marx in his letter to

Kugelmann)[100]. This does not mean that a given commodity producer A is only connected by production relations to given commodity producers B, C and D, who enter with him into a contract of purchase and sale, and is not related to any other member of society. Entering into direct production relations with his buyers B, C and D, our commodity producer A is actually connected, by a thick network of indirect production relations, with innumerable other people (for example, with all buyers of the same product, with all producers of the same product, with all the people from whom the producer of the given product buys means of production, and so on), in the final analysis, with all members of society. This thick network of production relations is not interrupted at the moment when commodity producer A terminates the act of exchange with his buyers and returns to his shop, to the process of direct production. Our commodity producer makes products for sale, for the market, and thus already in the process of direct production he must take into account the expected conditions of the market, i.e. he is forced to take into account the working activity of other members of society, to the extent that it influences the movement of commodity prices on the market.

Thus the following elements can be found in the structure of the commodity economy: 1) individual cells of the national economy, i.e. separate private enterprises, formally independent from each other; 2) they are materially related with each other as a result of the social division of labor; 3) the direct connection between individual commodity producers is established in exchange, and this, indirectly, influences their productive activity. In his enterprise each commodity producer is formally free to produce, at will, any product that pleases him and by any means he chooses. But when he takes the final product of his labor to the market to exchange it, he is not free to determine

---

[100] Karl Marx and Frederick Engels, Selected Works, Volume II, Moscow: Foreign Languages Publishing House, 1962, p. 461.

the proportions of the exchange, but must submit to the conditions (the fluctuations) of the market, which are common to all producers of the given product. Thus, already in the process of direct production, he is forced to adapt his working activity (in advance) to the expected conditions of the market. The fact that the producer depends on the market means that his productive activity depends on the productive activity of all other members of society. If clothiers supplied too much cloth to the market, then clothier Ivanov, who did not expand his production, did not thereby suffer less from the fall of cloth prices, and he had to decrease his production. If other clothes introduced improved means of production (for example, machines), lowering the value of cloth, then our clothier was also forced to improve his production technology. The separate commodity producer, formally independent from others in terms of the orientation, extent and methods of his production, is actually closely related to them through the market, through exchange. The exchange of goods influences the working activity of people; production and exchange represent inseparably linked, although specific, components of reproduction. "The capitalist process of production taken as a whole represents a synthesis of the processes of production and circulation" (C., III, p. 25). Exchange becomes part of the very process of reproduction or the working activity of people, and only this aspect of exchange, the proportions of exchange, the value of commodities, is the subject of our research. Exchange interests us mainly as the social form of the process of reproduction which leaves a specific mark on the phase of direct production (see below, Chapter Fourteen), not as a phase of the process of reproduction which alternates with the phase of direct production.

This role of exchange, as an indispensable component of the process of reproduction, means that the working activity of one member of society can influence the working activity of another only through things. In the market society, "the seeming mutual independence of the individuals is supplemented by a system of general and mutual dependence through or by means of the products" (C., I, p. 108). Social production relations inevitably take on a reified form - and to the extent that we speak of the relations between individual commodity producers and not of relations within separate private firms - they exist and are realized only in that form.

In a market society, a thing is not only a mysterious "social hieroglyphic" (C., I, p. 74), it is not only "a receptacle" under which social production relations among people are hidden. A thing is an intermediary in social relations, and the circulation of things is inseparably related to the establishment and realization of the productive relations among people. The movement of the prices of things on the market is not only the reflection of the productive relations among people; it is the only possible form of their manifestation in a market society. The thing acquires specific social characteristics in a market economy (for example, the properties of value, money, capital, and so on), due to which the thing not only hides the production relations among people, but it also organizes them, serving as a connecting link between people. More accurately, it conceals the production relations precisely because the production relations only take place in the form of relations among things. "When we bring the products of our labor into relation with each other as values, it is not because we see in these articles the material receptacles of homogeneous human labor. Quite the contrary: whenever, by an exchange, we equate as values our different products, by that very act, we also equate, as human labor, the different kinds of labor expended upon them. We are not aware of this, nevertheless we do it" (C., I, p. 74). Exchange and the equalization of things on the market bring about a social connection among the commodity producers and unify the working activity of people.

We consider it necessary to mention that by "things" we mean only the products of labor, just as Marx did. This qualification of the concept of "thing" is not only permissible, but indispensable, since we are analyzing the circulation of things on the market as they are connected with the working activity of people.We are interested in those things whose market regulation influences the working activity of commodity producers in a particular way. And the products of labor are such things. (On the price of land, see below, Chapter Five.)

The circulation of things - to the extent that they acquire the specific social properties of value and money - does not only express production relations among men, but it creates them.[101] "By the currency of the circulating medium, the connexion between buyers and sellers is not merely expressed. This connexion is originated by, and exists in, the circulation alone" (C., I, p. 137). As a matter of fact, the role of money as a medium of circulation is contrasted by Marx with its role as a means of payment, which "expresses a social relation that was in existence long before" (Ibid.). However, it is obvious that even though the payment of money takes place, in this case, after the act of purchase and sale, namely after the establishment of social relations between the seller and the buyer, the equalization of money and commodities took place at the instant when the act took place, and thus created the social relation. "[Money] serves as an ideal means of purchase. Although existing only in the promise of the buyer to pay, it causes the commodity to change hands" (C., I, p. 136).

Thus money is not only a "symbol," a sign, of social production relations which are concealed under it. By uncovering the naivete of the monetary system, which assigned the characteristics of money to its material or natural properties, Marx at the same time threw out the opposite view of money as a "symbol" of social relations

---

[101] The way this social property of things, which are expressions of production relations among people, takes part in the creation of production relations among particular individuals, will be explained below, in Chapter 3.

which exist alongside money (C., I, p. 91). According to Marx, the conception which assigns social relations to things per se is as incorrect as the conception which sees a thing only as a "symbol," a "sign" of social production relations. The thing acquires the property of value, money, capital, etc., not because of its natural properties but because of those social production relations with which it is connected in the commodity economy. Thus social production relations are not only "symbolized" by things, but are realized through things.

Money, as we have seen, is not only a "symbol." In some cases, particularly in the commodity metamorphosis C-M-C, money represents only a "transcient and objective reflex of the prices of commodities" (C., I, p. 129). The transfer of money from hand to hand is only a means for the transfer of goods. In this case, "Its functional existence absorbs, so to say, its material existence" (C., I, p. 129), and it can be replaced by the mere symbol of paper money. But even though "formally" separated from metallic substance, paper money nevertheless represents an "objectification" of production relations among people. [102]

In the commodity economy, things, the products of labor, have a dual essence: material (natural-technical) and functional (social). How can we explain the close connection between these two sides, the connection which is expressed in the fact that "socially determined labor" takes on "material traits," and things, "social traits"?

---

[102] One cannot agree with Hilferding's conception that paper money does away with the "objectification" of production relations. "Within the limits of a minimal quantity of means of circulation, the material expression of social relations is replaced by consciously regulated social relations. This is possible because metallic money represents a social relation even though it is disguised by a material shell" (R. Hilferding, Das Finanzkapital, Wien: Wiener Volksbuchhandlung, 1910). Commodity exchange by means of paper money is also carried out in an unregulated, spontaneous, "objectified" form, as is the case with metallic money. Paper money is not a "thing" from the point of view of the internal value of the material from which it is made. But it is a thing in the sense that through it are expressed, in "objectified" form, social production relations between buyer and seller. But if Hilferding is wrong, then the opposite view of Bogdanov, who holds that paper money represents a higher degree of fetishism of social relations than metallic money, has even less foundation. Bogdanov, Kurs politicheskoi ekonomii (Course in Political Economy), Vol. II, Part 4, p. 161.

Chapter 2: The Production Process and its Social Form

The close connection between the social-economic and the material-physical is explained by the particular connection between the material-technical process and its social form in the commodity economy. The capitalist production process "is as much a production process of material conditions of human life as a process taking place under specific historical and economic production relations, producing and reproducing these production relations themselves, and thereby also the bearers of this process, their material conditions of existence and their mutual relations, i.e., their particular socioeconomic form" (C., III, p. 818). There is a close connection and correspondence between the process of production of material goods and the social form in which it is carried out, i.e., the totality of production relations among men. The given totality of production relations among men is adjusted by a given condition of productive forces, i.e. the material production process. This totality makes possible, within certain limits, the process of production of material products indispensable for society. The correspondence between the material process of production, on the one hand, and the production relations among the individuals who participate in it, on the other, is achieved differently in different social formations. In a society with a regulated economy, for example in a socialist economy, production relations among individual members of society are established consciously in order to guarantee a regular course of production. The role of each member of society in the production process, namely his relationship to other members, is consciously defined. The coordination of the working activity of separate individuals is established on the basis of previously estimated needs of the material-technical process of production. The given system of production relations is in some sense a closed entity managed by one will and adapted to the material process of production as a whole.

Obviously changes in the material process of production may lead to inevitable changes in the system of production relations; but these changes take place within the system and are carried out by its own internal forces, by decisions of its managing bodies. The changes are brought about by changes in the production process. The unity which exists at the starting point makes possible a correspondence between the material-technical process of production and the production relations which shape it. Later on, each of these sides develops on the basis of a previously determined plan. Each side has its internal logic, but due to the unity at the start, no contradiction develops between them.

We have an example of such an organization of production relations in commodity-capitalist society, particularly in the organization of labor within an enterprise (technical division of labor), as opposed to the division of labor between separate private producers (social division of labor). Let us assume that an enterpriser owns a large textile factory which has three divisions: spinning mill, weaving mill, and dye-works. The engineers, workers and employees were assigned to different divisions previously, according to a determined plan. They were connected, in advance, by determined, permanent production relations in terms of the needs of the technical production process. And precisely for this reason, things circulate in the process of production from some people to others depending on the position of these people in production, on the production relations among them. When the manager of the weaving division receives the yarn from the spinning mill, he transformed it into fabric, but he did not send the fabric back to the manager of the spinning mill as an equivalent for the previously received yarn. He sent it forward to the dye-works, because the permanent production relations which connect the workers in the given weaving mill with the workers in the given dye-works determine, in advance, the forward movement of the objects, the products of labor, from the people employed in the earlier process of production (weaving) toward the people employed in the later process (dyeing). The production relations among people are organized in advance for the purpose of the material production of things, and not by means of things. On the other hand, the object moves in the production process from some people to others on the basis of production relations which exist among them, but the movement does not create production relations among them. Production relations among people have exclusively a technical character. Both of these sides are adjusted to each other, but each has a different character.

The entire problem is essentially different when the spinning mill, weaving mill and dye-works belong to three different enterprises, A, B and C. Now A no longer delivers the finished yarn to B only on the basis of B's ability to transform it into fabric, i.e., to give it the form useful to society. He has no interest in this; now he no longer wants simply to deliver his yarn, but to sell it, i.e. to give it to an individual who, in exchange will give him a corresponding sum of money, or in general, an object of equal value, an equivalent. It is all the same to him who this individual is. Since he is not connected by permanent production relations with any determined individuals, A enters into a production relation of purchase and sale with every individual who has and agrees to give him an equivalent sum of money for the yarn. This production relation is limited to the transfer of things, namely the yarn goes from A to the buyer and the money from the buyer to A. Even though our commodity producer A cannot in any way pull out of the thick network of indirect production relations which connect him with all members of society, he is not connected in advance by direct production relations with determined individuals. These production relations do not exist in advance but are established by means of the transfer of things from one individual to another. Thus they not only have a social, but also a material character. On the other hand the object passes from one determined individual to another, not on the basis of production relations established between them in advance, but on the basis of purchase and sale which is limited to the transfer of these objects. The transfer of things establishes a direct production relation between determined individuals; it has not only a technical, but also a social significance.

Thus in a commodity society which develops spontaneously, the process is carried out in the following way. From the point of view of the material, technical process of production, each product of labor must pass from one phase of production to the next, from one production unit to another, until it receives its final form and passes from the production unit of the final producer or intermediate merchant into the economic unit of the consumer. But given the autonomy and independence of the separate economic units, the transfer of the product from one individual economic unit to another is only possible through purchase and sale, through agreement between two economic units, which means that a particular production relation is established between them: purchase and sale. The basic relation of commodity society, the relation between commodity owners, is reduced to "a capacity in which they appropriate the produce of the labor of others, by alienating that of their own labor" (C., I, p. 108-109). The totality of production relations among men is not a uniformly connected system in which a given individual is connected by permanent connections, determined in advance, with given individuals. In the commodity economy, the commodity producer is connected only with the indetermined market, which he enters through a discrete sequence of individual transactions that temporarily link him with determined commodity producers. Each stage in this sequence closely corresponds to the forward movement of the product in the material process of production. The passage of the product through specific stages of production is brought about by its simultaneous passage through a series of private production units on the basis of agreements among them, and of exchange. Inversely, the production relation connects two private economic units at the point where the material product passes from one economic unit to the other. The production relation between determined persons is established on the occasion when things are transferred, and after the transfer it is broken once again.

We can see that the basic production relation in which determined commodity producers are directly connected, and thus for each of them the established connection between his working activity and the working activity of all members of society, namely purchase and sale, is carried on regularly. This type of production relation differs from production relations of an organized type in the following ways: 1) it is established between the given persons voluntarily, depending on its advantages for the participants; the social relation takes the form of a private transaction; 2) it connects the participants for a short time, not creating a permanent connection between them; but these momentary and discontinuous transactions, taken as a whole, have to maintain the constancy and continuity of the social process of production; and 3) it unites particular individuals on the occasion of the transfer of things between them, and it is limited to this transfer of things; relations among people acquire the form of equalization among things. Direct production relations between particular individuals are established by the movement of things between them; this movement must correspond to the needs of the process of material reproduction. "The exchange of commodities is a process in which the social exchange of things, i.e., the exchange of particular products of private individuals simultaneously represents the establishment of determined social production relations which individuals enter when exchanging things" (Zur Kritik der politischen Oekonomie, 1907, p.

32).¹⁰³ Or, as Marx put it, the process of circulation includes Stoff- und Formwechsel (Content and Form of Exchange) (Das Kapital, Volume III Part 2, 1894, p. 363), it includes the exchange of things and the transformation of their form, i.e., the movement of things within the material production process and the transformation of their social-economic form (for example, the transformation of commodities into money, money into capital, money capital into productive capital, etc.), which corresponds to the different production relations among people.

Social-economic (relations among people) and material-objective (movement of things within the process of production) aspects are indissolubly united in the process of exchange. In the commodity-capitalist society these two aspects are not organized in advance and are not adjusted to each other. For this reason every individual act of exchange can be realized only as the result of the joint action of both of these aspects; it is as if each aspect stimulated the other. Without the presence of particular objects in the hands of given individuals, the individuals do not enter into the production relation of exchange with each other. Yet, inversely, the transfer of things cannot take place if their owners do not establish particular production relations of exchange. The material process of production, on one hand, and the system of production relations among individual, private economic units, on the other, are not adjusted to each other in advance. They must be adjusted at each stage, at each of

---

¹⁰³ In the Russian translation by P. Rumyantsev, this is incorrectly translated as "result" - Kritika politicheskoi ekonomii (Critique of Political Economy), Petersburg, 1922, p. 53. Marx said Erzeugung (production, establishment) and not Erzeugniss (product, result). [Below, when Rubin quotes from the Russian translation, we will quote from K. Marx, A Contribution to the Critique of Political Economy (translated by N.I. Stone), Chicago: Charles H. Kerr and Co., 1904, and in future citations we will refer to this edition as Critique.]

the single transactions into which economic life is formally broken up. If this does not take place, they will inevitably diverge, and a gap will develop within the process of social reproduction. In the commodity economy such a divergence is always possible. Either production relations which do not stand for real movements of products in the process of production are developed (speculation), or production relations indispensable for the normal performance of the production process are absent (sales crisis). In normal times such a divergence does not break out of certain limits, but in times of crisis it becomes catastrophic.

In essence, the connection between the production relations among people and the material process of production have the same character in a capitalist society stratified into classes. As before, we leave aside production relations within an individual enterprise, and deal only with relations between separate, private enterprises, relations which organize them into a unified national economy. In the capitalist society, different factors of production (means of production, labor force and land) belong to three different social classes (capitalists, wage laborers and landowners) and thus acquire a particular social form, a form which they do not have in other social formations. The means of production appear as capital, labor as wage labor, land as an object of purchase and sale. The conditions of labor, i.e., means of production and land, which are "formally independent" (C., III, p. 825) from labor itself in the sense that they belong to different social classes, acquire a particular social "form," as was mentioned above. If the individual technical factors of production are independent, and if they belong to separate economic subjects (capitalist, worker and landowner), then the process of production cannot begin until a direct production relation is established among particular individuals who belong to the three social classes mentioned above. This production relation is brought about by concentrating all the technical factors of production in one economic unit which belongs to a capitalist. This combination of all the factors of production, of people and things, is indispensable in every social form of economy, but "the specific manner in which this union is accomplished distinguishes the different economic epochs of the structure of society from one another" (C., II, pp. 36-37).

Let us imagine feudal society, where the land belongs to the landlord, and the labor and means of production, usually very primitive, belong to the serf. Here a social relation of subordination and domination between the serf and landlord precedes and makes possible the combination of all the factors of production. By force of common law the serf uses a plot of land which belongs to the landlord, and he must pay rent and serve a corvee, i.e., work a given number of days on the manor, usually with his own means of production. Permanent production relations which exist between the landlord and the serf make possible the combination of all factors of production in two places: on the peasant's plot, and on the manor.

In capitalist society, as we have seen, such permanent, direct relations between determined persons who are owners of different factors of production, do not exist. The capitalist, the wage laborer, as well as the landowner, are commodity owners who are formally independent from each other. Direct production relations among them have yet to be established, and then in a form which is usual for commodity owners, namely in the form of purchase and sale. The capitalist has to buy, from the laborer, the right to use his labor force, and from the landlord, the right to use his land. To do this he must possess enough capital. Only as the owner of a given sum of value (capital) which enables him to buy means of production and to make it possible for the laborer to buy necessary means of subsistence, does he become a capitalist, an organizer and manager of production. Capitalists use the authority of directors of production "only as the personification of the conditions of labor in contrast to labor, and not as political or theocratic rulers as under earlier modes of production" (C., III, p. 881). The capitalist "is a capitalist and can undertake the process of exploiting labor only because, being the owner of the conditions of labor, he confronts the laborer as the owner of only labor-power" (C., III, p. 41). The capitalist's status in production is determined by his ownership of capital, of means of production, of things, and the same is true of the wage laborer as the owner of labor power, and the landlord as owner of the land. The agents of production are combined through the factors of production; production bonds among people are established through the movement of things. The independence of the factors of production, which is based on private ownership, makes possible their material-technical combination, indispensable for the production process, only by establishing the production process of exchange among their owners. And inversely: direct production relations which are established among the representatives of the different social classes (the capitalist, worker and landlord), result in a given combination of technical factors of production, and are connected with the transfer of things from one economic unit to another. This tight connection of production relations among people with the movement of things in the process of material production leads to the "reification" of production relations among people.

Chapter 3: Reification of Production Relations among People and Personification of Things

As we have seen, in commodity-capitalist society separate individuals are related directly to each other by determined production relations, not as members of society, not as persons who occupy a place in the social process of production, but as owners of determined things, as "social representatives" of different factors of production. The capitalist "is merely capital personified" (C., III, pp. 819, 824). The landlord "appears as the personification of one of the most essential conditions of production," land (C., III, pp. 819, 824). This "personification," in which critics of Marx saw something incomprehensible and even mystical,[104] indicates a very real phenomenon: the dependence of production relations among people on the social form of things (factors of production) which belong to them, and which are personified by them.

If a given person enters a direct production relation with other determined persons as owner of certain things, then a given thing, no matter who owns it, enables its owner to occupy a determined place in the system of production relations. Since the possession of things is a condition for the establishment of direct production relations among people, it seems that the thing itself possesses the ability, the virtue, to establish production relations. If the given thing gives its owner the possibility to enter relations of exchange with any other commodity owner, then the thing possesses the special virtue of exchangeability, it has "value." If the given thing connects two commodity owners, one of whom is a capitalist and the other a wage laborer, then the thing is not only a "value," it is "capital" as well. If the capitalist

---

[104] Cf. Passow, Richard, Kapitalismus. Jena: G. Fischer, 1918, p. 84.

enters into a production relation with a landlord, then the value, the money, which he gives to the landlord and through the transfer of which he enters the production bond, represents "rent." The money paid by the industrial capitalist to the money capitalist for the use of capital borrowed from the latter, is called "interest." Every type of production relation among people gives a specific "social virtue," "social form," to the things by means of which determined people enter into direct production relations. The given thing, in addition to serving as a use value, as a material object with determined properties which make it a consumer good or a means of production, i.e., in addition to performing a technical function in the process of material production, also performs the social function of connecting people.

Thus in the commodity-capitalist society people enter direct production relations exclusively as commodity owners, as owners of things. On the other hand, things, as a result, acquire particular social characteristics, a particular social form. "The social qualities of labor" acquire "material characteristics," and objects, "social characteristics" (C., I, p. 91). Instead of "direct social relations between individuals at work," which are established in a society with an organized economy, here we observe "material relations between persons and social relations between things" (C., I, p. 73). Here we see two properties of the commodity economy: "personification of things and conversion of production relations into entities [relations among things]" (C., III, p. 830), "The materialization of the social features of production and the personification of the material foundations of production" (Ibid., p. 880).

By the "materialization of production relations" among people, Marx understood the process through which determined production relations among people (for example, between capitalists and workers) assign a determined social form, or social characteristics, to the things by means of which people relate to one another (for instance, the social form of capital).

By "personification of things" Marx understood the process through which the existence of things with a determined social form, for example capital, enables its owner to appear in the form of a capitalist and to enter concrete production relations with other people.

At first sight both of these processes may appear to be mutually exclusive processes. On one hand, the social form of things is treated as the result of production relations among people. On the other hand, these same production relations are established among people only in the presence of things with a specific social form. This contradiction can be resolved only in the dialectical process of social production, which Marx considered as a continuous and ever-recurring process of reproduction in which each link is the result of the previous link and the cause of the following one. The social form of things is at the same tune the result of the previous process of production and of expectations about the future.[105]

Every social form related to the products of labor in capitalist society (money, capital, profit, rent, etc.), appeared as the result of a long historical and social process, through constant repetition and sedimentation of productive relations of the same type. When the given type of production relations among people is still rare and exceptional in a given society, it cannot impose a different and permanent social character on the products of labor which exist in it. "The momentary social contact" among people gives the products of their labor only a momentary social form which appears together with the social contacts which are created, and disappears as soon as the social contacts end (C., I, p. 88). In undeveloped exchange, the product of labor determines value only during the act of exchange, and is not a value either before

---

[105] Below we give a brief presentation of conclusions developed more fully in our article, "Production Relations and Material Categories," Pod znamenem marksizma (Under the Banner of Marxism), 1924, No. 10-11.

or after that act. When the participants in the act of exchange compare the products of their labor with a third product, the third product performs the function of money in embryonic form, not being money either before or after the act of exchange.

As productive forces develop, they bring about a determined type of production relations among people. These relations are frequently repeated, become common and spread in a given social environment. This "crystallization" of production relations among people leads to the "crystallization" of the corresponding social forms among things. The given social form is "fastened," fixed to a thing, preserved within it even when the production relations among people are interrupted. Only from that moment can one date the appearance of the given material category as detached from the production relations among people from which it arose and which it, in turn, affects. "Value" seems to become a property of the thing with which it enters into the process of exchange and which the thing preserves when it leaves. The same is true of money, capital and other social forms of things. Being consequences of the process of production, they become its prerequisites. From this point on, the given social form of the product of labor serves not only as an "expression" of a determined type of production relations among people, but as their "bearer." The presence of a thing with a determined social form in the hands of a given person induces him to enter determined production relations, and informs him of its particular social character. "The reification of production relations" among people is now supplemented by the "personification of things." The social form of the product of labor, being the result of innumerable transactions among commodity producers, becomes a powerful means of exerting pressure on the motivation of individual commodity producers, forcing them to adapt their behavior to the dominant types of production relations among people in the given society. The impact of society on the individual is carried out through the social form of things. This objectification, or "reification," of the production relations among people in the social form of things, gives the economic system greater durability, stability and regularity. The result is the "crystallization" of production relations among people.

Only at a determined level of development, after frequent repetition, do the production relations among people leave some kind of sediment in the form of certain social characteristics which are fixed to the products of labor. If the given type of production relations have not yet spread widely enough in the society, they cannot yet give to things an adequate social form. When the ruling type of production was crafts production, where the goal was the "maintenance" of the craftsman, the craftsman still considered himself a "master craftsman" and he considered his income the source of his "maintenance" even when he expanded his enterprise and had, in essence, already become a capitalist who lived from the wage labor of his workers. He did not yet consider his income as the "profit" of capital, nor his means of production as "capital." In the same way, due to the influence of dominant agriculture on precapitalist social relations, interest was not viewed as a new form of income, but was for a long time considered a modified form of rent. The renowned economist Petty tried to derive interest from rent in this manner.[106] With this approach, all economic forms are "subsumed" under the form which is dominant in the given mode of production (C., III, p. 876). This explains why a more or less extended period of development has to take place before the new type of production relations are "reified" or "crystallized" in the social forms which correspond to the products of labor.

Thus the connection between the production relations among people and the material categories must be presented in the following manner. Every type of

---

[106] Cf. I. Rubin, Istoriya ekonomicheskoi mysli (History of Economic Thought), Second Edition, 1928, Chapter VII.

production relation which is characteristic for a commodity-capitalist economy ascribes a particular social form to the things for which and through which people enter the given relation. This leads to the "reification" or "crystallization" of production relations among people. The thing which is involved in a determined production relation among people and which has a corresponding social form, maintains this form even when the given, concrete, single production relation is interrupted. Only then can the production relation among people be considered truly "reified," namely "crystallized" in the form of a property of the thing, a property which seems to belong to the thing itself and to be detached from the production relation. Since the things come forth with a determined, fixed social form, they, in turn, begin to influence people, shaping their motivation, and inducing them to establish concrete production relations with each other. Possessing the social form of "capital," things make their owner a "capitalist" and in advance determine the concrete production relations which will be established between him and other members of society. It seems as if the social character of things determines the social character of their owners. Thus the "personification of things" is brought about. In this way the capitalist glows with the reflected light of his capital, but this is only possible because he, in turn, reflects a given type of production relation among people. As a result, particular individuals are subsumed under the dominant type of production relations. The social form of things conditions individual production bonds among particular people only because the social form itself is an expression of social production bonds. The social form of things appears as a condition for the process of production which is given in advance, ready-made, and permanently fixed, only because it appears as the congealed, crystallized result of a dynamic, constantly flowing and changing social process of production. In this way, the apparent contraction between the "reification of people" and the "personification of things" is resolved in the dialectical, uninterrupted process of reproduction. This apparent contradiction is between the determination of the social form of things by production relations among people and the determination of the individual production relations among people by the social form of things.

Of the two sides of the process of reproduction which we have mentioned, only the second side - "personification of things" - lies on the surface of economic life and can be directly observed. Things appear in a ready-made social form, influencing the motivation and the behavior of individual producers. This side of the process is reflected directly in the psyche of individuals and can be directly observed. It is much more difficult to trace the formation of the social forms of things from the production relations among people. This side of the process, i.e., the "reification" of production relations among people, is the heterogeneous result of a mass of transactions of human actions which are deposited on top of each other. It is the result of a social process which is carried on "behind their backs," i.e., a result which was not set in advance as a goal. Only by means of profound historical and social-economic analysis did Marx succeed in explaining this side of the process.

From this perspective, we can understand the difference which Marx often drew between the "outward appearance," the "external connection," the "surface of phenomena," on the one hand, and "internal connection," "concealed connection," "immanent connection," the "essence of things," on the other hand.[107] Marx reproached vulgar economists for limiting themselves to an analysis of the external side of a phenomenon. He reproached Adam Smith for wavering between "esoteric" (external) and "exoteric" (internal) perspectives. It was held that the meaning of these statements by Marx was very obscure. Critics of Marx, even the most generous, accused him of economic metaphysics for his desire to explain the concealed

---

[107] See C., III, p. 817; and other works.

connections of phenomena. Marxists sometimes explained Marx's statements in terms of his desire to differentiate between methods of crude empiricism and abstract isolation.[108] We feel that this reference to the method of abstraction is indispensable, but far too inadequate to characterize Marx's method. He did not have this in mind when he drew an opposition between the internal connections and the external connections of a phenomenon. The method of abstraction is common to Marx and many of his predecessors, including Ricardo. But it was Marx who introduced a sociological method into political economy. This method treats material categories as reflections of production relations among people. It is in this social nature of material categories that Marx saw their "internal connections." Vulgar economists study only outward appearances which are "estranged" from economic relations (C., III, p. 817), i.e., the objectified, ready-made form of things, not grasping their social character. They see the process of the "personification" of things which takes place on the surface of economic life, but they have no idea of the process of "reification of production relations" among people. They consider material categories as given, ready-made "conditions" of the process of production which affect the motives of producers and which are expressed in their consciousness; they do not examine the character of these material categories as results of the social process. Ignoring this internal, social process, they restrict themselves to the "external connection between things as this connection appears in competition. In competition, then, everything appears inside out, and always seems to be in reverse."[109] Thus production

---

[108] J Kunov, "K ponimaniyu metoda issledovaniya Marksa" (Towards an Understanding of Marx's Method of Research):" Osnovnye problemy politicheskoi ekonomii. 1922, pp. 57-58.

[109] Marx, Teorii pribavochnoi stoimosli (Theories of Surplus Value), Vol. II, p. 57.

relations among people appear to depend on the social forms of things, and not the other way around.

Vulgar economists who do not grasp that the process of "personification of things" can only be understood as a result of the process of "reification of production relations among people," consider the social characteristics of things (value, money, capital, etc.) as natural characteristics which belong to the things themselves. Value, money, and so on, are not considered as expressions of human relations "tied" to things, but as the direct characteristics of the things themselves, characteristics which are "directly intertwined" with the natural-technical characteristics of the things. This is the cause of the commodity fetishism which is characteristic of vulgar economics and of the commonplace thinking of the participants in production who are limited by the horizon of the capitalist economy. This is the cause of "the conversion of social relations into things, the direct coalescence of the material production relations with their historical and social determination" (C., III, p. 830). "An element of production [is] amalgamated with and represented by a definite social form." (Ibid., p. 816). "The formal independence of these conditions of labor in relation to labor, the unique form of this independence with respect to wage-labor, is then a property inseparable from them as things, as material conditions of production, an inherent, immanent, intrinsic character of them as elements of production. Their definite social character in the process of capitalist production bearing the stamp of a definite historical epoch is a natural, and intrinsic substantive character belonging to them, as it were, from time immemorial, as elements of the production process" (Ibid., p. 825).[110]

The transformation of social production relations into social, "objective" properties of things is a fact about commodity-capitalist economy, and a consequence of the distinctive connections between the process of material production and the movement of production relations. The error of vulgar economics does not lie in the fact that it pays attention to the material forms of capitalist economy, but that it does not see their connection with the social form of production and does not derive them from this social form but from the natural properties of things. "The effects of determined social forms of labor are assigned to things, to the products of that labor; the relation itself comes forth in a fantastic manner in the form of things. We have seen that this is a specific property of commodity production. .. Hodgskin sees in this a purely subjective illusion behind which the deceit and interest of the exploiting classes is concealed. He does not see that the manner of presentation is a result of the actual relation itself, and that the relation is not an expression of the manner of

---

[110] Only by viewing this "coalescence" of social relations and material conditions of production from this point of view does Marx's theory of the dual nature of commodities become clear to us, as well as his statement that use values appear as the "material depositories of exchange value" (C., I, p. 36). Use value and value are not two different properties of things, as is held by Bohm-Bawerk. The contrast between them is caused by the contrast between the method of natural science, which deals with the commodity as a thing, and the sociological method, which deals with social relations "coalesced with things." "Use value expresses a natural relationship between a thing and a man, the existence of things for man. But exchange value represents the social existence of things" (Theorien uber den Mehrwert, 1910, Vol. III, p. 355).

presentation, but the other way around" (Theorien uber den Mehrwert, 1910, Vol. III, pp. 354-355).

Vulgar economists commit two kinds of errors: 1) either they assign the "economic definiteness of form" to an "objective property" of things (C., II, p. 164), i.e., they derive social phenomena directly from technical phenomena; for example, the ability of capital to yield profit, which presupposes the existence of particular social classes and production relations among them, is explained in terms of the technical functions of capital in the role of means of production; 2) or they assign "certain properties materially inherent in instruments of labor" to the social form of the instruments of labor (Ibid.), i.e., they derive technical phenomena directly from social phenomena; for example, they assign the power to increase the productivity of labor which is inherent in means of production and represents their technical function, to capital, i.e., a specific social form of production (the theory of the productivity of capital).

These two mistakes, which at first glance seem contradictory, can actually be reduced to the same basic methodological defect; the identification of the material process of production with its social form, and the identification of the technical functions of things with their social functions. Instead of considering technical and social phenomena as different aspects of human working activity, aspects which are closely related but different, vulgar economists put them on the same level, on the same scientific plane, so to speak. They examine economic phenomena directly in those closely intertwined and "coalesced" technical and social aspects which are inherent in the commodity economy. The result of this is a "wholly incommensurable [relation] between a use-value, a thing, on one side, and a definite social production relation, surplus-value, on the other" (C., III, p. 818); ". ... a social relation conceived as a thing is made proportional to Nature, i.e., two incommensurable magnitudes are supposed to stand in a given ratio to one another" (Ibid., p. 817). This identification of the process of production with its social forms, the technical properties of things with social relations "materialized" in the social form of things, cruelly revenges itself. Economists are often struck with naive astonishment "when what they have just thought to have defined with great difficulty as a thing suddenly appears as a social relation and then reappears to tease them again as a thing, before they have barely managed to define it as a social relation" (Critique, p. 31).

It can easily be shown that "the direct coalescence of material relations of production with their historical-social form," as Marx put it, is not only inherent in the commodity-capitalist economy, but in other social forms as well. We can observe that social production relations among people are causally dependent on the material conditions of production and on the distribution of technical means of production among the different social groups in other types of economy as well. From the point of view of the theory of historical materialism, this is a general sociological law which holds for all social formations. No one can doubt that the totality of production relations between the landlord and the serfs was causally determined by the production technique and by the distribution of the technical factors of production, namely the land, the cattle, the tools, between the landlord and the serfs, in feudal society. But the fact is that in feudal society production relations among people are established on the basis of the distribution of things among them and for things, but not through things. Here people are directly related with each other; "the social relations between individuals in the performance of their labor, appear at all events as their own mutual personal relations, and are not disguised under the shape of social relations between the products of labor" (C., I, p. 77). However, the specific nature of the commodity-capitalist economy resides in the fact that production relations among people are not established only for things, but through things. This is precisely what gives production relations among people a "materialized," "reified" form and gives birth to commodity fetishism, the confusion between the material-technical and the social-economic aspect of the production process, a confusion which was removed by the new sociological method of Marx.[111]

---

[111] In general, the connection between things and social relations among people is more complex and many-sided. Thus, for example, taking into consideration only phenomena which are closely related with our theme, we can observe: 1) in the economic sphere of various social formations, the causal dependence of production relations among people on the distribution of things among them (the dependence of production relations on the structure and distribution of productive forces); 2) in the economic sphere of the commodity-capitalist economy, the realization of production relations among people through things, their "coalescence" (commodity fetishism in the precise meaning of the words); 3) in various spheres of various social formations, the symbolization of relations among people in things (general social symbolization or fetishization of social relations among people). Here we are only concerned with the second topic, commodity fetishism in the precise meaning of the words, and we hold it indispensable to make a sharp distinction between this topic and the first (The confusion between the two is noticeable in N. Bukharin's Historical Materialism [English language edition: New York: Russell and Russell, Inc., 1965], Russian edition, 1922, pp. 161-162) and between this topic and the third (A. Bogdanov's theory of fetishism suffers from this confusion).

Chapter 4: Thing and Social Function (Form)

The new sociological method which Marx introduced into political economy applies a consistent distinction between productive forces and production relations, between the material process of production and its social form, between the process of labor and the process of value formation. Political economy deals with human working activity, not from the standpoint of its technical methods and instruments of labor, but from the standpoint of its social form. It deals with production relations which are established among people in the process of production. But since in the commodity-capitalist society people are connected by production relations through the transfer of things, the production relations among people acquire a material character. This "materialization" takes place because the thing through which people enter definite relations with each other plays a particular social role, connecting people - the role of "intermediary" or "bearer" of the given production relation. In addition to existing materially or technically as a concrete consumer good or means of production, the thing seems to acquire a social or functional existence, i.e., a particular social character through which the given production relation is expressed, and which gives things a particular social form. Thus the basic notions or categories of political economy express the basic social-economic forms which characterize various types of production relations among people and which are held together by the things through which these relations among people are established.

In his approach to the study of the "economic structure of society" or "the sum total of the relations of production" among people, Marx[112] separated particular

---

[112] Marx, "Preface" to A Contribution to the Critique of Political Economy, Chicago: Kerr and Co., 1904.

forms and types of production[113] Marx analyzed these relations among people in a capitalist society types of production relations in the following sequence. Some of these relations among people presuppose the existence of other types of production relations among the members of a given society, and the latter relations do not necessarily presuppose the existence of the former: thus the former assume the latter. For example, the relation between financial capitalist C and industrial capitalist B consists of B's receiving a loan from C; this relation already presupposes the existence of production relations between industrial capitalist B and laborer A, or more exactly, with many laborers. On the other hand, the relations between the industrial capitalist and the laborers do not necessarily presuppose that capitalist B had to borrow money from the financial capitalist. Thus it is clear that the economic categories "capital" and "surplus value" precede the categories "interest-bearing capital" and "interest." Furthermore, the relation between the industrial capitalist and the workers has the form of purchase and sale of labor-power, and in addition presupposes that the capitalist produces goods for sale, i.e., that he is connected with other members of society by the production relations of commodity owners with each other. On the other hand, relations among the commodity owners do not necessarily presuppose a production bond between the industrial capitalist and the workers. From this it is clear that the categories "commodity" and "value" precede the category "capital." The logical order of the economic categories follows from the character of the production relations which are expressed by the categories. Marx's economic system analyzes a series of production relations of increasingly complex types. These production relations are expressed in a series of social forms of increasing complexity - these being the social forms acquired by things. This connection between

---

[113] We have in mind various forms or types of production relations among people in a capitalist society, and not various types of production relations which characterize different types of social formations.

a given type of production relation among people and the corresponding social function, or form, of things, can be traced in all economic categories.

The basic social relation among people as commodity-producers who exchange the products of their labor gives to the products the special property of exchangeability, which then seems to be a natural property of the products: the special "form of value." Regular exchange relations among people, in the context of which the social activity of commodity owners has singled out a commodity (for example gold) to serve as a general equivalent which can be directly exchanged for any other commodity, give this commodity the particular function of money, or the "money form." This money form, in turn, carries out several functions, or forms, depending on the character of the production relation among buyers and sellers.

If the transfer of goods from the seller to the buyer and the inverse transfer of money are carried out simultaneously, then money assumes the function, or has the form of a "medium of circulation." If the transfer of goods precedes the transfer of money, and the relation between the seller and the buyer is transformed into a relation between debtor and creditor, then money has to assume the function of a "means of payment." If the seller keeps the money which he received from his sale, postponing the moment when he enters a new production relation of purchase, the money acquires the function or form of a "hoard." Every social function or form of money expresses a different character or type of production relation among the participants in exchange.

With the emergence of a new type of production relation - namely a capitalistic relation which connects a commodity owner (a capitalist) with a commodity owner (a worker), and which is established through the transfer of money - the money acquires a new social function or form: it becomes "capital." More exactly, the money which directly connects the capitalist with the workers plays the role, or has the form, of "variable capital." But to establish production relations with the workers, the capitalist must possess means of production or money with which to buy them. These means of production or money which serve indirectly to establish a production relation between the capitalist and the workers has the function or form of "constant capital." To the extent that we consider production relations between the class of capitalists and the class of laborers in the process of production, we are considering "productive capital" or "capital in the stage of production." But before the process of production began, the capitalist appeared on the market as a buyer of means of production and labor power. These production relations between the capitalist as buyer and other commodity owners correspond to the function, or form, of "money capital." At the end of the production process the capitalist appears as a seller of his goods, which acquires an expression in the function, or form of, "commodity capital." In this way the metamorphosis or "transformation of the form" of capital reflects different forms of production relations among people.

But this still does not exhaust the production relations which connect the industrial capitalist with other members of society. In first place, industrial capitalists of one branch are connected with the industrial capitalists of all other branches through the competition of capital and its transfer from one branch to another. This relation is expressed in the formation of "the general average rate of profit," and the sale of goods at "prices of production." In addition, the class of capitalists is itself subdivided into several social groups or subclasses: industrial, commercial and money (financial) capitalists. Besides these groups, there is still a class of landowners. Production relations among these different social groups create new social and economic "forms": commercial capital and commercial profit, interest-bearing capital and interest, and ground-rent. "Stepping beyond its inner organic life, so to say, it [capital] enters into relations with outer life, into relations in which it is not capital and labor which confront one another, but capital and capital in one case, and individuals, again simply as buyers and sellers, in the other" (C., III, p. 44).[114] The subject here is the different types of production relations, and particularly production relations: 1) between capitalists and workers; 2) between capitalists and the members of society who appear as buyers and sellers; 3) among particular groups of industrial capitalists and between industrial capitalists as a group and other groups of capitalists (commercial and financial capitalists). The first type of production relation, which is the basis of capitalist society, is examined by Marx in Volume I of Capital, the second type in Volume II, and the third in Volume III. The basic production relations of commodity society, the relations among people as commodity-producers, are examined by Marx in A Contribution to the Critique of Political Economy, and are reexamined in Part I of the first volume of Capital, which has the heading "Commodities and Money" and which can be treated as an introduction to Marx's system (in the first draft Marx intended to call this part: "Introduction. Commodities, Money." See Theorien uber den Mehrwert, 1910, Vol. III, p. VIII). Marx's system examines various types of production relations of increasing complexity as well as the increasingly complex corresponding economic forms of things.

The basic categories of political economy thus express various types of production relations which assume the form of things. "In reality, value, in itself, is only a material expression for a relation between the productive activities of people" (Theorien uber den Mehrwert, III, p. 218). "When, therefore, Galiani says: Value is a relation between persons - 'La Ricchezza e una ragione tra due persone' - he ought to have added: a relation between persons expressed as a relation between things" (C., I, p. 74). "To it [monetary system] gold and silver, when serving as money, did not represent a social relation between producers" (C., I, p. 82). "Capital is a social relation of production. It is a historical production

---

[114] Emphasis added.

relation."[115] Capital is "a social relation expressed (darstellt) in things and through things" (Theorien uber den Mehrwert, III, p. 325). "Capital is not a thing, but rather a definite social production relation, belonging to a definite historical formation of society, which is manifested in a thing and lends this thing a specific social character" (C., III, p. 814).[116]

Marx explained his conception of economic categories as the expression of production relations among people in greatest detail when he dealt with the categories value, money and capital. But he more than once pointed out that other notions of political economy express production relations among people. Surplus value represents "a definite historical form of social process of production" (C., III, p. 816). Rent is a social relation taken as a thing (C., III, p. 815). "Supply and demand are neither more nor less relations of a given production than are individual exchanges."[117] Division of labor, credit, are relations of bourgeois production (Ibid., pp. 126-145). Or as Marx stated in a general form, "economic categories are only the theoretical expressions, the abstractions of the social relations of production (Ibid., p. 109).

---

[115] K. Marx, Wage Labour and Capital, in Marx and Engels, Selected Works, Moscow: Foreign Languages Publishing House, 1962. In this edition, the passage cited above is translated: "Capital, also, is a social relation of production. It is a bourgeois production relation, a production relation of bourgeois society," p. 90.

[116] Marx most often said that a production relation "is represented" (sich darstellt) in a thing, and a thing "represents" (darstellt) a production relation.

[117] K. Marx, The Poverty of Philosophy, New York: International Publishers, 1963, p. 43.

Thus the basic concepts of political economy express different production relations among people in capitalist society. But since these production relations connect people only through things, the things perform a particular social function and acquire a particular social form which corresponds to the given type of production relation. If we said earlier that economic categories express production relations among people, acquiring a "material" character, we can also say that they express social functions, or social forms, which are acquired by things as intermediaries in social relations among people. We will begin our analysis with the social function of things.

Marx often spoke of the functions of things, functions which correspond to the different production relations among people. In the expression of value one commodity "serves as an equivalent" (C., I, p. 48 and p. 70). "The function of money" represents a series of different functions: "Function as a measure of value" (Ibid., p. 117), "function as a medium of circulation" or "function as coin" (Ibid., p. 117 and p. 126), "function as means of payment" (Ibid., pp. 127, 136, 139), "function of hoards" (p. 144) and "the function of money of the world" (p.144). The different production relations between buyers and sellers correspond to different functions of money. Capital is also a specific social function: "...the property of being capital is not inherent in things as such and in any case, but is a function with which they may or may not be invested, according to circumstances" (C., II, p. 207). In money capital, Marx carefully differentiated the "money function" from the "capital function" (C., II, pp. 36, 79). The subject here, obviously, is the social function which capital performs, connecting different social classes and their representatives, capitalists and wage workers; the subject clearly is not the technical function which the means of production perform in the material production process. If capital is a social function then, as Marx says, "its subdivision is justified and relevant." Variable and constant capital differ in terms of the different functions which they perform in the "process of expanding" capital (C., I, pp. 208-209); variable capital directly connects the capitalist with the worker and transfers the labor-power of the worker to the capitalist; constant capital serves the same purpose indirectly. A "functional difference" exists between them (C., I, p. 210). The same is true of the division into fixed and circulating capital. "It is not a question here of definitions [of fixed and circulating capital - I.R.] which things must be made to fit. We are dealing here with definite functions which must be expressed in definite categories (C., II, p. 230; emphasis added). This distinction between the functions of fixed and circulating capital refers to different methods of transferring the value of capital to the product, i.e., to the fuller partial restoration of the value of capital during one turnover period (Ibid., pp. 167-168). This distinction between social functions in the process of transferring value (i.e., in the process of circulation) is often confused by economists with a distinction between technical functions in the process of material production, namely with a distinction between the gradual wear and tear of the instruments of labor and the total consumption of raw materials and accessories. In the second part of Volume II of Capital, Marx devoted a great deal of energy to showing that the categories of fixed and circulating capital express precisely the above-mentioned social functions of transferring value. These functions are, in fact, related to particular technical functions of means of production, but they do not coincide with them. Not only do different parts of productive capital (constant and variable, fixed and circulating) differ from each other by their functions, but the division of capital into productive, money and commodity capital, is also based on differences in function. The "functions of commodity and commercial capital" are distinguished from the "functions of productive capital" (C., II, pp. 127, 79; C, III, p. 269, and elsewhere).

Thus different categories of political economy describe different social functions of things, corresponding to different production relations among people. But the social function which is realized through a thing gives this thing a particular social character, a determined social form, a "determination of form" (Formbestimmtheit),[118] as Marx frequently wrote. A specific social function or "economic form" of things corresponds to each type of production relations among people. Marx more than once pointed out the close relationship between the function and the form. "The coat officiates as equivalent, or appears in equivalent form" (C., I, p. 48). "This specific function in the process of circulation gives money, as a medium of circulation, a new determination of form" (Kritik der Politischen Oekonomie, p. 92). If the social function of a thing gives the thing a specific social-economic form, then it is clear that the basic categories of political economy (which we considered above as expressions of different production relations and social functions of things) serve as expressions of social-economic forms which correspond to things. These forms give things their function as "bearers" of the production relations among people. Most often Marx called the economic phenomena which he

---

[118] The concept of Formbestimmtheit or Formbestimmung plays a large role in Marx' system. The system is concerned above all with the analysis of social forms of economy, namely production relations among people. Instead of Formbestimmrheit, Marx often said Bestimmrheit. V. Bazarov and I. Stepanov sometimes very correctly translate the latter term with the word "form" (Cf. Kapital, Vol. III, Book II, pp. 365-366, and the Russian translation, p. 359). It is completely impermissible to translate "Bestimmtheit" with the word "nomination" ("naznachenie"), as is often done by P. Rumyantsev (Kritik der Politischen Oekonomie, p. 10, and the Russian translation, p. 40). The translation "formal determination" ("formal'noe opredelenie") also misses Marx's point. (Nakoplenie kapitali i krizisy, The Accumulation of Capital and Crises, by S. Bessonova.) We prefer a precise translation: "determination of form" or "definition of form."

analyzed, "economic forms," "definitions of forms." Marx's system examines a series of increasingly complex "economic forms" of things or "definitions of forms"(Formbestimmtheiten) which correspond to a series of increasingly complex production relations among people. In the Preface to the first edition of the first volume of Capital, Marx pointed out the difficulties of "analyzing economic forms," particularly "the form of value" and "the money form." The form of value, in turn, includes various forms: on one hand, every expression of value contains a "relative form" and an "equivalent form," and on the other hand, the historical development of value is expressed in the increasing complexity of its forms: from an "elementary form" through an "expanded form," value passes to a "general form" and a "money form." The formation of money is a "new definition of form" (Kritik der Politischen Oekonomie, p. 28). Different functions of money are at the same time different "definitions of form" (Ibid., p. 46). Thus, for example, money as a measure of value and as a standard of price are "different definitions of form," the confusion of which has led to erroneous theories (Ibid., p. 54).[119] "The particular functions of money which it performs, either as the mere equivalent of commodities, or as means of circulation, or means of payment, as hoard or as universal money, point, according to the extent and relative preponderance of the one function or the other, to very different stages in the process of social production" (C., I, p. 170; emphasis added). What is emphasized here is the close connection between the forms (functions) of money and the development of production relations among people.

The transition of money into capital indicates the emergence of a new economic form. "Capital is a social form which is acquired by means of reproduction when they are used by wage labor" (Theorien uber den Mehrwert, Vol III, p. 383), a particular "social

---

[119] Translated as "distinct forms of expression" in the English edition of the Critique, 1904, p. 81. (tr.)

determination" (Ibid., p. 547). Wage labor is also "a social determination of labor" (Ibid., p. 563), i.e., a determined social form of labor. The component parts of productive capital (constant and variable, fixed and circulating, examined in terms of the differences of their functions, also represent different forms of capital (C., II, pp. 167-168, and elsewhere). Fixed capital represents a "determination of form" (C., II, p. 169). In the same way, money, productive capital, and commodity capital are different forms of capital (C., II, p. 50). A particular social function corresponds to each of these forms. Money and commodity capital are "special, differentiated forms, modes of existence corresponding to special functions of industrial capital" (C., II, p. 83). Capital passes "from one functional form to another, so that the industrial capital... exists simultaneously in its various phases and functions" (Ibid., p. 106). If these functions become independent from each other and are carried out by the separate capitals, then these capitals take on independent forms of commodity-commercial capital and money commercial capital "through the fact that the definite forms and functions which capital assumes for the moment appear as independent forms and functions of a separate portion of the capital and are exclusively bound up with it" (C., III p. 323).

Thus economic categories express different production relations among people and the social functions which correspond to them, or the social-economic forms of things. These functions or forms have a social character because they are inherent, not in things as such, but in things which are parts of a definite social environment, namely things through which people enter into certain production relations with each other. These forms do not reflect the properties of things but the properties of the social environment. Sometimes Marx simply spoke of "form" or "determination of form," but what he meant was precisely "economic form," "social form," "historical-social form," "social determination of form," "economic determination of form," "historical-social determination" (See, for example, C., I, p. 146, 147,

149; C., III, p. 816, 830; Kapital, Vol. III, Book II, pp. 351, 358, 360, 366; Theorien uber den Mehrwert, Vol. III, pp. 484-485, 547, 563; Kritik der Politischen Oekonomie, p. 20, and elsewhere). Sometimes Marx also says that the thing acquires a "social existence," "formal existence" (Formdasein), "functional existence," "ideal existence." (Cf, C., I, pp. 125, 129; Theorien uber den Mehrwert, Vol. III, pp. 314, 349; Kritik der Politischen Oekonomie, p. 28, 101, 100, 94.) This social or functional existence of things is opposed to their "material existence," "actual existence," "direct existence," "objective existence" (C., I, p 129; Kritik der Politischen Oekonomie, p. 102; Kapital, Vol. III, Book II, pp. 359, 360, and Vol. III, Book I, p. 19; Theorien uber den Mehrwert, Vol. III, p. 193, 292, 320, 434). In the same way the social form or function is opposed to the "material content," "material substance," "content," "substance," "elements of production," material and objective elements and conditions of production (C., I, p. 36, 126, 146, 147, 149; C., III, pp 824-5; Kritik der Politischen Oekonomie, pp. 100-104, 121; Theorien uber den Mehrwert, Vol. III, p. 315, 316, 318, 326, 329, 424, and elsewhere).[120] All these expressions which distinguish between the technical and social functions of things, between the technical role of instruments and conditions of labor and their social form, can be reduced to the basic difference which we formulated earlier. We are dealing with the basic distinction between the material process of production

---

[120] It must be pointed out that sometimes Marx uses the terms "function" and "form" in a material-technical sense, the first term very often, the second more rarely. This creates a terminological inconvenience, but in essence this does not prevent Marx from making clear distinctions between the two senses of these terms, except for some passages which are unclear and contradictory (for example, in Volume II, part II of Capital). On the other hand, the terms "substance" and "content" are used by Marx not only to refer to the material process of production, but also to its social forms.

and its social forms, with two different aspects (technical and social) of the unified process of human working activity. Political economy deals with the production relations among people, i.e., with the social forms of the process of production, as opposed to its material-technical aspects.

Does this not mean that Marx's economic theory isolated the production relations among people from the development of productive forces when he analyzed the social form of production in isolation from its material-technical side? No at all. Every social-economic form analyzed by Marx presupposes, as given, a determined stage of the material-technical process of production. The development of the forms of value and money presupposes, as we have seen, constant "exchange of matter" (Stoffwechsel), the passage of material things. Value presupposes use value. The process of the formation of value presupposes the process of producing use values. Abstract labor presupposes a totality of different kinds of concrete labor applied in different branches of production. Socially necessary labor presupposes a different productivity of labor in various enterprises of the same branch. Surplus value presupposes a given level of development of productive forces. Capital and wage labor presuppose a social form of technical factors of production: material and personal. After the capitalist's purchase of labor power, the same difference between material and personal factors of production acquires the form of constant and variable capital. The relation between constant and variable capital, i.e., the organic composition of capital, is based on a certain technical structure. Another division of capital, into fixed and circulating, also presupposes a technical difference between the gradual wear and tear of instruments of labor and the complete consumption of the objects of labor and of labor power. The metamorphoses, or changes, of form of capital are based on the fact that productive capital directly organizes the material process of production. Money or commodity capital are more indirectly related to the material process of production, because directly they represent the stage of exchange. Thus on the one hand there is a difference between enterprise profit, commercial profit and interest, and on the other hand between productive and unproductive labor (employed in trade). The reproduction of capital presupposes the reproduction of its material component parts. The formation of a general average profit rate presupposes different technical and organic compositions of capital in individual industrial branches. Absolute rent presupposes a difference between industry, on the one hand, and agriculture on the other. Different levels of productivity of labor in different agricultural enterprises and extractive industries, caused by differences in fertility and location of plots, is expressed in the form of differential rent.

Thus we see that production relations among people develop on the basis of a certain state of productive forces. Economic categories presuppose certain technical conditions. But in political economy, technical conditions do not appear as conditions for the process of production treated from its technical aspects, but only as presuppositions of the determined social-economic forms which the production process assumes. The productive process appears in a given social-economic form, namely in the form of commodity-capitalist economy. Political economy treats precisely this form of economy and the totality of production relations which are proper to it. Marx's renowned theory according to which use value is the presupposition and not the source of exchange value must be formulated in a generalized way: Political economy deals with "economic forms," types of production relations among people in capitalist society. This society presupposes given conditions of the material process of production and of the technical factors which are its components. But Marx always protested against the transformation of the conditions of the material process of production from presuppositions of political economy into its subject matter. He rejected theories which derived value from use value, money from the technical properties of gold, and capital from the technical productivity of means of production. Economic categories, (or social forms of things) are of course very closely related to the material process of production, but they cannot be derived from it directly, but only by means of an indirect link: the production relations among people. Even in categories where technical and economic aspects are closely related and almost cover each other, Marx very skillfully distinguished one from another by considering the former as the presupposition of the latter. For example, the technical development of personal and material factors of production is a presupposition or basis on which the "functional," "formal" or social-economic distinction between variable and constant capital develops. But Marx decidedly refused to draw a distinction between them on the basis of the fact that they serve "as payment for a materially different element of production" (C., III, p. 32). For him this difference lay in their functionally different roles in the process of "the expansion of capital" (Ibid). The difference between fixed and circulating capital lies in the different ways that their value is transferred to products, and not in how fast they wear out physically. The latter distinction gives a material basis, a presupposition, a "point of departure" for the former, but not the distinction we are looking for, which has an economic and not a technical character (C., II, p. 201, Theorien uber den Mehrwert, Vol. III, p. 558). To accept this technical presupposition as our subject matter would mean that the analysis would be similar to that of vulgar economists whom Marx charged with "crudity" of analytical method because they were interested in "distinctions of form" and considered them "only from their substantive side" (C., III, p. 323).

Marx's economic theory deals precisely with the "differences in form" (social-economic forms, production relations) which actually develop on the basis of certain material-technical conditions, but which must not be confused with them. It is precisely this that represents the completely new methodological formulation of economic problems which is Marx's great service and distinguishes his work from that of his predecessors, the Classical Economists. The attention of Classical Economists was directed to discovering the material-technical basis of social forms which they took as given and not subject to further analysis. It was Marx's goal to discover the laws of the origin and development of the social forms assumed by the material-technical production process at a given level of development of productive forces.

This extremely profound difference in analytical method between the Classical Economists and Marx reflects different and necessary stages of development of economic thought. Scientific analysis "begins with the results of the process of development ready to hand" (C., I, p. 75), with the numerous social-economic forms of things which the analyst finds already established and fixed in his surrounding reality (value, money, capital, wages, etc.). These forms "have already acquired the stability of natural, self - understood forms of social life, before man seeks to decipher, not their historical character, for in his eyes they are immutable, but their meaning." (Ibid., emphasis added.) In order to discover the content of these social forms, the Classical Economists reduced complex forms to simple (abstract) forms in their analyses, and in this way they finally arrived at the material-technical bases of the process of production. By means of such analysis they discovered labor in value, means of production in capital, means of workers' subsistence in wages, surplus product (which is brought about by increased productivity of labor) in profit. Starting with given social forms and taking them for eternal and natural forms of the process of production, they did not ask themselves how these forms had originated. For Classical Political Economy, "the genetic development of different forms is not a concern. It [Classical Political Economy] only wants to reduce them to their unity by means of analysis, since it starts with them as given assumptions" (Theorien uber den Mehrwert, Vol. III, p. 572). Afterwards, when the given social-economic forms are finally reduced to their material-technical content, the Classical Economists consider their task complete. But precisely where they stop their analysis is where Marx continues. Since he was not restricted by the horizon of the capitalist economy, and since he saw it as only one of past and possible social forms of economy, Marx asked: why does the material-technical content of the labor process at a given level of development of productive forces assume a particular, given social form? Marx's methodological formulation of the problem runs approximately as follows: why does labor assume the form of value, means of production the form of capital, means of workers' subsistence the form of wages, increased productivity of labor the form of increased surplus value? His attention was directed to the analysis of social forms of economy and the laws of their origin and development, and to "the process of development of forms (Gestaltungsprozess) in their various phases" (Ibid.). This genetic (or dialectical) method, which contains analysis and synthesis, was contrasted by Marx with the one-sided analytical method of the Classical Economists. The uniqueness of Marx's analytical method does not consist only of its historical, but also of its sociological character, of the intense attention which it paid to social forms of economy. Starting with the social forms as given, the Classical Economists tried to reduce complex forms to simpler forms by means of analysis in order finally to discover their material-technical basis or content. However, Marx, starting from a given condition of the material process of production, from a given level of productive forces, tried to explain the origin and character of social forms which are assumed by the material process of production. He started with simple forms and, by means of the genetic or dialectical method, he went on to increasingly complex forms. This is why, as we said earlier, Marx's dominant interest is in "economic forms," in "determinations of forms" (Formbestimmtheiten).

Chapter 5: Production Relations and Material Categories

At first glance all the basic concepts of Political Economy (value, money, capital, profit, rent, wages, etc.) have a material character. Marx showed that under each of them is hidden a definite social production relation which in the commodity economy is realized only through things and gives things a determined, objectively-social character, a "determination of form" (more precisely: a social form), as Marx often put it. Analyzing any economic category, we must first of all point to the social production relation expressed by it. Only if the material category is an expression of a precisely given, determined production relation, does it enter the framework of our analysis. If this material category is not related to a given production relation among people, we pull it out of the framework of our analysis and set it aside. We classify economic phenomena into groups and build concepts on the basis of the identity of the production relations which the phenomena express, and not on the basis of the coincidence of their material expressions. For example, the theory of value deals with exchange between autonomous commodity producers, with their interaction in the labor process through the products of their labor. The fluctuation of the value of products on the market interests economists not for itself, but as it is related to the distribution of labor in society, to the production relations among independent commodity producers. For example, if land (which is not the product of exchange) appears in exchange, then production relations in this case do not connect commodity producers with commodity producers, but with a landowner; if the price fluctuations of plots of land have a different influence on the course and distribution of the production process from the price fluctuations of the products of labor, then we are dealing with a different social relation, a different production relation, behind the same material form of exchange and value. This social relation is subject to special analysis, namely in the context of the theory of rent. Thus land, which has price, i.e., a money expression of value (as a material category), does not have "value" in the sense mentioned above, i.e., in the act of exchange the price of land does not express the functional social relation which relates the value of the products of labor with the working activity of independent commodity producers. This led Marx to the following formulation, which has often been misinterpreted: "Objects that in themselves are not commodities, such as conscience, honor, &c., are capable of being offered for sale by their holders, and of thus acquiring, through their price, the form of commodities. Hence an object may have a price without having value. The price in that case is imaginary, like certain quantities in mathematics. On the other hand, the imaginary price-form may sometimes conceal either a direct or an indirect real value relation; for instance, the price of uncultivated land, which is without value, because no human labor has been incorporated in it" (C., I, p. 102). These words of Marx, which have often puzzled and even provoked the mockery of critics,[121] express a profound idea about the possible divergence between the social form of working relations and the material form which corresponds to it.

---

[121] "Real phenomena, such as the value of land, are presented as 'imaginary' and 'irrational,' while imaginary concepts, such as the mysterious 'exchange value,' which does not appear in exchange, are identified as the only reality" (Tugan-Baranovskii, Teoreticheskie osnovy marksizma, Theoretical Bases of Marxism, 4th Ed., 1918, p. 118). The passage by Marx which was cited above means that, even though the purchase and sale of land does not directly express relations between commodity producers through the products of their labor, it is nevertheless related to these relations and can be explained in terms of them. In other words, the theory of rent is derived from the theory of value. Riekes incorrectly interpreted this passage in the sense that the protection of landed property requires expenditures, i.e., labor, which is expressed in the price of land (Riekes, Hugo, Wert und Tauschwert, Berlin: L. Simion, [n.d.] p. 27).

The material form has its own logic and can include other phenomena in addition to the production relations which it expresses in a given economic formation. For example, in addition to the exchange of products of labor among independent commodity producers (the basic fact of the commodity economy), the material form of exchange includes the exchange of plots of land, the exchange of goods which cannot be multiplied by labor, exchange in a socialist society, etc. From the standpoint of the material forms of economic phenomena, the sale of cotton and the sale of a painting by Raphael or a plot of land do not in any way differ from each other. But from the standpoint of their social nature, their connection with production relations, and their impact on the working activity of society, the two phenomena are of a different order and have to be analyzed separately.

Marx frequently emphasized that one and the same phenomenon appears in a different light depending on its social form. Means of production, for example, are not capital in the workshop of a craftsman who works with them, though the same things become capital when they express and help to realize a production relation between wage laborers and their employer-capitalist. Even in the hands of a capitalist, means of production are capital only within the limits of the production relation between the capitalist and the wage laborers. In the hands of a money-capitalist, the means of production play a different social role. "Means of production are capital if, from the worker's standpoint, they function as his non-property, i.e., as someone else's property. In this form, they function only as opposed to the labor. The existence of these conditions in the form of an opposition to labor transforms their owner into a capitalist, and the means of production which belong to him, into capital. But in the hands of money-capitalist A, capital lacks this quality of opposition which transforms his money into capital, and thus the ownership of money into the ownership of capital. The real determination of form (Formbestimmtheit) through which money or commodities are transformed into capital has disappeared in this case. Money capitalist A is not in any way related to a worker, but only to another capitalist, B" (Theorien uber den Mehrwert, Vol. III, pp. 530-531, emphasis by Marx). Determination of social forms, which depends on the character of production relations, is the basis for the formation and classification of economic concepts.

Political Economy deals with determined material categories if they are connected with social production relations. Inversely, the basic production relations of the commodity economy are realized and expressed only in material form, and they are analyzed by economic theory precisely in this material form. The specific character of economic theory as a science which deals with the commodity capitalist economy lies precisely in the fact that it deals with production relations which acquire material forms. Of course the cause of this reification of production relations lies in the spontaneous character of the commodity economy. Precisely because commodity production, the subject of economic theory, is characterized by spontaneity, Political Economy as the science of the commodity economy, deals with material categories. The logical specificity of theoretical-economic knowledge must be derived precisely from that material character of economic categories, and not directly from the spontaneity of the national economy. The revolution in Political Economy which Marx carried out consists in his having considered social production relations behind material categories. This is the genuine subject of political economy as a social science. With this new "sociological" approach, economic phenomena appeared in a new light, in a different perspective. The same laws which had been established by the Classical

Economists were given a completely different character and meaning in Marx's system.[122]

Chapter 6: Struve on the Theory of Commodity Fetishism

Marx's approach to economic categories as expressions of social production relations (which we treated in the previous chapter) provoked criticism from P. Struve in his book, Khozyaistvo i Tsena (Economy and Price). Struve recognizes the merit of Marx's theory of fetishism in the sense that it revealed, behind capital, a social production relation between classes of capitalists and workers. But he does not consider it correct to stretch the theory of fetishism to the concept of value and to other economic categories. Struve and other critics of Marx transform the theory of fetishism from a general, fundamental basis of Marx's system into a separate, even if brilliant, digression.

Struve's critique is closely related to his classification of all economic categories into three classes: 1) "Economic" categories which express "economic relations of each economic agent with the outside world,"[123] for example, subjective value (tsennost). 2) "Intereconomic" categories which express "phenomena arising from interactions among autonomous economic units" (p. 17), for example, objective (exchange) value. 3) "Social" categories which express "phenomena which arise from interactions

---

[122] Ignorance of this essential distinction between Marx's theory of value and the theory of the Classical Economists accounts for the weakness of Rosenberg's book (Isaiah Rosenberg, Ricardo und Marx als Werttheoreriker; eine Kritische Studie, Wien: Kommissionsverlag von I. Brand, 1904).

[123] Khozyaisrvo i Tsena (Economy and Price), Vol. I, p. 17.

among economic agents who occupy different social positions" (p. 27), for example, capital.

Struve places only the third group ("social" categories) within the concept of social production relations. In other words, in the place of social production relations, he puts a narrower concept, namely production relations between social classes. From this starting point, Struve admits that production relations (i.e., social and class relations) are concealed behind the category of capital, but by no means behind the category of value (Struve uses the term "tsennost"), which expresses relations among equal, independent, autonomous commodity producers and thus is related to the second class of "intereconomic" categories. Marx correctly discovered the fetishism of capital, but he was mistaken in his theory of the fetishism of commodities and commodity value.

The inaccuracy of Struve's reasoning is a result of his unfounded classification of economic categories into three classes. First of all, to the extent that "economic" categories are expressions of "pure economic" activities (within the economic unit), cut off from all social forms of production, they are altogether outside the limits of Political Economy as a social science. "Intereconomic" categories cannot be as sharply distinguished from social categories as Struve suggests. The "interaction among autonomous economic units" is not only a formal characteristic which applies to different economic formations and to all historical epochs. It is a determined social fact, a determined "production relation" between individual economic units based on private ownership and connected by the division of labor, i.e., a relation which presupposes a society with a given social structure and which is fully developed only in the commodity capitalist economy.

Finally, when we examine the "social" categories, it must be pointed out that Struve limited them, without adequate foundation, to the "interaction among economic agents who occupy different social positions." But it has already been shown that the "equality" between commodity producers is a social fact, a determined production relation. Struve himself grasped the close connection between the "intereconomic" category (which expresses equality between commodity producers) and the "social" category (which expresses social inequality). He says that social categories "in every society are built according to the type of economic intercourse, and seem to acquire the form of intereconomic categories...The fact that social categories, in intereconomic intercourse, wear the clothes of intereconomic categories, creates an appearance of identity between them" (p. 27). Actually, this is not an instance of wearing the wrong clothes. What we are confronting is one of the basic, highly characteristic features of the commodity-capitalist society. It consists of the fact that in economic life social relations do not have the character of direct social domination of some social groups over others, but that they are realized by means of "economic constraint," i.e., by means of the interaction of individual, autonomous economic agents, on the basis of agreements between them. Capitalists use power "not as political or theocratic rulers" but as "the personification of the conditions of labor in contrast to labor" (C., III, p. 881). Relations among classes have, as their starting point, relations between capitalists and workers as autonomous economic agents. These relations cannot be analyzed or understood without the category of "value."

Struve himself could not consistently maintain his point of view. In his view, capital is a social category. However, he defines it as a "system of interclass and intraclass social relations" (pp. 31-32), i.e., relations between classes of capitalists and workers on the one hand, and relations between individual capitalists in the process of distribution of the total profit among them, on the other hand. But relations between individual capitalists are not brought about "by the interaction of economic agents who occupy different social positions." Why are they then subsumed under the "social" category, capital? This means that the "social" categories do not only include interclass relations, but also intraclass relations, i.e., relations between persons who are in the same class position. Yet what prevents us from seeing value as a "social" category, from seeing relations among autonomous commodity producers as social production relations, or in Struve's terminology, as social relations?

We thus see that Struve himself did not maintain a sharp distinction of social-production relations into two types: inter-economic and social. Thus he is wrong when he sees a "scientific inconsistency in the construction" by Marx according to which the "social category, capital, as a social 'relation' is derived from the economic category, value" (tsennost) (p. 29). First of all it must be pointed out that Struve himself, on page 30, contradicts himself when he classifies value (tsennost) as an "intereconomic" and not an economic category. Apparently Struve relates subjective value (tsennost) to "economic" categories, and objective, exchange value, to "intereconomic" categories. (This can be seen by comparing this statement with his reasoning on page 25.) But Struve is very familiar with the fact that Marx derived (the concept of) capital from objective, and not subjective, value, i.e., according to Struve's own terminology, from the intereconomic, and not the economic, category. It is because of this that Struve attacks Marx. As a matter of fact, the "social" category, capital, as well as the "intereconomic" category, value, belong to the same group of categories in Marx's system. These are social-production relations, or as Marx sometimes said, social-economic relations, i.e., each expresses an economic aspect and its social form, as opposed to their artificial separation by Struve.

By narrowing the concept of production relations to the concept of "social" or more precisely, class relations, Struve is aware that Marx uses this concept in a wider sense. Struve says: "In The Poverty of Philosophy, supply and demand, division of labor, credit, money, are relations of production. Finally, on page 130 we read: 'a modern factory, based on the application of machinery, is a social production relation, an economic category.' It is obvious that all the generally used economic concepts of our time are treated here as social production relations. This is undoubtedly correct if the content of these concepts refers in one way or another to social relations among people in the process of economic life" (p. 30). But not negating, one might say, the accuracy of Marx's conception of production relations, Struve nevertheless finds this concept "exceptionally undetermined" (p. 30), and he considers it more correct to confine the scope of this concept to "social" categories. This is highly characteristic of some critics of Marxism. After Marx's analysis, it is no longer possible to ignore the role of the social aspect of production, i.e., its social form. If one does not agree with Marx's conclusions, all that remains is to separate the social aspect from the economic, and to disregard the social aspect, to assign it to a separate field. This was done by Struve; this was done by Bohm-Bawerk, who based his theory on the motives of "pure economic activity," i.e., on the motives of the economic agent isolated from a given social and historical context - promising that later on, sometime in the future, the role and significance of the "social" categories will be examined.

Restricting the theory of fetishism to the field of "social" categories, Struve considers it wrong to stretch the theory to intereconomic categories, for example to the concept of value. This accounts for the duality of his position. On one hand, he has high regard for Marx's theory of capital as a social relation. But on the other hand, with respect to other economic categories, he himself supports a fetishistic point of view. "All intereconomic categories thus always express phenomena and objective relations, but at the same time human relations - relations among people. Thus subjective value, which is transformed into objective (exchange) value, from a state of mind, from a feeling fixed to objects (things) becomes their property" (p. 25). Here it is impossible not to see a contradiction. On one hand, we analyze "objective, and at the same time human" relations, i.e., social production relations which are realized through things and are expressed in things. On the other hand, here we are dealing with the "property" of the things themselves. Thus Struve concluded: "From here it is clear that 'reification,' 'objectification' of human relations, i.e., the phenomenon which Marx called the fetishism of the commodity world, appears in economic intercourse as a psychological necessity. If scientific analysis, consciously or unconsciously, restricts itself to economic intercourse, the fetishistic point of view manifests itself methodologically as the only accurate point of view" (p 25). If Struve had wanted to prove that economic theory cannot remove material categories, and that it has to examine the production relations of a commodity economy in their material form, then he would obviously be right. But the question is whether, following Marx, we analyze the material categories as the form in which the given production relations are manifested, or as the property of things, which is Struve's inclination.

Struve, with yet another argument, tried to advocate a fetishistic, material interpretation of "intereconomic" categories. "Considering inter-economic categories Marx forgot that in their concrete and real manifestations they are inseparably connected with the relations of man toward the external world, to nature and to things" (p. 26). In other words, Struve emphasized the role of the process of material production. Marx took sufficient account of that role in his theory of the dependence of production relations on the development of productive forces. However, when we study social forms of production, i.e., production relations, we cannot draw conclusions about the significance of material categories from the significance of things in the process of material production. Marx threw light on the question of the particular interrelationship between the material process of production and its social form in a commodity-capitalist society. It is on this, in fact, that he built his theory of commodity fetishism.

Some of Marx's critics have tried to restrict the theory of fetishism in a manner which is just the opposite from Struve's. Struve recognizes the fetishism of capital, but not the fetishism of value. To some extent we find just the opposite in Hammacher. According to Hammacher, in the first volume of Marx's great work, "capital is defined as the totality of commodities which represent accumulated labor," i.e., a material definition of capital is given, and only in Volume III does the "fetishism of capital" appear. Hammacher holds that Marx transferred to capital the characteristics of commodities purely by analogy, considering "commodities and capital as being only quantitatively different."[124]

The assertion that in the first volume of Capital, capital is defined as a thing and not as a social relation does not even have to be disproved, because it contradicts the entire content of the first volume of Capital. It is just as mistaken to think that Marx saw only a "quantitative" difference between commodities and capital. Marx pointed out that capital "announces from its first appearance a new epoch in the process of social production" (C., I, p. 170). But commodities as well as capital conceal within themselves determined social relations in a material form. The fetishism of commodities as well as the resulting fetishism of capital are equally present in the capitalist society. However, it is inaccurate to confine Marx's theory of fetishism only to the field of capital, as Struve does, or only to the field of simple commodity exchange. The materialization of social production relations lies at the very basis of the unorganized commodity economy, and it leaves its imprint on all the basic categories of everyday economic reasoning and also on Political Economy as the science of the commodity capitalist economy.

---

[124] Hammacher, Emit, Das philosophisch-okonomische System des Marxismus, Leipzig: Duncker and Humbtot, 1909, p. 546.

Chapter 7: Marx's Development of the Theory of Fetishism

The question of the origin and development of Marx's theory of fetishism has until now remained completely unexamined. Though Marx was very thorough in pointing out the origins of his labor theory of value in all his predecessors (in three volumes of Theories of Surplus Value he presented a long list of their theories), Marx was very stingy in his remarks on the theory of fetishism. (In Volume III of Theorien uber den Mehwert, pp. 354-5, 1910 edition, Marx mentions an embryonic form of the theory of fetishism in Hodgskin's work. In our opinion, the remarks are very unclear, and refer to a particular instance.) Although the question of the relation of Marx's theory of value to the theory of the Classical Economists was discussed in economic literature with great zeal though without particular success, the development of Marx's ideas on commodity fetishism has not attracted particular attention.

A few observations on the origin of Marx's theory of commodity fetishism can be found in Hammacher's book (cited earlier). In his view, the origins of this theory are purely "metaphysical." Marx simply transferred to the field of economics Feuerbach's ideas on religion. According to Feuerbach, the development of religion represents a process of man's "self-alienation": man transfers his own essence to the external world, transforms it into god, estranges it from himself. At first Marx applies this theory of "alienation" to ideological phenomena: "the entire content of consciousness represents an alienation from economic conditions on the basis of which ideology must then be explained" (Hammacher, op. cit., p. 233). Later Marx expands this theory to the field of economic relations and in them he reveals an "alienated" material form. Hammacher says that "for almost all earlier historical epochs, the mode of production itself represented a universal self-alienation; social relations became things, i.e., the thing expressed what was actually a relation. Feuerbach's theory of alienation thus receives a new character" (Ibid., p. 233). "Human needs are realized and appear in the form of alienated essences in religion, according to Feuerbach, just as economic relations do in social life according to Marx" (p. 234). Thus Marx's theory of fetishism represents "a specific synthesis of Hegel, Feuerbach and Ricardo" (p. 236), with a primary influence of Feuerbach, as we have seen. The theory of fetishism transfers Feuerbach's religious-philosophical theory of "alienation" into the field of economics. Thus it can be seen that this theory does not contribute in any way to an understanding of economic phenomena in general and commodity forms in particular, according to Hammacher. "The key to the understanding of Marx's theory lies in the metaphysical origin of the theory of fetishism, but it is not a key for unveiling the commodity form" (p. 544). The theory of fetishism contains an extremely valuable "critique of contemporary culture," a culture which is reified and which represses living man; but "as an economic theory of value, commodity fetishism is mistaken" (p.546). "Economically untenable, the theory of fetishism becomes an extremely valuable sociological theory" (p. 661).

Hammacher's conclusion on the sterility of Marx's theory of fetishism for understanding the entire economic system and particularly the theory of value is a result of Hammacher's inaccurate understanding of the "metaphysical" origins of this theory. Hammacher refers to The Holy Family, a work written by Marx and Engels at the end of 1844, when Marx was still under strong influence of utopian socialist ideas, particularly Proudhon's. Actually in that work we find the embryo of the theory of fetishism in the form of a contrast between "social," or "human" relations, and their "alienated," materialized form. The source of this contrast was the widespread conception of Utopian Socialists on the character of the capitalist system. According to the Utopian Socialists, this system is characterized by the fact that the worker is forced to "self-alienate" his personality, and that he "alienates" the product of his labor from himself. The domination of "things," of capital over man, over the worker, is expressed through this alienation.

We can quote certain citations from The Holy Family. The capitalist society is "in practice, a relation of alienation of man from his objectified essence, as well as an economic expression of human self-alienation" (Literatunoye nasledie, Literacy Legacy, Vol. II, Russian translation, 1908, pp. 163-4). "The definition of purchase already includes the manner in which the worker relates to his product, as toward an object which is lost for him, which is alienated" (p. 175). "The class of the propertied and the class of the proletariat represent human self-alienation to the same extent. But the first class experiences itself as satisfied and confirmed in this self-alienation. It sees in this alienation a confirmation of its power. In this alienation it holds an image of its human existence. However, the second class experiences itself annihilated in this alienation. It sees its own weakness in this alienation, and the reality of its inhuman existence" (p. 155).

It is against this "apex of inhumanity" of capitalist exploitation, against this "separation from everything human, even from the appearance of the human" (p. 156) that Utopian Socialism raises its voice in the name of eternal justice and of the interest of the oppressed working masses. "Inhuman" reality is contrasted with Utopia, the ideal of the "human." This is precisely why Marx praised Proudhon, contrasting him to bourgeois economists. "Sometimes political economists stress the significance of the human element, though only one aspect of this element, in economic relations, but they do this in exceptional cases, namely when they attack a particular abuse; sometimes (in the majority of cases) they take these relations as they are given, with their obviously expressed negation of everything human, namely in their strict economic sense" (p. 151). "All the conclusions of political economy presuppose private property. This basic assumption is, in their eyes, an incontestable fact which is not susceptible to further investigation. ... However, Proudhon exposes the basis of political economy, namely private property, to critical examination " (p. 149). "By making working time (which is the direct essence of human activity as such) the measure of wages and the value of the product, Proudhon makes the human element decisive. However, in old political economy the decisive factor was the material power of capital and landed property" (p. 172).

Thus in the capitalist society the "material" element, the power of capital, dominates. This is not an illusory, erroneous interpretation (in the human mind) of social relations among people, relations of domination and subordination; it is a real, social fact. "Property, capital, money, wage labor and similar categories, do not, in themselves, represent phantoms of the imagination, but very practical, very concrete products of the self-alienation of the worker" (pp. 176-177). This "material" element, which in fact dominates in economic life, is opposed by the "human" element as an ideal, as a norm, as that which should be. Human relations and their "alienated forms" - these are two worlds, the world of what should be and the world of what is; this is a condemnation of capitalist reality in the name of a socialist ideal. This opposition between the human and the material element reminds us of Marx's theory of commodity fetishism, but in essence it moves in a different world of ideas. In order to transform this theory of "alienation" of human relations into a theory of "reification" of social relations (i.e., into the theory of commodity fetishism), Marx had to create a path from Utopian to Scientific socialism, from praises of Proudhon to a sharp critique of his ideas, from negating reality in the name of an ideal to seeking within reality itself the forces for further development and motion. From The Holy Family Marx had to move toward The Poverty of Philosophy. In the first of these works Proudhon was praised for taking as the starting point of his observations the negation of private property, but later Marx built his economic system precisely by analyzing the commodity economy based on private property. In The Holy Family, Proudhon is given credit for his conception that the value of the product is constituted on the basis of working time (as "the direct essence of human activity"). But in The Poverty of Philosophy, Proudhon is subjected to criticism for this theory. The formula on "the determination of value by labor time" is transformed in Marx's mind from a norm of what should be into a "scientific expression of the economic relations of present-day society." (The Poverty of Philosophy, cited earlier, p. 69). From Proudhon, Marx partially returns to Ricardo, from Utopia he passes to the analysis of the actual reality of the capitalist economy.

Marx's transition from Utopian to Scientific Socialism introduced an essential change into the above-mentioned theory of "alienation." If the opposition which he had earlier described between human relations and their "material" form meant an opposition between what should be and what is, now both opposing factors are transferred to the world as it is, to social being. The economic life of contemporary society is on the one hand the totality of social production relations, and on the other a series of "material" categories in which these relations are manifested. Production relations among people and their "material" form is the content of a new opposition, which originated in the earlier opposition between the "human" element in the economy and its "alienated" forms. The formula of commodity fetishism was found in this way. But several stages were still necessary before Marx gave this theory its final formulation.

As can be seen from the citations from The Poverty of Philosophy, Marx said more than once that money, capital and other economic categories are not things, but production relations. Marx gave a general formulation to these thoughts in the following words: "Economic categories are only the theoretical expressions, the abstractions of the social relations of production" (The Poverty of Philosophy, p. 109). Marx already saw social production relations behind the material categories of the economy. But he did not yet ask why production relations among people necessarily receive this material form in a commodity economy. This step was taken by Marx in A Contribution to the Critique of Political Economy, where he says that "labor, which creates exchange value, is characterized by the fact that even social relations of men appear in the reverse form of a social relation of things" (Critique, p. 30). Here the accurate formulation of commodity fetishism is given. The material character which is present in the production relations of the commodity economy is emphasized, but the cause of this "materialization" and its necessity in an unregulated national economy are not yet pointed out.

In this "materialization" Marx apparently sees above all a "mystification" which is obvious in commodities and more obscure in money and capital. He explains that this mystification is possible because of the "habits acquired in everyday life." "It is only through the habit of everyday life that we come to think it perfectly plain and commonplace, that a social relation of production should take on the form of a thing, so that the relation of persons in their work appears in the form of a mutual relation between things, and between things and persons" (p. 30). Hammacher is completely right when he finds that this explanation of commodity fetishism in terms of habits is very weak. But he is profoundly mistaken when he states that this is the only explanation given by Marx. "It is startling," Hammacher says, "that Marx neglected the grounds for this essential point; in Capital no explanation whatever is given" (Hammacher, op. cit., p. 235). If in Capital these "habits" are not mentioned, it is because the whole section of Chapter I on commodity fetishism contains a complete and profound explanation of this phenomenon. The absence of direct regulation of the social process of production necessarily leads to the indirect regulation of the production process through the market, through the products of labor, through things. Here the subject is the "materialization" of production relations and not only "mystification" or illusion. This is one of the characteristics of the economic structure of contemporary society. "In the form of society now under consideration, the behavior of men in the social process of production is purely atomic. Hence their relations to each other in production assume a material character independent of their control and conscious individual action. These facts manifest themselves at first by products as a general rule taking the form of commodities" (C., I, pp. 92-93). The materialization of production relations does not arise from "habits" but from the internal structure of the commodity economy. Fetishism is not only a phenomenon of social consciousness, but of social being. To hold, as Hammacher does, that Marx's only explanation of fetishism was in terms of "habits" is to neglect altogether this definitive formulation of the theory of commodity fetishism which we find in Volume I of Capital and in the chapter on "The Trinity Formula" in Volume III.

Thus in The Holy Family, the "human" element in the economy is contrasted to the "material," "alienated" element just as ideal to reality. In The Poverty of Philosophy Marx disclosed social production relations behind things. In A Contribution to the Critique of Political Economy, emphasis is placed on the specific character of the commodity economy, which consists of the fact that social production relations are "reified." A detailed description of this phenomenon and an explanation of its objective necessity in a commodity economy is found in Volume I of Capital, chiefly as it applies to the concepts of value (commodity), money and capital. In Volume III, in the chapter on "The Trinity Formula," Marx gives a further, though fragmentary, development of the same thoughts as they apply to the basic categories of the capitalist economy, and in particular he emphasizes the specific "coalescence" of social production relations with the process of material production.

II

Marx's Labor Theory of Value

Introduction

Marx's critics often fling at him the reproach that he did not completely prove his labor theory of value, but merely decreed it as something obvious. Other critics have been ready to see some type of proof in the first pages of Capital, and they aimed their heavy artillery against the statements with which Marx opens his work. This is the approach of Bohm-Bawerk in his critique (Karl Marx and the Close of his System; Positive Theory of Capital). Bohm-Bawerk's arguments at first glance seem so convincing that one may boldly say that not a single later critique was formulated without repeating them. However, Bohm-Bawerk's entire critique stands or falls together with the assumptions on which it is built: namely, that the first five pages of Capital contain the only basis on which Marx built his theory of value. Nothing is more erroneous than this conception. In the first pages of Capital, Marx, by means of the analytic method, passes from exchange value to value, and from value to labor. But the complete dialectical ground of Marx's theory of value can only be given on the basis of his theory of commodity fetishism which analyzes the general structure of the commodity economy. Only after one finds the basis of Marx's theory of value does it become clear what Marx says in the famous first chapter of Capital. Only then do Marx's theory of value as well as numerous critiques of it appear in a proper light. Only after Hilferding's work[125] did one begin to understand accurately the sociological character of Marx's theory of value. The point of departure of the labor theory of value is a determined social environment, a society with a determined production structure. This conception was often repeated by Marxists; but until Hilferding's time, no one made it the foundation-stone of the entire edifice of Marx's theory of value. Hilferding deserves great praise for this,

---

[125] "Bohm-Bawerks Marx-Kritik," Marx-Studien, Wien, 1904, and the previously cited article, "Zur Problemstellung der theoretischen Oekonomie bei Karl Marx," Die Neue Zeit, Stuttgart, 1904.

but unfortunately he confined himself to a general treatment of the problems of the theory of value, and did not systematically present its basis.

As was shown in Part I, on commodity fetishism, the central insight of the theory of fetishism is not that political economy discloses production relations among people behind material categories, but that in a commodity-capitalist economy, these production relations among people necessarily acquire a material form and can be realized only in this form. The usual short formulation of this theory holds that the value of the commodity depends on the quantity of labor socially necessary for its production; or, in a general formulation, that labor is hidden behind, or contained in, value: value = "materialized" labor. It is more accurate to express the theory of value inversely: in the commodity-capitalist economy, production work relations among people necessarily acquire the form of the value of things, and can appear only in this material form; social labor can only be expressed in value. Here the point of departure for research is not value but labor, not the transactions of market exchange as such, but the production structure of the commodity society, the totality of production relations among people. The transactions of market exchange are then the necessary consequences of the internal structure of the society; they are one of the aspects of the social process of production. The labor theory of value is not based on an analysis of exchange transactions as such in their material form, but on the analysis of those social production relations expressed in the transactions.

Chapter 8: Basic Characteristics of Marx's Theory of Value

Before approaching Marx's theory of value in detail, we consider it necessary to describe its main characteristics. If this is not done, the presentation of the separate aspects and individual problems of the theory of value (which are very complex and interesting) can conceal from the reader the main ideas on which the theory is based and which impregnate every part of it. Obviously the general characteristics of Marx's theory which we present in this chapter can be fully developed and grounded only in the following chapters. On the other hand, in the following chapters the reader will come across repetitions of the ideas expressed in this chapter, though presented in greater detail.

All the basic concepts of political economy express, as we have seen, social production relations among people. If we approach the theory of value from this point of view, then we face the task of demonstrating that value: 1) is a social relation among people, 2) which assumes a material form and 3) is related to the process of production.

At first glance value, as well as other concepts of political economy, seems to be a property of things. Observing the phenomena of exchange we can see that each thing on the market exchanges for a determined quantity of any other thing, or - in conditions of developed exchange - it exchanges for a given quantity of money (gold) for which one can buy any other thing on the market (within the limits of this sum, of course). This sum of money, or price of things, changes almost every day, depending on market fluctuations. Today there was a shortage of cloth on the market and its price went up 3 roubles and 20 kopeks per arshin [1 arshin = 28 inches-tr.]. In one week the quantity of cloth supplied to the market exceeds the normal supply, and the price falls to 2 roubles 75 kopeks per arshin. These everyday fluctuations and deviations of prices, if taken over a longer period of time, oscillate around some average level, around some average price which is, for example, 3 roubles per arshin. In capitalist society this average price is not proportional to the labor value of the product, i.e., to the quantity of labor necessary for its production, but is proportional to the so-called "price of production," which equals the costs of production for the given product plus the average profit on the invested capital. However, to simplify the analysis we can abstract the fact that the cloth is produced by the capitalist with the help of wage laborers. Marx's method, as we have seen above, consists of separating and analyzing individual types of production relations which only in their entirety give a picture of the capitalist economy. For the time being we are concerned only with one basic type of production relation among people in a commodity economy, namely the relation among people as commodity producers who are separate and formally independent from each other. We know only that the cloth is produced by the commodity producers and is taken to the market to be exchanged or sold to other commodity producers. We are dealing with a society of commodity producers, with a so-called "simple commodity economy" as opposed to a more complex capitalist economy. In conditions of a simple commodity economy the average prices of products are proportional to their labor value. In other words, value represents that average level around which market prices fluctuate and with which the prices would coincide if social labor were proportionally distributed among the various branches of production. Thus a state of equilibrium would be established among the branches of production.

Every society based on a developed division of labor necessarily assumes a given allocation of social labor among the various branches of production. Every system of divided labor is at the same time a system of distributed labor. In the primitive communistic society, in the patriarchal peasant family, or in socialist society, the labor of all the members of a given economic unit is allocated in advance, and consciously, among the individual tasks, depending on the character of the needs of the members of the group and on the level of productivity of labor. In a commodity economy, no one controls the distribution of labor among the individual branches of production and the individual enterprises. No clothmaker knows how much cloth is needed by society at a given time nor how much cloth is produced at a given time in all cloth-making enterprises. The production of cloth thus either outruns the demand (overproduction) or lags behind it (underproduction). In other words, the quantity of social labor which is expended on the production of cloth is either too large or not large enough. Equilibrium between cloth production and other branches of production is constantly disturbed. Commodity production is a system of constantly disturbed equilibrium.

But if this is so, then how does the commodity economy continue to exist as a totality of different branches of production which complement each other? The commodity economy can exist only because each disturbance of equilibrium provokes a tendency for its reestablishment. This tendency to reestablish equilibrium is brought about by means of the market mechanism and market prices. In the commodity economy, no commodity producer can direct another to expand or contract his production. Through their actions in relation to things some people affect the working activity of other people and induce them to expand or contract production (though they are themselves not aware of this). The overproduction of cloth and the resulting fall of price below value induce clothmakers to contract production; the inverse is true in case of underproduction. The deviation of market prices from values is the mechanism by means of which the overproduction and underproduction is removed and the tendency toward the reestablishment of equilibrium among the given branches of production of the national economy is set up.

The exchange of two different commodities according to their values corresponds to the state of equilibrium among two given branches of production. In this equilibrium, all transfer of labor from one branch to another comes to an end. But if this happens, then it is obvious that the exchange of two commodities according to their values equalizes the advantages for the commodity producers in both branches of production, and removes the motives for transfer from one branch to another. In the simple commodity economy, such an equalization of conditions of production in the various branches means that a determined quantity of labor used up by commodity producers in different spheres of the national economy furnishes each with a product of equal value. The value of commodities is directly proportional to the quantity of labor necessary for their production. If three hours of labor are on the average necessary for the production of an arshin of cloth, given a certain level of technique (the labor spent on raw materials, instruments of production, etc., is also counted), and 9 hours of labor are necessary for the production of a pair of boots (assuming that the labor of the clothmaker and the bootmaker are of equal skill), then the exchange of 3 arshins of cloth for one pair of boots corresponds to the state of equilibrium between both given sorts of labor. An hour of labor of the bootmaker and an hour of labor of the clothmaker are equal to each other, each of them representing an equal share of the total labor of society distributed among all the branches of production. Labor, which creates value, thus appears not only as quantitatively distributed labor, but also as socially equalized (or equal) labor, or more briefly, as "social" labor which is understood as the total mass of homogeneous, equal labor of the entire society. Labor has these social characteristics not only in a commodity economy but also, for example, in a socialist economy. In a socialist economy organs of labor-accounting examine the labor of individuals in advance as part of the united, total labor of society, expressed in conventional social labor-units. However, in the commodity economy the process of socialization, equalization and distribution of labor is carried out in a different manner. The labor of individuals does not directly appear as social labor. It becomes social only because it is equalized with some other labor, and this equalization of labor is carried out by means of exchange. In exchange the concrete use values and the concrete forms of labor are completely abstracted. Thus labor, which we earlier considered as social, as socially equalized and quantitatively distributed, now acquires a particular qualitative and quantitative characteristic which is only inherent in a commodity economy: labor appears as abstract and socially necessary labor. The value of commodities is determined by the socially necessary labor, i.e., by the quantity of abstract labor.

But if value is determined by the quantity of labor which is socially necessary for the production of a unit of output, then this quantity of labor in turn depends on the productivity of labor. The increase of productivity of labor decreases the socially necessary labor and lowers the value of a unit of goods. The introduction of machines, for example, makes possible the production of a pair of boots in 6 hours instead of 9 hours which were necessary earlier. In this way their value is lowered from 9 roubles to 6 roubles (if one assumes that an hour of a bootmaker's labor, which we assume to be average labor, creates a value of 1 rouble). The cheaper boots begin to penetrate into the countryside, chasing out bast sandals and homemade boots. The demand for shoes increases and shoe production expands. In the national economy a redistribution of productive forces takes place. In this way the moving force which transforms the entire system of value originates in the material-technical process of production. The increase of productivity of labor is expressed in a decrease of the quantity of concrete labor which is factually used up in production, on the average. As a result of this (because of the dual character of labor, as concrete and abstract), the quantity of this labor, which is considered "social" or "abstract," i.e., as a share of the total, homogeneous labor of the society, decreases. The increase of productivity of labor changes the quantity of abstract labor necessary for production. It causes a change in the value of the product of labor. A change in the value of products in turn affects the distribution of social labor among the various branches of production. Productivity of labor-abstract labor-value-distribution of social labor: this is the schema of a commodity economy in which value plays the role of regulator, establishing equilibrium in the distribution of social labor among the various branches of the national economy (accompanied by constant deviations and disturbances). The law of value is the law of equilibrium of the commodity economy.

The theory of value analyzes the laws of exchange, the laws of the equalization of things on the market, only if these laws are related to the laws of production and distribution of labor in the commodity economy. The terms of exchange between any two commodities (we are considering average terms of exchange, and not accidental market prices) correspond to a given level of productivity of labor in the branches which manufacture these goods. The equalization of various concrete forms of labor as components of the total social labor, allocated among various branches, takes place through the equalization of things, i.e., the products of labor as values. Thus the current understanding of the theory of value as a theory which is confined to exchange relations among things is erroneous. The equilibrium of labor [allocation] behind the regularity in the equalization of things [in the process of exchange]. It is also incorrect to view Marx's theory as an analysis of relations between labor and things, things which are products of labor. The relation of labor to things refers to a given concrete form of labor and a given, concrete thing. This is a technical relation which is not, in itself, the subject of the theory of value. The subject matter of the theory of value is the interrelations of various forms of labor in the process of their distribution, which is established through the relation of exchange among things, i.e., products of labor. Thus Marx's theory of value is completely consistent with the above-given general methodological postulates of his economic theory, which does not analyze relations among things nor relations of people with things, but relations among people who are connected to each other through things.

Until now we have considered value mainly from its quantitative aspect. We dealt with the magnitude of value as the regulator of the quantitative distribution of social labor among individual branches of production. In this analysis we were led to the concept of abstract labor which was also treated predominantly from its quantitative aspect, namely as socially necessary labor. Now we must briefly examine the qualitative aspect of value. According to Marx, value is not only a regulator of the distribution of social labor, but also an expression of the social production relations among people. From this point of view, value is a social form which is acquired by the products of labor in the context of determined production relations among people. From value seen as a quantitatively determined magnitude, we must pass to value which we treat as a qualitatively determined social form. In other words, from the theory of the "magnitude of value" we must pass to the theory of the "form of value" (Wertform).[126]

As we have already pointed out, in a commodity economy value plays the role of regulating the distribution of labor. Does this role of value originate in the technical or social characteristics of the commodity economy, i.e., from the state of its productive forces or from the form of its production relations among people? The question has only to be asked in order to be answered in terms of the social characteristics of the commodity economy. Every distribution of social labor does not give the product of labor the form of value, but only that

---

[126] By form of value we do not mean those various forms which value assumes in the course of its development (for example, elementary form, expanded form, and so on), but value conceived from the standpoint of its social forms, i.e., value as form.

distribution of labor which is not organized directly by society, but is indirectly regulated through the market and the exchange of things. In a primitive communistic community, or in a feudal village, the product of labor has "value" (tsennost) in the sense of utility, use value, but it does not have "value" (stoimost). The product acquires value (stoimost) only in conditions where it is produced specifically for sale and acquires, on the market, an objective and exact evaluation which equalizes it (through money) with all other commodities and gives it the property of being exchangeable for any other commodity. In other words, a determined form of economy (commodity economy), a determined form of organization of labor through separate, privately-owned enterprises, are assumed. Labor does not, in itself, give value to the product, but only that labor which is organized in a determined social form (in the form of a commodity economy). If producers are related to each other as formally independent organizers of economic activity and as autonomous commodity producers, then the values of their labor confront each other on the market as "values." The equality of commodity producers as organizers of individual economic units and as contractors of production relations of exchange, is expressed in equality among the products of labor as values. The value of things expresses a determined type of production relations among people.

If the product of labor acquires value only in a determined social form of organization of labor, then value does not represent a "property" of the product of labor, but a determined "social form" or "social function" which the product of labor fulfills as a connecting link between dissociated commodity producers, as an "intermediary" or as a "bearer" of production relations among people. Thus at first glance value seems to be simply a property of things. When we say: "a painted, round oak table costs, or has the value of 25 roubles," it can be shown that this sentence gives information on four properties of the table. But if we think about it, we will be convinced that the first three properties of the table are radically different from the fourth. The properties characterize the table as a material thing and give us determined information on the technical aspects of the carpenter's labor. A man who has experience with these properties of the table can get a picture of the technical side of production, he can get an idea of the raw materials, the accessories, the technical methods and even the technical skill of the carpenter. But no matter how long he studies the table he will not learn anything about the social (production) relations between the producers of the table and other people. He cannot know whether or not the producer is an independent craftsman, an artisan, a wage laborer, or perhaps a member of a socialist community or an amateur carpenter who makes tables for personal use. Characteristics of the product expressed by the words: "the table has the value of 25 roubles" are of a completely different nature. These words show that the table is a commodity, that it is produced for the market, that its producer is related to other members of society by production relations among commodity owners, that the economy has a determined social form, namely the form of commodity economy. We do not learn anything about the technical aspects of the production or about the thing itself, but we learn something about the social form of the production and about the people who take part in it. This means that "value" (stoimost) does not characterize things, but human relations in which things are produced. It is not a property of things but a social form acquired by things due to the fact that people enter into determined production relations with each other through things. Value is a "social relation taken as a thing," a production relation among people which takes the form of a property of things. Work relations among commodity producers or social labor are "materialized" and "crystallized" in the value of a product of labor. This means that a determined social form of organization of labor is consistent with a particular social form of product of labor. "Labor, which creates (or more exactly, determines, seztende) exchange value, is a specific social form of labor." It "creates a determined social form of wealth, exchange value"[127] (Italics added). The definition of value as the expression of production relations among people does not contradict the definition of value as an expression of abstract labor which we gave earlier. The difference lies only in the fact that earlier we analyzed value from its quantitative aspect (as a magnitude), and now from its qualitative aspect (as a social form). Consistently with this, abstract labor was presented earlier in terms of its quantitative side, and is now being treated in terms of its qualitative side, namely as social labor in its specific form which presupposes production relations among people as commodity producers.

Marx's theory of the "form of value" (i.e., of the social form which the product of labor assumes) is the result of a determined form of labor. This theory is the most specific and original part of Marx's theory of value. The view that labor creates value was known long before Marx's time, but in Marx's theory it acquired a completely different meaning. Marx carried through a precise distinction between the material-technical process of production and its social forms, between labor as the totality of technical methods (concrete labor) and labor seen from the standpoint of its social forms in the commodity-capitalist society (abstract or human labor in general). The specific character of the commodity economy consists of the fact that the material-technical process of production is not directly regulated by society but is directed by individual commodity producers. Concrete labor is directly connected with the private labor of separate individuals. Private labor of separate commodity producers is connected with the labor of all other commodity producers and becomes social labor only if the product of one producer is equalized as a value with all other commodities. This equalization of all products as values is, at the same time (as we have shown) an equalization of all concrete forms of labor expended in the various spheres of the national economy. This means that the private labor of separate individuals does not

---

[127] *Kritik der politischen Oekonomie*, p. 13.

acquire the character of social labor in the concrete form in which it was expended in the process of production, but through exchange which represents an abstraction from the concrete properties of individual things and individual forms of labor. Actually, since commodity production is oriented to exchange already during the process of production, the commodity producer already in the process of direct production, before the act of exchange, equalizes his product with a determined sum of value (money), and thus also his concrete labor with a determined quantity of abstract labor. But, first of all, this equalization of labor carries with it a preliminary character "represented in consciousness." The equalization must still be realized in the actual act of exchange. Secondly, even in its preliminary form, the equalization of labor, even though it precedes the act of exchange, is carried out through an equalization of things as values "represented in consciousness." However, since the equalization of labor through the equalization of things is a result of the social form of the commodity economy in which there is no direct social organization and equalization of labor, abstract labor is a social and historical concept. Abstract labor does not express a psychological equality of various forms of labor, but a social equalization of different forms of labor which is realized in the specific form of equalization of the products of labor.

The special character of Marx's theory of value consists of the fact that it explained precisely the kind of labor that creates value. Marx "analyzed labor's value-producing property and was the first to ascertain what labor it was that produced value, and why and how it did so. He found that value was nothing but congealed labor of this kind."[128] It is precisely this

---

[128] F. Engels, "Preface" to Volume II of Capital, p. 16. (Italics by Engels.)

explanation of the "two-fold character of labor" which Marx considered the central part of his theory of value.[129]

Thus the two-fold character of labor reflects the difference between the material-technical process of production and its social form. This difference, which we explained in the chapter on commodity fetishism, is the basis of Marx's entire economic theory, including the theory of value. This basic difference generates the difference between concrete and abstract labor, which in turn is expressed in the opposition between use value and value. In Chapter 1 of Capital, Marx's presentation follows precisely the opposite order. He starts his analysis with market phenomena which can be observed, with the opposition between use and exchange value. From this opposition, which can be seen on the surface of phenomena, he seems to dive below toward the two-fold character of labor (concrete and abstract). Then at the end of Chapter 1, in the section on commodity production, he reveals the social forms which the material-technical process of production assumes. Marx approaches human society by starting with things, and going through labor. He starts with things which are visible and moves to phenomena which have to be revealed by means of scientific analysis. Marx uses this analytical method in the first five pages of Capital in order to simplify his presentation. But the dialectical course of this thought must be interpreted in the reverse order. Marx passes from the difference between the process of production and its social form, i.e., from the social structure of the commodity economy, to the two-fold character of labor treated from its technical and social aspects, and to the two-fold nature of the commodity as use value and exchange value. A superficial reading of Capital may lead one to think that by opposing use value and exchange value, Marx designated a property of things themselves (such is the interpretation of Bohm-Bawerk and other critics of

---

[129] Capital, I, p. 41; Letters of Marx and Engels (Russian translation by V. Adoratski, 1923, p. 168).

Marx). Actually the problem is the difference between the "material" and the "functional" existence of things, between the product of labor and its social form, between things and the production relations among people "coalesced" with things, i.e., production relations which are expressed by things. Thus what is revealed is an inseparable connection between Marx's theory of value and its general, methodological bases formulated in his theory of commodity fetishism. Value is a production relation among autonomous commodity producers; it assumes the form of being a property of things and is connected with the distribution of social labor. Or, looking at the same phenomenon from the other side, value is the property of the product of labor of each commodity producer which makes it exchangeable for the products of labor of any other commodity producer in a determined ratio which corresponds to a given level of productivity of labor in the different branches of production. We are dealing with a human relation which acquires the form of being a property of things and which is connected with the process of distribution of labor in production. In other words, we are dealing with reified production relations among people. The reification of labor in value is the most important conclusion of the theory of fetishism, which explains the inevitability of "reification" of production relations among people in a commodity economy. The labor theory of value did not discover the material condensation of labor (as a factor of production) in things which are the products of labor; this takes place in all economic formations and is the technical basis of value but not its cause. The labor theory of value discovered the fetish, the reified expression of social labor in the value of things. Labor is "crystallized" or formed in value in the sense that it acquires the social "form of value." The labor is expressed and "reflected" (sich darstellt). The term "sich darstellen" is frequently used by Marx to characterize the relationship between abstract labor and value. One can only wonder why Marx's critics did not notice this inseparable connection between his labor theory of value and his theory of the reification or fetishization of the production relations among people. They understood Marx's theory of value in a mechanical-naturalistic, not in a sociological, sense.

Thus Marx's theory analyzes the phenomena related to value from qualitative and quantitative points of view. Marx's theory of value is built on two basic foundations: 1) the theory of the form of value as a material expression of abstract labor which in turn presupposes the existence of social production relations among autonomous commodity producers, and 2) the theory of the distribution of social labor and the dependence of the magnitude of value on the quantity of abstract labor which, in turn, depends on the level of productivity of labor. These are two sides of the same process: the theory of value analyzes the social form of value, the form in which the process of distribution of labor is performed in the commodity capitalist economy. "The form in which this proportional distribution of labor operates, in a state of society where the interconnection of social labor is manifested in the private exchange of the individual products of labor, is precisely the exchange value of these products."[130] Thus value appears, qualitatively and quantitatively, as an expression of abstract labor. Through abstract labor, value is at the same time connected with the social form of the social process of production and with its material-technical content. This is obvious if we remember that value, as well as other economic categories, does not express human relations in general, but particularly production relations among people. When Marx treats value as the social form of the product of labor, conditioned by a determined social form of labor, he puts the qualitative, sociological side of value in the foreground. When the process of distribution of labor and the development of productivity of labor is carried out in

---

[130] "Letter of Marx to L. Kugelmann, July 11, 1868" in Karl Marx and Frederick Engels, Selected Works, Moscow: Foreign Languages Publishing House, 1962, Volume II, p. 461. (Marx's italics.) 6

a given social form, when the "quantitatively determined masses of the total labor of society"[131] (subsumed under the law of proportional distribution of labor) are examined, then the quantitative (one may say, mathematical) side of the phenomena which are expressed through value, becomes important. The basic error of the majority of Marx's critics consists of: 1) their complete failure to grasp the qualitative, sociological side of Marx's theory of value, and 2) their confining the quantitative side to the examination of exchange ratios, i.e., quantitative relations of value among things; they ignored the quantitative interrelations among the quantities of social labor distributed among the different branches of production and different enterprises, interrelations which lie at the basis of the quantitative determination of value.

We have briefly examined two aspects of value: qualitative and quantitative (i.e., value as a social form and the magnitude of value). Each of these analytical paths leads us to the concept of abstract labor which in turn (like the concept of value) appeared before us either primarily in terms of its qualitative side (social form of labor), or in terms of its quantitative side (socially-necessary labor). Thus we had to recognize value as the expression of abstract labor in terms of its qualitative and its quantitative sides. Abstract labor is the "content" or "substance" which is expressed in the value of a product of labor. Our task is also to examine value from this standpoint, namely from the standpoint of its connection with abstract labor as the "substance" of value.

As a result we come to the conclusion that complete knowledge of value, which is a highly complex phenomenon, requires thorough examination of value in terms of three aspects: magnitude of value, form of value and substance (content) of value. One may also say that value must be examined: 1) as a regulator of the

---

[131] Ibid.

quantitative distribution of social labor, 2) as an expression of social production relations among people, and 3) as an expression of abstract labor.

This three-fold division will help the reader follow the order of our further explanation. First of all, we must treat the entire mechanism which connects value and labor. Chapters Nine to Eleven are devoted to this problem. In Chapter Nine, value is considered as a regulator of the distribution of labor. In Chapter Ten, value is treated as an expression of production relations among people, and in Chapter Eleven it is treated from the standpoint of its relation with abstract labor. Only such thorough analysis of the mechanism which connects value and labor in its entirety can give us the foundations of Marx's theory of value (this is why the content of Chapters Nine to Eleven can be considered the foundation of the labor theory of value). This analysis prepares us for an analysis of the component parts of this mechanism: 1) value which is created by labor, and 2) labor which creates value. Chapter Twelve is devoted to an analysis of value treated in terms of its form, content (substance) and magnitude. Finally, chapters Thirteen to Sixteen present an analysis of labor (which creates value) in terms of the same three aspects. Since value is an expression of social relations among people, we must first of all give a general characterization of social labor (Chapter Thirteen). In a commodity economy, social labor acquires a more precise expression in the form of abstract labor which is the "substance" of value (Chapter Fourteen). The reduction of concrete labor to abstract labor implies the reduction of skilled labor to simple labor (Chapter Fifteen), and thus the theory of skilled labor is a completion of the theory of abstract labor. Finally, the quantitative aspect of abstract labor appears in the form of socially necessary labor (Chapter Sixteen).

Chapter 9: Value as the Regulator of Production

After the publication of Volume I of Capital, Kugelmann told Marx that in the opinion of many readers, Marx had not proved the concept of value. In the previously cited letter of July 11, 1868, Marx responded quite angrily to this objection: "Every child knows that a nation which ceased to work, I will not say for a year, but even for a few weeks, would perish. Every child knows, too, that the masses of products corresponding to the different needs require different and quantitatively determined masses of the total labor of society. That this necessity of the distribution of social labor in definite proportions cannot possibly be done away with by a particular form of social production but can only change the form in which it appears, is self-evident. No natural laws can be done away with. What can change, in historically different circumstances, is only the form in which these laws operate. And the form in which this proportional distribution of labor operates, in a state of society where the interconnection of social labor is manifested in the private exchange of the individual products of labor, is precisely the exchange value of these products."[132]

Here Marx mentioned one of the basic foundations of his theory of value. In the commodity economy, no one consciously supports or regulates the distribution of social labor among the various industrial branches to correspond with the given state of productive forces. Since individual commodity producers are autonomous in the management of production, the exact repetition and reproduction of an already given process of social production is completely impossible. Furthermore,

---

[132] Marx's letter to L. Kugelmann, July 11, 1868, in Karl Marx and Frederick Engels, Selected Works in Two Volumes, Volume II, Moscow: Foreign Languages Publishing House, 1962, p. 461.

proportional expansion of the process is impossible. Since the actions of the separate commodity producers are not connected or constant, daily deviations in the direction of excessive expansion or contraction of production are inevitable. If every deviation tended to develop uninterruptedly, then the continuation of production would not be possible; the social economy, based on a division of labor, would break down. In reality every deviation of production, whether up or down, provokes forces which put a stop to the deviation in the given direction, and give birth to movements in the opposite direction. Excessive expansion of production leads to a fall of prices on the market. This leads to a reduction of production, even below the necessary level. The further reduction of production stops the fall of prices. Economic life is a sea of fluctuating motion. It is not possible to observe the state of equilibrium in the distribution of labor among the various branches of production at any one moment. But without such a theoretically conceived state of equilibrium, the character and direction of the fluctuating movement cannot be explained.

The state of equilibrium between two branches of production corresponds to the exchange of products on the basis of their values. In other words, this state of equilibrium corresponds to the average level of prices. This average level is a theoretical conception. The average prices do not correspond to the actual movements of concrete market prices, but explain them. This theoretical, abstract formula of the movement of prices is, in fact, the "law of value." From this it can be seen that every objection to the theory of value which is based on the fact that concrete market prices do not coincide with theoretical "values," is nothing more than a misunderstanding. Total agreement between market price and value would mean the elimination of the unique regulator which prevents different branches of the social economy from moving in opposite directions. This would lead to a breakdown of the economy. "The possibility, therefore, of quantitative incongruity between price and magnitude of value, or the deviation of the former from the latter, is inherent in the price form itself. This is no defect, but, on the contrary, admirably adapts the price-form to a mode of production whose inherent laws impose themselves only as the mean of apparently lawless irregularities that compensate one another" (C., I, p. 102).

A given level of market prices, regulated by the law of value, presupposes a given distribution of social labor among the individual branches of production, and modifies this distribution in a given direction. In one section, Marx speaks of the "barometrical fluctuations of the market prices" (C., I, p. 356). This phenomenon must be supplemented. The fluctuations of market prices are in reality a barometer, an indicator of the process of distribution of social labor which takes place in the depths of the social economy. But it is a very unusual barometer; a barometer which not only indicates the weather, but also corrects it. One climate can replace another without an indication on a barometer. But one phase of the distribution of social labor replaces another only through the fluctuation of market prices and under their pressure. If the movement of market prices connects two phases of the distribution of labor in the social economy, we are right if we assume a tight internal relation between the working activity of economic agents and value. We will look for the explanation of these relations in the process of social production, i.e., in the working activity of people, and not in phenomena which lie outside the sphere of production or which are not related to it by a permanent functional connection. For example, we will not look for an explanation in the subjective evaluations of individuals or in mathematical interrelations of prices and quantities of goods if these interrelations are treated as given and isolated from the process of production. The phenomena related to value can only be grasped in close relation with the working activity of society. The explanation of value must be sought in social "labor." This is our first and most general conclusion.

The role of value as the regulator of the distribution of labor in society was explained by Marx not only in his letter to Kugelmann, but also in various sections of Capital. Perhaps these observations are presented in their most developed form in Chapter 12, section 4 of the first volume of Capital [Chapter 14, section 4, in the English translation] (the section on the "Division of Labor and Manufacture"): "While within the workshop, the iron law of proportionality subjects definite numbers of workmen to definite functions, in the society outside the workshop, chance and caprice have full play in distributing the producers and their means of production among the various branches of industry. The different spheres of production, it is true, constantly tend to an equilibrium: for, on the one hand, while each producer of a commodity is bound to produce a use-value, to satisfy a particular social want, and while the extent of these wants differs quantitatively, still there exists an inner relation which settles their proportions into a regular system, and that system one of spontaneous growth; and, on the other hand, the law of the value of commodities ultimately determines how much of its disposable working-time society can expend on each particular class of commodities. But this constant tendency to equilibrium, of the various spheres of production, is exercised only in the shape of a reaction against the constant upsetting of this equilibrium. The a priori system on which the division of labor, within the workshop, is regularly carried out, becomes in the division of labor within the society, an a posteriori, nature-imposed necessity, controlling the lawless caprice of the producers, and perceptible in the barometrical fluctuations of the market-prices" (C, I, pp. 355-356).

The same idea is presented by Marx in Volume III: "The distribution of this social labor and the mutual supplementing and interchanging of its products, the subordination under, and introduction into, the social mechanism, are left to the accidental and mutually nullifying motives of individual capitalists... Only as an inner law, vis-a-vis the individual agents, as a blind law of nature, does the law of value exert its influence here and maintain the social equilibrium of production amidst its accidental fluctuations" (C., III, p. 880).

Thus without a proportional distribution of labor among the various branches of the economy, the commodity economy cannot exist. But this proportional distribution of labor can only be realized if the profound internal contradictions which lie at the very basis of the commodity society are overcome. On one hand, the commodity society is unified into a single social economy by means of the division of labor. Individual parts of this economy are closely related to each other and influence each other. On the other hand, private ownership and autonomous economic activity of individual commodity producers shatter the society into a series of single, independent economic units. This shattered commodity society "becomes a society only through exchange, which is the single economic process known to the economy of this society."[133] The commodity producer is formally autonomous. He acts according to his own one-sided judgment, guided by his own interest as he conceives it. But due to the process of exchange he is related to his co-negotiator (buyer or seller) and through him he is indirectly connected to the entire market, i.e., with the totality of buyers and sellers, in conditions of competition which tend to reduce market terms to the same level. The production connection between individual commodity producers in the same branch of production is created through exchange, through the value of the product of labor. Such a connection is also created between different branches of production, between different places in the country, and between different countries. This connection does not only mean that commodity producers exchange with one another, but also that they become socially related to each other. Since they are connected in exchange through the products of labor,

---

[133] Rudolf Hilferding, Finanzkapital (Russian edition, 1923, p. 6).

they also become connected in their productive processes, in their working activity, because in the process of direct production they mUst take into account the presumed conditions on the market. Through exchange and the value of commodities, the working activity of some commodity producers affects the working activity of others, and causes determined modifications. On the other hand, these modifications influence the working activity itself. Individual parts of the social economy adjust to each other. But this adjustment is only possible if one part influences another through the movement of prices on the market, a movement which is determined by the "law of value." In other words, it is only through the "value" of commodities that the working activity of separate independent producers leads to the productive unity which is called a social economy, to the interconnections and mutual conditioning of the labor of individual members of society. Value is the transmission belt which transfers the movement of working processes from one part of society to another, making that society a functioning whole.

Thus we face the following dilemma: in a commodity economy where the working activity of individuals is not regulated and is not subjected to direct mutual adjustment, the productive-working connection between individual commodity producers can either be realized through the process of exchange, in which the products of labor are equalized as values, or it cannot be realized at all. But the interconnection between the individual parts of the social economy is an obvious fact. This means that the explanation of this fact must be sought in the movement of the values of commodities. Behind the movement of value, we must uncover the interrelations between the working activities of individuals. Thus we confirm the connection between the phenomena related to value and the working activity of people. We confirm the general connection between "value" and "labor." Here our starting point is not value, but labor. It is erroneous to represent the matter as if Marx had started with the phenomena related to value in their material expression and, analyzing them, had come to the conclusion that the common property of exchanged and evaluated things can only be labor. Marx's train of thought moves precisely in the opposite direction. In the commodity economy, the labor of individual commodity producers, which directly has the form of private labor, can acquire the character of social labor, i.e., can be subjected to the process of mutual connection and coordination, only through the "value" of the products of labor. Labor as a social phenomenon can only be expressed in "value." The specific character of Marx's labor theory of value lies in the fact that Marx does not base his theory on the properties of value, i.e., on the acts of equalization and evaluation of things, but on the properties of labor in the commodity economy, i.e., on the analysis of the working structure and production relations of labor. Marx himself noted this specific character of his theory when he said: "Political Economy has indeed analyzed, however incompletely, value and its magnitude, and has discovered what lies beneath these forms. But it has never once asked the question why labor is represented by the value of its product and labor-time by the magnitude of that value" (C., I, p. 801 italics by I.R.). Starting with the working activity of people, Marx showed that in a commodity economy this activity inevitably has the form of the value of products of labor.

Critics of Marx's theory of value are particularly opposed to the "privileged" position which is given to labor in this theory. They cite a long list of factors and conditions which are modified when the prices of commodities on the market change. They question the basis according to which labor is isolated from this list and placed in a separate category. To this we must answer that the theory of value does not deal with labor as a technical factor of production, but with the working activity of people as the basis of the life of society, and with the social forms within which that labor is carried out. Without the analysis of the productive-working relations of society, there is no political economy. This analysis shows that, in a commodity economy, the productive-working connection between commodity producers can only be expressed in a material form, in the form of the value of products of labor.

One may object that our view of the internal causal connection between value and labor (a causal connection which necessarily follows from the very structure of the commodity economy) is too general and undoubtedly will be questioned by critics of Marx's theory of value. We will see below that the formulation of the labor theory of value which we give now in its most general form will later acquire a more concrete character. But in this general formulation, the presentation of the problem of value excludes, in advance, a whole series of theories and condemns to failure an entire series of attempts. Concretely, theories seeking the causes which determine value and its changes in phenomena which are not directly connected with the working activity of people, with the process of production, are excluded in advance (for example, the theory of the Austrian school, which starts with the subjective evaluations of individual subjects isolated from the productive process and from the concrete social forms in which this process is carried out). No matter how keen an explanation was given by such a theory, no matter how successfully it discovered certain phenomena in the change of prices, it suffers from the basic error which assures all its special successes in advance: it does not explain the productive mechanism of contemporary society nor the conditions for its normal functioning and development. By pulling value, the transmission belt, out of the productive mechanism of the commodity economy, this theory deprives itself of any possibility of grasping the structure and motion of this mechanism. We must determine the connection between value and labor not only to understand the phenomena related to "value," but in order to understand the phenomenon "labor" in contemporary society, i.e., the possibility of unity of the productive process in a society which consists of individual commodity producers.

Chapter 10: Equality of Commodity Producers and Equality of Commodities

The commodity-capitalist society, like every society based on a division of labor, cannot exist without a proportional distribution of labor among individual branches of production. This distribution of labor can only be created if the working activities of individuals are interconnected and mutually conditioned. This productive working connection can only be realized through the process of market exchange, through the value of commodities, if the commodity production is not socially regulated. Analysis of the process of exchange, of its social forms and its connections with the production of the commodity society, is in essence the subject of Marx's theory of value.[134]

In the first chapter of Capital, Marx tacitly assumed the sociological premises of the theory of value (which we presented earlier), and began directly by analyzing the act of exchange, where the equality of exchanged commodities is expressed. For the majority of Marx's critics, these sociological premises remained a closed book. They do not see that Marx's theory of value is a conclusion based on the analysis of social-economic relations which characterize the commodity economy. For them, this theory is nothing more than "a purely

---

[134] Simmel thinks that economic research begins, not with exchangeable things, but with the social-economic role of exchange: "Exchange is a sociological phenomenon sui generis, a primitive form and function of interindividual life; it is not in any way a logical consequence of those qualitative and quantitative properties of things which are called utility and scarcity" (Georg Simmel, Philosophie des Geldes, Leipzig: Duncker Br Humblot, 1907, p. 59).

logical proof, a dialectic deduction from the very nature of exchange."[135]

We know that Marx did not in fact analyze the act of exchange as such, isolated from a determined economic structure of society. He analyzed the production relations of a determined society, namely commodity-capitalist society, and the role of exchange in that society. If anyone built a theory of value on the basis of analysis of the act of exchange as such, isolated from a determined social-economic context, it was Bohm-Bawerk, not Marx.

But though Bohm-Bawerk is wrong in saying that Marx derived the equality of exchanged goods from a purely logical analysis of the act of exchange, he is right in holding that Marx put particular emphasis on equality in his analysis of the act of exchange in the commodity economy. "Let us take two commodities, e.g., corn and iron. The proportions in which they are exchangeable, whatever those proportions may be, can always be represented by an equation in which a given quantity of corn is equated to some quantity of iron: e.g., 1 quarter corn = x cwt. iron. What does this equation tell us? It tells us that in two different things - in 1 quarter of corn and x cwt. of iron, there exists in equal quantities something common to both. The two things must therefore be equal to a third, which in itself is neither the one nor the other. Each of them, so far as it is exchange-value, must therefore be reducible to this third" (C., I, p. 37). It is this passage which Marx's critics see as the central point and only foundation of his theory of value, and it is against this passage that they direct their main blows. "I should like to remark, in passing," says Bohm-Bawerk, "that the first assumption, according to which an 'equality' must be manifested in the exchange of two things, appears to me to be very old-fashioned, which would not, however,

---

[135] Eugen von Bohm-Bawerk, Karl Marx and the Close of his System, New York: Augustus M. Kelley, 1949, p. 68.

matter much were it not also very unrealistic. In plain English, it seems to me to be a wrong idea. Where equality and exact equilibrium obtain, no change is likely to occur to disturb the balance. When, therefore, in the case of exchange the matter terminates with a change of ownership of the commodities, it points rather to the existence of some inequality or preponderance which produces the alteration."[136]

It may be superfluous to mention that Bohm-Bawerk's objections miss their target. Marx never maintained that exchange is carried out in conditions of "exact equilibrium"; he more than once pointed out that the qualitative "inequality" of commodities is the necessary result of the division of labor and represents, at the same time, a necessary stimulus of exchange. Bohm-Bawerk's attention was turned to the exchange of commodities as use values and to subjective evaluations of the utility of commodities, which stimulate exchange on the part of the individuals who take part in it. Thus he very correctly emphasized the fact of "inequality." But Marx was interested in the act of exchange as an objective social fact, and by emphasizing the equality he brought out essential characteristics of this social fact. However, he did not have in mind any kind of fantastic state of "exact equilibrium."[137]

Critics of Marx's theory of value usually see its center of gravity in its defining the quantitative equality of labor inputs which are necessary for the production of commodities, and which are equalized with each other in

---

[136] Bohm-Bawerk, Op. Cit., p. 68.

[137] "The act of exchange itself and the price which results from it influence ... the behavior of all later buyers and sellers, and thus do not exert influence in the form of inequality, but in the form of equality, i.e., as expressions of equivalence" (Zwiedineck, "Über den Subjektivismus in der Preislehre," Archiv fur Sozialwissenschaft u. Sozialpolitik, 1914, Vol. 38, Part II, pp. 22-23.

the act of exchange. But Marx more than once pointed to the other side of his theory of value, to the qualitative side, so to speak, as opposed to the quantitative side mentioned above. Marx was not interested in the qualitative properties of commodities as use values. But his attention was turned to the qualitative characteristics of the act of exchange as a social-economic phenomenon. It is only on the basis of these qualitative and essentially sociological characteristics that one can grasp the quantitative aspect of the act of exchange. Almost all critics of Marx's theory of value suffer from a complete ignorance of this side of Marx's theory. Their views are as one-sided as the opposite conception which holds that the phenomenon of value, as treated by Marx, is not in any way related to exchange proportions, i.e., to the quantitative side of value.[138]

Leaving aside the question of the quantitative equality of exchanged commodities, we must point out that in a commodity economy the contacts between individual private economic units are carried out in the form of purchase and sale, in the form of equalization of values given and received by individual economic units in the act of exchange. The act of exchange is an act of equalization. This equalization of exchanged commodities reflects the basic social characteristic of the commodity economy: the equality of commodity producers. We are not referring to their equality in the sense of owning equal material means of production, but to their equality as autonomous commodity producers independent from each other. No one among them can directly affect another unilaterally, without a formal agreement with the other. In other words, one producer may influence another, as an independent economic subject, through the terms of the agreement. The absence of non-economic coercion, the organization of the working activity of individuals, not on principles of public law but on the basis of civil law and so-called free

---

[138] See, for example, F. Petry, Der soziale Gehalt der Marxschen Werttheorie, Jena, 1916, pp. 27-28.

contract, are the most characteristic features of the economic structure of contemporary society. In this context, the basic form of production relations among private economic units is the form of exchange, i.e., the equalization of exchanged values. The equality of commodities in exchange is the material expression of the basic production relation of contemporary society: the connection among commodity producers as equal, autonomous and independent economic subjects.

We consider the following passage in Capital to be crucial for an understanding of the ideas of Marx which have been presented: "There was, however, an important fact which prevented Aristotle from seeing that, to attribute value to commodities, is merely a mode of expressing all labor as equal human labor, and consequently as labor of equal quality. Greek society was founded upon slavery, and had, therefore, for its natural basis, the inequality of men and of their labor-powers. The secret of the expression of value, namely, that all kinds of labor are equal and equivalent, because, and so far as they are human labor in general, cannot be deciphered, until the notion of human equality has already acquired the fixity of a popular prejudice. This, however, is possible only in a society in which the great mass of the produce of labor takes the form of commodities, in which, consequently, the dominant relation between man and man, is that of owners of commodities" (C., I, pp. 59-60).[139] The equality of the autonomous and independent commodity producers is the foundation for the equality of the exchanged goods. This is the basic characteristic of the commodity

---

[139] Obviously here we are not interested in determining whether or not Marx understood Aristotle accurately, or if his understanding of Aristotle is a type of "scientific subjectivism," as was stated by V. Zheleznov (Ekonomicheskoe mirovozzrenie dvernih grekov [Economic Weltanschauung of the Ancient Greeks], Moskva, 1919, p. 244), without adequate grounds, in our opinion.

economy, of its "cell structure," so to speak. The theory of value examines the process of formation of the productive unity called a social economy from separate, one might say independent, cells. It is not without reason that Marx wrote, in the preface to the first edition of the first volume of Capital, that the "commodity form of the product of labor or the form of value of the commodity is the form of the economic cell of bourgeois society." This cell structure of the commodity society represents, in itself, the totality of equal, formally independent, private economic units.

In the cited passage on Aristotle, Marx emphasizes that in slave society the concept of value could not be deduced from "the form of value itself," i.e., from the material expression of the equality of exchanged commodities. The mystery of value can only be grasped from the characteristics of the commodity economy. One should not be astonished that critics who missed the sociological character of Marx's theory of value should have interpreted the cited passage without discernment. According to Dietzel, Marx "was guided by the ethical axiom of equality." This "ethical foundation is displayed in the passage where Marx explains the shortcomings of Aristotle's theory of value by pointing out that the natural basis of Greek society was the inequality among people and among their labor-powers."[140] Dietzel does not understand that Marx is not dealing with an ethical postulate of equality, but with the equality of commodity producers as a basic social fact of the commodity economy. We repeat, not equality in the sense of equal distribution of material goods, but in the sense of independence and autonomy among economic agents who organize production.

If Dietzel transforms the society of equal commodity producers from an actual fact into an ethical postulate, Croce sees in the principle of equality a

---

[140] Heinrich Dietzel, Theoretische Sozialoekonomik, Leipzig: C.F. Winter, 1895, p. 273.

theoretically conceived type of society thought up by Marx on the basis of theoretical considerations and for the purpose of contrast and comparison with the capitalist society, which is based on inequality. The purpose of this comparison is to explain the specific characteristics of the capitalist society. The equality of commodity producers is not an ethical ideal but a theoretically conceived measure, a standard with which we measure capitalist society. Croce recalls the passage where Marx says that the nature of value can only be explained in a society where the belief in the equality of people has acquired the force of a popular prejudice.[141] Croce thinks that Marx, in order to understand value in a capitalist society, took as a type, as a theoretical standard, a different (concrete) value, namely that which would be possessed by goods which can be multiplied by labor in a society without the imperfections of capitalist society, and in which labor power would not be a commodity. From this, Croce derives the following conclusion on the logical properties of Marx's theory of value. "Marx's labor-value is not only a logical generalization, it is also a fact conceived and postulated as typical, i.e., something more than a mere logical concept."[142]

Dietzel transforms the society of equal commodity producers into an ethical postulate, while Croce makes of it a "thought-up" concrete image which confronts the capitalist society in order to explain more clearly the characteristics of this society. However, in reality this society of equal commodity producers is no more than an abstraction and a generalization of the basic characteristics of commodity economy in general and capitalist economy in particular. The theory of value and its premise of a society of equal commodity producers

---

[141] Benedetto Croce, Historical Materialism and the Economics of Karl Marx, London: Frank Cass & Co., 1966, pp. 60-66.

[142] Ibid., p. 56.

gives us an analysis of one side of the capitalist economy, namely the basic production relation which unites autonomous commodity producers. This relation is basic because it generates the social economy (the subject of political economy) as an unquestionable, though flexible, whole. Marx lucidly expressed the logical character of his theory of value when he said: "Up to this point we have considered men in only one economic capacity, that of owners of commodities, a capacity in which they appropriate the produce of the labor of others, by alienating that of their own labor" (C., I, pp. 108-109). The theory of value does not give us a description of phenomena in some imaginary society which is the opposite of capitalist society; it gives us a generalization of one aspect of capitalist society.

Finally, in capitalist society, production relations among people as members of different social groups are not confined to relations among them as independent commodity producers. However, relations among the members of different social groups in capitalist society are carried out in the form and on the basis of their interrelations as equal and autonomous commodity producers. The capitalist and the workers are connected to each other by production relations. Capital is the material expression of this relation. But they are connected, and enter into agreement with each other, as formally equal commodity producers. The category of value serves as an expression of this production relation, or more exactly, of this aspect of the production relation which connects them. Industrial capitalists and landlords, industrialists and financial capitalists, also enter agreements with each other as equal, autonomous commodity owners. This aspect of production relations among various social groups is expressed in the theory of value. Thus one characteristic of political economy as a science is explained. The basic concepts of politicaleconomy are built on the basis of value, and at first glance they even appear to be logical emanations of value. The first encounter with Marx's theoretical system may lead to agreement with Bohm-Bawerk's view that

Marx's system is a logical-deductive development of abstract concepts and their immanent, purely logical development, by Hegel's method. By means of magical, purely logical modifications, value is transformed into money, money into capital, capital into augmented capital (i.e., capital plus surplus value), surplus value into enterprise profit, interest and rent, etc. Bohm-Bawerk, who takes apart Marx's entire theory of value, notes that the more developed parts of Marx's system are a well composed whole consistently derived from an erroneous starting point. "In this middle part of the Marxian system the logical development and connection present a really imposing closeness and intrinsic consistency.... However wrong the starting point may be, these middle parts of the system, by their extraordinary logical consistency, permanently establish the reputation of the author as an intellectual force of the first rank."[143] Coming from Bohm-Bawerk, a thinker who is prone precisely to the logical development of concepts, this represents great praise. But in reality, the power of Marx's theory does not reside in its internal logical consistency as much as in the fact that the theory is thoroughly saturated with complex, rich social-economic content taken from reality and elucidated by the power of abstract thought. In Marx's work, one concept is transformed into another, not in terms of the power of immanent logical development, but through the presence of an entire series of accompanying social-economic conditions. An enormous historical revolution (described by Marx in the chapter on primitive capitalist accumulation) was necessary for the transformation of money into capital.

But here we are not interested in that side of the question. One concept grows out of another only in the presence of determined social-economic conditions. The fact is that every later concept carries the stamp of the previous one in Marx's theory. All the basic concepts of the economic system seem like logical varieties of the concept of value. Money - this is a value which serves as a

---

[143] Bohm-Bawerk, Op. Cit., pp. 88-89.

general equivalent. Capital - a value which creates surplus value. Wages-the value of the labor force. Profit, interest, rent are parts of surplus value. At first glance this logical emanation of the basic economic concepts from the concept of value seems inexplicable. But it can be explained by the fact that the production relations of capitalist society, which are expressed in the mentioned concepts (capital, wages, profit, interest, rent, etc.) appear in the form of relations among independent commodity producers, relations which are expressed through the concept of value. Capital is a variety of value because the production relation between the capitalist and the workers takes the form of a relation between equal commodity producers, i.e., autonomous economic agents. The system of economic concepts grows out of the system of production relations. The logical structure of political economy as a science expresses the social structure of capitalist society.[144]

The labor theory of value gives a theoretical formulation of the basic production relation of commodity society, a production relation between equal commodity producers. This explains the vitality of this theory, which has been at the forefront of economic science throughout the stormy current of economic ideas

---

[144] F. Oppenheimer sees Marx's "methodological fall" and his basic mistake in the fact that he took the "premise of social equality among the participants in the act of exchange," which is the basis of the theory of value, as the starting point for the analysis of the capitalist society with its class inequality. He quotes, with sympathy, the following statement by Tugan-Baranovskii: "Assuming social equality among the participants in the act of exchange, we abstract from the internal structure of the society in which this act is brought about" (Franz Oppenheimer, Wert und Kapitalprofit, Jena: G. Fischer, 1916, p. 176). Oppenheimer reproaches Marx for having ignored the class inequality of capitalist society in his theory of value. Liefmann throws an opposite objection against Marx's economic theory, namely that it "assumes beforehand the existence of determined classes" (Robert Liefmann, Grundsatze er Volkswirtschaftslehre, Stuttgart & Berlin: Deutsche Verlagsanstalt, 1920, p. 34). In essence, Liefmann is right: Marx's economic theory does assume the class inequality of capitalist society beforehand. But since the relations among classes in capitalist society take the form of relations among independent commodity producers, the starting point of analysis is value, which assumes social equality among the participants in the act of exchange. Marx's theory of value overcomes the one-sidedness of Oppenheimer and Liefmann. A detailed critique of Oppenheimer's and Liefmann's views is given in our work Sovremennye ekonomisty na Zapade (Contemporary Western Economists), 1927.

which replaced one another, and throughout all the attacks which were directed at it, always in new shapes and fresh formulations. Marx noted this quality of the labor theory of value in his letter to Kugelmann of July 11, 1868: "The history of the theory certainly shows that the concept of the value relation has always been the same - more or less clear, hedged more or less with illusions or scientifically more or less precise."[145] Hilferding also mentioned the vitality of this theory: "Economic theory - with the scope which Marx gives to it in his Theories of Surplus Value - is an explanation of capitalist society, which is based on commodity production. This basis of economic life, which remained unchanged through enormous and stormy development, explains the fact that economic theory reflects that development, retaining basic laws which were discovered earlier and developing them further, but not eliminating them completely. This means that the logical development of the theory accompanies the actual development of capitalism. Starting with the first formulations of the law of labor value in Petty and Franklin, and ending with the most subtle considerations of Volumes II and III of Capital, the process of development of economic theory is manifested as a logical unfolding."[146] This continuity of the historical development of the theory of value explains its central logical place in economic science. This logical place can only be understood in terms of the particular role which the basic relation among separate commodity producers as equal and autonomous economic agents plays in the system of production relations of capitalist society.

This makes obvious the inaccuracy of the attempts to consider the labor theory of value completely inapplicable to the explanation of capitalist society, and to restrict it to an imaginary society or to a simple commodity society which precedes capitalist society.

---

[145] Loc. cit., p. 462.

[146] Hilferding, "Aus der Vorgeschichte der Marxchen Oekonomie," Neue Zeit, 1910-1911, Vol. II.

Croce asks "why Marx, in analyzing the economic phenomena of the second or third sphere (i.e., the phenomena of profit and rent - I.R.), ever used concepts whose place was only in the first one" (i.e., in the sphere of labor value - I.R.). "If the correspondence between labor and value is only realized in the simplified society of the first sphere, why insist on translating the phenomena of the second into terms of the first?"[147] Similar criticisms are based on a one-sided understanding of the theory of value as an explanation of exclusively quantitative proportions of exchange in a simple commodity economy, on a total neglect of the qualitative side of the theory of value. If the law of quantitative proportions of exchange is modified in capitalist exchange, compared to simple commodity exchange, the qualitative side of exchange is the same in both economies. Only the analysis of the qualitative side makes it possible to approach and to grasp the quantitative proportions. "The expropriation of one part of society and monopoly ownership of means of production by the other part obviously modify exchange, since the inequality among the members of society can only become manifest in exchange. But since the act of exchange is a relation of equality, then inequality takes the form of equality - no longer as equality of value, but as equality of production price."[148] Hilferding should have extended his idea and translated it to the language of production relations.

The theory of value, which takes as its starting point the equality of exchanged commodities, is indispensable for the explanation of capitalist society with its inequality, because production relations between capitalists and workers take the form of relations between formally equal, independent commodity producers. All attempts to separate the theory of value from the theory of the capitalist economy are incorrect, whether or not

---

[147] Croce, Op. Cit., p. 134.

[148] Hilferding, Das Finanzkapital, Wien, 1910 (Russian edition. 1918, p. 23).

they restrict the sphere of activity of the theory of value to an imaginary society (Croce) or to a simple commodity economy, or even to a transformation of labor value into a purely logical category (Tugan-Baranovski) - or, finally, to a sharp separation of inter-economic categories, i.e., the separation of value from social categories, like capital (Struve). (Cf, Chapter Six, "Struve on the Theory of Commodity Fetishism.")

Chapter 11: Equality of Commodities and Equality of Labor

The equality of commodity producers as autonomous economic agents is expressed in the exchange-form: exchange is in essence an exchange of equivalents, an equalization of exchanged commodities. The role of exchange in the national economy is not confined to its social form. In the commodity economy, exchange is one of the indispensable components of the process of reproduction. It makes possible an adequate distribution of labor and the continuation of production. In its form, exchange reflects the social structure of the commodity economy. In terms of its content, exchange is one of the phases of the labor process, the process of reproduction. Formally, the act of exchange refers to an equalization of commodities. From the standpoint of the production process, it is closely connected to the equalization of labor.

Just as value expresses the equality of all products of labor, so labor (the substance of value) expresses the equality of labor in all forms and of all individuals. The labor is "equal." But what does the equality of this labor consist of? To answer this question, we must distinguish three types of equal labor:

1) Physiologically equal labor

2) Socially equalized labor

3) Abstract labor.

Since we will not treat the first form of labor here (see Chapter Fourteen), we must explain the difference between the second and third form of labor.

In an organized economy, the relations among people are relatively simple and transparent. Work acquires a directly social form, i.e., there is a certain social organization and determined social organs which distribute labor among individual members of society. Thus the labor of every individual directly enters the social economy as concrete labor with all of its concrete material properties. The labor of each individual is social precisely because it is different from the labor of other members of the community, and it represents a material supplement to their labor. Work in its concrete form is directly social labor. Thus it is also distributed labor. The social organization of labor consists of the distribution of labor among the different members of the community. Inversely, the division of labor is based on the decision of some social organ. Labor is at the same time social and allocated, which means that in its material-technical, concrete, or useful form, labor possesses both of these properties.

Is this labor also socially-equalized?

If we leave aside social organizations which were based on an extreme inequality of sexes and individual groups, and if we consider a large community with a division of labor (for example, a large family-community - zadruga - of Southern Slavs), then we can observe that the process of equalization had to, or at least could, take place in such a community. Such a process will be even more necessary in a large socialist community. Without the equalization of the labor of different forms and different individuals, the organ of the socialist community cannot decide whether or not it is more useful to spend one day of qualified labor or two days of simple labor, one month of the labor of individual A or two months of the labor of individual B, to produce certain goods. But in an organized community, such a process of equalization of labor is basically different from the equalization which takes place in a commodity economy. Let us imagine some socialist community where labor is divided among the members of the community. A determined social organ equalizes the labors of various individuals with each other, since without this equalization a more or less extensive social plan cannot be realized. But in such a community, the process of equalization of labor is secondary and supplements the process of socialization and allocation of labor. Labor is first of all socialized and allocated labor. We can also include here the quality of socially equalized labor as a derived and additional characteristic. The basic characteristic of labor is its characteristic of being social and allocated labor, and a supplementary characteristic is its property of being socially equalized labor.

Let us now examine the changes that would take place in the organization of labor of our community if we imagined the community, not as an organized entity, but as a union of separate economic units of private commodity producers, i.e., as a commodity economy.

The social characteristics of labor which we traced through an organized community are also found in a commodity economy. Here too we can see social labor, allocated labor, and socially equalized labor. But all of these processes of socialization, equalization and allocation of labor are carried out in an altogether different form. The combination of these properties is completely different. First of all, in a commodity economy there is no direct social organization of labor. Labor is not directly social.

In a commodity economy, the labor of a separate individual, of a separate, private commodity producer, is not directly regulated by society. As such, in its concrete form, labor does not yet directly enter the social economy. Labor becomes social in a commodity economy only when it acquires the form of socially equalized labor, namely, the labor of every commodity producer becomes social only because his product is equalized with the products of all other producers. Thus the labor of the given individual is equalized with the labor of other members of the society and with other forms of labor. There is no other property for determining the social character of labor in a commodity economy. Here there is no previously designed plan for the socialization and allocation of labor. The only indication of the fact that the labor of a given individual is included in the social system of the economy is the exchange of products of the given labor for all other products.

Thus if a commodity economy is compared to a socialist community, the property of social labor and the property of socially equalized labor seem to have changed places. In the socialist community, the property of labor as equal or equalized was the result of the production process, of the production decision of a social organ which socialized and distributed labor. In the commodity economy, labor becomes social only in the sense that it becomes equal with all other forms of labor, in the sense that it becomes socially equalized. Social or socially-equalized labor in the specific form which it has in the commodity economy can be called abstract labor.

We can present some citations from Marx's works which confirm what we have said.

The most striking place is in the Contribution to the Critique of Political Economy, where Marx says that labor becomes "social only because it takes the form of abstract universal labor," i.e., the form of equalization with all other forms of labor" (Critique, p. 30). "Abstract and in that form social labor," - Marx often characterizes the social form of labor in a commodity economy with these words. We can also cite the well-known sentence from Capital that in a commodity economy, "the specific social character of private labor carried on independently, consists in the equality of every kind of that labor, by virtue of its being human labor" (C., I, p. 74).

Thus in a commodity economy, the center of gravity of the social property of labor moves from its characteristic of being social to its characteristic of being equal or socially equalized labor, equalized through the equalization of the products of labor. The concept of equality of labor plays such a central role in Marx's theory of value precisely because in the commodity economy, labor becomes social only if it has the property of being equal.

In a commodity economy, the characteristics of social labor as well as allocated labor have their source in the equality of labor. The distribution of labor in the commodity economy is not a conscious distribution consistent with determined, previously manifested needs, but is regulated by the principle of equal advantage of production. The distribution of labor among different branches of production is carried out in such a way that commodity producers, through the expenditure of equal quantities of labor, acquire equal sums of value in all branches of production.

We can see that the first property of abstract labor (i.e., socially equalized labor in the specific form which it has in a commodity economy) consists of the fact that it becomes social only if it is equal. Its second property consists of the fact that the equalization of labor is carried out through the equalization of things.

In a socialist society the process of equalization of labor and the process of equalization of things (products of labor) are possible, but are separate from each other. When the plan for the production and distribution of different forms of labor is established, the socialist society performs a certain equalization of different forms of labor, and simultaneously it equalizes things (products of labor) from the standpoint of social usefulness. "It is true that even then (in socialism) it will still be necessary for society to know how much labor each article of consumption requires for its production. It will have to arrange its plan of production in accordance with its means of production, which include, in particular, its labor forces. The useful effects of the various articles of consumption, compared with each other and with the quantity of labor required for their production, will in the last analysis determine the plan."[149] When the process of production is finished, when the distribution of the produced things among the individual members of society takes place, a certain equalization of things for the purpose of distribution, society's conscious evaluation of these things, is probably indispensable.[150] It is obvious that the socialist society does not have to evaluate the things during their equalization (during their evaluation) in precise proportion to the labor expended on their production. A society directed by the goals of social policy may, for example, consciously introduce a lower estimate of the things which satisfy the cultural needs of the broad popular masses, and a higher estimate for luxury goods. But even if the socialist society should evaluate things exactly in proportion to the labor expended on them, the decision on the equalization of things will be separate from the decision on the equalization of labor.

It is otherwise in a commodity society. Here there is no independent social decision on the equalization of labor. The equalization of various forms of labor is carried out only in the form and through the equalization of things, products of labor. The equalization of things in the form of values on the market affects the division of labor of society, and it affects the working activity of the participants in production. The equalization and distribution of commodities on the market are closely connected with the process of equalization and distribution of labor in social production.

Marx frequently pointed out that in a commodity economy the social equalization of labor is realized only in a material form and through the equalization of commodities: "When we bring the products of our labor

---

[149] Frederick Engels, Anti-Duhring, New York: International Publishers, 1966, p. 338.

[150] Here we have in mind the first period of the socialist economy, when society will still regulate the distribution of products among its individual members.

into relation with each other as values, it is not because we see in these articles the material receptacles of homogeneous human labor. Quite the contrary: whenever, by an exchange, we equate as values our different products, by that very act, we also equate, as human labor, the different kinds of labor expended upon them. We are not aware of this, nevertheless we do it" (C., I, p. 74). Social equalization of labor does not exist independently; it is carried out only through the equalization of things. This means that the social equality of labor is realized only through things. "The exchange of products as commodities is a determined method of exchange of labor, a method of dependence of the labor of one on another" (Theorien uber den Mehrwert, III, p. 153). "The equality of all sorts of human labor is expressed objectively by their products all being equally values" (Kapital, I, p. 39; C., I, p. 72).[151] "The social character that his [the individual's] particular labor has of being the equal of all other particular kinds of labor, takes the form that all the physically different articles that are the products of labor, have one common quality, viz., that of having value" (C., I, p. 73-74).

There is nothing more erroneous than to interpret these words as meaning that the equality of things as values represents nothing more than an expression of physiological equality of various forms of human labor (see, below, the chapter on Abstract Labor). This mechanical-materialistic conception is foreign to Marx. He speaks of the social character of the equality of various types of work, of the social process of equalization of labor indispensable for every economy based on an extensive division of labor. In the commodity economy,

---

[151] In the original German edition, Marx did not speak of the "substance of value" (namely labor), but of "labor objectiveness" (Wertgegenstandlichkeit) or, more simply, of value (this is the way this term is translated in the French edition of Capital, edited by Marx). In the Russian translation this term was frequently translated erroneously as "substance of value" (i.e., labor).

this process is realized only through the equalization of the products of labor as values. This "materialization" of the social process of equalization in the form of an equalization of things does not mean the material objectification of labor as a factor of production, i.e., its material accumulation in things (products of labor).

"The labor of every individual, as far as it is expressed in exchange value, possesses this social character of equality and finds expression in exchange value only in so far as it is a relation of equality with the labor of all other individuals" (Critique, p. 26). In these words, Marx clearly expressed the interconnection and mutual conditioning of the processes of equalization of labor and equalization of commodities as values in the commodity economy. This explains the specific role which the process of exchange plays in the mechanism of the commodity economy, as an equalizer of the products of labor as values. The process of equalization and distribution of labor is closely connected with the equalization of values. Changes in the magnitude of value of commodities depend on the socially necessary labor expended on the commodities, not because the equalization of things is not possible without the equality of labor expended on them (according to Bohm-Bawerk, this is how Marx gives a foundation to his theory), but because the social equalization of labor is carried out, in a commodity economy, only in the form of an equalization of commodities. The key to the theory of value cannot be found in the act of exchange as such, in the material equalization of commodities as values, but in the way the labor is equalized and distributed in the commodity economy. We again come to the conclusion that Marx revealed the properties of "value" by analyzing "labor" in a commodity economy.

This makes it obvious that Marx analyzes the act of exchange only to the extent that it plays a specific role in the process of reproduction and is closely connected with that process. Marx analyzes the "value" of commodities in its connection with "labor," with the equalization and distribution of labor in production. Marx's theory of value does not analyze every exchange of things, but only that exchange which takes place: 1) in a commodity society, 2) among autonomous commodity producers, 3) when it is connected with the process of reproduction in a determined way, thus representing one of the necessary phases of the process of reproduction. The interconnection of the processes of exchange and distribution of labor in production leads us (for the purpose of theoretical analysis) to concentrate on the value of products of labor (as opposed to natural goods which may have a price; see above, Chapter Five), and then only those products which can be reproduced. If the exchange of natural goods (for example land) is a normal phenomenon of the commodity economy, connected to the process of production, we must include it within the scope of political economy. But this must be analyzed separately from phenomena related to the value of products of labor. No matter how much the price of land influences the process of production, the connection between them will be different from the functional connection between the value of products of labor and the process of distribution of labor in social production. The price of land, and, in general, the price of goods which cannot be multiplied, is not an exception to the labor theory of value, but is at the borders of this theory, at its limits - limits which the theory itself draws, as a sociological theory which analyzes the laws determining the changes of value and the role of value in the production process of the commodity society.

Thus Marx does not analyze every exchange of things, but only the equalization of commodities through which social equalization of labor is carried out in a commodity economy. We analyze the value of commodities as a manifestation of the "social equality of labor." We must connect the concept of "social equality of labor" with the concept of equilibrium among individual forms of labor. The "equality of labor" corresponds to a determined state of distribution of labor in production, namely to a theoretically conceived state of equilibrium in which the transfer of labor from one branch of production to another ceases. It is obvious that transfers of labor will always take place and are indispensable if there is a constant distortion of proportionality in the distribution of labor due to the spontaneity of the economy. But these transfers of labor serve precisely to remove the distortions, to remove the deviations from the average, theoretically-conceived equilibrium among individual branches of production. The state of equilibrium takes place (theoretically) when the motives which stimulate commodity producers to pass from one branch to another disappear, when equal advantages for production are created in different branches. The exchange of products of labor among different branches according to their values, the social equality of different types of labor, corresponds to the state of social equilibrium of production.

The laws of this equilibrium, examined from their qualitative aspect, are different for the simple commodity economy and for the capitalist economy. This difference can be explained by the fact that objective equilibrium in the distribution of social labor is created through competition, through the transfer of labor from one branch to another, a transfer which is connected with the subjective motives of commodity producers.[152] The different roles of commodity producers in the social process of production thus create different laws of equilibrium in the distribution of labor. In a simple commodity economy, equal advantage of production for commodity producers employed in different branches is realized through the exchange of commodities in accordance with the quantity of labor necessary for the production of these commodities. S. Frank is suspicious of this proposition. According to Frank, "Equal income propensity in different branches of the economy presupposes that the price of the product will be

---

[152] The following comment by Bortkiewicz is to the point: "The law of value is left suspended in mid-air if one does not assume that producers who produce for the market try to obtain as great an advantage as they can by expending the least effort, and that they are also in a position to change their employment" (Bortkiewicz, "Wertrechnung und Preisrechnung in Marxschen System," Archiv fur Sozialwissenschaft u. Sozialpolitik, 1906, XXIII, Issue I, p. 39). But Bortkiewicz wrongly considers this proposition a basic contradiction of Hilferding's interpretation of Marx's theory. Hilferding does not ignore competition nor the interrelations between supply and demand, but this interconnection "is regulated by the price of production" (Hilferding, Bohm-Bawerk's Criticism of Marx, New York: Augustus Kelley, 1949, p. 193). Hilferding understands that economic actions are carried out by means of the motives of economic agents, but he points out: "Nothing but the tendency to establish the equality of economic relations can be derived from the motives of economic agents, motives which are in turn determined by the nature of economic relations" (Finanzkapital, Russian edition, p. 264). This tendency is the premise for the explanation of phenomena of the commodity capitalist economy, but not the only explanation. "The motivation of agents of capitalist production must be derived from the social function of economic actions in a given mode of production" (Ibid., p. 241).

proportional to the producer's expenditures, so that a certain sum of income will come from a certain sum of production expenditures. However, this proportionality does not presuppose equality between the social labor expended by the producer, and the quantities of labor which he gets in exchange for his production."[153]

However, S. Frank does not ask what the content of the production expenditure is for the simple commodity producer, if it is not the labor spent on the production. For the simple commodity producer, the difference in the conditions of production in two different branches appear as different conditions for the engagement of labor in them. In a simple commodity economy, the exchange of 10 hours of labor in one branch of production, for example shoemaking, for the product of 8 hours of labor in another branch, for example clothing production, necessarily leads (if the shoemaker and clothesmaker are equally qualified) to different advantages of production in the two branches, and to the transfer of labor from shoemaking to clothing production. Assuming complete mobility of labor in the commodity economy, every more or less significant difference in the advantage of production generates a tendency for the transfer of labor from the less advantageous branch of production to the more advantageous. This tendency remains until the less advantageous branch is confronted by a direct threat of economic collapse and finds it impossible to continue production because of unfavorable conditions for the sale of its products on the market.

Starting with these considerations, we cannot agree with the interpretation of the theory of value given by A. Bogdanov. "In a homogeneous society with a division of labor, every economic unit must receive, in exchange for its goods, a quantity of products (for its own

---

[153] S. Frank, Teoriya tsennosti Marksa i yeyo znachenie (Marx's Theory of Value and its Significance), 1900, pp. 137-138.

consumption) which is equal in value to its own products, in order to maintain economic life at the same level as in the previous period." "If individual economic units receive less than this, they begin to weaken and collapse and they cease to be able to perform their earlier social role."[154] Exchange of products which is not proportional to the labor expended in the production of these products means that individual economic units receive from society less labor-energy than they give. This leads to their collapse and to the interruption of production. This means that the normal course of production is only possible when the exchange of products is proportional to labor expenditures.[155]

However original and seductive this interpretation of the labor theory of value based on "energy" may be, it is not satisfactory for the following reasons: 1) It presupposes a total absence of surplus product, and this presupposition is superfluous for the analysis of the commodity economy and does not correspond to reality. 2) If such a premise is accepted, the law of exchange of products in proportion to their labor costs will be seen to be effective in all cases of interaction among different economic units, even if the foundations of a commodity economy do not exist. What one gets is a formula applicable to all historical periods and abstracted

---

[154] Kratkii kurs ekonomicheskoi nauki (Short Course in Economic Science), 1920, p. 63. The same reasoning can be found in his Kurs politicheskoi ekonomii (Course in Political Economy), Vol. II, 4th Part, pp. 22-24.

[155] Such arguments can also be found in rudimentary form in the work of N. Ziber. "Exchange which was not based on equal quantities of labor would lead to the devouring of some economic forces by others. This could not in any case last for an extended period. Nevertheless only a long period is fit for scientific analysis" (N. Ziber, Teoriya tsennosli i Rikardo [Ricardo's Theory of Value and Capital), 1871, p. 88).

from the properties of the commodity economy. 3) A. Bogdanov's argument presupposes that the given economy must receive (as a result of exchange) a determined quantity of products in kind which is necessary for the continuation of production, i.e., he has in mind the quantity of products in physical terms, and not the sum of values. A. Bogdanov describes the absolute limit beyond which the exchange of things between a given economic unit and other economic units becomes destructive to the first, and deprives it of the ability to continue production. However, in analyzing the commodity economy, the decisive role is played by the relative advantage of production for commodity producers in different branches, and the transfer of labor from less advantageous to more advantageous branches. In conditions of simple commodity production, equal advantage of production in different branches presupposes an exchange of commodities which is proportional to the quantities of labor expended on their production.

In the capitalist society, where the commodity producer does not expend his labor but his capital, the same principle of equal advantage is expressed by a different formula: equal profit for equal capital. The rate of profit regulates the distribution of capital among different branches of production, and this distribution of capital in turn directs the distribution of labor among these branches. The movement of prices on the market is related to the distribution of labor through the distribution of capital. The movement of prices is determined by labor value, through the price of production. Many critics of Marxism were disposed to see in this the bankruptcy of Marx's theory of value.[156] They overlooked the fact that the theory analyzed not only the quantitive, but above all the qualitive (social) side of the phenomena related to value. "Reification" or fetishization of working relations; production relations expressed in the value of products; equality among commodity producers as economic agents; the role of value in the distribution of

---

[156] Thus, for example, Hainisch says: "What is labor value after these explanations (in Capital, Volume III - I.R.)? It is an arbitrarily constructed concept, and not the exchange value of economic reality. It is not the real fact which was the starting point of our analysis and which we wanted to explain" (Hainisch, Die Marxsche Mehrwerttheorie, 1915, p. 22). Hainisch's words are typical of a whole field of criticism of Marxism which was provoked by the publication of Volume III of Capital. The more acute critics did not attach any significance to the ostensible "contradiction" between Volume I and Volume III of Capital, or at least they did not consider it essential (See J. Schumpeter, "Epochen der Dogmen und Methodengeschichte," Grundriss der Sozialoekonomik, I, 1914, p. 82, and F. Oppenheimer, Wert und Kapitalprofit, Jena: G. Fischer, 1916, p. 172-173). They direct sharp criticisms at the basic premises of Marx's theory of value. On the other hand, critics who insist on the contradictions between Marx's theory of value and his theory of production price, recognize that the logic of the theory of value cannot be challenged. "In fact it is possible to adduce formal objections to the deductions applied in Marx's theory of value, and in reality they have been adduced. But without doubt, these objections have not achieved their goal" (Heimann, "Methodologisches zu den Problemen des Wertes," Archiv fur Sozialwissenschaft u. Sozialpolitik, 1913, XXXVII, Issue No. 3, p. 775). The impossibility of "refuting Marx, starting from the theory of value," was even recognized by Dietzel. He saw the Achilles' heel of Marx's system in the theory of crises (Dietzel, Vom Lehrwert der Wertlehre, Leipzig: A.Deichert, 1921, p. 31).

labor among the different branches of production - this whole chain of phenomena, which was not adequately examined by Marx's critics and was elucidated by Marx's theory of value, refers equally to a simple commodity economy and to a capitalist economy. But the quantitative side of value also interested Marx, if it was related to the function of value as regulator of the distribution of labor. The quantitative proportions in which things exchange are expressions of the law of proportional distribution of social labor. Labor value and price of production are different manifestations of the same law of distribution of labor in conditions of simple commodity production and in the capitalist society.[157] The equilibrium and the allocation of labor are the basis of value and its changes both in the simple commodity economy and in the capitalist economy. This is the meaning of Marx's theory of "labor" value.

In the previous three chapters we dealt with the mechanism which connects labor and value. In Chapter Nine, value was first of all treated as the regulator of the distribution of social labor; in Chapter Ten, as the expression of social production relations among people; in Chapter Eleven, as the expression of abstract labor. Now we can turn to a more detailed analysis of the concept of value.

---

[157] See below, Chapter Eighteen, "Value and Production Price."

Chapter 12: Content and Form of Value

In order to grasp what the concept of the "value" of a product means in Marx's work, as opposed to Marx's conception of exchange value, we must first of all examine how Marx approached the concept of "value." As is widely known, the value of a product, for example, 1 quarter of wheat, can only be expressed on the market in the form of a determined concrete product which is acquired in exchange for the first product, for example, in the form of 20 pounds of shoe polish, 2 arshins of silk, 1/2 ounce of gold, etc. Thus the "value" of the product can only appear in its "exchange value," or more precisely, in its different exchange values. However, why did not Marx confine his analysis to the exchange value of the product, and particularly to the quantitative proportions of exchange of one product for another? Why did he consider it necessary to construct the concept of value parallel with the concept of exchange value and different from it?

In the Contribution to the Critique of Political Economy, Marx did not yet sharply distinguish between exchange value and value. In the Critique, Marx began his analysis with use value, then moved to exchange value, and from there passed directly to value (which he still called Tauschwert). This transition is smooth and imperceptible in Marx's work, as if it were something obvious.

But Marx makes this transition very differently in Capital, and it is very interesting to compare the first two pages of the Critique and of Capital.

The first two pages of both works accord perfectly with each other. The exposition in both begins with use value and then passes to exchange value. The statement that exchange value is a form of quantitative interrelation or proportion in which products exchange for one another is found in both books. But after that, the two texts diverge. If in the Critique Marx passed imperceptibly from exchange value to value, in Capital he seems, on the contrary, to remain on a given point, as if foreseeing objections from his opponents. After the statement which is common to both books, Marx points out: "exchange-value appears to be something accidental and purely relative, and consequently an intrinsic value, i.e., an exchange-value that is inseparably connected with, inherent in commodities, seems a contradiction in terms. Let us consider the matter a little more closely"(C, I, p. 36).

One can see that here Marx had in mind an opponent who wanted to show that nothing exists except relative exchange values, that the concept of value is thoroughly superfluous in political economy. Who was the opponent alluded to by Marx?

This opponent was [Samuel] Bailey, who held that the concept of value is thoroughly unnecessary in political economy, that one must restrict oneself to the observation and analysis of individual proportions in which various goods are exchanged. Bailey, who was more successful in his superficiality than in his witty critique of Ricardo, tried to undermine the foundations of the labor theory of value. He maintained that it is wrong to speak of the value of a table. We can only say that the table is exchanged once for three chairs, another time for two pounds of coffee, etc.; the magnitude of the value is something thoroughly relative, and it varies in different instances. From this Bailey drew conclusions which led to the negation of the concept of value as a concept which differs from the relative value of a given product in a given act of exchange. Let us imagine the following case: the value of a table equals three chairs. A year later, the table is exchanged for six chairs. We think we are right if we say that even though the exchange value of the table has changed, its value has remained unchanged. Only the value of the chairs fell, to half their former value. Bailey finds this statement meaningless. Since the relation of exchange between the table and the chairs changed, the relation of the chairs to the table changed also, and the value of the table consists only of this.

In order to disprove Bailey's theory, Marx considered it necessary to develop (in Capital) the conception that exchange value cannot be grasped if it is not reduced to some common factor, namely to value. The first section of Chapter 1 of Capital is devoted to giving a foundation to this idea of the transition from exchange value to value and from value to the common basis under both, namely labor. Section 2 is a completion of Section 1, since here the concept of labor is analyzed in greater detail. We may say that Marx passed from the differences which are manifested in the sphere of exchange value to the common factor which is at the basis of all exchange values, namely to value (and in the last analysis, to labor). Here Marx shows the inaccuracy of Bailey's conception of the possibility of restricting analysis to the analysis of the sphere of exchange value. In Section 3, Marx undertakes the opposite course and explains the way the value of a given product is expressed in its various exchange values. Earlier Marx had been led by analysis to the common factor, and now he moves from the common factor to the differences. Earlier he refuted Bailey's conception, and now he completes Ricardo's theory, which did not explain the transition from value to exchange value. In order to refute Bailey's theory, Marx had to develop Ricardo's theory further.

Actually, Bailey's attempt to show that there is no value other than exchange value, was facilitated significantly by Ricardo's onesidedness. Ricardo could not show how value is expressed in a determined form of value. Thus Marx had two tasks: 1) he had to show that value must be revealed behind exchange value; 2) he had to prove that the analysis of value necessarily leads to different forms of its manifestation, to exchange value.

How did Marx make the transition from exchange value to value?

Usually, critics and commentators of Marx hold that his central argument consists of his famous comparison of wheat and iron on page 3 of the first volume of the German edition of Capital. If wheat and iron are equated with each other, Marx reasoned, then there must be something common to both and equal in magnitude. They must be equal to a third thing, and this is precisely their value. One usually holds that this is Marx's main argument. Almost all critiques of Marx's theory are directed against this argument. Unfortunately, every work directed against Marx maintains that Marx tried to prove the necessity of the concept of value by means of purely abstract reasoning.

But what has been completely overlooked is the following circumstance. The paragraph in which Marx treats the equality of the wheat and the iron is merely a deduction from the previous paragraph, which says: "A given commodity, e.g., a quarter of wheat is exchanged for x blacking, y silk, or z gold, &c. - in short, for other commodities in the most different proportions. Instead of one exchange-value, the wheat has, therefore, a great many. But since x blacking, y silk, or z gold, &c., each represent the exchange-value of one quarter of wheat, x blacking, y silk, z gold, &c., must, as exchange-values, be replaceable by each other, or equal to each other. Therefore, first: the valid exchange-values of a given commodity express something equal; secondly, exchange-value, generally, is only the mode of expression, the phenomenal form, of something contained in it, yet distinguishable from it" (C, I, p. 37).

As can be seen from this passage, Marx does not examine the individual case of equalization of one commodity for another. The starting-point of the argument is a statement of a well-known fact about the commodity economy, the fact that all commodities can be equalized with each other, and the fact that a given commodity can be equated with an infinity of other commodities. In other words, the starting point of all of Marx's reasoning is the concrete structure of the commodity economy, and not the purely logical method of comparison of two commodities with each other.

Thus Marx starts from the fact of manyfold equalization of all commodities with each other, or from the fact that every commodity can be equated with many other commodities. However, this premise in itself is still not enough for all the conclusions which Marx reached. At the basis of these conclusions there is still a tacit assumption which Marx formulates in various other places.

Another premise consists of the following: we assume that the exchange of one quarter of wheat for any other commodity is subsumed by some regularity. The regularity of these acts of exchange is due to their dependence on the process of production. We reject the premise that the quarter of wheat can be exchanged for an arbitrary quantity of iron, coffee, etc. We cannot agree with the premise that the proportions of exchange are established every time, in the act of exchange itself, and thus have a completely accidental character. On the contrary, we affirm that all the possibilities for the exchange of a given commodity for any other commodity are subsumed under certain regularities based on the production process. In such a case, Marx's entire argument takes the following form.

Marx says: Let us take, not the chance exchange of two commodities, iron and wheat, but let us take exchange in the form in which it actually takes place in a commodity economy. Then we will see that every object can be equalized with all other objects. In other words, we see an infinity of proportions of exchange of the given product with all others. But these proportions of exchange are not accidental; they are regular, and their regularity is determined by causes which lie in the production process. Thus we reach the conclusion that the value of a quarter of wheat is expressed once in two pounds of coffee, another time in three chairs, and so on, independently of the fact that the value of a quarter of wheat has remained the same in all these cases. If we assumed that in each of the infinite proportions of exchange, the quarter of wheat has another value (and this is what Bailey's statement can be reduced to), then we would admit complete chaos in the phenomenon of price formation, in the grandiose phenomenon of the exchange of products by means of which the comprehensive interrelation of all forms of labor is carried out.

The above reasoning led Marx to the conclusion that even though the value of the product is necessarily manifested in exchange value, he would have to subsume the analysis of value under that of exchange value and independently of it. "The progress of our investigation will show that exchange-value is the only form in which the value of commodities can manifest itself or be expressed. For the present, however, we have to consider the nature of value independently of this, its form" (C., I, p. 38). Consistently with this, in the first and second sections of Chapter 1 of Capital, Marx analyzed the concept of value in order to pass to exchange value. This distinction between value and exchange value leads us to ask: what is value as opposed to exchange value.

If we take the most popular and most widely held view, then, unfortunately, we can say that value is usually considered to be the labor which is necessary for the production of given commodities. However, the exchange value of given commodities is seen as another product for which the first commodity is exchanged. If a given table is produced in three hours of labor and is exchanged for three chairs, one usually says that the value of the table, equal to three hours of labor, was expressed in another product different from the table itself, namely in three chairs. The three chairs make up the exchange value of the table.

This popular definition usually leaves unclear whether the value is determined by the labor or whether the value is the labor itself. Obviously, from the point of view of Marx's theory, it is accurate to say that exchange value is determined by labor, but then we must ask: what is the value determined by labor, and to this question we usually do not find an adequate answer in the popular explanations.

This is why the reader frequently forms the idea that the value of the product is nothing other than the labor necessary for its production. One gets a false impression of the complete identity between labor and value.

Such a conception is very widespread in anti-Marxist literature. One may say that a large number of the misunderstandings and misinterpretations which can be found in anti-Marxist literature are based on the false impression that, according to Marx, labor is value.

This false impression often grows out of the inability to grasp the terminology and meaning of Marx's work. For example, Marx's well-known statement that value is "congealed" or "crystallized" labor is usually interpreted to mean that labor is value. This erroneous impression is also created by the double meaning of the Russian verb "represent" (predstavlyat'). Value "represents" labor - this is how we translate the German verb "darstellen." But this Russian sentence can be understood, not only in the sense that value is a representation, or expression, of labor - the only sense which is consistent with Marx's theory - but also in the sense that value is labor. Such an impression, which is the most widespread in critical literaturedirected against Marx, is of course completely false. Labor cannot be identified with value. Labor is only the substance of value, and in order to obtain value in the full sense of the word, labor as the substance of value must be treated in its inseparable connection with the social "value form" (Wertform).

Marx analyzes value in terms of its form, substance and magnitude (Wertform, Wertsubstanz, Wertgrosse). "The decisive, crucial point consists of revealing the necessary internal connection between the form, substance and magnitude of value" (Kapital, 1, 1867, p. 34). The connection between these three aspects was hidden from the eyes of the analyst because Marx analyzed them separately from each other. In the first German edition of Capital, Marx pointed out several times that the subject was the analysis of various aspects of one and the same object: value. "Now we know the substance of value. It is labor. We know the measure of its magnitude. It is labor-time. What still remains is its form, which transforms value into exchange value" (Ibid., p. 6; Marx's italics). "Up to now we have defined only the substance and magnitude of value. Now we turn to the analysis of the form of value" (Ibid., p. 13). In the second edition of Volume I of Capital, these sentences were excluded, but the first chapter is divided into sections with separate headings: the heading of the first section says, "Substance of Value and Magnitude of Value"; the third section is titled: "Form of Value or Exchange Value." As for the second section, which is devoted to the two-fold character of labor, it is only a supplement to the first section, i.e., to the theory of the substance of value.

Leaving aside here the quantitative aspect, or the magnitude of value, and limiting ourselves to the qualitative aspect, we can say that value has to be considered in terms of "substance" (content) and "form of value."[158] The obligation to analyze value in terms of both of the factors included within it means an obligation to keep to a genetic (dialectic) method in the analysis.

---

[158] Here and later, "form of value" (Wertform) does not mean the various forms which value acquired in its development (for example, accidental, expanded, and general forms of value), but of value itself, which is considered as the social form of the product of labor. In other words, here we do not have in mind the various "forms of value," but "value as form."

This method contains analysis as well as synthesis.[159] On one hand, Marx takes as his starting-point the analysis of value as the finished form of the product of labor, and by means of analysis he uncovers the content (substance) which is contained in the given form, i.e., labor. Here Marx follows the road which was paved by the Classical Economists, particularly Ricardo, and which Bailey refused to follow. But on the other hand, because Ricardo had confined himself to the reduction of form (value) to content (labor) in his analysis, Marx wants to show why this content acquires a given social form. Marx does not only move from form to content, but also from content to form. He makes the "form of value" the subject of his examination, namely value as the social form of the product of labor - the form which the Classical Economists took for granted and thus did not have to explain.

Reproaching Bailey for limiting his analysis to the quantitative aspect of exchange value and for ignoring value, Marx observes that the classical school, on the other hand, ignored the "form of value" even though it subjected value itself (namely the content of value, its dependence on labor) to analysis. "Political Economy has indeed analyzed, however incompletely, value and its magnitude, and has discovered what lies beneath these forms. But it has never once asked the question why labor is represented by the value of its product and labor-time by the magnitude of that value" (C., I, p. 80). The Classical Economists uncovered labor under value; Marx showed that the working relations among people and social labor necessarily take the material form of the value of products of labor in a commodity economy. The classics pointed to the content of value, to labor expended in the production of the product. Marx studied above all the "form of value,"

---

[159] On these methods, see above, the end of Chapter Four.

i.e., value as the material expression of the working relations among people and social (abstract) labor.[160]

"The form of value" plays an important role in Marx's theory of value. However, it did not attract the attention of critics (except Hilferding).[161] Marx himself mentions "the form of value" in variouspassages incidentally. The third section of Chapter I of Capital has the title "Form of Value or Exchange Value." But Marx does not remain on the explanation of the form of value, and quickly passes to its various modifications, to the individual "forms of value": accidental, expanded, general and monetary. These different "forms of value," which are included in every popular presentation of Marx's theory, overshadowed the "form of value" as such. Marx elaborated the "form of value" in greater detail in the passage mentioned above: "It is one of the chief failings of

---

[160] We leave aside the controversial question of whether or not Marx interpreted the Classics correctly. We suppose that in relation to Ricardo, Marx was right when he said that Ricardo examined the quantity and partially the content of value, ignoring the form of value (See Theorien uber den Mehwert, Vol. II, Book I, p. 12 and Vol. III, p. 163, 164). For more detailed analysis, see our article, "Basic Characteristics of Marx's Theory of Value and Its Difference from Ricardo's Theory," included in Rozenberg, Teoriya stoimosti u Rikardo i Marksa (Theory of Value in Ricardo and Marx), Moskva: Moskovskii Rabochii, 1924.

[161] The significance of the form of value for an understanding of Marx's theory was noticed by S. Bulgakov in his old and interesting articles ("Chto takoye trudovaya tsennost" [What is Labor Value] in Sbornike pravovedeniya i obshcheslvennykh znanii [Essays on Jurisprudence and Social Science], 1896, V, VI, p. 234, and "O nekotorykh osnovnykh ponyatiyakh politicheskoi ekonimii" [On Some Basic Concepts of Political Economy] in Nauchnom Obozrenii [Scientific Survey], 1898, No. 2, p. 337.

classical economy that it has never succeeded, by means of its analysis of commodities, and in particular, of their value, in discovering that form under which value becomes exchange-value. Even Adam Smith and Ricardo, the best representatives of the school, treat the form of value as a thing of no importance, as having no connection with the inherent nature of commodities. The reason for this is not solely because their attention is entirely absorbed in the analysis of the magnitude of value. It lies deeper. The value-form of the product of labor is not only the most abstract, but is also the most universal form, taken by the product in bourgeois production, and stamps that production as a particular species of social production, and thereby gives it its special historical character. If then we treat this mode of production as one eternally fixed by Nature for every state of society, we necessarily overlook that which is the differentia specifica of the value-form, and consequently of the commodity-form, and of its further developments, money-form, capital-form, &c." (C., I, pp. 80-81, footnote. Rubin's italics).

Thus the "value form" is the most general form of the commodity economy; it is characteristic of the social form which is acquired by the process of production at a determined level of historical development. Since political economy analyzes a historically transient social form of production, commodity capitalist production, the "form of value" is one of the foundation stones of Marx's theory of value. As can be seen from the sentences quoted above, the "form of value" is closely related to the "commodity form," i.e., to the basic characteristic of the contemporary economy, the fact that the products of labor are produced by autonomous, private producers. A working connection between producers is brought about only by means of the exchange of commodities. In such a "commodity" form of economy, social labor necessary for the production of a given product is not expressed directly in working units, but indirectly, in the "form of value," in the form of other products which are exchanged for the given product. The product of labor is transformed into a commodity; it has use value and the social "form of value." Thus social labor is "reified," it acquires the "form of value," i.e., the form of a property attached to things and which seems to belong to the things themselves. This "reified" labor (and not social labor as such) is precisely what represents value. This is what we have in mind when we say that value already includes within itself the social "form of value."

However, what is that "form of value" which, as opposed to exchange value, is included in the concept of value?

I will mention only one of the dearest definitions of the form of value in the first edition of Capital: "The social form of commodities and the form of value (Wertform), or form of exchangeability (form der Austauschbarkeit) are, thus, one and the same (Kapital, 1, 1867, p. 28; Marx's italics). As we can see, the form of value is called a form of exchangeability, or a social form of the product of labor which resides in the fact that it can be exchanged for any other commodity, if this exchangeability is determined by the quantity of labor necessary for the production of the given commodity. In this way, when we have passed from exchange value to value, we have not abstracted from the social form of the product of labor. We have abstracted only from the concrete product in which the value of the commodity is expressed, but we still have in mind the social form of the product of labor, its capacity to be exchanged in a determined proportion for any other product.

Our conclusion can be formulated in the following way: Marx analyzes the "form of value" (Wertform) separately from exchange value (Tauschwert). In order to include the social form of the product of labor in the concept of value, we had to split the social form of the product into two forms: Wertform and Tauschwert. By the first we mean the social form of the product which is not yet concretized in determined things, but represents some abstract property of commodities. In order to include in the concept of value the properties of the social form of the product of labor and thus show the inadmissibility of identifying the concept of value with the concept of labor, an identification which was often approached by popular presentations of Marx, we have to prove that value must be examined not only from the aspect of the substance of value (i.e., labor), but from the aspect of the "form of value." In order to include the form of value in the concept of value itself, we have to separate it from exchange value, which is treated separately from value by Marx. Thus we have broken down the social form of the product into two parts: the social form which has not yet acquired a concrete form (i.e., "form of value"), and the form which already has a concrete and independent form (i.e., exchange value).

After we have examined the "form of value," we must pass on to the examination of the content or substance of value. All Marxists agree that labor is the content of value. But the problem is, what kind of labor is under consideration. It is known to us that the most different forms may be hidden under the word "labor." Precisely what kind of labor makes up the content of value?

After having drawn a distinction between socially equalized labor in general, which can exist in different forms of social division of labor, and abstract labor, which exists only in a commodity economy, we must ask the following question: does Marx understand, by substance or content of value, socially equalized labor in general (i.e., social labor in general), or rather abstractly universal labor? In other words, when we speak of labor as the content of value, do we include in the concept of labor all those characteristics which were included in the concept of abstract labor, or do we take labor in the sense of socially equalized labor, not including in it those properties which characterize the social organization of labor in the commodity economy? Does the concept of labor as the "content" of value coincide with the concept of "abstract" labor which creates value? At first glance, one can find in Marx's work arguments in favor of both of these meanings of the content of value. We can find arguments which seem to hold that labor as the content of value is something poorer than abstract labor, i.e., labor without those social properties which belong to it in a commodity economy.

What arguments do we find in favor of this solution?

By content of value, Marx often referred to something which may acquire the social form of value but can also take on another social form. By content is understood something which can take various social forms. Socially equalized labor has precisely this capacity, but not abstract labor (i.e., labor which has already acquired a determined social form). Socially equalized labor may take on the form of labor organized in a commodity economy and the form of labor organized, for example, in a socialist economy. In other words, in a given case we take the social equalization of labor abstractly, not paying attention to the modifications which are called forth in the content (i.e., labor) by one or the other of its forms.

Can one find the concept of content of value in this sense in Marx's work? We can answer this question affirmatively. We remember, for example, in Marx's words, that "exchange-value is a definite social manner of expressing the amount of labor bestowed upon an object" (C., I, p. 82). It is obvious that labor is here treated as the abstract content which can take this or that social form. When Marx, in the well-known letter to Kugelmann of July 11, 1868, says that the social division of labor is manifested in the commodity economy in the form of value, he again treats socially allocated labor as the content which can take this or that social form. In the second paragraph of the section on Commodity Fetishism, Marx says directly that "the content of the determination of value" can be found not only in the commodity economy but also in the patriarchal family or on the feudal estate. Here, too, as we can see, labor is treated as the content which can take various social forms.

However, in Marx's work one can also find arguments in favor of the opposite viewpoint, according to which we must consider abstract labor as the content of value. First of all, we find in Marx's work some statements which directly say this, for example the following: "They (commodities) are related to abstract human labor as to their general social substance" (Kapital, 1, 1867, p. 28. Italics by I. R.). This statement seems to leave no doubt about the fact that abstract labor is not only the creator of value, but also the substance and content of value. We reach this same conclusion on the basis of methodological considerations. Socially equalized labor acquires the form of abstract labor in the commodity economy, and only from this abstract labor follows the necessity of value as the social form of the product of labor. From this it follows that the concept of abstract labor in our schema directly precedes the concept of value. One might say that this concept of abstract labor must be taken as the basis, as the content and substance of value. One cannot forget that, on the question of the relation between content and form, Marx took the standpoint of Hegel, and not of Kant. Kant treated form as something external in relation to the content, and as something which adheres to the content from the outside. From the standpoint of Hegel's philosophy, the content is not in itself something to which form adheres from the outside. Rather, through its development, the content itself gives birth to the form which was already latent in the content. Form necessarily grows out of the content itself. This is a basic premise of Hegel's and Marx's methodology, a premise which is opposed to Kant's methodology. From this point of view, the form of value necessarily grows out of the substance of value. Therefore, we must take abstract labor in all the variety of its social properties characteristic for a commodity economy, as the substance of value. And, finally, if we take abstract labor as the content of value, we achieve a significant simplification of Marx's entire schema. In this case, labor as the content of value does not differ from labor which creates value.

We have reached the paradoxical position that Marx sometimes takes social (or socially equalized) labor, and sometimes abstract labor, as the content of value.

How can we get out of this contradiction? The contradiction disappears if we remember that the dialectical method includes both methods of analysis which we treated above: the method of analysis from form to content, and the method from content to form. If we start from value as a determined, previously given social form, and if we ask what is the content of this form, then it is clear that this form only expresses, in general, the fact that social labor is expended. Value is seen as a form which expresses the fact of social equalization of labor, a fact which does not only take place in a commodity economy but can take place in other economies. Passing analytically from finished forms to their content, we find socially equalized labor as the content of value. But we will reach another conclusion if we take as our starting point, not the finished form, but the content itself (i.e., labor), from which the form necessarily follows (i.e., value). In order to pass from labor, considered as the content, to value as the form, we must include the concept of labor in the social form which belongs to it in the commodity economy, i.e., we must now recognize abstractly universal labor as the content of value. It is possible that the seeming contradiction in the determination of the content of value which we find in Marx's work can be explained precisely in terms of the difference between the two methods.

Since we have separately analyzed the form and the content of value, we must treat the relation between them. What relation exists between labor and value? The general answer to this question is: value is the adequate and exact form for expressing the content of value (i.e., labor). In order to clarify this idea, we return to the previous example: the table is exchanged for three chairs. We say that this process of exchange is determined by a certain regularity and depends on the development and changes in productivity of labor. But exchange value is the social form of the product of labor which not only expresses the changes of labor, but which also masks and hides these changes. It hides them because of the simple reason that exchange value presupposes a value relation between two commodities - between the table and the chairs. Thus changes in the exchange proportion between these two objects do not tell us whether the quantity of labor expended on the production of the table or the quantity of labor expended on the production of the chairs has changed. If the table, after a certain time, is exchanged for six chairs, the exchange value of the table has changed. However, the value of the table itself may not have changed at all. In order to analyze, in pure form, the dependence of the change of the social form of the product on the quantity of labor expended on its production, Marx had to divide the given event into two parts, to split it, and to say that we must analyze separately the causes which determine the "absolute" value of the table and the causes which determine the "absolute" value of the chairs; and that one and the same act of exchange (namely the fact that the table now exchanges for six chairs instead of three) may be brought about either by causes which act on the table, or by causes whose roots lie in the production of the chairs. To treat separately the effect of each of these causal chains, Marx had to split the changes of exchange value of the table into two parts, and to assume that these changes were brought about by causes which lay exclusively in the table, i.e., changes in the productivity of labor necessary for the production of the table. In other words, he had to assume that the chairs as well as all other commodities for which our table would exchange, maintain their previous value. Only with this assumption is value a completely accurate and adequate form for expressing labor in its qualitative and quantitative aspects.

Until now we have examined the connection between the substance and the form of value from its qualitative aspect. Now we must examine this same connection from its quantitative aspect. Thus we pass from the substance and form to the third aspect of value, the magnitude of value. Marx treats social labor not only from its qualitative aspect (labor as the substance of value), but from the quantitative as well (amount of labor). In the same way, Marx examines value from the qualitative aspect (as form, or form of value), and from the quantitative aspect (magnitude of value). From the qualitative aspect, the interrelations between the "substance" and "form of value" signify interrelations between socially abstract labor and its "reified" form? i.e., value. Here Marx's theory of value directly approaches his theory of commodity fetishism. From the quantitative aspect, we are concerned with the interrelations between the quantity of abstract, socially necessary labor and the magnitude of the value of the product, whose change is the basis for the regular movement of market prices. The magnitude of value changes in dependence on the quantity of abstract, socially-necessary labor, but because of the twofold character of labor the changes in the quantity of abstract, socially-necessary labor are caused by changes in the quantity of concrete labor, i.e., by the development of the material-technical process of production, in particular the productivity of labor. Thus, the entire system of value is based on a grandiose system of spontaneous social accounting and comparison of the products of labor of various types and performed by different individuals as parts of the total social abstract labor. This system is hidden and cannot be seen on the surface of events. In turn, this system of total social abstract labor is put into motion by the development of material productive forces which are the ultimate factor of development of society in general. Thus Marx's theory of value is connected with his theory of historical materialism.

In Marx's theory we find a magnificent synthesis of the content and form of value on the one hand, and the qualitative and quantitative aspects of value on the other. In one passage Marx points out that Petty confused two definitions of value: "value as the form of social labor" and "the magnitude of value which is determined by equal labor time, according to which labor is treated as the source of value" (Theorien uber den Mehrwert, V. I, 1905, p. 11). Marx's greatness lies precisely in the fact that he gave a synthesis of both of these definitions of value. "Value as the material expression of the production relations among people," and "value as a magnitude determined by the quantity of labor or labor-time" - both of these definitions are inseparably connected in Marx's work. The quantitative aspect of the concept of value, on the analysis of which the classical economists predominantly concentrated, is examined by Marx on the basis of analysis of the qualitative aspect of value. It is precisely the theory of the form of value or of "value as the form of social labor" which represents the most specific part of Marx's theory of value as opposed to the theory of the classical economists. Among bourgeois scientists, one can frequently find the idea that the characteristic feature of Marx's work in comparison with the classical economists consists of his recognition of labor as the "source" or "substance" of value. As can be seen from the passages by Marx which we cited, the recognition of labor as the source of value can also be found among economists who are mainly interested in the quantitative phenomena related to value. In particular, the recognition of labor as the source of value can also be found in Smith and Ricardo. But we would look in vain to these writers for a theory of "value as the form of social labor."

Before Marx, the attention of the classical economists and their epigones was drawn either to the content of value, mainly its quantitative aspect (amount of labor), or to relative exchange value, i.e., to the quantitative proportions of exchange. Two extreme ends of the theory of value were subjected to analysis: the fact of development of productivity of labor and technique as the internal cause of changes of value, and the fact of relative changes of value of commodities on the market. But the direct connection was missing: the "form of value", i.e., value as the form which is characterized by the reification of production relations and the transformation of social labor into a property of the products of labor. This explains Marx's reproaches of his predecessors, which one might at first glance say are contradictory. He reproaches Bailey for examining the proportions of exchange, i.e., exchange value, ignoring value. He sees the shortcoming of the classics in the fact that they examined value and the magnitude of value, the content, and not the "form of value." Marx's predecessors, as was pointed out, paid attention to the content of value mainly from the quantitative aspect (labor and the magnitude of labor), and in the same way, the quantitative aspect of exchange value. They neglected the qualitative aspect of labor and value, the characteristic property of the commodity economy. Analysis of the "form of value" is precisely what gives a sociological character and specific traits to the concept of value. This "form of value" brings together the ends of the chain: the development of productivity of labor, and market phenomena. Without the form of value, these ends separate and each of them is transformed into a one-sided theory. We acquire labor expenditures from the technical side, independent from the social form of the material process of production (labor value as the logical category), and relative changes of prices on the market, a theory of prices which seeks to explain the fluctuations of prices outside of the sphere of the labor process and cut off from the basic fact of the social economy, from the development of productive forces.

Showing that without the form of value there is no value, Marx acutely grasped that this social form, without the labor content which fills it, remains empty. Noticing the neglect of the form of value on the part of the classical economists, Marx warns us of another danger, namely of overestimating the social value-form at the expense of its labor-content. "This led to the rise of a restored mercantile system (Ganilh, &c.), which sees in value nothing but a social form, or rather the unsubstantial ghost of that form"(C., I, p. 81, footnote.)[162]

In another place Marx said of the same Ganilh:

"Ganilh is quite right when he says of Ricardo and most economists that they consider labor without exchange, although their system, like the whole bourgeois system, rests on exchange value."[163]

Ganilh is right when he emphasizes the meaning of exchange, i.e., the determined social form of working activity among people which is expressed in the "form of value." But he exaggerates the meaning of exchange at the expense of the productive-labor process: "Ganilh imagines, with the Mercantilists, that the magnitude of value is itself the product of exchange, whereas in fact it is only the form of value or the form of commodity which the product receives through exchange."[164]

The form of value is supplemented by the labor content, the magnitude of value depends on the amount of abstract labor. In its turn labor, which is closely connected with the system of value by its social or

---

[162] In the German original, Marx simply says: substanzlosen Schein (p. 47). Translators who did not pay adequate attention to the distinction between the form and the content (substance) felt it necessary to include the word "independent," which Marx did not include. Struve translates substanzlosen with the words "without content," which accurately translates Marx's concept, which saw in the "substance" of value its content, as opposed to its form.

[163] Theories of Surplus Value, Moscow: Foreign Languages Publishing House, 1956, Part I, p. 199.

[164] Ibid., p. 200.

abstract aspect, is closely related to the system of material production by its material-technical, or concrete, aspect.

As a result of the analysis of value from the aspect of its content (i.e., labor) and its social form, we acquire the following advantages. We straight away break with the widespread identification of value and labor and thus we define the relationship of the concept of value to the concept of labor more accurately. We also define the relation between value and exchange value more accurately. Earlier, when value was treated simply as labor and was not given distinct social characteristics, value was equated with labor on one hand, and was separated from exchange value by an abyss on the other hand. In the concept of value economists frequently duplicated the same labor. From this concept of value they could not move to the concept of exchange value. Now when we consider value in terms of content and form, we relate value with the concept which precedes it, abstract labor (and in the last analysis with the material process of production), the content. On the other hand, through the form of value we have already connected value with the concept which follows it, exchange value. In fact, once we have determined that value does not represent labor in general, but labor which has the "form of exchangeability" of a product, then we must pass from value directly to exchange value. In this way, the concept of value is seen to be inseparable from the concept of labor on one hand, and from the concept of exchange value on the other.

Chapter 13: Social Labor

We have reached the conclusion that in a commodity economy the equalization of labor is carried out through the equalization of the products of labor. Individual acts of social equalization of labor do not exist in the commodity economy. This is why it is erroneous to present the problem in a way that suggests that someone equalized different forms of labor in advance, comparing them by means of given measuring units, after which the products of labor were exchanged proportionally, according to the already measured and equalized quantities of labor which they contained. Starting from this viewpoint, which ignores the anarchic, spontaneous character of the commodity capitalist economy, economists frequently thought the task of economic theory was to find a standard of value which would make it possible in practice to compare and measure the quantity of various products in the act of market-exchange. It seemed to them that the labor theory of value emphasized labor precisely as this practical standard of value. This is why their critique aimed to demonstrate that labor could not be accepted as a convenient standard of value due to the absence of precisely established units of labor with which to measure various forms of labor different from each other in terms of intensity, qualification, danger to health, etc.

The above-mentioned economists could not free themselves from an erroneous idea which had built itself a nest in political economy and which attributed to the theory of value a task which was not its own, namely to find a practical standard of value. In reality the theory of value has a completely different task, theoretical and not practical. It is not necessary for us to seek a practical standard of value which would make possible the equalization of the products of labor on the market. This equalization takes place in reality every day in the process of market exchange. In this process, spontaneously, a standard of value is worked out, namely money, which is indispensable for this equalization. This market exchange does not need any type of standard which is thought up by economists. The task of the theory of value is completely different, namely to grasp and explain theoretically the process of equalization of commodities which takes place regularly on the market, in close connection with the equalization and distribution of social labor in the process of production, i.e., to uncover the causal relation between both of these processes and the laws of their changes. The causal analysis of the actually realized processes of equalization of various commodities and various forms of labor, and not the finding of practical standards for their comparison - this is the task of the theory of value.

The essential confusion of the standard of value and the law of the changes of value in Smith's work led to great damage in political economy and can still be felt today. The great service of Ricardo consists of his having put aside the problem of finding a practical standard of value and placing the theory of value on a strict scientific basis of causal analysis of the changes of market prices depending on changes in productivity of labor.[165] His follower in this sense is Marx, who sharply criticized views of labor as an "unchanging standard of value." "The problem of an unchanging standard of value is in reality only an erroneous expression of the search for the concepts and nature of value itself" (Theorien uber den Mehrwert, III, p. 159). "The service of Bailey consists of the fact that, with his objections, he revealed the confusion of the 'standard of value' (as it is represented in money, a commodity which exists together with other commodities) with the immanent standard and substance of value" (Ibid., p. 163). The theory of value does not seek an "external standard" of value, but its "cause," "the genesis and immanent nature of value" (Ibid., pp. 186, 195). Causal analysis of the changes of value of commodities which depend on changes in the

---

[165] See I. Rubin, Istoriya ekonomicheskoi mysli (History of Economic Thought), 2nd Edition, 1928, Chapters XXII and XXVIII.

productivity of labor the analysis of these real events from qualitative and quantitative points of view is what Marx calls the study of the "substance" and "immanent standard" of value. "Immanent standard" does not here mean the quantity which is taken as a unit of measure, but a "quantity which is connected with some kind of existence or some kind of quality."[166] Marx's statement that labor is an immanent standard of value must be understood only in the sense that quantitative changes of labor necessary for the production of the product bring about quantitative changes in the value of the product. Thus the term "immanent standard" was transferred by Marx, along with many other terms, from philosophy to political economy. It cannot be treated as completely successful, since in a superficial reading this term makes the reader think mainly about a measure of equalization rather than of causal analysis of quantitative changes of events. This unsuccessful terminology connected with the incorrect interpretation of Marx's reasoning in the first pages of Capital has led even Marxists to introduce into the theory of value a problem which is foreign to it, namely that of finding a practical standard of value.

The equalization of labor in a commodity economy is not established by some previously determined unit of measurement, but is carried out through the equalization of commodities in exchange. Due to the process of exchange, the product as well as the labor of the commodity producer is subject to substantial changes. Here we are not speaking of natural, material changes. The sale of frocks cannot lead to any changes in the natural form of the frock itself, nor ill the labor of the tailor, nor in the totality of the already finished concrete

---

[166] O. Bauer, "Istoriya Kapitala," Sbornik Osnovnye problemy politicheskoi ekonomii (Basic Problems of Political Economy), 1922, p. 47. This is Hegel's well-known definition of measure. See Kuno Fischer, Geschichte der neuern Philosophie, Vol. 8, Heidelberg: C. Winter, 1901, p. 490, and G. F. Hegel, Samtliche Werke, Vol. III, Book I, Leipzig: F. Meiner, 1923, p. 340.

labor processes. But the sale of the product changes its form of value, its social function or form. Sale indirectly affects the working activity of commodity producers. It places their labor in a determined relation with the labor of other commodity producers of the same profession, i.e., it changes the social function of labor. Changes through which the product of labor is subject to the process of exchange can be characterized in the following way: 1) the product acquires the capacity to be directly exchanged for any other product of social labor, i.e., it exhibits its character of being a social product; 2) the product acquires this social character in such a form that it is equalized with a determined product (gold) which possesses the quality of being directly exchangeable for all other products; 3) the equalization of all products with each other, which is carried out by their comparison with gold (money) also includes the equalization of various forms of labor which differ by the different levels of qualification, i.e., the length of training, and 4) the equalization of products of a given kind and quality produced in different technical conditions, i.e., with an expenditure of different individual quantities of labor.

The listed changes which the product undergoes through the process of exchange are accompanied by analogous changes in the labor of the commodity producer: 1) the labor of the separate private commodity producer displays its character as social labor; 2) the given concrete form of labor is equalized with all other concrete form of labor. This manyfold equalization of labor also includes: 3) the equalization of different forms of labor which differ in terms of qualifications, and 4) the equalization of different individual labor expenditures which are spent in the production of exemplars of productsof a given type and quality. This way, through the process of exchange, private labor acquires a supplementary characteristic in the form of social labor, concrete labor in the form of abstract labor, complex labor is reduced to simple, and individual to socially-necessary labor. In other words, the labor of the commodity producer, which in the process of production directly takes the form of private, concrete, qualified (i.e., different by a determined level of qualification, which in some cases may be said to equal zero) and individual, acquires social properties in the process of exchange which characterize it as social, abstract, simple, and socially-necessary labor.[167] We are not dealing with four separate processes of transformation of labor, as some analysts present the problem, these are different aspects of the same process of equalization of labor which is carried out through the equalization of the products of labor as values. The unified act of equalizing commodities as values puts aside and cancels the properties of labor as private, concrete, qualified and individual. All these aspects are so closely interrelated that in A Contribution to the Critique of Political Economy, Marx still did not give a clear enough distinction between them, and he erased the boundaries between abstract, simple, and socially-necessary labor (Critique, pp. 24-26). On the other hand, in Capital these definitions are developed by Marx with such clarity and rigor that the attention of the reader must grasp the close relation between them as expressions of different aspects of the equalization of labor in the process of its distribution. This process presupposes: 1) interconnection among all labor processes (social labor); 2) equalization of individual spheres of production or spheres of labor (abstract labor); 3) equalization of forms of labor with different qualifications (simple labor) and 4) equalization of labor

---

[167] In commodity production, i.e., production which is meant in advance for exchange, labor acquires the above-mentioned social properties already in the process of direct production, though only as "latent" or "potential" properties which must still be realized in the process of exchange. Thus labor possesses a dual character. It appears directly as private, concrete, qualified and individual labor, and at the same time as potentially social, abstract, simple and socially-necessary (see the next chapter).

applied in individual enterprises within a given sphere of production (socially-necessary labor).

Among the four definitions of value-creating labor (mentioned above), the concept of abstract labor is central. This is explained by the fact that in a commodity economy, as we will show below, labor becomes social only in the form of abstract labor. Furthermore, the transformation of qualified labor to simple labor is only one part of a larger process of transformation of concrete labor into abstract. Finally, the transformation of individual into socially necessary labor is only the quantitative side of the same process of transforming concrete labor into abstract labor. Precisely because of this, the concept of abstract labor is a central concept in Marx's theory of value.

As we have frequently pointed out, the commodity economy is characterized by formal independence among separate commodity producers on one hand, and material interrelations among their working activities on the other. However, in what way is the private labor of an individual commodity producer included in the mechanism of social labor and responsible for its motion? How does private labor become social labor, and how does the totality of separate, scattered private economic units become transformed into a relatively unified social economy characterized by the regularly repeating mass phenomena studied by political economy? This is the basic problem of political economy, the problem of the very possibility and the conditions of existence of the commodity-capitalist economy.

In a society with an organized economy, the labor of an individual in its concrete form is directly organized and directed by a social organ. It appears as part of total social labor, as social labor. In a commodity economy the labor of an autonomous commodity producer, which is based on the rights of private property, originally appeared as private labor. "We do not proceed from the labor of individuals as social labor, but, on the contrary, from special labor of private individuals which appears as universal social labor only by divesting itself of its original character in the process of exchange. Universal social labor is, therefore, no ready-made assumption, but a growing result" (Critique, p. 46). The labor of the commodity producer displays its social character, not as concrete labor expended in the process of production, but only as labor which has to be equalized with all other forms of labor through the process of exchange.

However, how can the social character of labor be expressed in exchange? If a frock is the product of the private labor of a tailor, then one may say that the sale of the flock, or its exchange for gold, equalizes the private labor of the tailor with another form of private labor, namely the labor of the producer of gold. How can the equalization of one private labor with another private labor give the first a social character? This is only possible in case the private labor of the gold producer is already equalized with all other concrete forms of labor, i.e., if his product, gold, can be directly exchanged for any other product and, consequently, if it plays the role of general equivalent, or money. The labor of the tailor, since it is equalized with the labor of the gold producer, is thus also equalized and connected with all concrete forms of labor. Equalized with them as a form of labor equal to them, the labor of the tailor is transformed from concrete to general or abstract. Being connected with the others in the unified system of total social labor, the labor of the tailor is transformed from private to social labor. The comprehensive equalization (through money) of all concrete forms of labor and their transformation into abstract labor simultaneously creates among them a social connection, transforming private into social labor. "The labor time of a single individual is directly expressed in exchange as universal labor time, and this universal character of individual labor is the manifestation of its social character" (Critique, pp. 26-27. Marx's italics).[168] Only as a "universal quantity" does labor become a "social quantity" (Ibid.). "Universal labor, and in this form social labor," Marx frequently said. In the first chapter of Capital, Marx lists three properties of the equivalent form of value: 1) use value becomes a form in which value is expressed; 2) concrete labor becomes a form of manifestation of abstract labor, and 3) private labor acquires the form of directly social labor (C, I, pp. 56-60). Marx starts his analysis with phenomena which take place on the surface of the market in material forms: he begins with the opposition between use value and exchange value. He seeks the explanation for this opposition in the opposition between concrete and abstract labor. Continuing with this analysis of the social forms of organization of labor, he turns to the central problem of his economic theory, the opposition between private and social labor. In the commodity economy the transformation of private into social labor coincides with the transformation of concrete into abstract labor. The social connection between the working activity of individual commodity producers is realized only through the equalization of all concrete forms of labor, and this equalization is carried out in the form of an equalization of all the products of labor as values. Inversely, the equalization of various forms of labor and the abstraction from their concrete properties is the unique social relation which transforms the totality of private economic units into a unified social economy. This explains the special attention which Marx gave to the concept of abstract labor in his theory.

---

[168] In A Contribution to the Critique of Political Economy, Marx called abstract labor "universal" labor.

Chapter 14: Abstract Labor

The theory of abstract labor is one of the central points of Marx's theory of value. According to Marx, abstract labor "creates" value. Marx attached decisive importance to the difference between concrete and abstract labor. "I was the first to point out and to examine critically this two-fold nature of the labor contained in commodities. As this point is the pivot on which a clear comprehension of Political Economy turns, we must go more into detail" (C., I, p. 41). After the publication of the first volume of Capital, Marx wrote Engels: "The best points in my book are: 1) the two-fold character of labor, according to whether it is expressed in use value or exchange value. (All understanding of the facts depends upon this.) It is emphasized immediately, in the first chapter; 2) the treatment of surplus value independently of its particular forms as profit, interest, ground rent, etc."[169]

When we see the decisive importance which Marx gave to the theory of abstract labor, we must wonder why this theory has received so little attention in Marxist literature. Some writers pass over this question in complete silence. For example, A. Bogdanov transforms abstract labor into "abstractly-simple labor" and, leaving aside the problem of concrete and abstract labor, he restricts himself to the problem of simple and qualified labor.[170] Many critics of Marxism also prefer to put simple labor in the place of abstract labor, for example Karl

---

[169] Letter of Marx to Engels, August 24, 1867, in Karl Marx and Frederick Engels: Selected Correspondence, Moscow: Progress Publishers, 1965, p. 192.

[170] A. Bogdanov, Kurs politicheskoi ekonomii (Course of Political Economy), Vol. II, part 4, p. 18.

Diehl.[171] In popular presentations of Marx's theory of value, writers paraphrase in their own words the definitions given by Marx in the second section of Chapter 1 of Capital, on the "two-fold character of labor embodied in commodities." Kautsky writes: "On the one hand, labor appears to us as the productive expenditure of human labor-power in general, on the other hand, as specific human activity for the attainment of a given object. The first aspect of labor forms the common element in all the productive activities carried on by men; the second varies with the nature of the activity."[172] This generally-accepted definition can be reduced to the following, very simple statement: concrete labor is the expenditure of human energy in a determined form (clothesmaking, weaving, etc.). Abstract labor is the expenditure of human energy as such, independently of the given forms. Defined in this way, the concept of abstract labor is a physiological concept, devoid of all social and historical elements. The concept of abstract labor exists in all historical epochs independently of this or that social form of production.

If even Marxists usually define abstract labor in the sense of expenditure of physiological energy, then we need not wonder that this concept is widespread in anti-Marxist literature. For example, according to P. Struve: "From the Physiocrats and their English successors, Marx accepted the mechanical-naturalistic point of view which is so striking in his theory of labor as the substance of value. This theory is the crown of all objective theories of value. It directly materializes value, transforming it into the economic substance of economic goods, similar to the physical matter which is the substance of physical things.

---

[171] Karl Diehl, Sozialwissenschaftliche Erlauterungen zu David Ricardos Grundgesetzen der Volkswirtschaft und Besteurung, Vol. I, Leipzig: F. Meiner, 1921, pp. 102-104.

[172] K. Kautsky, The Economic Doctrines of Karl Marx, London: A. & C.Black, 1925, p. 16.

This economic substance is something material, because the labor which creates value is understood by Marx in a purely physical sense as an abstract expenditure of nervous and muscular energy, independently of the concrete purposeful content of this expenditure, which is distinguished by infinite variety. Marx's abstract labor is a physiological concept, an ideal concept, and in the last analysis a concept which can be reduced to mechanical work" (Struve's foreword to the Russian edition of Volume I of Capital, 1906, p. 28). According to Struve, abstract labor is a physiological concept for Marx; that is why the value created by abstract labor is something material. This interpretation is shared by other critics of Marx. Gerlach noted that according to Marx, "value is something which is common to all commodities, it is the condition for their exchangeability, and represents a reification of abstract-human labor."[173] Gerlach directs his critical observations against this point of Marx's theory of value: "It is completely impossible to reduce human labor to simple labor physiologically. ... Since human labor is alwaysaccompanied and conditioned by consciousness, we must refuse to reduce it to the movement of muscles and nerves, because in this reduction there is always some kind of remainder which is not amenable to similar analysis" (Ibid., pp. 49-50). "Earlier attempts to show, experimentally, abstract human labor, that which is general in human labor, which is its specific distinction, did not succeed; the reduction of labor to nervous and muscular energy is not possible" (Ibid., p. 50). Gerlach's statement that labor cannot be reduced to the expenditure of physiological energy, because it always contains a conscious element, cannot be related in any way to the concept of "abstract labor" which was created by Marx on the basis of his analysis of the properties of the commodity economy. However, these arguments of Gerlach seem so convincing that they are often repeated by critics of Marx's theory of

---

[173] Otto Gerlach, Uber die Bedingungen wirtschaftlicher Thatigkeit, Jena:G. Fischer, 1890, p. 18.

value.[174] We find an even more striking version of a naturalistic conception of abstract labor in the work of L. Buch: labor, in abstract form, is treated "as the process of transformation of potential energy into mechanical work."[175] Here the attention is directed not so much to the quantity of physiological energy which was expended, but rather to the quantity of mechanical labor received. But the theoretical basis of the problem is purely naturalistic, completely neglecting the social aspect of the labor process, i.e., precisely the aspect which is the direct subject of political economy.

Only a few analysts understand that the characteristics of abstract labor do not in any way coincide with a physiological equality of different labor expenditures. "The universal character of labor is not a concept of natural science which includes only a physiological content. Private labor is abstract-universal and thus also social, as the expression of the activity of holders of rights."[176] But the general conception of Petry, for whom Marx's theory of value does not represent Wertgesetz but Wertbetrachtung, is not an explanation of a "real process in objects," but a "subjective condition of knowledge" (Ibid., p. 50). This deprives Petry

---

[174] For example, K. Diehl, Op. Cit., p. 104.

[175] Leo von Buch, Uber die Elemente der politischen Oekonomie, I Theil: Intensitat der Arbeit, Wert und Preis der Waren, Leipzig: Duncker & Humblot, 1896, p. 149.

[176] F. Petry, Der soziale Gehalt der Marxschen Werttheorie, Jena, 1916, pp. 23-24.

of any possibility of formulating the problem of abstract labor accurately.[177]

Another attempt to introduce a social aspect into the concept of abstract labor is found in the work of A. Nezhdanov (Cherevanin). According to Nezhdanov, the concept of abstract labor does not express a physiological equality of labor expenditures, but a social process of equalization of different forms of labor in production. This is "an important and indispensable social process which is carried out by every conscious social-economic organization.... This social process which characterizes the reduction of different forms of labor to abstract labor is carried out unconsciously in the commodity society."[178] Taking abstract labor as an expression of the process of equalization of labor in every economy, A. Nezhdanov neglects the particular form which the equalization of labor acquires in a commodity economy; here it is not carried out directly in the process of production, but through exchange. The concept of abstract labor expresses the specific historical form of equalization of labor. It is not only a social, but also a historical concept.

We can see that the majority of writers understood abstract labor in a simplified way - in the sense of physiological labor. This is due to the fact that these writers did not apply themselves to follow Marx's theory of abstract labor in its entirety. To do this they

---

[177] An excellent analysis and critique of Petry's book is given in an article by R. Hilferding, in Grunberg's Arhiv fur die Geschichte des Sozialismus und der Arbeiterbewegung, 1919, pp. 439-448. See also our Sovremennye ekonmisty na Zapade (Contemporary Economists in the West), 1927.

[178] "Teoriya tsennosti i pribyli Marksa pered sudom Fetishista" (Marx's Theory of Value and Profit before the Judgment of Fetishists), Nauchnoye Obozrenie (Scientific Survey), 1898, No. 8, p. 1393.

would have had to turn to a detailed analysis of Marx's text in the section on commodity fetishism, and in particular in A Contribution to the Critique of Political Economy, where Marx developed this theory most completely. Instead, these writers preferred to confine themselves to a literal repetition of a few sentences which Marx devoted to abstract labor in the second section of Chapter 1 of Capital.

In the above-mentioned section of Capital, Marx does, in fact, seem to give a basis for the interpretation of abstract labor precisely in a physiological manner. "Productive activity, if we leave out of sight its special form, viz., the useful character of the labor, is nothing but the expenditure of human labor-power. Tailoring and weaving, though qualitatively different productive activities, are each a productive expenditure of human brains, nerves, and muscles, and in this sense are human labor" (C., I, p. 44). And, in concluding, Marx stresses this idea still more sharply: "On the one hand all labor is, speaking physiologically, an expenditure of human labor-power, and in its character of identical abstract human labor, it creates and forms the value of commodities. On the other hand, all labor is the expenditure of human labor-power in a special form and with a definite aim, and in this, its character of concrete useful labor, it produces use-values" (C, I, p. 46). Supporters as well as opponents of Marx find support in the cited passages and understand abstract labor in a physiological sense. The first repeat this definition, not analyzing it critically. The others bring against it a whole series of objections and sometimes they make of this the starting-point for the refutation of the labor theory of value. Neither the former nor the latter notice that the simplified conception of abstract labor (which was presented above), at first glance based on a literal interpretation of Marx's words, cannot in any way be made consistent with the entirety of Marx's theory of value, not with a series of individual passages in Capital.

Marx never tired of repeating that value is a social phenomenon, that the existence of value

(Wertgegenstandlichkeit) has "a purely social reality" (C., I, p. 47), and does not include a single atom of matter. From this it follows that abstract labor, which creates value, must be understood as a social category in which we cannot find a single atom of matter. One of two things is possible: if abstract labor is an expenditure of human energy in physiological form, then value also has a reified-material character. Or value is a social phenomenon, and then abstract labor must also be understood as a social phenomenon connected with a determined social form of production. It is not possible to reconcile a physiological concept of abstract labor with the historical character of the value which it creates. The physiological expenditure of energy as such is the same for all epochs and, one might say, this energy created value in all epochs. We arrive at the crudest interpretation of the theory of value, one which sharply contradicts Marx's theory.

There can be only one way out of these difficulties: since the concept of value has a social and historical character in Marx's work (and this is precisely his service and the distinctive feature of his theory), then we must construct the concept of the abstract labor which creates value on the same basis. If we do not stay with the preliminary definitions which Marx gave on the first pages of his work, and if we apply ourselves to trace the further development of his thought, we will find in Marx's work enough elements for a sociological theory of abstract labor.

To grasp Marx's theory of abstract labor accurately, we cannot for a minute forget that Marx puts the concept of abstract labor into inseparable connection with the concept of value. Abstract labor "creates" value, it is the "content" or "substance" of value. Marx's task was (as we have frequently noted) not to reduce value analytically to abstract labor, but to derive value dialectically from abstract labor. And this is not possible if abstract labor is understood as nothing other than labor in a physiological sense. Thus it is not accidental that the writers who consistently hold a physiological interpretation of abstract labor are forced to reach conclusions which sharply contradict Marx's theory, namely to conclude that abstract labor in itself does not create value.[179] Whoever wants to maintain Marx's well-known statement that abstract labor creates value and is expressed in value, must renounce the physiological concept of abstract labor. But this does not mean that we deny the obvious fact that in every social form of economy the working activity of people is carried out through the expenditure of physiological energy. Physiological labor is the presupposition of abstract labor in the sense that one cannot speak of abstract labor if there is no expenditure of physiological energy on the part of people. But this expenditure of physiological energy remains precisely a presupposition, and not the object of our analysis.

In every social form of economy, human labor is at the same time material-technical and physiological labor. The first quality is possessed by labor only to the extent that the labor is subjected to a definite technical plan and directed to the production of products necessary for the satisfaction of human needs; the second quality is possessed by labor only to the extent that labor represents an expenditure of physiological energy which is accumulated in the human organism and which must regularly be restored. If labor did not create useful products, or if it was not accompanied by the expenditure of the energy of the human organism, the entire picture of the economic life of humanity would be completely different from what it actually is. Thus labor which is treated in isolation from this or that social organization of economy is a material-technical as well as a biological presupposition for all economic activity. But this presupposition of economic research cannot be

---

[179] See "Otvet kritikam" (Answer to Critics) in I.I. Rubin, Ocherki po teorii stoimosti Marksa (Essays on Marx's Theory of Value), Moskva: Gosudarstvennoe Izdatel'stvo, 1928, which was appended to the third edition.

transformed into the object of analysis. The expenditure of physiological energy as such isnot abstract labor and does not create value.

Until now we have examined the physiological version of abstract labor in its crudest form. The adherents to this crude form hold that the value of the product is created by abstract labor as an expenditure of a certain sum of physiological energy. But there are also finer formulations of this physiological interpretation, which approximately hold: the equality of products as values is created through the equality of all forms of human labor as expenditures of physiological energy. Here labor is no longer treated simply as the expenditure of a certain sum of physiological energy, but in terms of its physiological homogeneity with all other forms of labor. Here the human organism is not treated merely as the source of physiological energy in general, but also as the source which is able to furnish labor in any concrete form. The concept of physiological labor in general has been transformed into a concept of physiologically equal or homogeneous labor.

However, this physiologically homogeneous labor is not the object but rather the presupposition of economic research. In reality, if labor as the expenditure of physiological energy is a biological presupposition of any human economy, then the physiological homogeneity of labor is a biological presupposition of any social division of labor. The physical homogeneity of human labor is an indispensable presupposition for the transfer of people from one to another form of labor and, thus, for the possibility of the social process of redistribution of social labor. If people were born as bees and ants, with determined working instincts which in advance limited their working capacities to one form of activity, then the division of labor would be a biological fact, and not a social one. If social labor is to be carried out in one or another sphere of production, every individual must be able to pass from one form of labor to another.

Thus the physiological equality of labor is a necessary condition for the social equalization and distribution of labor in general. Only on the basis of the physiological equality and homogeneity of human labor, i.e., the variety and flexibility of the working activity of people, is the transfer from one activity to another possible. The origin of the social system of division of labor, and in particular the system of commodity production, is only possible on this basis. Thus when we speak of abstract labor, we presuppose labor which is socially equalized, and the social equalization of labor presupposes the physiological homogeneity of labor without which the social division of labor as a social process could not be carried out in any form.

The physiological homogeneity of human labor is a biological presupposition, and not a cause of the development of the social division of labor. (This presupposition, in turn, is a result of the long process of human development, and in particular of the development of instruments of labor and of some organs of the body: the hand and the brain.) The level of development and the forms of social division of labor are determined by purely social causes and they, in turn, determine the extent to which the variety of working operations which the human organism can potentially perform, are actually manifested in the variety of working operations of men as members of society. In a strictly enforced caste system, the physiological homogeneity of human labor cannot be expressed to a significant extent. In a small community based on a division of labor, the physiological homogeneity of labor is manifested in a small circle of people, and the human character of labor cannot be expressed. Only on the basis of commodity production, characterized by a wide development of exchange, a mass transfer of individuals from one activity to another, and indifference of individuals towards the concrete form of labor, is it possible to develop the homogeneous character of all working operations as forms of human labor in general. The physiological homogeneity of human labor was a necessary presupposition of the social division of labor, but only at a determined level of social development and in a determined social form of economy does the labor of the individual have the character of a form of manifestation of human labor in general. We would not be exaggerating if we said that perhaps the concept of man in general and of human labor in general emerged on the basis of the commodity economy. This is precisely what Marx wanted to point out when he indicated that the general human character of labor is expressed in abstract labor.

We have come to the conclusion that physiological labor in general, or physiologically equal labor, are not in themselves abstract labor, even though they are its assumptions. The equal labor which is expressed in the equality of value must be treated as socially equalized labor. Since the value of the product of labor is a social and not a natural function, so labor, which creates this value, is not a physiological but a "social substance." Marx expressed this idea clearly and briefly in his work Wages, Price and Profit: "As the exchangeable values of commodities are only social functions of those things, and have nothing at all to do with their natural qualities, we must first ask, What is the common social substance of all commodities? It is Labor. To produce a commodity a certain amount of labor must be bestowed upon it, or worked up in it. And I say not only Labor, but social Labor."[180] And to the extent that this labor is equal, what is under consideration is socially equal, or socially equalized, labor.

Thus we must not limit ourselves to the characteristic of labor as equal, but must distinguish three types of equal labor, as we mentioned in Chapter Eleven:

1) physiologically equal labor

---

[180] Wages, Price and Profit, in Karl Marx and Frederick Engels, Selected Works in Two Volumes, Moscow: Foreign Languages Publishing House, 1962, Volume I, p. 417.

2) socially equalized labor

3) abstract, or abstract-universal labor, i.e., socially equalized labor in the specific form which it acquires in a commodity economy.

Although abstract labor is a specific property of a commodity economy, socially equalized labor can be found, for example, in a socialist commune. Abstract labor does not only fail to coincide with physiologically equal labor but cannot be identified with socially equalized labor at all (see, above, Chapter Eleven). Every abstract labor is social and socially equalized labor, but not every socially equalized labor can be considered abstract labor. For socially equalized labor to take the specific form of abstract labor characteristic of the commodity economy, two conditions are necessary, as was accurately shown by Marx: It is necessary that: 1) the equality of different kinds of labor and of individuals expresses "the specific social character of private labor carried on independently" (C., I, P. 74), i.e., that labor become social labor only as equal labor, and 2) that this equalization of labor take place in a material form, i.e., "assumes in the product the form of value"(Ibid.).[181] I, the absence of these conditions, labor is physiologically equal. It can also be socially equalized, but it is not abstract-universal labor.

If some writers erroneously confuse abstract labor with physiologically equal labor, other writers commit an equally unacceptable, though not as crude, error: they confuse abstract labor with socially equalized labor. Their reasoning can be reduced to the following terms: the

---

[181] "In the particular form of production with which we are dealing, viz., the production of commodities, the specific social character of private labor carried on independently, consists in the equality of every kind of that labor, by virtue of its being human labor, which character, therefore, assumes in the product the form of value..." (C., I, p. 74).

organ of a socialist commune, as we have seen, equalizes labor of different forms and individuals, for the purpose of accounting and distribution of labor, i.e., it reduces all labor to a general unit which is necessarily abstract; thus labor acquires the character of abstract labor.[182] If these writers insist they are right in calling socially equalized labor "abstract," we can recognize their right to do this: every writer has the right to give any term he chooses to a phenomenon, even though such arbitrary terminology can be very dangerous and creates great confusion in science. But our argument is not over the term which is given to socially equalized labor, but over something different. We confront the question: what do we understand by that "abstract labor" which creates value and is expressed in value, according to Marx's theory. We must again mention that Marx did not only want to analytically reduce value to labor, but also to analytically derive value from labor. And from this point of view it is clear that neither physiologically equal nor socially equalized labor as such create value. The abstract labor which Marx treated is not only socially equalized labor but socially equalized labor in a specific form which is characteristic for a commodity economy. In Marx's system, the concept of abstract labor is inseparably related to the basic characteristics of the commodity economy. In order to prove this we must explain in greater detail Marx's views of the character of abstract labor.

Marx begins his analysis with commodities, in which he distinguishes two sides: the material-technical and the social (i.e., use value and value). Similar two sides

---

[182] An approximately similar view can be found in the article of I. Dashkovski, "Abstraktnyi trud i ekonomicheskie kategorii Marksa" (Abstract Labor and Marx's Economic Categories), Pod znamenem marksizma (Under the Banner of Marxism), 1926, No. 6. Dashkovski also confuses abstract labor with physiological labor. (See Rubin, "Otvet kritikam," Loc. Cit.)

are distinguished by Marx in the labor embodied in commodities. Concrete and abstract labor are two sides (material-technical and social) of one and the same labor embodied in commodities. The social side of this labor, which creates value and is expressed in value, is abstract labor.

We begin with the definition which Marx gives of concrete labor. "So far therefore as labor is a creator of use-value, is useful labor, it is a necessary condition, independent of all forms of society, for the existence of the human race; it is an eternal nature-imposed necessity, without which there can be no material exchanges between man and Nature, and therefore no life" (C., I, pp. 42-43; Rubin's italics). It is obvious that abstract labor is contrasted to concrete labor. Abstract labor is related to a definite "social form," and expresses determined relations of man to man in the process of production. Concrete labor is the definition of labor in terms of its material-technical properties. Abstract labor includes the definition of social forms of organization of human labor. This is not a generic and specific definition of labor, but the analysis of labor from two standpoints: the material-technical and the social. The concept of abstract labor expresses the characteristics of the social organization of labor in a commodity-capitalist society.[183]

For an accurate interpretation of the opposition between concrete and abstract labor, one must start with

---

[183] "We now see, that the difference between labor, considered on the one hand as producing utilities, and on the other hand, as creating value, a difference which we discovered by our analysis of a commodity, resolves itself into a distinction between two aspects of the process of production" (C.,I,p. 197), i.e., between the process of production in its technical aspect and its social aspect. See F. Petry, Der soziale Gehalt der Marxschen Werttheorie, Jena, 1916, p. 22.

the opposition which Marx drew between private and social labor, and which we have examined above.

Labor is social if it is examined as part of the total mass of homogeneous social labor or, as Marx frequently said, if it is seen in terms of its "relation to the total labor of society." In a large socialist community, the labor of the members of the community, in its concrete form (for example, the labor of a shoemaker), is directly included in the unified working mechanism of society, and is equalized with a determined number of units of social labor (if we refer to the early phase of a socialist economy, when the labor of individuals is still evaluated by society - see the end of this chapter for a more detailed examination of this topic). Labor in its concrete form is in this case directly social labor. It is different in a commodity economy where the concrete labor of producers is not directly social labor but private, i.e., labor of a private commodity producer, a private owner of means of production and an autonomous organizer of economic activity. This private labor can become social only through its equalization with all other forms of labor, through the equalization of their products (see above, Chapter Eleven). In other words, concrete labor does not become social because it has the form of concrete labor which produces concrete use values, for example shoes, but only if the shoes are equalized as values with a given sum of money (and through the money with all other products as values). Thus the labor materialized in the shoes is equalized with all other forms of labor and, consequently, sheds its determined concrete form and becomes impersonal labor, a particle of the entire mass of homogeneous social labor. Similarly, just as the concrete products of labor (for example shoes) display their character as value only if the product sheds its concrete form and is equalized with a given sum of abstract monetary units, so the private and concrete labor contained in the product displays its character as social labor only if it sheds its concrete form and is equalized, in a given proportion. with all other forms of labor, i.e., is equalized with a given quantity of impersonal, homogeneous, abstract labor, "labor in general." The transformation of private labor into social labor can only be carried out through the transformation of concrete labor into abstract labor. On the other hand, the transformation of concrete into abstract labor already signifies its inclusion in the mass of homogeneous social labor, i.e., its transformation into social labor. Abstract labor is the variety of social labor or socially equalized labor in general. It is social or socially equalized labor in the specific form which it has in a commodity economy. Abstract labor is not only socially equalized labor, i.e., abstracted from concrete properties, impersonal and homogeneous labor. It is labor which becomes social labor only as impersonal and homogeneous labor. The concept of abstract labor presupposes that the process of impersonalization or equalization of labor is a unified process through which labor is "socialized," i.e., is included in the total mass of social labor. This equalization of labor may take place, but only mentally and in anticipation, in the process of direct production, before the act of exchange. But in reality, it takes place through the act of exchange, through the equalization (even though it is mental and anticipated) of the product of the given labor with a definite sum of money. If this equalization precedes exchange, it must yet be realized in the actual process of exchange.

The role of labor we have described is characteristic of it precisely in a commodity economy and is especially striking if the commodity society is compared with other forms of economy. "Let us take the services and payments in kind of the Middle Ages. It was the specific[184] kind of labor performed by each individual in its natural form, the particular and nor the

---

[184] Marx wrote, "specific" (osobennyi) (Besonderheit), i.e., the concrete character of labor (Critique, p. 29). Translators often create confusion by translating the term "besondere" (i.e., specific or concrete) with the word "private."

universal[185] aspect of labor, that constituted then the social tie. Or, let us finally take labor carried on in common in its primitive natural form, as we find it at the dawn of history of all [cultures]. It is clear that in this case labor does not acquire its social character from the fact that the labor of the individual takes on the abstract form of universal labor or that his product assumes the form of a universal equivalent. The very nature of production under a communal system makes it impossible for the labor of the individual to be private labor and his product to be a private product; on the contrary, it makes individual labor appear as the direct function of a member of a social organism. On the contrary, labor, which is expressed in exchange value, at once appears as the labor of a separate individual. It becomes social labor only by taking on the form of its direct opposite, the form of abstract universal labor" (Critique, pp. 29-30; Rubin's italics). The same idea was repeated by Marx in Capital. He says of medieval society: "Here the particular and natural form of labor, and not, as in a society based on production of commodities, its general abstract form is the immediate social form of labor" (C, I, p. 77). In the same way, in the agricultural production of a patriarchal peasant family, "the different kinds of labor, such as tillage, cattle tending, spinning, weaving and making clothes, which result in the various products, are in themselves, and such as they are, direct social functions" (Ibid., p. 78).

Thus, as opposed to a patriarchal family or a feudal estate, where labor in its concrete form had a directly social character, in the commodity society the only social relation among independent, private economic units is realized through a many-sided exchange and equalization of the products of the most varied concrete forms of labor, i.e., through abstraction from their concrete properties, through the transformation of concrete to abstract labor. The expenditure of human energy as such,

---

[185] In the Critique, Marx calls abstract labor "universal," as we mentionedearlier.

in a physiological sense, is still not abstract labor, labor which creates value, even though this is its premise. Abstraction from the concrete forms of labor, the basic social relation among separate commodity producers, is what characterizes abstract labor. The concept of abstract labor presupposes a determined social form of organization of labor in a commodity economy: the individual commodity producers are not directly connected in the production process itself to the extent that this process represents the totality of concrete working activities; this connection is realized through the process of exchange, i.e., through abstraction from those concrete properties. Abstract labor is not a physiological category, but a social and historical category. Abstract labor differs from concrete labor not only in terms of its negative properties (abstraction from concrete forms of labor) but also in terms of its positive property (the equalization of all forms of labor in a many-sided exchange of the products of labor). "The labor realized in the values of commodities is presented not only under its negative aspect, under which abstraction is made from every concrete form and useful property of actual work, but its own positive nature is made to reveal itself expressly. The general value-form is the reduction of all kinds of actual labor to their common character of being human labor generally, of being the expenditure of human labor-power" (C., I p. 67). In other passages Marx emphasizes that this reduction of concrete forms of labor to abstract labor is carried out definitively in the process of exchange. However, in the process of direct production this reduction has an anticipated or ideal character, since production is designated for exchange (see below). In Marx's theory of value, the transformation of concrete into abstract labor is not a theoretical act of abstracting for the purpose of finding a general unit of measurement. This transformation is a real social event. The theoretical expression of this social event, namely the social equalization of different forms of labor and not their physiological equality, is the category of abstract labor. The neglect of this positive, social nature of abstract labor has led to the interpretation of abstract labor as a calculation of labor expenditures in a physiological sense, namely a purely negative property of abstracting from the specific forms of concrete labor.

Abstract labor appears and develops to the extent that exchange becomes the social form of the process of production, thus transforming the production process into commodity production. In the absence of exchange as the social form of production, there can be no abstract labor. Thus to the extent that the market and the sphere of exchange is widespread, to the extent that individual economic units are drawn into exchange, to the extent that these units are transformed into a unified social economy and later into a world economy, the characteristic properties of labor which we have called abstract labor are strengthened. Thus Marx wrote: "only foreign trade, the development of the market into a world market, transform money into world money and abstract labor into social labor. Abstract wealth, value, money - consequently abstract labor, are developed to the extent that concrete labor develops into the totality of the varied forms of labor encompassed by the world market" (Theorien uber den Mehrwert, III, p. 301; Marx's italics). When exchange is restricted within national boundaries, abstract labor does not yet exist in its most developed form. The abstract character of labor achieves its completion when international trade connects and unifies all countries, and when the product of national labor loses its specific concrete properties because it is delivered to the world market and equalized with the products of labor of the most varied national industries. This concept of abstract labor is indeed far from the concept of labor expenditures in a physiological sense, without reference either to the qualitative properties of working activity or to the social forms of the organization of labor.

In production based on exchange, the producer is not interested in the use value of the product he makes, but exclusively in its value. The products do not interest him as results of concrete labor, but as the result of abstract labor, i.e., to the extent that they can shed their innate useful form and be transformed into money, and through money into an infinite series of different use values. If, from the standpoint of value, a given occupation is less advantageous for a producer than another occupation, he passes from one concrete activity to another, presupposing that in the commodity economy there is full mobility of labor. Exchange creates the indifference of the producer towards his concrete labor (obviously in the form of a tendency which is interrupted and weakened by counteracting influences). "The indifference to the particular kind of labor corresponds to a form of society in which individuals pass with ease from one kind of work to another, which makes it immaterial to them what particular kind of work may fall to their share. Labor has become here, not only categorically but really, a means of creating wealth in general and is no longer grown together with the individual into one particular destination. This state of affairs has found its highest development in the most modern of bourgeois societies, the United States. It is only here that the abstraction of the category 'labor,' 'labor in general,' labor sans phrase, the starting point of modern political economy, becomes realized in practice. Thus, the simplest abstraction which modern political economy sets up as its starting point, and which expresses a relation dating back to antiquity and prevalent under all forms of society, appears in this abstraction truly realized only as a category of the most modern society. ....This example of labor strikingly shows how even the most abstract categories, in spite of their applicability to all epochs - just because of their abstract character - are by the very definiteness of the abstraction a product of historical conditions as well, and are fully applicable only to and under those conditions."[186] We have cited this long excerpt from Marx's work because here he definitively

---

[186] K. Marx "Introduction to the Critique of Political Economy," in A Contribution to the Critique of Political Economy, Chicago: Charles Kerr,1904, pp. 299-300. Also see Rubin, "Otvet kritikam," Loc. Cit.

demonstrated the impossibility of defining "abstract labor" or "labor in general" physiologically. "Labor in general" at first glance exists in all forms of society, but in reality it is a product of historical conditions of a commodity economy and "possesses full significance" only in this economy. Abstract labor becomes a social relation among the members of society if it is realized through exchange and through equalization of products of the most varied forms of labor: "in the world of commodities the character possessed by all labor of being human labor constitutes its specific social character" (C., I, p. 67), and only this social character of labor abstracted from concrete properties gives it the character of abstract labor which creates value. In value "the general character of individual labor" appears "as its social character" - Marx repeats this idea constantly in A Contribution to the Critique of Political Economy.

Thus, to the extent that value can be dialectically derived from labor, we must understand by labor that labor which is organized in the determined social form which exists in a commodity economy. When we speak of physiologically equal or even of socially equalized labor in general, this labor does not create value. One can approach another, less concrete concept of labor only by restricting the task to a purely analytical reduction of value to labor. If we start with value as a finished, given social form of the product of labor (which does not require a particular explanation) and if we ask, to what labor can this value be reduced, we answer briefly: to equal labor. In other words, if value can be dialectically derived only from abstract labor which is distinguished by a concrete social form, the analytical reduction of value to labor can be restricted to the definition of the character of labor as socially equalized in general,[187] or even physiologically equal labor. It is possible that precisely this explains the fact that in the second section of Chapter

---

[187] See above, in Chapter Twelve, the citations in which Marx recognizes socially equalized labor as the substance of value.

I of the first volume of Capital, Marx reduced value to labor by the analytical method and underlined the character of labor as physiologically equal, no longer dwelling on the social form of organization of labor in the commodity economy.[188] On the other hand, wherever Marx wants to derive value dialectially from abstract

---

[188] In the first German edition of Capital, Marx summarized the difference between concrete and abstract labor as follows: "From what has been said it follows that a commodity does not possess two different forms of labor but one and the same labor is defined in different and even opposed ways depending on whether it is related to the use value of commodities as to its *product*, or to *commodity value as to its material expression*" (Kapital, I, 1867, p. 13. Marx's italics). Value is not the product of labor but is a material, fetish expression of the working activity of people. Unfortunately in the second edition Marx replaced this summary which underlines the social character of social labor by the well-known concluding sentence of section two of Chapter I which has given many commentators a basis for understanding abstract labor in a physiological sense: "all labor is, speaking physiologically, an expenditure of human labor-power" (C., I, p. 46). It seems that Marx himself knew the inaccuracy of the preliminary characterization of abstract labor which he gave in the second edition of Capital. Striking proof of this is the fact that in the French edition of Volume I of Capital (1875), Marx felt it necessary to complete this characterization: here, on page 18, Marx simultaneously gave both definitions of abstract labor; first of all he repeats the above cited definition from the first edition of Capital, after which follows the definition of the second edition. It must not be forgotten that as a general rule, in the French edition of Capital, Marx simplified and in places shortened his exposition. However, on this given point he felt it necessary to supplement and complicate the characterization of abstract labor, thus recognizing, it would seem, the inadequacy of the definition of abstract labor given in the second edition.

labor, he emphasizes the social form of labor in the commodity economy as the characteristic of abstract labor.

Since we have explained the social nature of abstract labor and its relation to the process of exchange, we must answer certain critical observations[189] which were raised against our conception of abstract labor. Some critics say that our conception may lead to the conclusion that abstract labor originates only in the act of exchange, from which it follows that value also originates only in exchange. However, from Marx's point of view, value, and thus also abstract labor, must already exist in the process of production. This borders on a very serious and profound question of the relation between production and exchange. How should we resolve this problem? On one hand, value and abstract labor must already exist in the process of exchange, yet on the other hand, Marx in several passages says that abstract labor presupposes the process of exchange.

We can cite several examples. According to Marx, Franklin perceived labor as abstract, but did not grasp that it was abstractly general, social labor which arises from the complete alienation of individual labor (Critique, pp. 62-64). Franklin's main error was thus that he did not take into consideration the fact that abstract labor arises from the alienation of individual labor.

This case does not refer to an isolated phrase in Marx's work. In later editions of Capital, Marx, with increasing sharpness, underlined the idea that in a commodity economy only exchange transforms concrete labor into abstract labor.

We can examine the well-known passage which we cited earlier: "when we bring the products of our labor into relation with each other as values, it is not because

---

[189] See Rubin's "Otvet kritikam," Loc. Cit.

we see in these articles the material receptacles of homogeneous human labor. Quite the contrary: whenever, by an exchange, we equate as values our different products, by that very act, we also equate, as human labor, the different kinds of labor expended upon them" (C., I, p. 74). In the first edition of Capital this passage had precisely the opposite meaning. In Marx's original work this passage said: "People relate their products to each other as values to the extent that these things are for them only material shells of homogeneous human labor," etc. (Kapital, 1, 1867, p. 38.) In order to avoid being interpreted to mean that people consciously equalize their labor with each other in advance as abstract, Marx completely changed the meaning of his sentence in the second edition, and he underlined the meaning that the equalization of labor as abstract labor takes place only through the exchange of products of labor. This is a significant change between the first and the second editions.

But as we mentioned, Marx did not restrict himself to the second edition of Volume I of Capital. He still corrected the later text for the French edition of 1875. There he wrote that he had introduced those changes which he had not been able to include in the second German edition. On this basis Marx assigned to the French edition of Capital an independent scientific value parallel with that of the German original.

In the second edition of Capital we find the well-known sentence: "The equalization of the most different kinds of labor can be the result only of an abstraction from their inequalities, or of reducing them to their common denominator, viz., expenditure of human labor-power or human labor in the abstract" (C., I, p. 73). In the French edition Marx, at the end of this sentence, replaced the period with a comma and added: "and only exchange brings about this reduction, opposing the products of different forms of labor with each other on the basis of equality" (French edition of Capital, 1875, p 29). This insertion is significant and strikingly shows how far Marx was from the physiological interpretation of abstract labor. How can we reconcile these statements of Marx, which can be multiplied, with his basic view that value is created in production?

It is not hard to reconcile these views.

The problem is that in treating the question of the relation between exchange and production two concepts of exchange are not adequately distinguished. We must distinguish exchange as a social form of the process of reproduction from exchange as a particular phase of this process of reproduction, alternating with the phase of direct production.

At first glance it seems that exchange is a separate phase of the process of reproduction. We can see that the process of direct production comes first, and the phase of exchange comes next. Here exchange is separate from production and stands opposite from it. But exchange is not only a separate phase of the process of reproduction; it puts its specific imprint on the entire process of reproduction. It is a particular social form of the social process of production. Production based on private exchange - these are words with which Marx frequently characterized a commodity economy. From this point of view, "the exchange of products as commodities is a determined form of social labor or social production" (Theorien uber den Mehrwert, III, 1921, p. 153). If we pay attention to the fact that exchange is a social form of the production process, a form which leaves its imprint on the course of the process of production itself, then many of Marx's statements will become completely clear. When Marx constantly repeats that abstract labor is only the result of exchange, this means that it is the result of a given social form of the production process. Only to the extent that the process of production acquires the form of commodity production, i.e., production based on exchange, labor acquires the form of abstract labor and products of labor acquire the form of value.

Thus exchange is above all a form of production process, or a form of social labor. Since exchange is actually the dominant form of the process of production, it leaves its imprint on the phase of direct production. In other words, since a person produces after he has entered the act of exchange, and before he enters the next act of exchange, the process of direct production acquires determined social properties which correspond to the organization of the commodity economy based on exchange. Even though the commodity producer is still in his workshop and in a given moment does not enter into exchange with other members of society, he already feels the pressure of all those persons who enter the market as his buyers, competitors, people who buy from his competitors, etc., in the last analysis, the pressure of all members of society. This economic relation and these production relations, which are directly realized in exchange, extend their influence even after the given concrete acts of exchange have ended. These acts leave a sharp social imprint on the individual and on the product of his labor. Already in the very process of direct production, the producer appears as a commodity producer, his labor has the character of abstract labor, and his product has the character of value.

Here, however, it is necessary to beware of the following errors. Many writers think that since the process of direct production already possesses determined social properties, this means that the products of labor, and labor, in the phase of direct production, are characterized point by point by the same social properties which characterize them in the phase of exchange. Such an assumption is erroneous because, even though both phases (the phase of production and the phase of exchange) are closely related to each other, this does not mean that the phase of production has become the phase of exchange. There is a certain similarly between the two phases, but a certain difference has also been preserved. In other words we recognize that from the moment when exchange becomes the dominant form of social labor and people produce especially for exchange, the character of the product of labor as a value is taken into consideration in the phase of direct production. But this character of the product of labor as a value is not yet that character which it acquires when it is in fact exchanged for money, when, in Marx's terms, its "ideal" value is transformed into "real" value, and the social form of commodities is substituted by the social form of money.

This is also true of labor. We know that commodity producers, in their acts of production, take into consideration the state of the market and of demand during the process of direct production. They produce exclusively in order to transform their product into money, and thus their private and concrete labor into social and abstract labor. But this inclusion of the labor of the individual into the working mechanism of the entire society is only preliminary and surmised: it is still subject to very rough verification in the process of exchange, verification which can give positive or negative results for the given commodity producer. Thus the working activity of commodity producers in the phase of production is directly private and concrete labor, and it is social labor only indirectly, or latently, as Marx put it.

Thus when we read Marx's work, and particularly his descriptions of how exchange influences value and abstract labor, we must always ask what Marx had in mind in a given case - exchange as the form of the production process itself, or exchange as a separate phase which is opposed to the phase of production. To the extent that he deals with exchange as a form of the production process, Marx clearly says that without exchange there is neither abstract labor nor value. Labor acquires the character of abstract labor only to the extent that exchange develops. When Marx speaks of exchange as a separate phase which stands in opposition to production, he says that even before the process of exchange, labor and the product of labor possess determined social characteristics but that these characteristics must be realized in the process of exchange. In the process of direct production labor is not yet abstract labor in the full sense of the word, it must still become (werden) abstract labor. Numerous statements to this effect can be found in Marx's works. We can cite two passages from the Critique: "As a matter of fact, the individual labors which are represented in these particular use-values, become [werden] universal, and, in this form, also social labor, only when they are actually exchanged for one another in proportion to the labor-time contained in them. Social labor-time exists in these commodities in a latent state, so to say, and is first revealed [offenbart sich] in the process of exchange" (Critique, p. 46). Elsewhere Marx writes: "Commodities now confront one another in a double capacity: actually as use-values, ideally as exchange values. The twofold aspect of labor contained in them is reflected in their mutual relations; the special concrete labor being virtually present as their use-value, while universal abstract labor-time is ideally represented [vorgestelltes Dasein] in their price" (Ibid., p. 80).

Marx holds that commodities and money do not lose their differences because of the fact that every commodity must be transformed into money; each of these is in reality what the other is ideally, and ideally what the first is in reality. All of these statements show that we must not think of the problem too literally. We should not think that, since in the process of direct production commodity producers are directly connected to each other by production relations, therefore their products and their labor already possess a directly social character. Reality is not like this. The labor of commodity producers is directly private and concrete, but it acquires a supplementary, "ideal" or "latent" social property in the form of abstract-general and social labor. Marx always laughed at the Utopians who dreamed of the disappearance of money and believed in the dogma that "the isolated labor of the individual contained in [a commodity] is direct social labor" (Critique, p. 106).

Now we must answer the following question: can abstract labor, which we treat as a purely "social substance," have a quantitative determination, i.e., a determined magnitude? It is obvious that from the standpoint of Marx's theory, abstract labor has a determined magnitude, and precisely because of this the product of labor does not only acquire the social form of value but has a value of determined magnitude. In order to grasp the possibility of the quantitative characterization of abstract labor, we must again resort to the comparison of abstract labor with the socially equalized labor which is found in a socialist community. We suppose that the organs of the socialist community equalize labor of different types and of different individuals. For example, one day of simple labor is taken as 1 unit, and a day of qualified labor as 3 units; a day of the labor of experienced worker A is taken as equal to two days of the labor of inexperienced worker B, and so on. On the basis of these general principles, the organs of social accounting know that worker A expended in the social process of production 20 units of labor, and worker B, 10 units of labor. Does this mean that A really worked two times longer than B? Not at all. Even less does this computation mean that A spent two times more physiological energy than B. From the point of view of the actual length of time of their work, it is possible that A and B worked an equal number of hours. It is possible that from the standpoint of the quantity of physiological energy expended in the process of labor, A spent less energy than B. Nevertheless, the quantity of "social labor" which is the share of A is larger than the quantity of labor which is the share of B. This labor represents a purely "social substance." The units of this labor are units of a homogeneous mass of social labor, calculated and equalized by social organs. At the same time, this social labor has a thoroughly determined magnitude but (and one must not forget this) a magnitude of a purely social character. The 20 units of labor which are the share of A do not represent a number of working hours, and not a sum of actually expended physiological energy, but a number of units of social labor, i.e., a social magnitude. Abstract labor is precisely a social magnitude of this type. In a spontaneous commodity economy, it plays the role which socially equalized labor plays in a consciously organized socialist economy. Thus Marx constantly mentions that abstract labor is a "social substance" and its magnitude a "social magnitude."

Only through such a sociological interpretation of abstract labor can we understand Marx's central proposition that abstract labor "creates" value or finds its expression in the form of value. The physiological conception of abstract labor could easily lead to a naturalistic concept of value, to a conception which sharply contradicts Marx's theory. According to Marx, abstract labor and value are distinguished by the same social nature and represent purely social magnitudes. Abstract labor means "social determination of labor," and value, the social property of the product of labor. Only abstract labor, which presupposes determined production relations among people, creates value, and not labor in the material-technical or physiological sense.[190] The relations between abstract labor and value cannot be thought of as relations between physical causes and physical effects. Value is a material expression of social labor in the specific form which labor possesses in a commodity economy, i.e., abstract labor. This means that value is "congealed" labor, "a mere congelation of homogeneous human labor," "crystals of the social substance" of labor (C., I, p. 38). For these remarks, Marx was frequently attacked and accused of a "naturalistic"

---

[190] This is why Stolzmann is wrong. He writes: "If the meaning and character of all economic events follows from their 'social functions,' why is this not true of labor as well, why does labor not find its character in its social function, i.e., in the function which belongs to it within the present economic order which is the subject to be explained?" (Stolzmann, Der Zweck in der Volkswirtschaft, 1909, p. 533). Actually the labor which creates value was not viewed by Marx as a technical factor of production, but from the point of view of the social forms of its organization. According to Marx, the social form of labor does not hang in a vacuum: it is closely related to the material process of production. Only through a complete misinterpretation of the social form of labor in Marx's system is it possible to assert that 'Saber for Marx is simply a technical factor of production" (S. Prokopovich, K kritike Marksa (Towards a Critique of Marx), 1901, p. 16), or to consider it "a fundamental error of Marx that in explaining value in terms of labor he neglects the different evaluations of different forms of labor" as a factor of production (G. Cassel, "Grundriss einer elementaren Preislehre," Zeitschrift fur die gesamte Staatswissenschaft, 1899, No. 3, p. 447). Even Marshall sees Marx's error in his having ignored the "quality of labor" (Marshall, Principles of Economics, 1910, p. 503). The question is whether we are interested in the social or the technical properties of labor. Marx was interested in the social forms or social quality of labor in a commodity economy, a form which is expressed in the act of abstraction from the technical properties of different forms of labor.

construction of the theory of value. But these remarks can be grasped properly only by comparing them with Marx's theory of commodity fetishism and the "reification" of social relations. Marx's first postulate is that social production relations among people are expressed in a material form. From this it follows that social (namely abstract) labor is expressed in the form of value. Thus value is "reified," "materialized" labor and simultaneously it is an expression of production relations among people. These two definitions of value contradict each other if one deals with physiological labor; but they perfectly supplement each other if one deals with social labor. Abstract labor and value have a social and not a material-technical or physiological nature. Value is a social property (or a social form) of a product of labor, just as abstract labor is a "social substance" which lies at the basis of this value. Nevertheless abstract labor, just as the value which it creates, does not only have a qualitative but also a quantitative side. It has a determined magnitude, in the same sense that the social labor accounted for by the organs of a socialist community has a determined magnitude.

In order to be done with the question of the quantitative determination of abstract labor, we must explain a possible misunderstanding which might arise. At first glance it might seem that if abstract labor is the result of social equalization of labor through the equalization of the products of labor, the only criterion of equality or inequality of two labor expenditures is the fact of equality (or inequality) in the process of exchange. From this standpoint we cannot speak of equality or inequality of two labor expenditures before the moment of their social equalization through the process of exchange. On the other hand, if in the process of exchange these labor expenditures are socially equalized, we must consider them equal even though they are not equal (for example, with respect to the number of hours of labor) in the process of direct production.

Such an assumption leads to false conclusions. It deprives us of the right to say that in the process of exchange equal quantities of labor, and sometimes very unequal quantities (for example, in the exchange of the products of very qualified labor for the products of unqualified labor, or in the exchange of products by their prices of production in a capitalist economy, etc.), are socially equalized. We would have to admit that the social equalization of labor in the process of exchange is carried out in isolation of dependence on quantitative aspects which characterize labor in the process of direct production (for example, the length, intensity, length of training for a given level of qualification, and so on), and thus, the social equalization would lack any regularity since it would be exclusively determined by market spontaneity.

It is easy to show that the theory of abstract labor developed earlier has nothing in common with the false impression mentioned above. We can again return to the example of the socialist community. The organs of the socialist community recognized worker A's right to 20 hours of social labor, and worker B's right to 10 hours of social labor. These calculations would be carried out by the organs of the socialist community on the basis of the properties which characterize the labor in the material-technical process of production (for example, its length, intensity, quantity of produced goods, and so on). If the organs of the socialist community would take as the decisive single criterion, the quantity of physiological energy expended by the workers (we suppose that this quantity can be determined by means of psycho-physiological research) to determine each worker's quantitative share, we would say that the grounds for the social equalization of labor are those properties of labor which characterize it in terms of its physiological and not its material-technical side. But this would not change the problem. In both cases we could say that the act of social equalization of two labor expenditures is carried out on the basis of characteristics which lie outside the act of equalization itself. But from this it does not follow in any sense that the social equality of two labor expenditures, determined on the basis of their physiological equality, is identical with their physiological equality. Even if we assume that a given numerical expression of two quantities of social labor (20 hours and 10 hours of social labor) exactly coincides with the numerical expression of two quantities of physiological energy (20 units and 10 units of physiological energy), there is still an essential difference between the nature of social labor and the expenditure of physiological energy, the social equalization of labor and its physiological equality. This is even more so in those cases when the social equalization is not regulated on the basis of one but on the basis of a whole series of properties which characterize labor in its material-technical or its physiological aspects. In this case, socially - equal labor is not only qualitatively different from physiologically - equal labor, but the quantitative determination of the first can only be understood as the result of social equalization of labor. The qualitative as well as the quantitative characteristics of social labor cannot be grasped without analysis of the social form of the process of production in which the social equalization of labor takes place.

This is precisely the state of affairs which we find in a commodity economy. The equality of two amounts of abstract labor signifies their equality as parts of total social labor - an equality which is only established in the process of social equalization of labor by means of the equalization of the products of labor. Thus we assert that in a commodity economy, the social equality of two labor expenditures or their equality in the form of abstract labor is established through the process of exchange. But this does not prevent us from ascertaining a series of quantitative properties which distinguish labor in terms of its material-technical and its physiological aspects, and which causally influence the quantitative determination of abstract labor before the act of exchange and independent of it. The most important of these properties are: 1) the length of labor expenditure, or the quantity of working time; 2) the intensity of labor;

3) the qualification of labor; and 4) the quantity of products produced in a unit of time. We can briefly examine each of these properties.

Marx considers the quantity of working time expended by the worker the basic property which characterizes the quantitative determination of labor. This method of quantitative determination of labor according to labor-time is characteristic of Marx's sociological method. If we were considering the quantitative determination of labor in a psycho-physiological laboratory, we would have to take as a unit of labor a certain amount of expended physiological energy. But when we consider the distribution of total social labor among individuals and branches of production - a distribution which is carried out consciously in a socialist community and spontaneously in a commodity economy - different quantities of labor appear as different quantities of labor-time. Thus Marx frequently replaces labor with labor-time, and examines labor-time as the substance materialized in the product (Critique, pp. 23, 26).

Thus Marx takes labor-time or "the extensive magnitude of labor" as the basic measure of labor (C., I, p. 519). Together with this property Marx puts the intensity of labor, the "intensive magnitude of labor," i.e., "the quantity of labor expended in a given time," as a supplementary and secondary property (Ibid.). One hour of labor of greater intensity is recognized to be equal, for example, to 1 1/2 hours of labor of normal intensity. In other words, the more intensive labor is recognized as equal to longer labor. Intensity is translated into units of labor-time, or intensive magnitude is calculated as extensive magnitude. This reduction of intensity of labor to labor-time strikingly testifies to what extent Marx subordinated the properties characteristic of labor from its physiological aspect under the properties of a social character which play a decisive role in the social process of distribution of labor.

The subordinate role of intensity of labor with respect to labor-time is even more strikingly displayed in Marx's later observations. According to Marx, the property of intensity of labor is taken into consideration to determine a quantity of abstract labor only when the given labor expenditures differ to a lesser or greater extent in comparison with the average level. But "if the intensity of labor were to increase simultaneously and equally in every branch of industry, then the new and higher degree of intensity would become the normal degree for the society, and would therefore cease to be taken account of" (C., I, p. 525).[191] In other words, if, in a given country, today or fifty years ago, one million working days (eight hours each) are expended for production every day, the sum of values created every day remains unchanged even though the average intensity of labor increases, for example 1 1/2 times, during the half century, and thus the quantity of expended physiological energy increases. This reasoning on Marx's part proves that one cannot confuse physiological with abstract labor, and that the amount of physiological energy cannot be taken as the basic qualitative property which determines the amount of abstract labor and the magnitude of created value. Marx considers labor-time the measure of

---

[191] Marx expressed the same idea more sharply in Theorien uber denMehrwert, III, pp. 365-366: "If this intensification of labor would become general, the value of commodities would then have to fall consistently with the smaller amount of labor-time expended on them." If, with a general increase of intensity of labor, 12 hours are expended instead of an earlier 15 hours on a given product, then in Marx's view the value of the product falls (since it is determined by labor-time and by the number of expended hours). The amount of physiological energy expended on the products has not changed (i.e., in 12 hours just as much energy is expended now as was expended in 15 hours earlier). Thus from the point of view of the advocates of a physiological interpretation of labor value, the value of the product would have to remain unchanged.

labor, and the intensity of labor has only a supplementary and subordinate role.

We will devote the next chapter to the problem of qualified labor. Here we will only point out that Marx, faithful to his general view of labor-time as the measure of labor, reduced a day of qualified labor to a given number of days of simple labor, i.e., again to labortime.

Until now we have examined the equalization of amounts of labor expended in various branches of production. If we consider different expenditures of labor in the same branch of production (more precisely, expenditures for the production of goods of the same kind and quality), their equalization is subject to the following principle: two labor expenditures are recognized as equal if they create equal quantities of a given product, even though in fact these labor expenditures can be very different from each other in terms of length of labor-time, intensity, and so on. The working day of a worker who is more highly skilled, or who works with better means of production, is socially equalized with two days of labor of a less qualified worker, or a worker who works with poor means of production, even though the amount of physiological energy expended in the first case would be much smaller than in the second case. Here the decisive property which determines the quantitative characteristicof labor as abstract and socially-necessary does not in any sense represent an amount of expended physiological energy. Here too, Marx reduces the labor of a worker distinguished by his skill, or by better means of production, to socially necessary labor-time, i.e., Marx equalizes labor with a given amount of labor-time.

We can see that the quantitative characteristic of abstract labor is causally conditioned by a series of properties which characterize labor in terms of its material-technical and its physiological sides in the process of direct production, before the process of exchange and independent of it. But if two given labor expenditures, independent of the process of exchange, differ in terms of length, intensity, level of qualification and technical productivity, the social equalization of these labor expenditures is carried out in a commodity economy only through exchange. Socially equalized and abstract labor differ qualitatively and quantitatively from labor which is examined in terms of its material-technical or its physiological aspects.

Chapter 15: Qualified Labor

In the process of exchange, the products of different concrete forms of labor are equalized and thus labor is also equalized. If other conditions remain unchanged, differences in concrete forms of labor play no role in the commodity economy and the product of one hour of labor of the shoemaker is equalized with the product of one hour of labor of the tailor. However, the different forms of labor take place in unequal conditions; they differ from each other according to their intensiveness, their danger to health, the length of training, and so on. The process of exchange eliminates the differences in the forms of labor; at the same time it eliminates the different conditions and converts qualitative differences into quantitative ones. Due to these different conditions, the product of one day's labor of the shoemaker is exchanged, for example, for the product of two days' labor of an unqualified construction worker or excavator, or for the product of half a day's labor of a jeweller. On the market, products produced in unequal amounts of time are equalized as values. At first glance this conception contradicts the basic premise of Marx's theory, according to which the value of the product of labor is proportional to the labor-time expended on its production. Let us see how this contradiction can be resolved.

Among the different conditions of labor mentioned above, the most important are the intensiveness of the given form of labor and the length of training and preparation required for the given form of labor or the given profession. The question of the intensiveness of labor is not a special theoretical problem and we will treat it incidentally. However, our main attention will be devoted to the question of qualified labor.

First of all we will define qualified and simple labor. Simple labor is "the expenditure of simple labor-power, i.e., of the labor-power which, on an average, apart from any special development, exists in the organism of every ordinary individual" (C., I, p. 44; Rubin's italics). As opposed to simple labor, we will call qualified labor that labor which requires special training, i.e., "longer or professional training and more significant general education than the average for workers."[192] One should not think that simple, average labor is a magnitude which is equal among different people and which does not change in the course of historical development. Simple average labor has a different character in different countries and in different cultural epochs, but it represents a given magnitude for each determined society at a given moment of its development (C., I, p. 44). The labor which any average worker can perform in England would require some kind of preparation for the worker in Russia. The labor which the average Russian worker is able to carry out at present, would have been considered labor which was above average, in terms of complexity, in Russia a hundred years ago.

The difference of qualified from simple labor is manifested: 1) in the increased value of the products which are produced by the qualified labor, and 2) in the increased value of the qualified labor force, i.e., in the increased wage of the qualified wage laborer. On one hand, the product of one day of labor of the jeweller has a value which is two times larger than the product of a day's labor of the shoemaker. On the other hand, the jewel-worker gets from the jewel entrepreneur a larger wage than the shoemaker gets from his entrepreneur. The first phenomenon is a property of the commodity economy as such, and characterizes the relations among people as producers of commodities. The second phenomenon is a property of the capitalist economy only, and characterizes relations among people as relations between capitalists and wage laborers. Since in the theory of value, which

---

[192] Otto Bauer, "Qualifizierte Arbeit und Kapitalismus," Die Neue Zeit, Stuttgart, 1906, Bd. I, No. 20.

studies the properties of the commodity economy as such, we only deal with the value of commodities and not with the value of the labor force, in the present chapter we will consider only the value of products produced by qualified labor, leaving aside the question of the value of the qualified labor force.

The concept of qualified labor must be precisely distinguished from two other concepts which are frequently confused with it: ability (or dexterity) and intensiveness. Speaking of qualified labor we have in mind the level of average qualification (training) which is required for employment in the given form of labor, the given profession or specialty. This average qualification must be distinguished from the individual qualification of the single producer in the context of the same profession or specialty. The labor of the jeweller requires, on the average, a high level of qualification, but different jewellers display, in their work, different degrees of experience, training and skill; they differ from each other in terms of the dexterity or ability of their labor (C., I, pp. 38-39; 197). If shoemakers produce, on the average, one pair of shoes per day, and a given shoemaker who is abler and better trained produces two pairs, then naturally the product of one day's labor of the more qualified shoemaker (twopairs of shoes) will have two times more value than the product of one day's labor of the shoemaker of average ability (one pair of shoes). This is obvious since the value is determined, as will be shown in detail in the next chapter, not by the individual but by the labor socially necessary for the production. Differences in ability or dexterity among the two different shoemakers can be precisely measured in terms of the different quantities of products which they produced during the same time (given the same instruments of labor and other equal conditions). Thus the concept of ability or dexterity of labor enters into the theory of socially-necessary labor and does not present special theoretical difficulties. The question of qualified labor presents far larger problems. This is related to different values of products produced at the same time by two producers in different professions, producers whose products are not comparable with each other. Analysts who reduce qualified labor to ability simply circumvent the problem. Thus L. Boudin holds that the higher value of the product of qualified labor can be explained by the fact that the qualified laborer produces a larger quantity of products.[193] F. Oppenheimer says that Marx, who concentrated on "acquired" qualification, which results from "longer education and training," neglected "innate" qualification. But in our judgment, Oppenheimer included in this "innate" qualification the individual ability of particular producers, which is related to socially necessary, and not to qualified labor, where Oppenheimer placed it.[194]

Other analysts have tried to reduce qualified labor to more intensive labor. The intensity or tension of labor is determined by the quantity of labor which is expended in a unit of time. Just as we can observe individual differences in the intensity of labor between two producers in the same profession, so we can observe the different average intensity of labor in two different professions (C., I, p. 409, 524, 561). Goods produced by labor of the same duration but of different intensity have different value since the quantity of abstract labor depends not only on the length of the labor-time expended, but also on the intensity of the labor. (See the end of the previous chapter.)

Some analysts, as was mentioned above, have tried to resolve the problem of qualified labor by seeing in

---

[193] Louis B. Boudin, The Theoretical System of Karl Marx in the Light of Recent Criticism, Chicago: Charles H. Kerr & Co., 1907.

[194] Franz Oppenheimer, Wert und Kapitalprofit, Jena: Ct. Fischer, 2nd edition, 1922, p. 63, pp. 65-66. A detailed critique of Oppenheimer's views is given in our Sovremennye ekonomisty na Zapade (Contemporary Economists in the West), 1927.

qualified labor, labor of higher intensity or tension. "Complex labor can produce greater value than simple labor only in conditions in which it is more intense than simple labor," says Liebknecht.[195] This greater intensity of qualified labor is expressed, first of all, in a greater expenditure of mental energy, in greater "attention, intellectual effort, and mental expenditure." Let us assume that the shoemaker spends 1/4 of a unit of mental energy per unit of muscular labor, and the jeweller expends 1 1/2 units. In this example, one hour of labor of the shoemaker represents the expenditure of 1 1/4 units of energy (muscular as well as mental), and one hour of labor of the jeweller represents 2 1/2 units of energy, i.e., the labor of the jeweller creates two times more value. Liebknecht himself is aware that such an assumption has a "hypothetical" character.[196] We think this assumption is not only unfounded, but is belied by the facts. We are taking into account forms of qualified labor which create commodities of higher value due to the length of training. But in terms of intensity, they do not exceed the intensity of less qualified forms of labor. We must explain why qualified labor, independent of the level of its intensity, creates a product of higher value.[197]

---

[195] Wilhelm Liebkneckt, Zur Geschichte der Werttheorie in England, Jena: G. Fischer, 1902, p. 102. The author of this book is the son of Wilhelm Liebknecht and the brother of Karl Liebkneckt. A detailed critique of Liebknecht's views was given in our introduction to the Russian translation of Liebknecht's History of the Theory of Value in England.

[196] Ibid., p. 103.

[197] In P. Rumyantsev's Russian translation of A Contribution to the Critique of Political Economy, complex labor is called "labor of higher tension" (1922, p. 38). This term should not confuse the reader, since it is not Marx's term. In the original edition, Marx called it "labor of higher potential" (p. 6).

We face the following problem: why does the expenditure of equal labor-time in two professions with different average levels of qualification (length of training) create commodities of different value? In Marxist literature it is possible to note two different approaches to the solution of this question. One approach can be found in the work of A. Bogdanov. He notes that a qualified labor force "can function normally only on condition that more significant and varied needs of the worker himself are satisfied, i.e., on condition that he consume a larger quantity of different products. Thus complex labor-power has greater labor value, and costs the society a greater amount of its labor. This is why this labor power gives society a more complex, i.e.,'multiplied,' living labor."[198] If the qualified laborer absorbs consumer goods and, consequently, social energy which is five times greater than the simple laborer, then one hour of labor of the qualified laborer will produce a value which is five times greater than one hour of simple labor.

We consider Bogdanov's argument unacceptable, first of all in terms of its methodology. In essence, Bogdanov deduces the higher value of the product of qualified labor from the higher value of the qualified labor-power. He explains the value of commodities in terms of the value of the labor power. However, Marx's analytical path was just the opposite. In the theory of value, when he explains the value of commodities produced by qualified labor, Marx analyzes the relations among people as commodity producers, or the simple commodity economy; at this stage of the examination, the value of labor-power in general, and of qualified labor in particular, do not yet exist for Marx (C., I, p. 44,

---

[198] A. Bogdanov, and I. Stepanov, Krus politicheskoi ekonomii (Course in Political Economy), Vol. II, No. 4, p. 19. Bogdanov's italics.

footnote).[199] In Marx's work, the value of commodities is determined by abstract labor which in itself represents a social quantity and does not have value. However, in Bogdanov's work, labor, or labor-time, which determines value, in turn also has value. The value of commodities is determined by the labor-time materialized in them, and the value of this labor-time is determined by the value of the consumer goods necessary for the subsistence of the laborer.[200] Thus we get a vicious circle which A. Bogdanov tries to get out of, by means of an argument which, in our opinion, is not convincing.[201]

Independently of these methodological defects, we must note that Bogdanov indicates only the minimal absolute limit below which the value of the products of qualified labor cannot go. The value must, under all circumstances, be sufficient to preserve the qualified labor force on its previous level, so that it will not be forced to de-qualify (sink to a lower level of qualification). But as we have pointed out, except for the minimal absolute limit, the relative advantage of different forms of labor plays a decisive role in the commodity economy.[202] Let us assume that the value of the product of a given type of qualified labor is completely adequate to maintain the qualified labor-power of the producer, but is not sufficient to make labor in the given profession relatively more advantageous than labor in other

---

[199] In one passage Marx deviates from his usual method and tends to treat the value of the product of qualified labor as dependent on the value of the qualified labor power. See Theorien uber den Mehrwert, III, pp. 197-198.

[200] See F. Engels, Anti-Duhring, New York: International Publishers, 1966, P. 210.

[201] Op. cit., p. 20.

[202] See our similar objections to A. Bogdanov in the chapter on "Equality of Commodities and Equality of Labor."

professions which require a shorter training period. In these conditions, a transfer of labor out of the given profession will start; this will continue until the value of the product of the given profession is raised to a level which establishes a relative equality in conditions of production and a state of equilibrium among the different forms of labor. In the analysis of the problems of qualified labor, we must take as our starting point, not the equilibrium between the consumption and the productivity of the given form of labor, but the equilibrium among different forms of labor. Thus we approach the basic starting-point of Marx's theory of value, we approach the distribution of social labor among different branches of the social economy.

In earlier chapters we developed the idea that the exchange of products of different forms of labor in terms of their values corresponds to the state of equilibrium between two given branches of production. This general position is completely applicable to cases where products of two forms of labor are exchanged, forms of labor which have different levels of qualification. The value of the product of qualified labor must exceed the value of the product of simple labor (or of less qualified labor in general) by the amount of value which compensates for the different conditions of production and establishes equilibrium among these forms of labor. The product of one hour of labor of the jeweller is equalized on the market with the product of two hours of labor of the shoemaker because equilibrium in the distribution of labor between these two branches of production is established precisely in the given exchange proportion, and the transfer of labor from one branch to the other ceases. The problem of qualified labor is reduced to the analysis of the conditions of equilibrium among different forms of labor which differ in terms of qualification. This problem is not yet solved, but it is accurately posed. We have not yet answered our question, but we have already outlined the method, the path which will lead us to our goal.

A large number of Marxist analysts have taken this path.[203] They concentrated their main attention on the fact that the product of qualified labor is not only the result of the labor which is directly expended on its production, but also of that labor which is necessary for the training of the laborer in the given profession. The latter labor also enters into the value of the product and makes it correspondingly more expensive. "In what it has to give for the product of skilled labor, society consequently pays an equivalent for the value which the skilled labors would have created had they been directly consumed by society,"[204] and not spent on training a qualified labor force. These labor processes are composed of the master craftsman's and the teacher's labor, which is expended for training a laborer of a given profession, and of the labor of the student himself during the training period. Examining the question whether or not the labor of the teacher enters into the value of the product of qualified labor, O. Bauer is perfectly right in taking as the starting-point of his reasoning conditions of equilibrium among different branches of production. He reaches the following conclusions: "Together with the value created by labor, expended in the direct process of production, and with the value transferred from the teacher to the qualified labor force, value which is created by the teacher in the process of training is also one of the determining factors in the value of the products which are produced by qualified labor at the stage of simple commodity production."[205]

---

[203] R. Hilferding, Bohm-Bawerk's Criticism of Marx (New York: Augustus M. Kelley, 1949). H. Deutsch, Qualifizierle Arbeit und Kapitalismus, Wien: C.W. Stern, 1904. Otto Bauer, Op. Cit. V.N. Poznyakov, Kvalifitsirovannyi trud i teoriya tsennosti Marksa (Qualified Labor and Marx's Theory of Value), 2nd edition.

[204] Hilferding, Op. Cit., p. 145.

[205] Bauer, Op. Cit., pp. 131-132.

Thus, the labor expended in training the producers of a given profession enters into the value of the product of qualified labor. But in professions which differ in terms of higher qualifications and greater complexity of labor, the training of laborers is usually carried out by means of selection, from a larger number of the most capable students. From among three individuals studying engineering, perhaps only one graduates and achieves the goal. Thus, the expenditure of the labor of three students, and the corresponding increased expenditure of labor by the instructor, are required for the preparation of one engineer. Thus the transfer of students to a given profession, among whom only one third has a chance of reaching the goal, takes place to a sufficient extent only if the increased value of the products of the given profession can compensate the unavoidable (and to some extent wasted) expenditures of labor. Other conditions remaining equal, the average value of the product of one hour of labor in professions where training requires expenditures of labor by numerous competitors will be greater than the average value of one hour of labor in professions in which these difficulties do not exist.[206] This circumstance raises the value of the product

---

[206] This view, which is already found in Adam Smith, was particularly emphasized by L. Lyubimov (Kurs politicheskoi ekonomii - Course of Political Economy - 1923, pp. 72-78). Unfortunately, L. Lyubimov mixed together the question of what determines the average value of products of a highly qualified profession, for example, engineers, artists, etc., with the question of what determines the individual price of a given unreproducible object (a painting by Raphael). When he treats reproducible mass-produced goods (for example the labor of an engineer can be treated as labor which produces - with small exceptions - homogeneous and reproducible products), we can obtain the value of a unit of product by dividing the value of the entire production of a given profession by the number of homogeneous products produced by that profession. But this is not possible with respect to individual, unreproducible objects. The fact that the wasted expenditure of labor of thousands of painters who failed is compensated in the price of a painting by Raphael, or that the wasted expenditure of labor of hundreds of unsuccessful painters is compensated in the price of a painting by Salvador Rosa, cannot in any way be derived from the fact that the average value of the product of one hour of labor of a painter is equal to the value of the product of five hours of simple labor (to each hour of the painter's labor is added one hour of labor spent by the painter for his training and three hours of labor expended on the training of three painters who failed). L. Lyubimov is completely right when he subsumes the value of the product of a highly qualified laborer under the law of value. But he cannot deny the fact of monopoly in relation to the individual price of unreproducible objects. P. Maslov commits the opposite error. He ascribes a monopolistic character to the average value of products of highly qualified labor as well (See his Kapitalizm - Capitalism - 1914, pp. 191-192).

of highly qualified labor.[207]

As we can see, the reduction of qualified to simple labor is one of the results of the objective social process of equalization of different forms of labor which, in capitalist society, is carried out through the equalization of commodities on the market. We do not have to repeat the mistake of Adam Smith, who "fails to see the objective equalization of different kinds of labor which the social process forcibly carries out, mistaking it for the subjective equality of the labors of individuals" (Critique, p. 68). The product of one hour of the jeweller's labor is not exchanged for the product of two hours of the shoemaker's labor because the jeweller subjectively considers his labor to be two times more valuable than that of the shoemaker. On the contrary, the subjective, conscious evaluations of the producers are determined by the objective process of equalization of different commodities, and through the commodities, by the equalization of different forms of labor on the market. Finally, the jeweller is motivated by calculating in advance that the product of his labor will have two times more value than the product of the shoemaker's labor. In his consciousness he anticipates what will happen on the market only because his consciousness fixes and generalizes previous experience. What happens here is analogous to what Marx described when he explained the higher rate of profit which is acquired in those branches of the capitalist economy which are connected with special risk, difficulty, and so on. "After average prices, and their corresponding market-prices, become stable for a time it reaches the consciousness of the individual capitalists that this equalization balances definite differences, so that they include these in their mutual

---

[207] In capitalist society, the interest on training expenditures is sometimes added; in some cases this is treated as invested capital. See Maslov, Op. Cit., p. 191, and Bauer, Op. Cit., p. 142. However, what takes place here is not the production of new value, but only a redistribution of value produced earlier.

calculations" (C., III, p. 209, Marx's italics). In just the same way, in the act of exchange the jeweller takes his high skill into account in advance. This high skill "is taken into account once and for all as valid ground for compensation" (C., III, p. 210). But this computation is only a result of the social process of exchange, a result of colliding actions of a large number of commodity producers. If we take the labor of an unqualified laborer (digging) as simple labor, and if we take one hour of this labor as a unit, then one hour of the jeweller's labor is equal, let us say, to 4 units, not because the jeweller evaluates his labor and assigns it the value of 4 units, but because his labor is equalized on the market with 4 units of simple labor. The reduction of complex to simple labor is a real process which takes place through the process of exchange and in the last analysis is reduced to the equalization of different forms of labor in the process of distribution of social labor, not to the different evaluations of different forms of labor or to the definition of different values of labor.[208] Since the equalization of different forms of labor takes place, in the commodity economy, through the equalization of the products of labor as values, the reduction of qualified to simple labor cannot take place any other way than through the equalization of the products of labor. "A commodity may be the product of the most skilled labor, but its value, by equating it to the product of simple unskilled labor, represents a definite quantity of the latter labor alone" (C., I, p. 44). "The value of the most varied commodities is everywhere expressed in money, i.e., in a determined quantity of gold or silver. And precisely because of this, the different forms of labor represented by these values are reduced, in different proportions, to determined quantities of one and the same form of simple labor, namely that labor which

---

[208] As is stated by Oppenheimer and others. See Oppenheimer, *Wert und Kapitalprofit*, 2nd edition, 1922, pp. 69-70.

produces gold and silver."[209] The assumption that the reduction of qualified to simple labor must take place in advance and precede exchange in order to make possible the act of equalization of the products of labor misses the very basis of Marx's theory of value.

As we can see, in order to explain the high value of the products of qualified labor we do not have to repudiate the labor theory of value; we must only understand clearly the basic idea of this theory as a theory which analyzes the law of equilibrium and distribution of social labor in the commodity-capitalist economy. From this point of view we can evaluate the arguments of those critics of Marx[210] who make the problem of qualified labor the main target of their attacks and see this as the most vulnerable part of Marx's theory. The objections of these critics can be reduced to two basic propositions: 1) no matter how Marxists might explain the causes of the high value of products of qualified labor, it remains a fact of exchange that the products of unequal quantities of labor are exchanged as equivalents, which contradicts the labor theory of value; 2) Marxists cannot show the criterion or standard by which we could equalize in advance a unit of qualified labor, for example one hour of a jeweller's labor, with a determined number of units of simple labor.

The first objection is based on the erroneous impression that the labor theory of value makes the equality of commodities dependent exclusively on the physiological equality of the labor expenditures necessary for their production. With this interpretation of the labor theory of value, one cannot deny the fact that one hour of the jeweller's labor and four hours of the shoemaker's labor represent, from a physiological point of view, unequal quantities of labor. Every attempt to represent

---

[209] [Rubin cites the Russian edition of the first volume of Capital, translated by V. Bazarov and I. Stepanov, 1923, p. 170.]

[210] See Bohm-Bawerk, Op. Cit.

one hour of qualified labor as physiologically condensed labor and equal, in terms of energy, to several hours of simple labor, seems hopeless and methodologically incorrect. Qualified labor is, in fact, condensed, multiplied, potential labor; it is not physiologically, but socially condensed. The labor theory of value does not affirm the physiological equality but the social equalization of labor which, in turn, of course takes place on the basis of properties which characterize labor from the material-technical and physiological aspects (see the end of the previous chapter). On the market, products are not exchanged in terms of equal, but of equalized quantities of labor. It is our task to analyze the laws of the social equalization of various forms of labor in the process of social distribution of labor. If these laws explain the causes of the equalization of one hour of the jeweller's labor with four hours of the unqualified worker's labor, then our problem is solved, irrespective of the physiological equality or inequality of these socially equalized quantities of labor.

The second objection of Marx's critics assigns to economic theory a task which is in no way proper to it: to find a standard of value which would make it operationally possible to compare different kinds of labor with each other. However, the theory of value is not concerned with the analysis or search for an operational standard of equalization; it seeks a causal explanation of the objective process of equalization of different forms of labor which actually takes place in a commodity capitalist society.[211] In the capitalist society, this process takes place spontaneously; it is not organized. The equalization of different forms of labor does not take place directly, but is established through the equalization of the products of labor on the market, it is a result of the colliding actions of a large number of commodity producers. In these conditions, "society is the only accountant competent to calculate the height of prices, and the method which society employs to this end is the method of

---

[211] See the Chapter on "Social Labor" above.

competition."[212] Those critics of Marx who assign to simple labor the role of a practical standard and a unit for the equalization of labor in essence put an organized economy in the place of capitalist society. In an organized economy, different forms of labor are equalized with each other directly, without market exchange or competition, without the equalization of things as values on the market.

Rejecting this confusion of theoretical and practical points of view, and consistently holding to a theoretical point of view, we find that the theory of value explains, in a thoroughly adequate manner, the cause of the high value of highly qualified labor as well as the changes of these values. If the period of training is shortened, or in general if the labor expenditures necessary for training in a given profession are shortened, the value of the products of this profession falls. This explains a whole series of events in economic life. Thus, for example, starting with the second half of the 19th century, the value of the product of labor of store clerks as well as the value of their labor power fell significantly. This can be explained by the fact that "the necessary training, knowledge of commercial practices, languages, etc., is more and more rapidly, easily, universally and cheaply reproduced with the progress of science and public education" (C., III, p. 300).

In this, as in the previous chapter, we took as our starting-point a state of equilibrium among the various branches of social production and the different forms of labor. But as we know, the commodity capitalist economy is a system in which equilibrium is constantly destroyed. Equilibrium appears only in the form of a tendency which is destroyed and delayed by countervailing factors. In the field of qualified labor, the tendency to establish

---

[212] Rudolf Hilferding, Bohm-Bawerk's Criticism of Marx (published together with Eugen von Bohm-Bawerk, Karl Marx and the Close of his System), New York: Augustus M. Kelley, 1949, pp. 146-147.

equilibrium among different forms of labor is weaker to the extent that a long period of qualification, or high costs of training in a given profession, put large obstacles on the transfer of labor from the given profession to other, simpler professions. When we apply a theoretical schema to living reality, the delayed effect of these obstacles must be taken into consideration. The difficulties of being admitted to higher professions gives these professions some form of monopoly. On the other hand, "a few [professions] of inferior kind, that are over-supplied with underpaid workmen" (C.,.I p. 440), are accessible. Frequently, the difficulty of being admitted to professions with higher skills, and the selection which takes place in this admission, throws many unsuccessful competitors into lower professions, thus increasing the over-supply in these professions.[213] In addition, the increasing technical and organizational complexity of the capitalist process of production intensifies the demand for new forms of qualified labor power, disproportionally increasing the payment for this labor force and for its products. This is, so to speak, a premium for the time expended to acquire qualifications (which may be shorter or longer). This premium arises in a dynamic process of change in the qualifications of labor. But just as the deviation of market prices from values does not disprove but makes possible the realization of the law of value, so the "premium for qualification," which signifies the absence of equilibrium among different forms of labor, in turn leads to the increase of qualified labor and to the distribution of productive forces in the direction of equilibrium of the social economy.

---

[213] Maslov, Kapitalizm (Capitalism), p. 192.

Chapter 16: Socially-Necessary Labor

In earlier chapters we concentrated mainly on the analysis of the qualitative aspect of labor which creates value; now we can turn to a more direct analysis of the quantitative aspect.

As is known, when Marx ascertained that changes in the magnitude of value of commodities depended on changes in the quantity of labor expended on their production, he did not have in mind the individual labor which was factually expended by a given producer on the production of the given commodity, but on the average quantity of labor necessary for the production of the given product, at a given level of development of productive forces. "The labor-time socially necessary is that required to produce an article under the normal conditions of production, and with the average degree of skill and intensity prevalent at the time. The introduction of power-looms into England probably reduced by one-half the labor required to weave a given quantity of yarn into cloth. The hand-loom weavers, as a matter of fact, continued to require the same time as before; but for all that, the product of one hour of their labor represented after the change only half an hour's social labor, and consequently fell to one-half its former value" (C, I, p. 39).

The magnitude of socially necessary labor-time is determined by the level of development of productive forces, which is understood in a broad sense as the totality of material and human factors of production. Socially-necessary labor-time changes in relation not only to changes in the "conditions of production," i.e., of material-technical and organizational factors, but also in relation to changes in the labor force, in the "ability and intensity of labor."

In the first stage of his analysis, Marx assumed that all exemplars of a given sort of product were produced in equal, normal, average conditions. The individual labor expended on every exemplar quantitatively coincides with the socially-necessary labor, and the individual value with the social or market value. Here the difference between individual labor and socially-necessary labor, between individual value and social (market) value, is not yet taken into account. Thus Marx speaks simply of "value," and not of "market value," in these passages (market value is not mentioned in the first volume of Capital).

In later stages of his analysis, Marx assumed that different exemplars of a given sort of commodity are produced in different technical conditions. Here the opposition between individual and social (market) value appears. In other words, the concept of value is developed further and is defined more accurately as social or market value. In the same way, socially necessary labor-time opposes individual labor-time which differs in enterprises of the same branch of production. Thus we express the property of the commodity economy that the same price is established for all commodities of a given type and quality which are exchanged on the market. This is independent of the individual technical conditions in which these commodities are produced, and independent of the quantity of individual labor expended on their production in different enterprises. A society based on a commodity economy does not directly regulate the working activity of people but regulates it through the value of the products of labor, through commodities. The market does not take into account the individual properties and deviations in the working activity of individual commodity producers in individual economic units. "Each individual commodity, in this connection, is to be considered as an average sample of its class" (C., I, p. 39). Every individual commodity is not sold according to its individual value, but according to the average social value, which Marx calls market value in Volume III of Capital.

All enterprises of the same branch of production can be arranged in a series according to their level of technical development, starting with the most productive and ending with the most backward. Regardless of differences in the individual value of the product in each of these enterprises or in each group of enterprises (for the sake of simplicity, we will follow Marx in distinguishing three types of enterprises: with high, average and low productivity), their goods are sold on the market for the same price, which is determined in the last analysis (through deviation and destruction) by the average or market value: "commodities whose individual value is below the market-value realize an extra surplus-value, or surplus-profit, while those whose individual value exceeds the market-value are unable to realize a portion of the surplus-value contained in them" (C., III, p. 178). This difference between market-value and individual value, which creates various advantages of production for enterprises with different levels of productivity of labor, is the prime mover of technical progress in capitalist society. Every capitalist enterprise tries to introduce the latest technical improvements, to lower the individual value of production in comparison with the average market-value, and to get the possibility to extract super-profit. Enterprises with a backward technology try to decrease the individual value of their products, if possible to the level of market-value; otherwise they are threatened by the competition of more productive enterprises and face economic collapse. The victory of large over small-scale production, the increase of technical progress and the concentration of production in larger and technically more perfect enterprises, are the consequences of the sale of commodities on the market according to average market-value, independent of individual value.

If we assume a given level of development of productive forces in a given branch of production (the branch is defined as the totality of enterprises, with very different levels of productivity), the market value is a determined magnitude. But it is erroneous to think that it is given or established in advance, that it is computed on the basis of a given technique. As was pointed out, the technique of different enterprises is different. Market-value is a magnitude which is established as a result of market conflict among large numbers of sellers-commodity producers who produce in different technical conditions and who deliver to the market commodities which possess different individual values. As was already pointed out in Chapter Thirteen, the transformation of individual into socially-necessary labor takes place through the same process of exchange which transforms private and concrete labor into social and abstract labor: "the different individual values must be equalized at one social value, the above-mentioned market-value, and this implies competition among producers of the same kind of commodities and, likewise, the existence of a common market in which they offer their articles for sale" (C., III, p. 180). The market value is a resultant of the market struggle among various producers in a given branch of production (in this we take into account normal conditions on the market, which presupposes a balance of supply and demand and thus equilibrium among the given branches of production and other branches; on this, see below). Similarly, socially-necessary labor, which determines market-value, is a resultant of different levels of productivity of labor in different enterprises. Socially-necessary labor determines the value of commodities only to the extent that the market puts together all producers of the given branch and places them in the same conditions of market exchange. Depending on the extension of the market and the subordination of the separate commodity producers to market forces, the market-value which is created is uniform for all commodities of a given sort and quality. In the same way, socially-necessary labor acquires importance. The market-value is established through competition among producers in the same branch of production. But in the developed capitalist society there is also competition of capitals invested in different branches of production. The transfer of capitals from one branch to another, i.e., "competition of capitals in different spheres... brings out the price of production equalizing the rates of profit in the different spheres" (Ibid.). Market-value acquires the form of price of production.

If market-value is established only as the result of the social process of competition among enterprises with different levels of productivity, then we must ask which group of enterprises determines this market-value. In other words, which magnitude represents the average socially-necessary labor which determines market value? "On the one hand, market-value is to be viewed as the average value of commodities produced in a single sphere, and, on the other, as the individual value of the commodities produced under average conditions of their respective sphere and forming the bulk of the products of that sphere" (C., III, p. 178). If we make the simplifying assumption that for the whole totality of commodities of a given branch of production, the market-value coincides with the individual value (even though it diverges from the individual value of individual exemplars), then the market value of commodities will equal the sum of all individual values of commodities of the given branch, divided by the number of commodities. But in a later phase of analysis we must assume that behind the entire branch of production, the sum of market-values may deviate from the sum of individual values (which, for example, takes place in agriculture); the coincidence of these two sums is preserved only for the totality of all branches of production or for the whole social economy. In this case, the market-value will no longer exactly coincide with the sum of all individual values divided by the number of commodities of a given type. In this case, the quantitative determination of market-values is subject to the following laws. In Marx's view, in normal conditions market-value approaches the individual value of the dominant mass of products of a given branch of production. If a large part of the commodities is produced in enterprises with average productivity of labor, and only an insignificant part is produced in the worst conditions, then the market value will be regulated by enterprises with average productivity, i.e., market-value approaches the individual value of the products produced by this type of enterprise. This is the most frequent case. If "the part of the mass produced under less favorable conditions forms a relatively weighty quantity as compared with the average mass and with the other extreme," i.e., produced under the best conditions, then "the mass produced under less favorable conditions regulates the market, or social, value" (C., III, p. 183), i.e., approaches the individual values of those commodities (completely coinciding with them only in some instances, for example in agriculture). Finally, if commodities produced in the best conditions dominate the market, then they will exert a decisive influence on market value. In other words, socially-necessary labor may approach labor of average productivity (this takes place in the majority of cases) as well as labor of higher or lower productivity. It is only necessary that labor of higher (or lower) productivity deliver to the market the greatest quantity of commodities, i.e., in order to become the average (not in the sense of average productivity, but in the sense of the most widespread productivity) labor of a given branch of production.[214]

According to the reasoning of Marx which we have presented, he presupposes a normal course of production, correspondence between the supply of

---

[214] K. Diehl inaccurately claims that Marx considers only labor expended in enterprises of average productivity as socially necessary labor. But if, in the given branch of production, the mass of products produced in the worst conditions is dominant, the market value will be determined by labor of lower productivity. "Here, as a result of determined conditions of supply, socially necessary labor-time is not the decisive factor, but rather a greater magnitude" (K. Diehl, Uber das Verhaltnis von Wert und Preis im okonomischen System von Marx, Jena, 1898, pp. 23-24). Such a view could only be relevant to cases of divergence between supply and demand which cause the deviation of prices from market-values: in such cases socially-necessary labor is not decisive, but rather a magnitude which exceeds it or which is lower. But Diehl grasps the fact that Marx's reasoning does not refer to such cases of deviation of prices from market-values (on this, see below), but refers precisely to the "correspondence of the general mass of the products with social needs" (Ibid., p. 24), i.e., equilibrium between the given branch of production and other branches. But if this equilibrium appears when the market-value is determined by labor of lower productivity, precisely this labor is considered socially-necessary. If Diehl considers only labor of average productivity as socially-necessary, other authors are disposed to recognize only labor of higher productivity, expended in the best technical conditions, as socially-necessary. "The actual exchange value of all values depends on the labor-time necessary with the most developed technical methods of production, on 'socially-necessary' labor-time" CW. Liebknecht, Zur Geschichte der Werttheorie in England, Jena, 1902, p. 94). As we saw from the text, this idea also disagrees with Marx's theory.

commodities and effective demand, i.e., those cases when buyers buy the entire amount of commodities of a given kind according to their normal market values. As we have seen, market value is determined by labor of high, average or low productivity; all these forms of labor may represent socially-necessary labor, depending on the technical structure of a given branch of production, and depending on the interrelations among enterprises with different levels of productivity in this branch. But all these different cases where market values are determined, under conditions of normal supply and demand, must be strictly distinguished from cases of divergence between supply and demand, when market price is higher than market-value (excessive demand) or when market price is lower than market-value (excessive supply). "We ignore here the overstocked market, in which the part produced under most favorable conditions always regulates the market-price. We are not dealing here with the market-price, in so far as it differs from the market-value, but with the various determinations of the market-value itself" (C., III, p. 183). How can we explain changes of market-value which depend on the numerical dominance of one or another group of enterprises (of high, average or low productivity)?

The answer to this question can be found in the mechanism of distribution of labor and equilibrium among different branches of social production. Market-value corresponds to the theoretically defined state of equilibrium among the different branches of production. If commodities are sold according to market values, then the state of equilibrium is maintained, i.e., the production of a given branch does not expand or contract at the expense of other branches. Equilibrium among different branches of production, the correspondence of social production with social needs, and the coincidence of market prices with market-values - all these factors are closely interrelated and concomitant. "For the market-price of identical commodities, each, however, produced under different individual circumstances, to correspond to the market-value and not to deviate from it either by rising above or falling below it, it is necessary that the pressure exerted by different sellers upon one another be sufficient to bring enough commodities to market to fill the social requirements, i.e., a quantity for which society is capable of paying the market-value" (C., III, pp. 180-181). The coincidence of prices with market values corresponds to the state of equilibrium among the different branches of production. Differences in the determination of market value by labor of high, average or low productivity become clear if we concentrate our attention on the role of market-values in the mechanism of distribution and equilibrium of labor. If enterprises with high productivity are dominant, more accurately, if masses of products produced in the best conditions are dominant, the market value cannot be regulated by the value of production in average or poor conditions, since this would bring about an increase of surplus profits in enterprises of higher productivity and would lead to significant expansion of production in these enterprises. This expansion of production (in the case of the dominant role of this group of enterprises) would lead on the market to excess demand and to the gravitation of prices to the level of value in enterprises of high productivity. Similar reasoning can be applied to cases of numerical predominance of another group of enterprises, namely those with average or low productivity. Different cases of regulation of market-values (or, which is the same thing, the determination of socially-necessary labor) call be explained by the different conditions of equilibrium of the given branch of production with other branches. This equilibrium depends oil the dominance of enterprises with different levels of productivity, i.e., in the last analysis, it depends on the level of development of productive forces.

Thus socially-necessary labor, which determines the market value of commodities in a given branch of production, can be labor of high, average or low productivity. Which labor is socially-necessary depends on the level of development of productive forces in the given branch of production, and first of all on the quantitative dominance of enterprises with different levels of productivity (as was already mentioned above, we are not considering the number of enterprises, but the mass of commodities produced in them).[215] But this is not all.

We suppose that two branches of production have completely equal quantitative distributions of enterprises with different levels of productivity. Let us say that enterprises of average productivity compose 40 percent, and enterprises with higher and lower productivity 30 percent each. However, there is the following essential difference among the two branches of production. In the first branch, production in enterprises with better equipment is open to quick and significant expansion (for example, because of particular advantages in the concentration of production: because of the ability to receive from abroad, or quickly to produce domestically, the necessary machines; because of the abundance of raw materials, the availability of a labor force fit for factory production, and so on). In the other branch, large-scale production can be expanded more slowly and to a smaller extent. It can be said in advance that in the first branch the market value will tend to be established (obviously if other conditions are the same) at a lower level than in the second branch, i.e., in the first branch the market-value will be closer to labor expenditures in enterprises with higher productivity. However, in the second branch the market-value may rise. If the market-value in the first branch rose as high as in the second branch, the result would be a quick and significant expansion of production in enterprises of higher productivity, an oversupply on the market, the breakdown of equilibrium between supply

---

[215] "Which group of enterprises (with different levels of productivity - I.R..) will, in the last analysis, determined the average value, depends on the numerical interrelations or the proportional quantitative interrelations among the class of enterprises in a given branch" (Theorien uber den Mehrwert, Vol. II, Book I, P. 56).

and demand, the fall of prices. For the first branch of production, the maintenance of equilibrium with other branches of production presupposes that market-value approaches expenditures in enterprises with higher productivity. In the second branch of production, the equilibrium of the social economy is possible with a higher level of market value, i.e., when prices approach labor expenditures in enterprises with average and low productivity.

Finally, cases are also possible where the equilibrium of the social economy takes place in conditions when market-value is not determined by individual labor expenditures in a given group of enterprises (for example of high productivity), but by the average amount of labor expenditures in the given group plus those in the group nearest to the given group. This can take place frequently if, in the given branch of production, enterprises are not divided into three groups according to their productivity, as we have assumed, but into two groups, of high and low productivity. It is obvious that the "average value" is not here considered as an arithmetic average: it can be closer to the expenditures of the group with higher or lower productivity, depending on the conditions of equilibrium between the given branch and other branches of production. Thus L. Boudin simplifies the problem excessively when he says that in the case of introducing technical improvements and new methods of production, "the value of the commodities produced...will not be measured by the average expenditure of labor, but either by that of the old or that of the new method."[216]

Thus the different cases of determination of market-value (namely the determination of socially-necessary labor) are explained by the different conditions of equilibrium between the given branch and other branches of the social economy, depending on the level of

---

[216] Louis B. Boudin, The Theoretical System of Karl Marx, Chicago: Charles H. Kerr & Co., 1907, p. 70.

development of productive forces. The growth of the productive power of labor in a given branch of production, which changes the conditions of equilibrium of this branch with other branches, changes the magnitude of socially-necessary labor and the market-value. Labor-time "changes with every variation in the productiveness of labor" (C., I, p. 40). "In general, the greater the productiveness of labor, the less is the labor-time required for the production of an article, the less is the amount of labor crystallized in that article, andthe less is its value; and vice versa, the less the productiveness of labor, the greater is the labor-time required for the production of an article, and the greater is its value" (Ibid.). In Marx's theory, the concept of socially-necessary labor is closely related to the concept of the productive power of labor In a commodity economy, the development of productive forces finds its economic expression in changes of socially-necessary labor and changes of market value of individual commodities, which are determined by socially-necessary labor. The movement of value on the market is a reflection of the process of development of the productivity of labor. A striking formulation of this idea was given by Sombart in his well-known article dedicated to Volume III of Capital. "Value is a specific historical form in which is expressed the productive power of social labor, which governs, in the last analysis, all economic phenomena."[217] However, Sombart was mistaken in seeing in the theory of socially-necessary labor the entire content of Marx's theory of value. The theory of socially-necessary labor encompasses only the quantitative, not the qualitative aspect of value. "The fact that the quantity of labor contained in commodities is a quantity socially-necessary for the production of commodities, and thus labor-time is necessary labor-time - this definition refers only to the magnitude of value" (Theorien uber den Mehrwert, III, pp. 160-161). Sombart restricted himself to

---

[217] Werner Sombart, "Zur Kritik des Oekonomischen Systems von Marx," Braun's Archiv fur soziale Gesetzgebung u. Statistik, 1894, Vol. VII, p. 577.

the aspect of Marx's theory which examined the dependence of changes in the magnitude of value on the movement of the material process of production, and he did not notice the most original part of Marx's theory, namely the theory of the "form of value."[218]

Above it was pointed out that the different cases of determination of market-value which we examined must be strictly distinguished from cases of deviation of prices from market-values which result from excessive supply or excessive demand. If market value is determined by average values in normal conditions, then, when there is excessive demand, the market price will deviate from market-value in an upward direction, approaching the expenditures of enterprises with low productivity. The opposite will take place in the case of excess supply. If the quantity of products on the market "besmaller or greater, however, than the demand for them, there will be deviations of the market-price from the market-value" (C., III, p. 185). Marx strictly distinguished those cases when market value is determined, for example, by the expenditures in enterprises with high productivity due to the fact that the greatest quantity of commodities is produced in these enterprises, from cases when market value is normally determined by average value, but because of oversupply, the market price is higher than the market-value and is determined by expenditures in enterprises with high productivity (See C., III, pp. 182 and 185-186). In the first case the sale of goods according to labor expenditures in enterprises with high productivity signifies a normal state of affairs on the market and there is equilibrium between the given branch of production and other branches. In the second case the sale of commodities according to the

---

[218] This basic shortcoming of Sombart's interpretation was noted by S. Bulgakov in his article, "Chto takoe trudovaya tsennost" (What is Labor Value), Sborniki pravovedeniya i obshchestvennykh znanii (Essays on Jurisprudence and Social Science), 1896, Vol. VI, p. 238.

same expenditures is caused by an abnormal oversupply on the market, and unavoidably causes a contraction of production in the given branch, i.e., it signifies an absence of equilibrium among the individual branches. In the first case, commodities are sold according to their market-values. In the second case, the price of commodities deviates from market values determined by socially-necessary labor.

In this context we can see clearly the mistake which is made by those interpreters of Marx who say that even in cases of oversupply (or shortage of commodities) on the market, commodities are sold according to the socially-necessary labor expended on their production. By socially-necessary labor they not only understand labor which is necessary for the production of one exemplar of a given commodity under a given level of development of productive forces, but the entire sum of labor which society as a whole can spend on the production of a given kind of commodity. If, with a given level of development of productive forces, the society can spend 1 million working days on the production of shoes (yielding one million pairs of shoes), and if the society spent 1,250,000 days, then the 1,250,000 pairs of shoes produced represent only one million days of socially necessary labor, and one pair of shoes represents 0.8 days of labor. One pair of shoes is not sold for 10 roubles (if we assume that the labor of one day creates a value of 10 roubles) but for 8 roubles. Can we say that because of excessive production the quantity of socially-necessary labor contained in one pair of shoes changed, even though the technique for producing shoes did not change in any way? Or perhaps we should say: even though the quantity of socially-necessary labor required for the production of one pair of shoes did not change, because of the excessive supply the shoes are sold according to a market price which is below the market-value determined by the socially-necessary labor. The interpreters of Marx mentioned above answer the question in the first sense, thus establishing an "economic" concept of necessary labor, i.e., recognizing that socially-necessary labor changes not only in relation to changes in the productive power of labor, but also in relation to changes in the balance between social supply and demand. Defining the dependence of socially-necessary labor on the productive power of labor, we have answered in the second sense. It is one thing when, because of the improvement of technique, the time necessary for the production of a pair of shoes decreases from 10 to 8 hours. This means a decrease of socially-necessary labor, a fall of value, a general fall of the price of shoes, as a permanent, normal phenomenon. It is quite another thing when, due to the oversupply of shoes, one pair of shoes is sold for 8 roubles, even though 10 hours are needed for the production of shoes, as before. This is an abnormal state of affairs on the market which leads to the contraction of shoe production; it is a temporary fall of prices, and they will tend to return to the earlier level. In the first case we have a change in the conditions of production, i.e., changes in the necessary labor-time.[219] In the second case, "even though every part of the product cost only the socially necessary labor-time (here we assume that other conditions of production remain the same), in this branch an excessive quantity of social labor was spent, a quantity which is larger than that necessary on the general mass."[220]

Those who propose extending the concept of socially-necessary labor commit the following fundamental methodological errors:

1) They confuse a normal state of affairs on the market with an abnormal state, the laws of equilibrium among different branches of production with cases of breakdown of equilibrium which can only be temporary.

---

[219] Marx, Theories of Surplus Value [Russian translation by V. Zheleznov, Vol. I, p. 151; Russian translation by Plekhanov, Vol. I, pp. 184-185].

[220] Ibid.

2) By doing this they destroy the concept of socially-necessary labor which presupposes equilibrium between the given branch of production and other branches.

3) They ignore the mechanism of deviation of market prices from values, inaccurately treating the sale of goods at any price in any abnormal conditions on the market, as sale which corresponds to value. Price is confused with value.

4) They break the close relation between the concept of socially-necessary labor and the concept of the productive power of labor, thus allowing the first to change without corresponding changes of the second.

We move on to a detailed analysis of the "economic" version of socially-necessary labor in the next chapter.

Chapter 17: Value and Demand

I: Value and Demand

Proponents of the so-called "economic" concept of socially-necessary labor say: a commodity can be sold according to its value only on condition that the general quantity of produced commodities of a given kind corresponds to the volume of social need for those goods or, which is the same thing, that the quantity of labor actually expended in the given branch of industry coincides with the quantity of labor which society can spend on the production of the given type of commodities, supposing a given level of development of productive forces. However, it is obvious that this later quantity of labor depends on the volume of social need for the given products, or on the amount of demand for them. This means that the value of commodities does not only depend on the productivity of labor (which expresses that quantity of labor necessary for the production of commodities under given, average technical conditions), but also on the volume of social needs or demand. Opponents of this conception object that changes in demand which are not accompanied by changes in productivity of labor and in production technique bring about only temporary deviations of market prices from market-values, but not long-run, permanent changes in average prices, i.e., they do not bring about changes in value itself. In order to grasp this problem it is necessary to examine the effect of the mechanism of demand and supply (or competition).[221]

"In the case of supply and demand... the supply is equal to the sum of sellers, or producers, of a certain kind of commodity, and the demand equals the sum of buyers or consumers (both productive and individual) of the same kind of commodity" (C., III, p. 1931). Let us first of all dwell on demand. We must define it more accurately: demand is equal to the sum of buyers multiplied by the average quantity of commodities which each of them buys, i.e., demand equals the sum of commodities which can find buyers on the market. At first glance it seems that the volume of demand is an accurately determined quantity which depends on the volume of social need for a given product. But this is not the case. "The definite social wants are very elastic and changing. Their fixedness is only apparent. If the means of subsistence were cheaper, or money-wages higher, the laborers would buy more of them, and a greater 'social need' would arise for them" (C., III, p. 188; Rubin's italics). As we can see, the volume of demand is determined, not only by the given need of the present day, but also by the size of income or by the buyers' ability to pay, and by the prices of commodities. A peasant population's demand for cotton can be expanded: 1) by the peasant population's greater need for cotton instead of homespun linen (we leave aside the question of the economic or social causes of this change of needs); 2) by an increase of income or

---

[221] The reader may find the history of the so-called "technical" or "economic" version of socially-necessary labor in the following books: T. Grigorovichi, Die Wertlehre bei Marx und Lasalle, Wien, 1910; Karl Diehl, Sozialwissenschaftliche Besteuerungen zu David Ricardos Grundgesetzen der Volkswirkschaft und Besteuerung, Vol. I, Leipzig; F. Meiner, 1921; also see the discussion in the journal Pod znamenem marksizma (Under the Banner of Marxism) for 1922-23, particularly articles by M. Dvolaitski, A. Mendelson, V. Motylev.

purchasing power among the peasants; 3) by a fall in the price of cotton. Assuming a given structure of needs and given purchasing power (i.e., given the distribution of income in the society), the demand for a particular commodity changes in relation to changes in its price. Demand "moves in a direction opposite to prices, swelling when prices fall, and vice versa" (C., III, p. 191). "The expansion or contraction of the market depends on the price of the individual commodity and is inversely proportional to the rise or fall of this price" (Ibid., p. 108). The influence of the indicated cheapening of commodities on the expanding consumption of these commodities will be more intense if this cheapening is not transitory but long-lasting, i.e., if the cheapening is the result of a rise in the productivity of labor in the given branch and of a fall in the value of the product (C., III, p. 657).

Thus the volume of demand for a given commodity changes when the price of the commodity changes. Demand is a quantity which is determined only for a given price of commodities. The dependence of the volume of demand on changes in price has an unequal character for different commodities. Demand for subsistence goods, for example bread, salt, etc., is characterized by low elasticity, i.e., the fluctuations of the volume of consumption of these commodities, and thus of the demand for these commodities, are not as significant as the corresponding price fluctuations. If the price of bread falls to half its former amount, the consumption of bread does not increase two times, but less. This does not mean that the cheapening of bread does not increase the demand for bread. The direct consumption of bread increases to some extent. Furthermore, "a part of the grain may be consumed in the form of brandy or beer; and the increasing consumption of both of these items is by no means confined within narrow limits" (C., III, p. 657). Finally, "price reduction in wheat production may result in making wheat, instead of rye or oats, the principal article of consumption for the masses" (Ibid.), which increases the demand for wheat.

Thus even subsistence goods are subsumed by the general law according to which the volume of consumption, and thus the volume of demand for a given commodity, changes inversely to the change in its price. This dependence of demand on price is perfectly obvious if we remember the restricted character of the purchasing power of the masses of population, and in first place of wage laborers in the capitalist society. Only cheap commodities are available to the working masses. Only to the extent that certain commodities become cheaper do they enter the consumption patterns of the majority of the population and become objects of mass demand.

In the capitalist society, social need in general, and also social need equipped with buying power, or the corresponding demand, do not represent, as we have seen, a fixed, precisely-determined magnitude. The magnitude of a particular demand is determined by a given price. If we say that the demand for cloth in a given country during a year is for 240,000 arshins, then we must certainly add: "at a given price," for example 2 roubles 75 kopeks per arshin. Thus demand may be represented on a schedule which shows different quantities of demand in relation to different prices. Let us examine the following demand schedule for cloth:[222]

Prices, in Roubles (per arshin)	Demand (in arshins)
7 r. - k	30,000
6 r. - k	50,000
5 r. - k	75,000
3 r. 50 k	100,000
3 r. 25 k	120,000

---

[222] The absolute figures and the rate of increase of demand are completely arbitrary.

Prices, in Roubles (per arshin)	Demand (in arshins)
3 r. - k	150,000
2 r. 75 k	240,000
2 r. 50 k	300,000
2 r. - k	360,000
1 r. - k	450,000

This schedule can be expanded in an upward or a downward direction: upward to the point when commodities will find a small number of buyers from the wealthy classes of society; downward to the point when the need for cloth of the majority of the population is satisfied so fully that a further cheapening of cloth will not cause a further expansion of demand. Between these two extremes, an infinite number of combinations of the volume of demand and the level of prices is possible. Which of these possible combinations takes place in reality? On the basis of the demand alone we cannot see if the volume of demand for 30,000 arshins at 7 roubles per arshin will be realized with a greater probability than a volume of demand for 450,000 arshins at 1 rouble per arshin, or if a combination which lies between these two extremes is more probable. The real volume of demand is determined by the magnitude of the productivity of labor, which is expressed in the value of an arshin of cloth.

Let us turn to the conditions in which the cloth is produced. Let us assume that all cloth factories produce cloth on the basis of the same technical conditions. The productivity of labor in cloth manufacturing is at a level at which it is necessary to expend 2¾ hours of labor (including expenditures on raw materials, machines, and so on) for the production of 1 arshin of cloth. If we assume that one hour of labor creates a value equal to one rouble, then we get a market-value of 2 roubles 75 kopeks for 1 arshin. In a capitalist economy, the average price of cloth is not equal to the labor-value, but to the production price. In this case, we assume that the production price is equal to 2 roubles 75 kopeks. In our further analysis, we will generally treat market-value as equal either to labor-value or to production price. A market-value of 2 roubles 75 kopeks is a minimum below which the price of cloth cannot fall for long, since such a fall in price would cause a reduction in the production of cloth and a transfer of capital to other branches. We also assume that the value of one arshin of cloth equals 2 roubles 75 kopeks regardless of whether a smaller or a larger quantity of cloth is produced. In other words, the increased production of cloth does not change the quantity of labor or the costs of production spent on the production of one arshin of cloth. In this case the market value of 2 roubles 75 kopeks, "the minimum with which the producers will be content, is also ... the maximum"[223] above which the price cannot rise for long, since such a price increase would cause a transfer of capital from other branches, and an expansion of cloth production. Thus from an infinite quantity of possible combinations of the volume of demand and price, only one combination can exist for long, namely that combination where the market value is equal to the price, i.e., a combination which in Table 1 occupies the seventh place from the top: 2 roubles 75 kopeks-240,000 arshins. Obviously that combination is not manifested exactly, but represents the state of equilibrium, the average level, around which actual market prices and the actual volume of demand will fluctuate. The market value of 2 roubles 75 kopeks determines the volume of effective demand, 240,000 arshins, and the supply (namely the volume of production) will be attracted to this amount. The increase of production, for example, to the level of 300,000 arshins, will bring about, as can be seen in the table, a fall in price below market value, approximately to 2 roubles 50 kopeks, which is disadvantageous for the producers and forces them to decrease production. The inverse will

---

[223] John Stuart Mill, Principles of Political Economy, New York: Augustus M. Kelley, 1965, pp. 451-452.

take place in the case of a contraction of production below 240,000 arshins. Normal proportions of production or supply will equal 240,000 arshins. Thus all combinations of our schedule except one can only exist temporarily, expressing an abnormal market situation, and indicating a deviation of market price from market-value. Among all the possible combinations, only the one which corresponds to the market-value: 2 roubles 75 kopeks for 240,000 arshins, represents a state of equilibrium. The market value of 2 roubles 75 kopeks can be called an equilibrium price or normal price, and the amount of production of 240,000 arshins can be called an equilibrium amount[224] which at the same time represent the normal demand and normal supply.

Among the infinity of unstable combinations of demand, we have found only one stable combination of equilibrium which consists of the equilibrium price (value) and its corresponding equilibrium amount. The stability of this combination can be explained in terms of the stability of the production price (value), not by the stability of the equilibrium amount. The mechanism of the capitalist economy does not explain why tne volume of demand tends to be for an amount of 240,000 arshins regardless of all upward and downward fluctuations. But this mechanism does fully explain that market prices must tend toward the value (or production price) of 2 roubles 75 kopeks, in spite of all fluctuations. Thus also the volume of demand tends toward 240,000 arshins. The state of technology determines the value of the product, and value in turn determines the normal volume of demand and the corresponding normal quantity of supply, if we suppose a given level of needs and a given

---

[224] The terras "equilibrium price" and "equilibrium amount" were used by Marshall, Principles of Economics, 1910, p. 345. The adjective "normal" is used here not in the sense of something that "should be," but in the sense of an average level which corresponds to the state of equilibrium and which expresses a regularity in the movement of prices.

level of income of the population. The deviation of actual from normal supply (i.e., overproduction or underproduction) brings about a deviation of market price from value. This price deviation in turn brings about a tendency to change the actual supply in the direction of normal supply. If this whole system of fluctuations or this mechanism of demand and supply revolves around constant quantities-values-which are determined by the technique of production, then changes of these values which result from the development of productive forces bring about corresponding changes in the entire mechanism of supply and demand. A new center of gravity is created in the market mechanism. Changes in values change the volume of normal demand. If, due to the development of productive forces, the quantity of socially necessary labor needed to produce one arshin of cloth decreased from 2¾ to 2½ hours, and thus the value of one arshin of cloth fell from 2 roubles 75 kopeks to 2 roubles 50 kopeks, then the amount of normal demand and normal supply would be established at the level of 300,000 arshins (if the needs and purchasing power of the population remained unchanged). Changes in value bring about changes in demand and supply. "Hence, if supply and demand regulate the market-price, or rather, the deviations of the market-price from the market-value, then, in turn, the market-value regulates the ratio of supply to demand, or the center round which fluctuations of supply and demand cause market-prices to oscillate" (C., III, p. 181). In other words, value (or normal price) determines normal demand and normal supply. Deviations of actual demand or supply from their normal levels determine "market prices, or more precisely, deviations of market price from market-value," deviations which in turn bring about a movement towards equilibrium. Value regulates price through normal demand and normal supply. We call the equilibrium stage between supply and demand the state in which commodities are sold according to their values. And since the sale of commodities by their values corresponds to the state of equilibrium between different branches of production, we are led to the following conclusion: equilibrium between demand and supply takes place if there is equilibrium between the various branches of production. We would commit a methodological error if we would take the equilibrium between demand and supply as the starting-point for economic analysis. The equilibrium in the distribution of social labor among the different branches of production remains the starting-point, as was the case in our earlier analysis.

Although Marx's views of demand and supply which he expressed in Chapter 10 of Volume III of *Capital* (and elsewhere) are fragmentary, this does not mean that we do not find in Marx's work indications which testify to the fact that he understood the mechanism of demand and supply in the sense presented above. According to Marx, market-price will correspond to market-value on condition that sellers "bring enough commodities to the market to fill the social requirements, i.e., a quantity for which society is capable of paying the market-value" (Ibid.,). In Marx's words, "social requirements" depend on the quantity of commodities which find buyers on the market at the price which is equal to value, i.e., the quantity which we called "normal demand" or "normal supply." Elsewhere Marx speaks of "the difference between the quantity of the produced commodities and that quantity of them at which they are sold at market-value" (Ibid., p. 186), i.e., of the difference between actual and "normal demand." Thus various passages in Marx's works are explained, passages where he speaks of "usual" social requirements and the "usual" volume of demand and supply. He has in mind "normal demand" and "normal supply," which correspond to a given value and which change if the value changes. Marx said, about an English economist: "The good man does not grasp the fact that it is precisely the change in the cost of production, and thus in the value, which caused a change in the demand, in the present case, and thus in the proportion between demand and supply, and that this change in the demand may bring about a change in the supply. This would prove just the reverse of what our good thinker wants to prove. It would prove that the change in the cost of production is by no means due to the proportion of demand and supply, but rather regulates this proportion" (C., III, p. 191, footnote; Rubin's italics).

We have seen that changes in value (if the requirements and purchasing power of the population are unchanged) bring about changes in the normal volume of demand. Let us now see if there is also an inverse relation here: if a long-range change in demand brings about a change in the value of the product, when the production technique remains unchanged. We are referring to long-range steady changes in demand, and not of temporary changes which only influence market-price. Such long-range changes (for example the increase of demand for a given product) which are independent of changes in the value of products, can take place either because of an increase of purchasing power of the population, or because of increased requirements for a given product. The intensity of needs can increase because of social or natural causes (for example, long-range changes in climactic conditions may create a larger demand for winter clothing). We will treat this question in greater detail below. For now we will accept as given that the schedule of demand for cloth changed, for example, because of increased requirements for winter clothing. Changes in this schedule are expressed by the fact that now a larger number of buyers agree to pay a higher price for cloth, namely that a larger number of buyers and a larger demand correspond to each price of cloth. The schedule takes on the following form:

Prices, in Roubles (per arshin)	Demand (in arshins)
7 r. - k	50,000
6 r. - k	75,000
5 r. - k	100,000
3 r. 50 k	150,000

Prices, in Roubles (per arshin)	Demand (in arshins)
3 r. 25 k	200,000
3 r. - k	240,000
2 r. 75 k	280,000
2 r. 50 k	320,000
2 r. - k	400,000
1 r. - k	500,000

The market-price which corresponded to value in Table 1 was 2 roubles 75 kopeks, and the normal volume of demand and supply was 240,000 arshins. The change in demand shown in Table 2 directly increased the market-price of cloth to about 3 roubles for one arshin, since there were only 240,000 arshins of cloth on the market. According to our schedule, this was the quantity sought by buyers at the price of 3 roubles. All producers sell their commodities, not for 2 roubles 75 kopeks as earlier, but for 3 roubles. Since the production technique did not change (by our assumption), producers received a superprofit of 25 kopeks per arshin. This brings about an expansion of production and, perhaps, even a transfer of capital from other spheres (through expansion of credits which banks give to the cloth industry). Production will expand until it reaches the point when the equilibrium between the cloth industry and other branches of production is reestablished. This takes place when the cloth industry increases its production from 240,000 to 280,000 arshins which will be sold for the previous price of 2 roubles 75 kopeks. This price corresponds to the state of technique and the market-value. The increase or decrease of demand cannot cause a rise or fall in the value of the product if the technical conditions of production do not change, but it may cause an increase or decrease of production in one branch. However, the value of the product is determined exclusively by the level of development of the productive forces and by the technique of production. Consequently, demand does not influence the magnitude of value; rather value, combined with demand which is partly determined by value, determines the volume of production in a given branch, i.e., the distribution of productive forces. "The urgency of needs influences the distribution of productive forces in society, but the relative value of the different products is determined by the labor expended on their production."[225]

If we recognize the influence of changes in demand on the volume of production, on its expansion and contraction, do we contradict the basic concept of Marx's economic theory that the development of the economy is determined by the conditions of production, by the composition and level of development of the productive forces? Not at all. If changes in the demand for a given commodity influence the volume of its production, these changes in demand are in turn brought about by the following causes: 1) changes in the value of a given commodity, for example its cheapening as a result of the development of productive forces in a given productive branch; 2) changes in the purchasing power or the income of different social groups; this means that demand is determined by the income of the different social classes (C., III, pp. 194-5) and "is essentially subject to the mutual relationship of the different classes and their respective economic position" (Ibid., p. 181), which, in turn, changes in relation to the change in productive forces; 3) finally, changes in the intensity or urgency of needs for a given commodity. At first glance it seems that in the last case we make production dependent on consumption. However, we must ask what causes changes in the urgency of needs for a given commodity. We assume that if the price of iron plows and the purchasing power of the population remain the same and the need for plows is increased by the substitution of iron plows for

---

[225] P. Maslov, Teoriya razvitiya narodnogo khozyaistva (Theory of the Development of the National Economy), 1910, p. 238.

wooden plows in agriculture, the increasing need brings about a temporary increase in the market price of plows above their value, and as a result increases the production of plows. The increased need or demand brings about an expansion of production. However, this increase of demand was brought about by the development of productive forces, not in the given productive branch (in the production of plows) but in other branches (in agriculture). Let us take another example, which is related to consumer goods. Successful anti-alcoholic propaganda decreases the demand for alcoholic beverages; their price temporarily falls below value, and as a result the production of distilleries decreases. We have purposely chosen an example where the reduction of production is brought about by social causes of an ideological and not an economic character. It is obvious that the successes of anti-alcoholic propaganda were brought about by the economic, social, cultural and moral level of different social groups, a level which in turn changes as a result of a complex series of social conditions which surround it. These social conditions can be explained, in the last analysis, by the development of the productive activities of society. Finally, we can move from the economic and social conditions which change demand to natural phenomena which may also influence the volume of demand in some cases. Sharp and long-range changes in climactic conditions could strengthen or weaken the need for winter clothes and bring about an expansion or contraction of cloth production. Here there is no need to mention that changes of demand brought about by purely natural causes and independent of social causes are rare. But even such cases do not contradict the view of the primacy of production over consumption. This view should not be understood in the sense that production is performed automatically, in some kind of vacuum, outside of a society of living people with their various needs which are based on biological requirements (food, protection from cold, etc.). But the objects with which man satisfies his needs and the manner of satisfying these needs are determined by the development of production, and they, in turn, modify the character of the given needs and may even create new needs. "Hunger is hunger; but the hunger that is satisfied with cooked meat eaten with fork and knife is a different kind of hunger from the one that devours raw meat with the aid of hands, nails and teeth."[226] In this particular form hunger is the result of a long historical and social development. In just the same way, changes in climactic conditions bring about needs for given goods, for cloth, namely for cloth of a determined quality and manufacture, i.e., a need whose character is determined by the preceding development of society and, in the last analysis, of its productive forces. The quantitative increase of demand for cloth is different for the different social classes, and depends on their incomes. If in a given period of production, a given level of needs for cloth (a need based on biological requirements) is a fact given in advance or a prerequisite of production, then such a state of needs for cloth is in turn the result of previous social development. "By the very process of production, they [the prerequisites of production] are changed from natural to historical, and if they appear during one period as a natural prerequisite of production, they formed in other periods its historical result" (Ibid., p. 287). The character and change of a requirement for a given product, even if basically a biological requirement, is determined by the development of productive forces which may take place in the given sphere of production or in other spheres; which may take place in the present or in an earlier historical period. Marx does not deny the influence of consumption on production nor the interactions between them (Ibid., p. 292). But his aim is to find social regularity in the changes of needs, a regularity which in the last analysis can be explained in terms of the regularity of the development of productive forces.

II: Value and Proportional Distribution of Labor

---

[226] Marx, "Introduction to the Critique of Political Economy," in A Contribution to the Critique of Political Economy, Chicago: 1904, p. 279.

We have reached the conclusion that the volume of demand for a given product is determined by the value of the product, and changes when the value changes (if the needs and productive power of the population are given). The development of productive forces in a given branch changes the value of a product and thus the volume of social demand for the product. As can be seen in demand schedule No. 1, a determined volume of demand corresponds to a given value of the product. The volume of demand equals the number of units of the product which are sought at the given price. The multiplication of the value per unit of product (which is determined by the technical conditions of production) times the number of units which will be sold at the given value, expresses the social need which is able to pay for the given product.[227] This is what Marx called the "quantitatively definite social needs" for a given product (C., III, p. 635), the "amount of social want" (Ibid., p. 185), the "given quantity of social want" (Ibid., p. 188). The "definite quantity of social output in the various lines of production" (Ibid.) the "usual extension of reproduction" (Ibid.), correspond to this social need. This usual, normal volume of production is determined by "whether the labor is therefore proportionately distributed among the different spheres in keeping with these social needs, which are quantitatively circumscribed" (C., III, p. 635).

---

[227] By social need, Marx often meant the quantity of products which are sought on the market. But these terminological differences do not concern us here. Our aim is not to define given terms, but to distinguish various concepts, namely: 1) value per unit of commodity; 2) the quantity of units of a commodity which is sought at the market at a given value; 3) the multiplication of the value per unit of commodity times the number of units which are sought on the market at a given value. What is important here is to emphasize that the volume of social need for products of a given kind is not independent of the value per unit of the commodity, and presupposes that value.

Thus a given magnitude of value per unit of a commodity determines the number of commodities which find buyers, and the product of these two numbers (value times quantity) expresses the volume of social need, by which Marx always understood social need which is able to pay (C., III, pp. 180-181, p. 188, pp. 192-193). If the value of one arshin is 2 roubles 75 kopeks, the number of arshins of cloth which are sought on the market equals 240,000. The volume of social need is expressed by the following quantities: 2 roubles 75 kopeks x 240,000 = 660,000 roubles. If one rouble represents a value created by one hour of labor, then 660,000 hours of average social labor are spent in the production of cloth, given a proportional distribution of labor among the particular branches of production. This amount is not determined in advance by anyone in the capitalist society; no one checks it, and no one is concerned with maintaining it. It is established only as a result of market competition, in a process which is constantly interrupted by deviations and breakdowns, a process in which "chance and caprice have full play" (C., I, p. 355), as Marx pointed out repeatedly (C., I, p. 188). This figure expresses only the average level or the stable center around which the actual volumes of demand and supply fluctuate. The stability of this amount of social need (660,000) is explained exclusively by the fact that it represents a combination or multiplication of two figures, one of which (2 roubles 75 kopeks) is the value per unit of commodity, which is determined by the productive techniques and represents a stable center around which market prices fluctuate. The other figure, 240,000 arshins, depends on the first. The volume of social demand and social production in a given branch fluctuates around the figure 660,000 precisely because market-prices fluctuate around the value of 2 roubles 75 kopeks. The stability of a given volume of social need is the result of the stability of a given magnitude of value as the center of fluctuations of market prices.[228]

Advocates of the "economic" interpretation of socially-necessary labor have placed the entire process on its head, taking its final result, the figure of 660,000 roubles, the value of the entire mass of commodities of a given branch, as the starting-point of their analysis. They say: given a particular level of development of productive forces, society can spend 660,000 hours of labor on cloth production. These hours of labor create a value of 660,000 roubles. The value of the commodities of the given branch must therefore be equal to 660,000 roubles; it can neither be larger nor smaller. This definitely fixed quantity determines the value of a particular unit of a commodity: this figure is equal to the quotient which results from dividing 660,000 by the number of produced units. If 240,000 units of cloth are produced, then the value of one arshin is equal to 2 roubles 75 kopeks; if production increases to 264,000 arshins, then the value falls to 2 roubles 50 kopeks; however, if production falls to 220,000 arshins, then the value rises to 3 roubles. Each of these combinations (2 r. 75 k. x 240,000; 2 r. 50 k. x 264,000; 3 r. x 220,000) equals 660,000. The value of a unit of product can change (2 r. 75 k., 2 r. 50 k., or 3 r.) even if the production technique does not change. The general value of all products (660,000 roubles) has a constant and stable character. The general amount of labor which is needed in a given sphere of production given a proportional distribution of labor (660,000 hours of labor) also has a stable and constant character. In given conditions, this constant magnitude can be combined in different ways with two factors: the value per unit of commodity and the number of manufactured goods (2 r. 75 k. x 240,000 = 2 r. 50 k. x 264,000 = 3 r. x 220,000 = 660,000). In this way, the value of the commodity is not determined by the amount of labor necessary for

---

[228] Here we have in mind stability at given conditions. This does not exclude changes if these conditions change.

the production of a unit of commodity, but by the total amount of labor allocated to the given sphere of production[229] divided by the number of manufactured goods.

This summary of the argument of advocates of the so-called "economic" version of socially-necessary labor is, in our view, inadequate for the following reasons:

1) Taking the quantity of labor allocated to a given sphere of production (the result of the complex process of market competition) for the starting-point of analysis, the "economic" version imagines the capitalist society according to the pattern of an organized socialist society in which the proportional distribution of labor is calculated in advance.

2) The interpretation does not examine the question of what determines the quantity of labor which is allocated to a given sphere, a quantity which, in capitalist society, is not determined by anyone nor consciously maintained by anyone. Such analysis would show that the indicated quantity of labor is the result or the product of the value per unit times the quantity of products demanded on the market at a given price. Value is not determined by the quantity of labor in the given sphere, but rather that quantity presupposes value as a magnitude which depends on the production technique.

3) The economic interpretation does not derive the stable, constant (in given conditions) volume of labor which is allocated to a given sphere (660,000 hours of labor) from the stable value per unit of commodity (2 roubles 75 kopeks or 2⅔ hours of labor). Instead, this interpretation derives the stable character of the value of

---

[229] By this term we understand, here and below, the quantity of labor which is allocated to a given sphere of production, given a proportional distribution of labor, i.e., a state of equilibrium.

the total mass of products of a given sphere from the multiplication of two different factors (value per unit and quantity). This means that it concludes that the magnitude of value per unit of product (2 roubles 75 kopeks, 2 roubles 50 kopeks, 3 roubles) is unstable and changing. Thus it completely denies the significance of the value per unit of product as the center of gravity of the price fluctuations, and as the basic regulator of the capitalist economy.

4) The economic interpretation does not take into account the fact that among all the possible combinations which yield 660,000 with a given state of technique (and precisely with the expenditure of 2¾ hours of socially-necessary labor on the production of one arshin of cloth), only one combination is stable: the constant equilibrium combination (namely 2 r. 75 k. x 240,000 = 660,000). However, the other combinations can only be temporary, transitional combinations of disequilibrium. The economic interpretation confuses the state of equilibrium with a state of disturbed equilibrium, value with price.

Two aspects of the economic interpretation must be distinguished: first, this interpretation tries to ascertain certain facts, and secondly, it tries to explain these facts theoretically. It asserts that every change in the volume of production (if technique does not change) brings about an inversely proportional change in the market price of the given product. Due to this inverse proportionality in the changes of both quantities, the product of the multiplication of these two quantities is an unchanged, constant quantity. Thus, if the production of cloth decreases from 240,000 to 220,000 arshins, i.e., by 11/12ths, the price per arshin of cloth increases from 2 r. 75 k to 3 r., i.e., by 12/11ths. The multiplication of the number of commodities by the price per unit in both cases equals 660,000. Going on to explain this, the economic interpretation ascertains that the quantity of labor allocated in a given sphere of production (660,000 hours of labor) is a constant magnitude and determines the sum of values and the market prices of all products of the given sphere. Since this magnitude is constant, the change in the number of goods produced in the given sphere causes inversely proportional changes of value and of the market price per unit of product. The quantity of labor spent in the given sphere of production regulates the value as well as the price per unit of product.

Even if the economic interpretation correctly ascertained the fact that changes in the quantity of products are inversely proportional to changes in the price per unit of product, its theoretical explanation would still be false. The increase of the price of one arshin of cloth from 2 r. 75 k. to 3 r. in the case of a decrease of production from 240,000 to 220,000 arshins would mean a change in the market price of cloth and its deviation from value, which would remain the same if the technical conditions do not change, i.e., it would be equal to 2 r. 75 k. This way, the quantity of labor allocated to a given sphere of production would not be the regulator of the value per unit of product, but would regulate only the market price. The market price of the product at any moment would equal the indicated quantity of labor divided by the number of manufactured goods. This is the way certain spokesmen of the "technical" interpretation represent the problem; they recognize the fact of inverse proportionality between the change in quantity and the market price of a product, but they reject the explanation given by the economic interpretation.[230] There is no doubt that this interpretation, according to which the sum of market prices of products of a given sphere of production represents, despite all price fluctuations, a constant quantity determined by the quantity of labor allocated to the given sphere, is supported by some of Marx's observations.[231] Nevertheless, we think the view of the inverse proportionality between changes in the

---

[230] L. Lyubimov, Kurs politicheskoi ekonomii (Course in Political Economy), 1923, pp. 244-245.

[231] In Theories of Surplus Value.

quantity and the market price of products runs into a whole series of very serious objections:

1) This view contradicts empirical facts which show, for example, that when the number of commodities doubles, the market price does not fall to half the former price, but above or below this price, in different amounts for different products. In this context, a particularly sharp difference can be observed between subsistence goods and luxury goods, According to some calculations, the doubling of the supply of bread lowers its price four or five times.

2) The theoretical conception of the inverse proportionality between the change in the quantity and price of products has not been proved. Why should the price rise from the normal price or value of 2 r. 75 k. to 3 r. (i.e., by 12/11ths of the original price) if production is reduced from 240,000 to 220,000, i.e., by 11/12ths of the previous volume? Is it not possible that (in cloth manufacturing) the price of 3 r. may not correspond to the quantity of production of 220,000 arshins (as the theory of proportionality assumes) but to the quantity of 150,000 arshins, as is shown in our demand schedule No. 1? Where, in capitalist society, is the mechanism which makes the market price of cloth invariably equal to 660,000 roubles?

3) The last question reveals the methodological weakness of the theory we have looked into. In capitalist society, the laws of economic phenomena have similar effects as "the law of gravity" which "asserts itself when a house falls about our ears" (C., I, p. 75), i.e., as tendencies, as centers of fluctuations and of regular deviations. The theory which we are discussing transforms a tendency or a law which regulates events into an empirical fact: the sum of market prices, not only in equilibrium conditions, i.e., as the sum of market values, but in any market situation and at any time, completely coincides with the quantity of labor allocated to the given sphere. The assumption of a "pre-

established harmony" is not only disproved, but also does not correspond to the general methodological bases of Marx's theory of the capitalist economy.

The objections we have listed force us to throw out the thesis of the inverse proportionality between changes in the quantity and the market price of products, namely the thesis of the empirical stability of the sum of market prices of the products of a given sphere. Marx's statements in this context must be understood, in our view, not in the sense of an exact inverse proportionality, but in the sense of an inverse direction between changes in the quantity and market price of products. Every increase of production beyond its normal volume brings about a fall in price below value and a decrease of production causes a rise in price. Both of these factors (the quantity of products and their market prices) change in inverse directions, even though not with inverse proportionality. Because of this, the quantity of labor which is allocated to a given sphere does not only play the role of a center of equilibrium, an average level of fluctuation towards which the sum of market prices tends, but represents to some extent a mathematical average of the sums of market prices which change daily. But this character of a mathematical average in no way means that the two quantities completely coincide, and in addition does not have a particular theoretical significance. In Marx's work we generally find a more cautious formulation of the inverse changes in the quantity of products and their market prices (C., III, p. 178; Theorien über den Mehrwert, III, p. 341). We feel all the more justified in interpreting Marx in this sense because in his work we sometimes find a direct negation of the inverse proportionality between changes in the quantity of products and their prices. Marx noted that in the case of a poor crop, "the total price of the diminished supply of grain is greater than the former total price of a larger supply of grain" (Critique, p. 134). This is an expression of the known law which was cited above, according to which the decrease of production of grain to half its former amount raises the price of a pood[232] of grain to more than twice its former price, so that the total sum of prices of grain rises. In another passage, Marx rejects Ramsey's theory, according to which the fall in the value of the product to half its former value due to the improvement of production will be accompanied by an increase of production to twice its former amount: "The value (of commodities) falls, but not in proportion to an increase in their quantity. For example, the quantity may double, but the value of individual commodities may fall from 2 to 1ff, and not to 1" (Theorien über den Mehrwert, III, p. 407), as would follow according to Ramsey and according to proponents of the view we are examining. If the cheapening of commodities (due to an improvement of technique) from 2 r. to WA r. may be accompanied by a doubling of the production of that product, then inversely an abnormal doubling of production may be accompanied by a fall in price from 2 r. to 1ffr., and not to 1 r. as would be required by the thesis of inverse proportionality.

Thus we consider incorrect the view according to which the quantity of labor allocated to a given sphere of production and - to the individual products manufactured in this sphere determines the value of a unit of product (as is held by proponents of the economic interpretation) or coincides precisely with the market price of a unit of product (as is held by proponents of the economic interpretation and some proponents of the technical interpretation). The value per unit of product is determined by the quantity of labor which is socially-necessary for its production. If the level of technique is given, this represents a constant magnitude which does not change in relation to the quantity of manufactured goods. The market price depends on the quantity of goods produced and changes in the opposite direction (but is not inversely proportional) to this change in quantity. However, the market price does not completely coincide with the quotient which results from a division of the

---

[232] A unit of weight equal to about 36.11 pounds

quantity of labor allocated to the given sphere with the number of goods produced. Does this mean that we are completely ignoring the quantity of labor which is allocated to a given sphere of production (given a proportional distribution of labor)? In no way. The tendency to a proportional distribution of labor (it would be more accurate to say, a determined, stable[233] distribution of labor) between different spheres of production which depends on the general level of development of productive forces, represents a basic event of economic life which is subject to our examination. But as we have observed more than once, in a capitalist society with its anarchy of production, this tendency does not represent the starting-point of the economic process, but rather its final result. This result is not manifested precisely in empirical facts, but only serves as a center of their fluctuations and deviations. We recognize that the quantity of labor which is allocated to a given sphere of production (given a proportional distribution of labor) plays a certain role as regulator in the capitalist economy, but: 1) this is a regulator in the sense of a tendency, an equilibrium level, a center of fluctuations, and in no way in the sense of an exact expression of empirical events, namely market prices; and 2) which is even more important, this regulator belongs to an entire system of regulators and is a result of the basic regulator of this system-value-as the center of fluctuations of market prices.

    Let us take an example with simple figures. Let us assume that: a) the quantity of labor socially necessary to produce one arshin of cloth (given average technique) is

---

[233] The term "proportional" should not be understood in the sense of a rational, predetermined distribution of labor, which does not exist in a capitalist society. We are referring to a regularity, to a certain constancy and stability (despite all daily fluctuations and deviations) in the distribution of labor among individual branches, depending on the level of development of productive forces.

equal to 2 hours, or the value of one arshin equals 2 roubles; b) given this value, the quantity of cloth which can be sold on the market, and thus the normal volume of production, consists of 100 arshins of cloth. From this it follows that: c) the quantity of labor required by the given sphere of production is 2 hours x 100 = 200 hours, or the total value of the product of the given sphere equals 2 r. x 100 = 200 roubles. We are facing three regulators or three regulating magnitudes, and each of them is a center of fluctuations of determined, empirical, actual magnitudes. Let us examine the first magnitude: a_1) to the extent that it expresses the quantity of labor necessary for the production of one arshin of cloth (two hours of labor), this magnitude influences the actual expenditure of labor in different enterprises of the cloth industry. If a given group of enterprises of low productivity does not spend two but three hours of labor per arshin, it will gradually be forced out by more productive enterprises, unless it adapts to their higher level of technique. If a given group of enterprises does not spend two hours but rather 1ffl, then this group will gradually force out the more backward enterprises, and in a period of time it will decrease the socially-necessary labor to 1ffl hours. In short, the individual and the socially-necessary labor (even though they do not coincide) display a tendency toward equalization. a_2) If the same magnitude indicates the value per unit of production (2 roubles), it is the center of the fluctuations of market prices. If market price falls below 2 roubles, production falls and there is a transfer of capital out of the given sphere. If prices rise above values, the opposite takes place. Value and market-price do not coincide, but rather the first is the regulator, the center of fluctuation, of the second.

Let us now move on to the second regulating magnitude, designated by the letter b: the normal volume of production, 100 arshins, is the center of fluctuations of the actual volume of production in the given sphere. If more than 100 arshins are produced, then the price falls below the value of 2 roubles per arshin and a reduction of production begins. The opposite takes place in the case of underproduction. As we can see, the second regulator (b) depends on the first (a₂), not only in the sense that the magnitude of value determines the volume of production (given the structure of needs and the purchasing power of the population) but also in the sense that the distortion of the volume of production (overproduction or underproduction) are corrected by the deviation of market prices from value. The normal volume of production, 100 arshins (b), is the center of fluctuations of the actual volume of production precisely because the value of 2 roubles (a₂) is the center of fluctuations of market prices.

Finally, we turn to the third regulating magnitude, c, which represents a product of the multiplication of the first two, namely 200 = 2 x 100, or c = ab. However, as we have seen, a can have two meanings: a, represents the quantity of labor expended on the production of one arshin of cloth (2 hours), a₂ represents the value of one arshin (2 roubles). If we take a₁b = 2 hours of labor x 100 = 200 hours of labor, then we get the quantity of labor which is allocated to a given sphere of production (given proportional distribution of labor), or the center of fluctuations of actual labor expenditures in the given sphere. If we take a₂b = 2 roubles x 100 = 200 roubles, then we get the sum of values of the products of the given sphere, or the center of fluctuations of the sums of market values of the products of the given sphere. Thus we do not in any way deny that the third magnitude, c = 200, also plays the role of regulator, of center of fluctuations. However, we derive its role from the regulative role of its components, a and b. As we can see, c = ab, and the regulative role of c is the result of the regulative roles of a and b. 200 hours of labor is the center of fluctuations of the quantity of labor expended in the given sphere precisely because 2 hours of labor indicates the average expenditure of labor per unit of product, and 100 arshins is the center of fluctuations of the volume of production. In just the same way, 200 roubles is the center of fluctuations of the sum of market prices of the given sphere precisely because 2 roubles, or value, is the center of fluctuations of market prices per unit of product, and 100 arshins is the center of fluctuations of the volume of production. All three regulative magnitudes, a, b, and c, represent a unified regulative system in which c is the resultant of a and b, and b, in turn, changes in relation to changes in a. The last magnitude (a), i.e., the quantity of labor socially necessary for the production of a unit of product (2 hours of labor), or the value of a unit of product (2 roubles) is the basic regulating magnitude of the entire system of equilibrium of the capitalist economy.

We have seen that c = ab. This means that c may change in relation to a change in a or to a change in b. This means that the quantity of labor expended in a given sphere diverges from the state of equilibrium (or from a proportional distribution of labor) either because the quantity of labor per unit of production is larger or smaller than what is socially necessary, given the normal quantity of manufactured goods, or because the quantity of units produced is too large or too small compared to the normal quantity of production, given the normal expenditure of labor per unit of production. In the first case 100 arshins are produced, but in technical conditions which may, for example, be below the average level, with an expenditure of three hours of labor per arshin. In the second case, the expenditure of labor per arshin is equal to the normal magnitude, 2 hours of labor, but 150 arshins are produced. In both cases the total expenditure of labor in the given sphere of production consists of 300 hours instead of the normal 200 hours. On this basis, proponents of the economic interpretation consider both cases equal. They assert that overproduction is equivalent to an excessive expenditure of labor per unit of production. This assertion is explained by the fact that all their attention is concentrated exclusively on the derived regulating magnitude c. From this point of view, in both cases there is excessive expenditure of labor in the given sphere: 300 hours of labor instead of 200. But if we do not remain on this derived magnitude, but move on to its components, the basic regulating magnitudes, then the picture changes. In the first case the cause of the divergence lies in the field of a (the expenditure of labor per unit of output), in the second case, in the field of b (the amount of produced goods). In the first case, equilibrium among enterprises with different levels of productivity within a given sphere, breaks down. In the second case, the equilibrium between the quantity of production in the given sphere and in other spheres, i.e., the equilibrium between different spheres of production, breaks down. This is why in the first case equilibrium will be established by the redistribution of productive forces from technically backward enterprises to more productive enterprises within the given sphere; in the second case, the equilibrium will be established by the redistribution of productive forces among different spheres of production. To confuse the two cases would mean to sacrifice the interests of scientific analysis of economic events for a superficial analogy and, as Marx often said, for the sake of "forced abstractions," i.e., the desire to squeeze phenomena of a different economic nature into the same concept of socially-necessary labor.

Thus the basic error of the "economic interpretation" does not lie in the fact that it fails to recognize the regulating role of the quantity of labor which is allocated to a given sphere of production (given a proportional distribution of labor) but in the fact that it: 1) wrongly interprets the role of a regulator in a capitalist economy, transforming it from a level of equilibrium, a center of fluctuations, into a reflection of empirical fact, and 2) it assigns to this regulator an independent and fundamental character, whereas it belongs to an entire system of regulators and actually has a derived character. Value cannot be derived from the quantity of labor allocated to a given sphere, because the quantity of labor changes in relation to changes in value which reflect the development of the productivity of labor. In spite of claims of its proponents, the "economic interpretation" does not complement the "technical" interpretation, but rather discards it: asserting that value changes in relation to the number of produced goods (given constant technique), it rejects the concept of value as a magnitude which depends on the productivity of labor. On the other hand, the "technical interpretation" is able to explain completely the phenomena of the proportional distribution of labor in society and the regulating role of the quantity of labor allocated to a given sphere of production, i.e., to explain those phenomena which the economic interpretation supposedly solved, according to its proponents.

III: Value and the Volume of Production

Above, in our schedules of demand and supply, we assumed that the expenditures of labor necessary for the production of a unit of output remained constant when the volume of output increased. Now we introduce a new assumption, namely that a new, additional quantity of products is produced under worse conditions than before. We can remember Ricardo's theory of differential rent. According to this theory, the increase of demand for grain due to the increase in population makes it necessary to farm less fertile land or plots of land which are further away from the market. Thus the quantity of labor necessary for the production of a pood of grain in the least favorable conditions (or for the transportation of grain) increases. And since precisely this quantity of labor determines the value of the entire mass of grain produced, the value of grain rises. The same phenomenon can be observed in mining, when there is a movement from rich mines to less abundant mines. The increase of production is accompanied by an increase in the value per unit of output, whereas earlier we treated the value of a unit of output as independent of the amount of production. An analogous situation can be found in branches of manufacturing where production takes place in enterprises with different levels of productivity. We assume that enterprises with the highest productivity, which could supply goods at the lowest price, cannot produce the quantity of goods which would be demanded on the market at such a low price. In view of the fact that the production must also take place in enterprises of average and low productivity, the market value of commodities is determined by the value of commodities produced in average or less favorable conditions (see the chapter on socially-necessary labor). Here too the increase of production means an increase of value and thus an increase in the price per unit of output. We present the following schedule of supply:

Volume of Production (in arshins)	Price of Production (or value in roubles)
100,000	2 r. 75 k
150,000	3 r. - k
200,000	3 r. 25 k

We assume that if the price level is below 2 r. 75 k., producers will not produce at all and will interrupt production (with the exception, perhaps, of insignificant groups of producers who are not taken into account). To the extent that the price is increased to the level of 3 r. 25 k., production will attract enterprises with average and low productivity. However, a price above 3 r. 25 k. would give such a high profit to entrepreneurs that we can consider the level of production at this price unlimited compared to the limited demand. Thus prices may fluctuate from 2 r. 75 k. to 3 r. 25 k., and the volume of production from 100,000 to 200,000 arshins. However, at what level will the price and the volume of production be established?

We return to demand schedule No. 1 and compare it to the supply schedule. We can see that the price is established at the level of 3 roubles and the volume of production at 150,000 arshins. Equilibrium between demand and supply is established and price coincides with labor-value (or with the price of production), which is determined by the labor expenditures in enterprises of average productivity. Now we assume (as we did above) that, because of this or that cause (because of the increase in the purchasing power of the population or the intensification of the urgency of needs), the demand for cloth increases and is expressed by demand schedule No. 2. The price of 3 roubles cannot be maintained, because at this price the supply consists of 150,000 arshins and the demand of 240,000. The price will rise because of this excess of demand until it reaches the level of 3 r. 25 k. At this price, demand as well as supply equal 200,000 arshins and are in a state of equilibrium. At the same time the new price of 3 r. 25 k. coincides with a new increased value (or price of production) which, due to the expansion of production from 150,000 to 200,000 arshins, is now regulated by the labor expenditures in enterprises with low productivity of labor.

If we said above that the increase in demand influences the volume of production, not influencing the magnitude of value (earlier the increase of production from 240,000 to 280,000 arshins took place at the same value of 2 r. 75 k.), in this case the increase in demand brings about an increase of production from 150,000 to 200,000 arshins, and is accompanied by an increase of value from 3 r. to 3 r. 25 k. Demand somehow determines value.

This conclusion is of decisive significance for representatives of the Anglo-American and mathematical schools in political economy, including Marshall.[234] Some of these economists hold that Ricardo subverted his own theory of labor-value with his theory of differential rent, and that he opened the door for a theory of demand and

---

[234] Information on these schools in the Russian language may be found in the following books: I. Blyumin, Subyektivnaya shkola v politicheskoi ekonomii (The Subjective School in Political Economy), 1928; N. Shaposhnikov, Teoriya tsennosti i raspredeleniya (Theory of Value and Distribution), 1912; L. Yurovskii, Ocherki po teorii tseny (Essays on the Theory of Price), Saratov, 1919; A. Bilimovich, K voprosu o rastsenke khozyaistvennykh blag (On the Question of the Evaluation of Economic Goods), Kiev, 1914.

supply which he rejected, and in the last analysis for a theory which defines the magnitude of value in terms of the magnitude of needs. These economists use the following argument. Value is determined by the labor expenditures on the worse plots of land, or in the least favorable conditions. This means that value increases with the extension of production to worse land or, in general, to less productive enterprises, i.e., to the extent that production increases. And since the increase in production is brought about by an increase in demand, then value does not regulate supply and demand, as Ricardo and Marx thought, but value itself is determined by demand and supply.

Proponents of this argument forget a very important circumstance. In the example we discussed, changes in the volume of production at the same time mean changes in the technical conditions of production in the same branch. Let us examine three examples.

In the first case, production takes place only in better enterprises which supply the market with 100,000 arshins at the price of 2 r. 75 k. In the second case (from which we started in our example), production takes place in the better and average enterprises, which together produce 150,000 arshins at the price of 3 roubles. In the third case, production takes place in the better, average and worse enterprises and reaches a level of 200,000 arshins at the price of 3 r. 25 k. In all three cases, which correspond to our schedule No. 3, not only the volumes of production are different, but also the technical conditions of production in the given branch. The value has changed precisely because the conditions of production changed in the given branch. From this example, we should not draw the conclusion that changes of value are determined by changes in demand and not by changes in technical conditions of production. Inversely, the conclusion can only be that changes in demand cannot influence the magnitude of value in any way except by changing the technical conditions of production in the given branch.

Thus the basic proposition of Marx's theory that changes in value are determined exclusively by changes in technical conditions remains valid. Demand cannot influence value directly, but only indirectly, namely by changing the volume of production and thus its technical

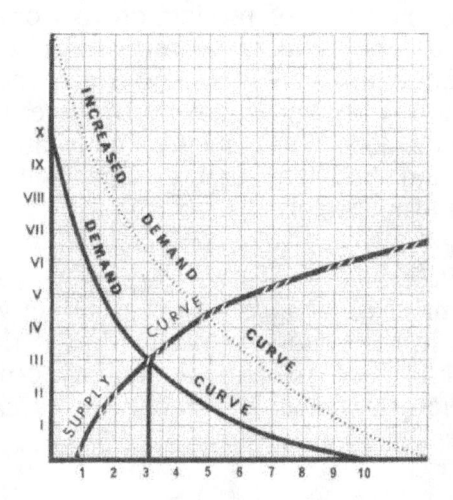

conditions. Does this indirect influence of demand on value contradict Marx's theory? In no way. Marx's theory defines the causal relationship between changes in value and the development of productive forces. But the development of productive forces, in turn, is subject to the influence of a whole series of social, political and even cultural conditions (for example, the influence of literacy and technical education on the productivity of labor). Has Marxism ever negated that tariff policy or enclosures influence the development of productive forces? These factors may, indirectly even lead to a change in the value of products. The prohibition of imports of cheap foreign raw materials and the necessity to produce them inside the country with large expenditures of labor raises the value of the product processed from these raw materials. Enclosures which pushed peasants to worse and more distant lands led to an increase in the price of grain. Does this mean that changes in value are caused by enclosures or tariff policies and not by changes in the technical conditions of production? On the contrary, from this we conclude that various economic and social conditions, which include changes in demand, may affect value, not side by side with the technical conditions of production, but only through changes in the technical conditions of production. Thus the technique of production remains the only factor which determines value. Marx considered such an indirect effect of demand on value (through changes in the technical conditions of production) entirely possible. In one passage Marx referred to the transfer from better to worse conditions of production which we examined. "In some lines of production it may also bring about a rise in the market-value itself for a shorter or longer period, with a portion of the desired products having to be produced under worse conditions during this period" (C., III, pp. 190-191).[235] On the other hand, the fall of demand can also influence the magnitude of the value of a product. "For instance, if the demand, and consequently the market-price, fall, capital may be withdrawn, thus causing supply to shrink. It may also be that the market-value itself shrinks and balances with the market-price as a result of inventions which reduce the necessary labor-time" (Ibid., p. 190). "In this case, the price of commodities would have changed their value, because of the effect on supply, on the costs of

---

[235] In the original, Marx said: "only market value increases for a longer or shorter period of time" (Kapital, III, 1894, Part 1, p. 170). The case which Marx mentions, where the increase of demand due to a transfer to worse conditions of production increases the value per unit of product, was known to Ricardo (Principles of Political Economy and Taxation, Volume I of Piero Sraffa, The Works and Correspondence of David Ricardo, London: Cambridge University Press, 1962, p. 93). It is possible to find numerous analogous examples in Capital and in Theorien über den Mehrwert, in chapters devoted to differential rent.

production."[236] it is known that the introduction of new technical methods of production which lower the value of products frequently takes place in conditions of crisis and decreasing sales. No one would say that in these cases the fall in value is due to the fall in demand and not the improvement of the technical conditions of production. And we can hardly say, from the example cited above, that the increase of value is the result of the increase of demand, and not of the worsening of the average technical conditions of production in the given branch.

Let us examine the same question from another angle. Proponents of the theory of demand and supply assert that only competition, or the point of intersection of the demand and supply curves, determines the level of prices. Proponents of the labor theory of value assert that the point of intersection and equilibrium of supply and demand does not change at random, but fluctuates around a given level which is determined by the technical conditions of production. Let us examine this question with the example we have been using.

The demand schedule shows numerous possible combinations of the volume of demand and the price; it does not give us any indication of the combinations which may take place in reality. No combination has greater chances than the others. But as soon as we turn to the supply schedule, we can say with confidence: the technical structure of the given branch of production and the level of productivity of labor in it are limited in advance to the extremities of the value fluctuations between 2 r. 75 k. and 3 r. 25 k. No matter what the volume of demand, the fall of prices below 2 r. 75 k. makes further production disadvantageous and impossible, given the technical conditions. However, a price rise above 3 r. 25 k. causes an immense increase of supply and an opposite movement of prices. This means that only three combinations of supply, determined by the technical

---

[236] Marx, Teorii pribavochnoi stoimosti (Theories of Surplus Value), Vol. II, Petersburg, 1923, p. 132.

conditions of the given branch, confront the infinity of possible demands. The maximum and minimum possible changes of value are established in advance. Our main task in analyzing supply and demand consists of finding "the regulating limits or limiting magnitudes" (C., HI, p. 363).

So far we only know the limits of the changes of value, but we do not yet know if value will equal 2 r. 75 k., 3 r., or 3 r. 25 k. Changes in the volume of production (100,000 arshins, 150,000 arshins or 200,000 arshins) and the extension of production to worse enterprises changes the average magnitude of socially-necessary labor per unit of output, i.e., changes the value (or price of production). These changes are explained by the technical conditions of a given branch.

Among the three possible levels of value, the one that takes place in reality is the level at which the volume of supply equals the volume of demand (in demand schedule No. 1, that value is 3 roubles, and in schedule no 2, 3 r. 25 k.). In both cases the value completely corresponds to the technical conditions of production. In the first case the production of 150,000 arshins takes place in better enterprises. In the second case, in order to produce 200,000 arshins, the worse enterprises must also produce. This increases the average expenditures of socially-necessary labor, and thus the value. Consequently we reach our previous conclusion that demand may indirectly influence only the volume of production. But since a change in the volume of production is equivalent to a change in the average technical conditions of production (given the technical properties of the branch), this leads to the increase of value. In every given case the limits of possible changes of value and the magnitude of value established in reality (obviously as the center of fluctuations of market prices) are completely determined by the technical conditions of production. Without reference to whole series of complicating conditions and round-about methods, our analysis (whose goal is to discover regularities in the seeming chaos of the movement of prices and in competition, in what are at first glance accidental relations of demand and supply) has led us directly to the level of development of productive forces which, in the commodity-capitalist economy, is reflected by the specific social form of value and by changes in the magnitude of value.[237]

IV: Demand and Supply Equation

After the preceding analysis, it will not be hard for us to determine value according to the well-known "demand and supply equation" in which the mathematical school formulates its theory of price. This school revives an old theory of supply and demand, eliminating its internal logical contradictions on a new methodological basis. If the earlier theory held that price is determined by the interrelations between demand and supply, the modern mathematical school rigorously understands that the volume of demand and supply depend on price. This way the proposition that there is a causal dependence of price on demand and supply becomes a vicious circle. The labor theory of value emerges from this vicious circle; it recognizes that even if price is determined by supply and demand, the law of value in turn regulates supply. Supply changes in relation to the development of productive

---

[237] The fact that costs of production increase together with an increase in the volume of production (calculated per unit of output) was placed at the foundation of Ricardo's theory of rent and was emphasized by representatives of the Anglo-American and mathematical schools. We have felt it necessary to devote special attention to this theory because of the theoretical interest which this question has for the theory of value. In practice, the given question has a great deal of significance for agriculture and for the extractive industry. However, in the context of manufacturing we more often meet cases of decreases of costs of production when the volume of production increases (calculated per unit of output).

forces and to changes in the quantity of socially-necessary labor. The mathematical school has found a different exit from this vicious circle: this school renounced the very question of the causal dependence between the phenomena of price and restricted itself to a mathematical formulation of the functional dependence between price, on the one hand, and the volume of demand and supply, on the other. This theory does not ask why prices change, but only shows how simultaneous changes in price and demand (or supply) take place. The theory illustrates this functional dependence among the phenomena in the following diagram[238]:

The segments along the horizontal axis, 1, 2, 3, etc. (the horizontal coordinates) show the price per unit of output: 1 rouble, 2 v., 3 r., etc. The segments along the vertical axis (the vertical coordinates) show the quantity of demand or supply, for example, / means 100,000 units, // means 200,000, etc. The demand curve slopes downward; it starts very high at low prices; if the price is near zero, demand is greater than X, i.e. 1,000,000. If the price is 10 roubles demand falls to zero. For every price there is a corresponding volume of demand. To know the volume of demand, for example when the price is 2 roubles, we must extend a vertical line to the point where it cuts the demand curve. The ordinate will be approximately IV i.e., at the price of 2 roubles the demand will be 400,000. The supply curve moves in an inverse sense from the demand curve. It increases if prices increase. The point of intersection of the demand and supply curves determines the price of commodities. If we extend a vertical projection from this point, we see that the point is approximately at 3, i.e., the price equals 3. The

---

[238] In the Russian language, this diagram may be found in the following books: Charles Gide, Osnovy politicheskoi ekonomii (Principles of Political Economy), 1916, p. 233; and his Istoryiya ekonomicheskikh uchenii (History of Economic Doctrines), 1918, p. 413; N Shaposhnikov, Teoriya tsennosti i raspredeleniya (Theory of Value and Distribution), 1910, Chapter 1.

amount of the vertical coordinate equals approximately HI, i.e., at the price of 3 roubles the demand and supply equal approximately 300,000, i.e., demand and supply balance each other; they are in equilibrium. This is the equalization of supply and demand which takes place in the given case of a price of 3 roubles. For any other price, equilibirum is impossible. If the price is below 3 roubles, demand will be greater than supply; if the price is above 3 roubles, the supply will exceed the demand.

From the diagram it follows that the price is determined exclusively by the point of intersection of the demand and supply curves. Since this point of intersection moves with every shift of one of the curves, for example the demand curve, then it seems at first glance that the change in demand changes the price, even if there are no changes in the conditions of production. For example, in the case of an increase in demand (the dotted curve of increased demand on the diagram) the demand curve will cross the same supply curve at a different point, a point which corresponds to the quantity 5. This means that in the case of the indicated increase of demand, the equilibrium between demand and supply will take place at a price of 5 roubles. It seems as if the price is not determined by the conditions of production, but exclusively by the demand and supply curves. The change in demand all alone changes the price which is identified with value.

Such a conclusion is the result of an erroneous construction of the supply curve. This curve is constructed according to the pattern of the demand curve, but in the opposite direction, starting with the lowest price. Actually, the mathematical economists grasp the fact that if the price is near zero, there is no supply of goods. This is why they start the supply curve, not at zero, but at a price which approaches 1, on our diagram close to 2/3, i.e., at 66 2/3kopeks. If a price is 66 2/3 then the supply approaches the midpoint towards I, i.e., it is equal to 50,000; if the price is 3 roubles, supply equals

777, i.e., 300,000. At the price of 10 roubles, the curve increases to approximately VI - VII, i.e., it is approximately equal to 650,000 units. Such a supply curve is possible if we are dealing with a market situation at a given moment. If we assume that the normal price is 3 roubles and the normal volume of supply is 300,000, it is possible that if prices fall catastrophically to 66 2/3 kopeks, only a small number of producers will really be forced to sell goods at such a low price, namely 50,000 units at this price. On the other hand, an unusual increase of prices to the level of 10 roubles forces producers to deliver to the market all stocks and inventories and to expand production immediately, if this is possible. It may happen, though it is not very likely, that in this way they will succeed in delivering to the market 650,000 units of goods. But from the accidental price of one day we pass to the permanent, stable, average price which determines the constant, average, normal volume of demand and supply. If we want to find a functional connection between the average level of prices and the average volume of demand and supply on the diagram, we will immediately notice the erroneous construction of the supply curve. If an average volume of supply of 300,000 corresponds to an average price of 3 roubles, then the fall of price to 66 2/3 kopeks, given the previous technique of production, will not result 'in a reduction of average supply to 50,000, but in a total stoppage of supply and a transfer of capital from the given branch to other branches. On the other hand, if the average price (given constant conditions of production) increased from 3 roubles to 10 roubles, this would cause a continuous transfer of capital from other branches, and an increase of the average volume of supply would not remain at 650,000, but would increase far beyond this magnitude. Theoretically, supply would increase until this branch completely devoured all the other branches of production. In practice, the quantity supplied would be larger than any volume of demand, and we could recognize it as an unlimited magnitude. As we can see, some instances of equilibrium between demand and supply, represented in our diagram, unavoidably lead to a destruction of equilibrium among the various branches of production, i.e., to the transfer of productive forces from one branch to another. Since such a transfer changes the volume of supply, this also leads to a destruction of equilibrium between demand and supply. Consequently, the diagram only gives us a picture of a momentary state of the market but does not show us a long-range, stable equilibrium between demand and supply, which may be theoretically understood only as the result of equilibrium between the various branches of production. From the standpoint of equilibrium in the distribution of social labor among the various branches of production, the form of the supply curve must be completely different from that shown in Diagram 1.

First of all let us assume (as we did at the beginning of this chapter) that the price of production (or value) per unit of output is a given magnitude (for example 3 roubles) independent of the volume of production, if technical conditions are constant. This means that, at the price of 3 roubles, equilibrium is established among the given branches of production and other branches, and the transfer of capital from one branch to another stops. From this it follows that the fall of price below 3 roubles will bring about a transfer of capital from the given sphere and a tendency to a total stoppage of supply of the given commodity. However, the increase of price above 3 roubles will bring about a transfer of capital from other spheres and a tendency to an unlimited increase of production (we may point out that we are, as earlier, not talking of a temporary increase or decrease of price, but of a constant, long-range level of prices, and of an average, long-range volume of supply and demand). Thus if the price is below 3 roubles, supply will stop altogether, and if the price is above 3 roubles, supply may be taken as unlimited in relation to the demand. We do not present any supply curve. The equilibrium between demand and supply can only be established if the level of prices coincides with value (3 roubles). The magnitude of the value (3 roubles) determines the volume of effective demand for a given commodity and the corresponding volume of supply (300,000 units of output). The diagram has the following form:

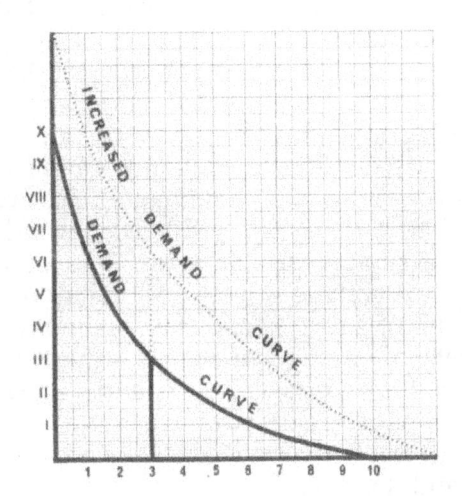

As we can see from this diagram, the technical conditions of production (or socially-necessary labor in a technical sense) determine value, or the center around which average prices fluctuate (in the capitalist economy such a center will not be labor value, but rather price of production). The vertical coordinate can be established only in relation to the quantity 3, which signifies a value of 3 roubles. However, the demand curve determines only the point which is expressed by the vertical coordinate, namely the volume of effective demand and the volume of production which, in the diagram, approaches the quantity III, i.e., 300,000. A shift of the demand curve, for example an increase of demand for one or another reason, can only increase the volume of supply (in the given example to VI-i.e.. to 600,000-as can be seen from the dotted curve in the diagram) but does not increase the average price which remains, as before, 3 roubles. This price is determined exclusively by the productivity of labor or by the technical conditions of production.

Let us now introduce (as we did earlier) an additional condition. Let us assume that in the given sphere, enterprises of higher productivity can supply to the market only a limited quantity of goods; the rest of the goods have to be produced in enterprises of average and low productivity. If the price of 2 r. 50 k. is the production price (or value) in the better enterprises, the volume of supply will be 200,000 units; if the price is 3 roubles, the supply is 300,000, and at 3 r. 50 k., 400,000. If the average price is below 2 r. 50 k., a tendency to complete stoppage of production will become dominant. If the average price is higher than 3 r. 50 k., a tendency toward unlimited expansion of supply will dominate. Because of this, the fluctuations of average prices are limited in advance by the minimum of 2 r. 50 k. and the maximum of 3 r. 50 k. Three levels of average prices or values are possible within these limits: 2 r. 50 k., 3 r., and 3 r. 50 k. Each of them corresponds to a determined volume of production (200,000, 300,000 and 400,000) and thus to a given level of productive technique. The diagram then has the following form:

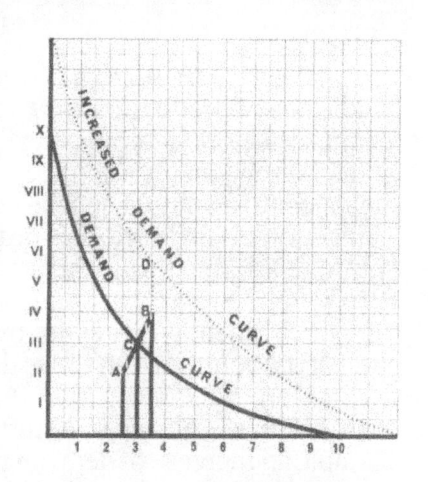

If in Diagram 2, the supply of goods (on the part of producers) took place at a price of 3 roubles, now the supply takes place if the price only reaches 2 r. 50 k. In this case the supply equals II, i.e., 200,000 (the quantity on the ordinate, which is a projection from the letter A). If the price is 3 roubles, supply will increase to III, i.e., to 300,000; on the diagram this corresponds to the letter C. If the price is 3 r. 50 k., supply equals IV, i.e., 400,000 (corresponds to the vertical coordinate of point B). Curve ACB is the supply curve. The point of intersection of this supply curve with the demand curve (at point C) determines the actual volume of supply and the corresponding value or center of price fluctuations. In the given example, the price is established at 3 roubles, and the volume of production equals III, i.e., 300,000. Production will take place in the better and average enterprises. In such technical conditions of production, value and average price are equal to 3 roubles. If the average demand curve would shift downward slightly because of a long-range decrease of demand, it could meet the supply curve at point A; in this case the average volume of supply would be equal to 200,000 units and production would take place only in the better enterprises; value would fall to 2 r. 50 k. If the demand curve would shift upward slightly because of an increase in demand, it could meet the supply curve at point B; the average volume of supply would equal IV, i.e., 400,000, and value, 3 r. 50 k. The interrelation between the demand and supply curves which was formulated by the mathematical school, and which this school represented in Diagram 1, exists in reality (if we are dealing with average price and average volume of demand and supply) only within the narrow limits of price fluctuations between 2 r. 50 k. and 3 r. 50 k., i.e., limits which are entirely established by the production techniques in enterprises with different levels of productivity and by the quantitative interrelations among these enterprises, i.e., by the average level of technique of a given branch. Only in these narrow limits does supply have the form of a rising curve. Every point of this curve then shows the quantity of production and its corresponding price. Only within these narrow limits do changes in the demand curve which shift the point of intersection of the demand curve with the supply curve (points A, C, or B) change the volume of production. Such changes influence the average technical conditions in which the total mass of products are produced and thus influence the magnitude of value (2 r. 50 k., 3 r., 3 r. 50 k.). But such an influence of demand on value takes place only through changes in the technical conditions of production and is restricted to narrow limits depending on the technical structure of the given branch. Since only demand can go beyond these limits, its direct influence (through production technique) on value ceases. Let us assume, for example, that demand increases, as is shown by the dotted curve on the diagram. In diagram No. 1, which was designed by the mathematical economists, such an increase of demand leads to the intersection of the demand curve with the supply curve at a point which corresponds to the price of 5 roubles. It seems that the increase of demand directly increases the value of the commodity. However, on diagram No. 3, the average price cannot be greater than 3 r. 50 k., since such an increase would bring about a tendency to an unlimited increase of supply, namely supply would outstrip demand. The supply curve does not extend beyond B. Thus the increasing demand curve does not intersect the supply curve; it intersects with the projection which goes through point B and which corresponds to the maximum average price of 3 r. 50 k. This means that if the volume of production increases to VII, i.e., to 700,000, because of increased demand, the value and average price will remain, as before, 3 r. 50 k. (more precisely, the price will be slightly greater than 3 r. 50 k., and will tend towards this value from above, since by our assumption, if the price is 3 r. 50 k. the quantity of production is only 400,000). Thus the differences between Diagram 1 and Diagram 3 consist of the following:

In Diagram 1, we have two curves (demand and supply) which are not regulated by the conditions of production. Their intersection may take place at any point, depending only on the direction of these curves; consequently, the point of intersection may be established by competition at any level. Every change of demand directly changes the price, which is considered identical with value.

In Diagram 3, supply does not, in advance, have the form of a curve which allows an infinite number of points of intersection, but has the form of a short line segment ACB, which is determined by technical conditions of production. Competition is regulated in advance by the conditions of production. These conditions establish the limits of changes of value or average prices. On the other hand, value, which is in every case established within these limits, corresponds exactly to the conditions of production which accompany the given volume of production. Demand cannot influence value directly and without limit but only indirectly, through changes in the technical conditions of production and within narrow limits which are also determined by these technical conditions. Consequently, the basic premise of Marx's theory remains in force: value and its changes are determined exclusively by the level and development of the productivity of labor, or by the quantity of social labor necessary for the production of a unit of output, given average technical conditions.

Chapter 18: Value and Production Price

After finishing his examination of the production relations among commodity producers (theory of value) and between capitalists and workers (theory of capital), Marx moves on to the analysis of production relations among industrial capitalists in the different branches of production (the theory of production price) in the third volume of Capital. The competition of capitals among different spheres of production leads to the formation of a general, average profit rate and to the sale of commodities at production prices which are equal to costs of production plus average profit and, quantitatively, they do not coincide with the labor-value of commodities. The magnitude of the costs of production and average profit as well as their changes are explained by changes in the productivity of labor and in the labor-value of commodities; this means that the laws of changes in production prices can be understood only if we start with the law of labor value. On the other hand, the average profit rate and the production price, which are regulators of the distribution of capital among various branches of production, indirectly (through the distribution of capitals) regulate the distribution of social labor among the different spheres of production. The capitalist economy is a system of distributed capitals which are in a dynamic equilibrium, but this economy does not cease to be a system of distributed labor which is in a dynamic equilibrium, as is true of any economy based on a division of labor. It is only necessary to see under the visible process of distribution of capital the invisible process of the distribution of social labor. Marx succeeded in showing clearly the relation between these two processes by explaining the concept which serves as the connecting link between them, namely the concept of the organic composition of capital. If we know the distribution of a given capital to constant and variable capital, and the rate of surplus value, we can easily determine the quantity of labor which this capital brings into action, and we can move from the distribution of capital to the distribution of labor.

Thus, if in the third volume of Capital Marx gives the theory of production price as the regulator of the distribution of capital, then this theory is linked to the theory of value in two ways: on one hand, production price is derived from labor-value; on the other hand, the distribution of capital leads to the distribution of social labor. Instead of the schema of a simple commodity economy: productivity of labor-abstract labor-value-distribution of social labor, for a capitalist economy we get a more complex schema: productivity of labor-abstract labor-value-production price-distribution of capital-distribution of social labor. Marx's theory of production price does not contradict the theory of labor-value. It is based on the labor theory of value and includes this theory as one of its components. This is clear if we remember that the labor theory of value analyzes only one type of production relation among people (among commodity producers). However, the theory of production price assumes the existence of all three basic types of production relations among people in the capitalist society (relations among commodity producers, relations among capitalists and workers, relations among individual groups of industrial capitalists). If we limit the capitalist economy to these three types of production relations, then this economy becomes similar to a three-dimensional space in which it is possible to determine a position only in terms of three dimensions or three planes. Since a three-dimensional space cannot be reduced to one plane, so the theory of the capitalist economy cannot be reduced to one theory, the labor theory of value. Just as in three-dimensional space it is necessary to determined the distance of each point from each of three planes, so the theory of the capitalist economy presupposes the theory of production relations among commodity producers, i.e., the labor theory of value. Critics of Marx's theory who see a contradiction between the labor theory of value and the theory of production price do not grasp Marx's method. This method consists of a consistent analysis of various types of production relations among people or, so to speak, of various social dimensions.

I: Distribution and Equilibrium of Capital

As we have seen, Marx analyzed the changes in the value of commodities closely related to the working activity of commodity producers. The exchange of two products of labor at their labor-value means that equilibrium exists between two given branches of production. Changes in the labor-value of a product destroy this labor equilibrium and cause a transfer of labor from one branch of production to another, bringing about a redistribution of productive forces in the social economy. Changes in the productive power of labor cause increases or decreases in the amount of labor needed for the production of given goods, bringing about corresponding increases or decreases in the values of commodities. Changes of value in turn bring about a new distribution of labor between the given productive branch and other branches. The productivity of labor influences the distribution of social labor through the labor-value.

This more or less direct causal relation between the labor-value of products and the distribution of social labor assumes that changes in the labor-value of products directly affect producers, namely the organizers of production, bringing about their transfer from one sphere to another and, consequently, the redistribution of labor. In other words, it is assumed that the organizer of production is a direct producer, a worker, and at the same time the owner of means of production, for example, a craftsman or a peasant. This petty producer tries to direct his labor to those spheres of production where the given quantity of labor yields him a product which is highly valued on the market. The result of the distribution of social labor among different spheres of production is that a determined quantity of labor of equal intensity, qualification, and so on, yields an approximately equal market-value to producers in all the spheres of production. Engaging their living labor in shoe production or in tailoring, the craftsmen at the same time engage past, accumulated labor, i.e., instruments and materials of labor (or means of production in a wide sense of these terms) which are necessary for production in their activity. These means of production are not usually very complicated; their value is relatively insignificant and thus, naturally, they do not lead to significant differences between individual spheres of crafts production. The distribution of labor (living labor) among individual branches of production is accompanied by the distribution of means of production (past labor) among these branches. The distribution of labor, which is regulated by the law of labor-value, has a primary, basic character; the distribution of instruments of labor has a secondary, derived character.

The distribution of labor is completely different in a capitalist economy. Since the organizers of production are in this case industrial capitalists, the expansion or contraction of production, i.e., the distribution of productive forces, depends on them. Capitalists invest their capitals in the sphere of production which is most profitable. The transfer of capital to the given sphere of production creates an increased demand for labor in that branch and consequently an increase of wages. This attracts hands, living labor, to the given branch.[239] The distribution of productive forces among individual spheres of the social economy takes the form of a distribution of capitals among these spheres. This distribution of capitals in turn leads to a corresponding distribution of living labor, or labor-power. If in a given country we observe an increase of capital invested in coal mining, and an increase in the number of workers employed in coal mining, we can ask ourselves which of these events was the cause of the other. Obviously, no one

---

[239] "Wage-labor subordinated by capital ... must submit to being transformed in accordance with the requirements of capital and to being transferred from one sphere of production to another" (C., III, p. 195).

will disagree about the answer: the transfer of capital led to the transfer of labor power, and not inversely. In the capitalist society, the distribution of labor is regulated by the distribution of capital. Thus if our goal (as before) is to analyze the laws of distribution of social labor in the social economy, we must resort to a round-about path and proceed to a preliminary analysis of the laws of distribution of capital.

The simple commodity producer spends his labor in production and tries to get a market value which is proportional to the labor he expends on his product. This market value must be adequate for his own and his family's subsistence, and for the continuation of production at the previous volume, or at a slightly expanded volume. However, the capitalist spends his capital for production. He tries to get a return of capital which is larger than his original capital. Marx formulated this difference in his well-known formulas of the simple commodity economy, C-M-C (commodity-money-commodity) and the capitalist economy, M-C-M + m (money-commodity-increased money). If we split this short formula we will see technical differences (small and large-scale production) and social differences (which social class organizes production) between the simple commodity economy and the capitalist economy. We will see differences in the motives of producers (the craftsman strives to secure his subsistence, the capitalist strives to increase value) as results of the different character of production and the different social position of the producer. "The expansion of value, which is the objective basis or mainspring of the circulation M-C-M, becomes his subjective aim" (C., I, p. 152). The capitalist directs his capital to one or another sphere of production depending on the extent to which the capital invested in the given sphere increases. The distribution of capital among different spheres of production depends on the rate of increase of the capital in them.

The rate of increase of capital is determined by the relation between m, incremental capital, and M, invested capital. In the simple commodity economy, the value of commodities is expressed by the formula: $C = c + (v + m)$.[240] The craftsman subtracts the value of the means of production which he used, namely c, from the value of the finished product, and the rest (v + m), which he added by his labor, is spent partly for his own and his family's subsistence goods (v) and the remainder represents a fund for the expansion of consumption or production (m). The same value of the product has the form $C = (c + v) + m$ for the capitalist. The capitalist subtracts $(c + v) = k$ of invested capital, or the costs of production, from the value of the commodity, whether this is spent on the purchase of means of production (c) or on the labor force (v). He considers the remainder, m, as his profit.[241] Consequently, $c + v = k$, and $m = p$. The formula $C = (c + v) + m$ is transformed into the formula $C = k + p$, i.e., "the value of a commodity = cost-price + profit" (C., III, p. 36). However, the capitalist is not interested in the absolute quantity of profit, but in the relation of the profit to the invested capital, namely in the rate of profit $p' = p/k$. The rate of profit expresses "the degree of self-expansion of the total capital advanced" (C., III, p. 45). Our earlier statement that the distribution of capital depends on its rate of increase in various spheres of production means that the rate of profit becomes the regulator of the distribution of capital.

The transfer of capital from spheres of production with low rates of profit to spheres of production with higher rates of profit creates a tendency toward the

---

[240] C means the value of the commodity; c = constant capital; v = variable capital; k = the whole capital; m = surplus value; m' = rate of surplus value, p = profit; p' = rate of profit. The categories c, v, and m are relevant only when they are applied to the capitalist economy. We use these categories in a conditional sense when we apply them to a simple commodity economy.

[241] Here we treat the entire surplus value as equal to profit.

equalization of profit rates in all spheres of production, a tendency toward the establishment of a general profit rate. Obviously this tendency is never realized completely in an unorganized capitalist economy, since in this economy complete equilibrium between the various spheres of production does not exist. But this absence of equilibrium, which is accompanied by differences in rates of profit, leads to the transfer of capital. This transfer tends to equalize profit rates and' to establish equilibrium among the different productive branches. This "incessant equilibration of constant divergences" (C., III, p. 196) provokes the striving of capital for the highest rate of profit. In capitalist production, "it is rather a matter of realizing as much surplus-value, or profit, on capital advanced for production, as any other capital of the same magnitude, or pro rata to its magnitude in whichever line it is applied... In this form capital becomes conscious of itself as a social power in which every capitalist participates proportionally to his share in the total social capital" (C., III, p. 195). In order to establish such a general average rate of profit, the existence of competition among capitalists engaged in different branches of production is necessary. The possibility for the transfer of capital from one branch to another is also necessary, since if this was not the case, various rates of profit could be established in different branches of production. If such competition of capitals is possible, equilibrium among the different productive branches can be theoretically assumed only in case the rates of profit which exist in these branches are approximately equal. Capitalists who work in average, socially necessary conditions in these productive branches will gain the general, average rate of profit.

Capitals of equal value invested in different spheres of production yield the same profit. Capitals which differ in size yield profit in proportion to their size. If capitals K and K_1 yield profits P and P_1, then

$$P/K = P_1/K_1 = p'$$

where p′ is the general, average rate of profit. But where does the capitalist get his profit? From the selling price of his commodity. The profit of the capitalist, p, is the surplus: the selling price of the commodity minus the costs of production. Thus, the selling prices of different commodities have to be set at a level at which capitalists, the producers of these commodities, will receive a surplus from the selling price, a profit, which is proportional to the size of the invested capital, after they reimburse, or pay for, their costs of production. The selling price of goods, which covers the costs of production and yields an average profit on the whole invested capital, is called the production price. In other words, production price is a price of commodities at which capitalists gain an average profit on their invested capital. Since equilibrium in the different branches of production presupposes, as we have seen, that capitalists in all branches of production receive an average profit, equilibrium between the different spheres of production presupposes that the products are sold at production prices. Production price corresponds to the equilibrium of the capitalist economy. This is a theoretically defined, average level of prices at which the transfer of capital from one branch to another no longer takes place. If the labor-value corresponded to the equilibrium of labor among the various spheres of production, then the production price corresponds to the equilibrium of capital invested in the different spheres. "... price of production ... is a prerequisite of supply, of the reproduction of commodities in every individual sphere" (C., Ill, p. 198), i.e., the condition of equilibrium among the different spheres of the capitalist economy.

The production price should not be confused with the market-price, which constantly fluctuates above and below it, sometimes exceeding the production price, sometimes falling below it. The production price is a theoretically defined center of equilibrium, a regulator of the constant fluctuations of market prices. In conditions of a capitalist economy, the production price performs the same social function which the market-price determined by labor expenditures performs in conditions of simple commodity production. The first as well as the second are "equilibrium prices," but labor value corresponds to a state of equilibrium in the distribution of labor among the various spheres of the simple commodity economy, and production price corresponds to the equilibrium state in the distribution of capitals among the different spheres in the capitalist economy. This distribution of capital in turn points to a certain distribution of labor. We can see that competition leads to the establishment of a different price level of commodities in different social forms of economy. As Hilferding said, very much to the point, competition can explain only the "tendency towards the establishment of equality in economic relations" for individual commodity producers. But what does the equality among these economic relations consist of? The equality depends on the objective social structure of the social economy. In one case it will be an equality of labor, in another case an equality of capital.

     As we have seen, production price equals costs of production plus the average profit on invested capital. If the average profit rate is given, then it is not difficult to calculate the production price. Let us assume that the invested capital is 100, the average rate of profit 22%. If the advanced capital is amortized during the year, then the production price is equal to the entire capital. The production price equals 100 + 22 = 122. The calculation is more complex if only one part of the fixed invested capital is used up during the year. If the capital of 100 consists of 20 v and 80 c, from which only 50 c are used up during the year, then the costs of production are equal to 50 c + 20 v = 70. To this sum is added 22%. This percentage is not calculated on the basis of the costs of production, 70, but of the entire invested capital, 100. Thus the production price is 70 + 22 = 92 (C., III, pp. 154-155). If from the same constant capital of 80 c, only 30 c were used up during the year, then the costs of production would be 30 c + 20 v = 50. To this sum, as before, is added the profit of 22. The production price of the commodity equals the costs of production plus the average profit on the entire invested capital.

II: Distribution of Capital and Distribution of Labor

To simplify our computations, we will assume that the entire invested capital is used up during the year, i.e., that the costs of production are equal to the invested capital. If two commodities are produced by means of capitals K and K₁ then the production price of the first commodity equals $K + p' K$, and of the second, $K_1 + p' K_1$. The production prices of two commodities are related to each other in the following way: [242]

---

[242] Marx usually uses the formula $K + Kp'$, understanding K as the costs of production, and not as capital (C., III, p. 165, p. 173). But elsewhere he says that equal capitals produce commodities which have the same production price "if we abstract the fact that a part of fixed capital enters the labor process without entering the process of increasing value" (Theorien über den Mehrwert, III, p. 76). The formula of the proportionality of production prices with capitals, which we cited above, can be maintained even with a partial consumption of fixed capital, if "the value of the unused part of the fixed capital is calculated in the product" (Ibid., p. 174). Let us assume that the first capital, 100, consists of 80 c + 20 v, and that the consumption of fixed capital is 50 c. Another capital of 100 consists of 70 c + 30 v, and the consumption of fixed capital is 20 c. The average rate of profit is 20%. The production price of the first product is 90, and of the second 70, namely the production prices are not equal even though the capitals are equal. However, if the unused part of the fixed capital, namely 30, is added to the number 90, and if we add 50 to 70, then in both cases we get 120. Production prices which include the unused part of fixed capital are proportional to capital. See the detailed calculation in Kautsky's note in Theorien über den Mehrwert, III, p. 74, and see also Capital, I, p. 213, especially the footnote.

$$(K + p'K)/(K_1 + p'K_1) = (K(1 + p'))/(K_1(1 + p')) = K/K_1$$

Production prices of commodities are proportional to the capitals by means of which the commodities are produced. Commodities have the same production price if they are produced with the same capitals. The equalization, on the market, of two commodities which are produced in different branches, means the equality of two capitals.

The market equalization of commodities produced with equal capitals means an equalization of commodities produced with unequal quantities of labor. Equal capitals with different organic compositions put different quantities of labor into action. Let us assume that one capital of 100 consists of 70 c and 30 v. Another capital of 100 consists of 90 c and 10 v. If the rate of surplus value is 100%, the living labor of workers is twice as large as the paid labor expressed by the variable capital (i.e., the wage). Thus 70 units of past labor and 60 units of living labor are expended on the production of the first commodity-a total of 130; 90 units of past labor and 20 units of living labor are expended on the production of the second commodity-a total of 110. Since both commodities were produced by equal capitals, they are equalized with each other on the market regardless of the fact that they were produced by unequal quantities of labor. The equality of capitals means the inequality of labor.

The divergence between the size of the capitals and the amount of labor is also due to differences in the turnover period of the variable part of the capital. We assume that the organic composition of both capitals is equal, namely 80 c + 20 v. However, the variable part of the first capital circulates once a year, and of the second capital, three times, i.e., every third of a year the capitalist pays his workers 20 v. The sum of wages paid to the workers during the year equals 60. It is obvious that the labor expenditures for the first commodity are 80 + 40 =

120, and for the second commodity, 80 + 120 = 200. But since the invested capitals, despite the differences in the turnover period, are 100 in both cases, the commodities are equalized with each other even though they are produced by unequal amounts of labor. It is necessary to mention that "the difference in the period of turnover is in itself of no importance, except so far as it affects the mass of surplus-labor appropriated and realized by the same capital in a given time" (C., III, p. 152}, i.e., if we are dealing with the difference in the turnover period of variable capital. The phenomena mentioned here, namely the differences in the organic composition of capital and in the turnover period, can in the last analysis be reduced to the fact that the size of capital in itself cannot serve as an indicator of the amount of living labor which it activates, since this amount of labor depends on: 1) the size of the variable capital, and 2) the number of its turnovers.

Consequently, we reach a conclusion which at first glance contradicts the labor theory of value. Starting with the basic law of equilibrium of the capitalist economy, namely from equal rates of profit for all spheres of production, from the sale of commodities by production prices which contain equal profit rates, we reach the following results. Equal capitals activate unequal quantities of labor. Equal production prices correspond to unequal labor-values. In the labor theory of value the basic elements of our reasoning were the labor-value of commodities as a function of the productivity of labor, and the distribution of labor among different spheres of production in a state of equilibrium. But the production price does not coincide with the labor value and the distribution of capital does not coincide with the distribution of labor. Does this mean that the basic elements of the labor theory of value are completely superfluous for analyzing the capitalist economy, that we must throw out this unnecessary theoretical ballast and concentrate our attention exclusively on the production price and the distribution of capital? We will try to show that the analysis of production prices and distribution of capital in turn presupposes labor-value, that these central links of the theory of the capitalist economy do not exclude the links of the labor theory of value which were treated above. On the contrary, in our further analysis we will show that production price and distribution of capitals lead to labor-value and distribution of labor and, parallel with them, are included in a general theory of equilibrium of the capitalist economy. We must build a bridge from the distribution of capitals to the distribution of labor, and from production price to labor-value. First of all, we will deal with the first half of this task.

We have seen that the distribution of capitals does not coincide with the distribution of labor, that the equality of capital means an inequality of labor. If a capital of 100, expended in a given sphere of production, is equalized, through the exchange of commodities on the market, with a capital of 100 spent in any other sphere of production, then, if there are differences in the organic composition of these capitals, this will mean that the given quantity of labor expended in the first branch will be equalized with another quantity of labor, expended in the second branch, which is not equal to the first quantity. Now we must still determine precisely what quantities of labor spent in different spheres of production are equalized with each other. Even though the size of the capitals does not coincide quantitatively with the amounts of labor which they activated, this does not mean that there is no close connection between these capitals and the labor. This connection can be observed if we know the organic composition of the capitals. If the first capital consists of 80 c + 20 v, and the second of 70 c + 30 v, and if the rate of surplus value is 100%, then the first capital activates 40 units of living labor and the second 60. At the given rate of surplus value, "a certain quantity of variable capital represents a definite quantity of labor-power set in motion, and therefore a definite quantity of materialized labor" (C., III, p. 144). "The variable capital thus serves here (as is always the case when the wage is given) as an index of the amount of labor set in motion by a definite total capital" (Ibid.). Thus we know that, in the first sphere of production, the total amount of labor expenditure consists of 120 (80 past and 40 living) and in the second of 130 (70 past and 60 living). Starting from a distribution of capitals among given spheres of production (100 each), we have arrived, through the organic composition of capital, to the distribution of social labor between these spheres (120 in the first and 130 in the second). We know that the amount of labor of 120, expended in the first branch, is equalized with a mass of labor of 130 expended in the second sphere. The capitalist economy establishes equilibrium between unequal quantities of labor if they are activated by equal capitals. Through the laws of equilibrium of capitals we have come to the equilibrium in the distribution of labor. Actually, in conditions of simple commodity production, equilibrium is established between equal quantities of labor, and in conditions of a capitalist economy, between unequal quantities. But the task of scientific analysis consists of clearly formulating the laws of equilibrium and distribution of labor no matter what form this formula takes. If we are dealing with a simple schema of distribution of labor which is determined by the labor-value (which in turn depends on the productivity of labor), then we get the formula of equal quantities of labor. If we assume that the distribution of labor is determined by the distribution of capital, which acquires meaning as an intermediate link in the causal chain, then the formula of the distribution of labor depends on the formula of the distribution of capitals: unequal masses of labor which are activated by equal capitals are equalized with each other. The subject of our analysis remains, as before, the equilibrium and the distribution of social labor. In the capitalist economy this distribution is realized through the distribution of capitals. This is why the formula on the equilibrium of labor becomes more complex than for the simple commodity economy; it is derived from the formula for the equilibrium of capitals.

As we have seen, the equalization of things on the market is closely connected with the equalization of labor in a capitalist society as well. If the products of two spheres are equalized on the market, and if they are produced with equal amounts of capital and with the expenditure of unequal masses of labor, this means that in the process of distribution of social labor among the different branches, unequal masses of labor activated by equal capitals are equalized with each other. Marx did not limit himself to pointing out the inequality of the labor-value of two commodities with equal production prices: he gave us a theoretical formula for the deviation of production price from labor-value. Nor did he limit himself to the assertion that in the capitalist economy, unequal masses of labor expended in different spheres are equalized with each other: he gave us a theoretical formula for the deviation of the distribution of labor from the distribution of capitals, i.e., he established a relation between both of these processes through the concept of the organic composition of capital.

To illustrate what we have outlined, we can cite the first half of Marx's table in Volume III of Capital (we have changed some of the headings). "Let us take five different spheres of production, and let the capital in each have a different organic composition" (C., III, p. 155). The total sum of social capital equals 500, and the rate of surplus value is 100%.

Distribution of Capital	Organic Composition of Capital	Distribution of Labor
100	80c + 20v	120
100	70c + 30v	130
100	60c + 40v	140
100	85c + 15v	115
100	95c + 5v	105

We have called the third column "distribution of labor." This column shows the amount of labor expended in each sphere. Marx called this column "Value of products," because the labor value of the total product of each sphere of production is determined by the quantity of labor expended in each sphere. Critics of Marx's theory hold that this title, "Value of the Product," is fictional, artificially constructed, and theoretically superfluous. They do not take into account that this column does not only show the labor value of the different spheres of production, but also the distribution of social labor among the different spheres of production, i.e., a phenomenon which exists objectively and has central significance for economic theory. Rejection of this column is equivalent to the rejection of economic theory, which analyzes the working activity of society. The table clearly shows how Marx bridged the distribution of capital, through the organic composition of capital, with the distribution of social labor.[243] Thus the causal chain of connections becomes more profound and acquires the following form: production price-distribution of capitals-distribution of social labor. Now we must turn to the analysis of the first link of this chain, production price, and to see if this link does not presuppose other, more primary links.

III: Production Price

Above we reached the following schema of causal relations: production price-distribution of capitals-distribution of labor. The starting point of this schema is

---

[243] Unfortunately, Marx did not succeed in developing in greater detail the question of the relation between the distribution of capitals and the distribution of labor, but it is clear that he thought he would return to this question. Marx dwells on the question "whether the labor is therefore proportionately distributed among the different spheres in keeping with these social needs, which are quantitatively circumscribed." In a parenthesis, Marx adds: "This point is to be noted in the distribution of capital among the various spheres of production" (C., III, pp. 635-636).

production price. Can we remain with production price in our analysis, or must we take the analysis further? What is production price? Costs of production plus average profit. But what do costs of production consist of? They consist of the value of the constant and variable capital spent in production. Let us take the next step by asking: what is the value of constant and variable capital equal to? It is obviously equal to the value of the commodities which are its components (namely machines, raw materials, subsistence goods, etc.). In this way all our arguments turn in a vicious circle: the value of commodities is explained by production prices, i.e., costs of production or value of capital, and the value of capital, in turn, is reduced to the value of commodities. "Determining the value of commodities by the value of capitals is the same as determining the value of commodities by the value of commodities" (Theorien über den Mehrwert, III, p. 82).

To prevent production price from becoming a vicious circle, we must find those conditions which lead to changes in production prices and in average rates of profit. We will begin with costs of production.

If the average rate of profit remains unchanged, then the production prices of commodities change when the costs of production change. Costs of production of given commodities change in the following instances: 1) when the relative quantities of means of production, and the labor necessary for production, change, namely when the productivity of labor in the given sphere of production changes, given constant prices; 2) when the prices of means of production change; this presupposes changes in the productivity of labor in branches which produce these means of production (if the relative quantity of means of production and labor force are constant). In both cases, costs of production change in relation to changes in the productivity of labor, and, consequently, in relation to changes in labor value. Thus, "the general rate of profit remains unchanged. In this case the price of production of a commodity can change only if its own value has changed. This may be due to more, or less, labor being required to reproduce the commodity in question, either because of a change in the productivity of labor which produces this commodity in its final form, or of the labor which produces those commodities that go into its production. The price of production of cotton yarn may fall, either because raw cotton is produced cheaper than before, or because the labor of spinning has become more productive due to improved machinery" (C., III, p. 206; also see p. 165). It is necessary to note that production prices expressed quantitatively do not exactly coincide with the labor-value of the commodities which are their constituents. "Since the price of production may differ from the value of a commodity, it follows that the cost-price of a commodity containing this price of production of another commodity may also stand above or below that portion of its total value derived from the value of the means of production consumed by it" (C., III, pp. 164-165). We can see that this circumstance, to which Tugan-Baronovskii attached such great significance in his critique of Marx's theory, was well known to Marx himself. Marx even cautioned "that there is always the possibility of an error if the cost-price of a commodity in any particular sphere is identified with the value of the means of production consumed by it" (C., III, p. 165). But this deviation does not in any way conflict with the fact that changes in labor-value which are caused by changes in the productivity of labor bring about changes in costs of production and thus in production prices. This is precisely what had to be proved. The fact that the quantitative expressions of different series of events diverge does not remove the existence of a causal relation among them nor deny that changes in one series depend on changes in the other. Our task is complete if we can only establish the laws of this dependence.

The second part of production price, besides costs of production, is average profit, i.e., the average rate of profit multiplied by the capital. We must now examine in greater detail the formation of average profit, its magnitude, and its changes.

The theory of profit analyzes the interrelations, and the laws of change, of the incomes of individual industrial capitalists and groups of capitalists. But the production relations among individual capitalists and their groups cannot be understood without a preliminary analysis of the basic production relation between the class of capitalists and the class of wage laborers. Thus the theory of profit, which analyzes the interrelations among the incomes of individual capitalists and their groups, is built by Marx on the basis of the theory of surplus value, in which he analyzed the interrelations between the income of the capitalist class and the class of wage laborers.

We know from the theory of surplus value that in capitalist society the value of a product is broken down to the following three components. One part (c) compensates the value of constant capital used up in production-this is a reproduced, and not a newly-produced value. When this value is subtracted from the value of the whole product ($C - c$), we get the value produced by living labor, "created" by it. This value is a result of the given process of production. It, in turn, is composed of two parts: one (v) reimburses the workers for the value of the subsistence goods, i.e., refunds their wages, or the variable capital. The remainder, $m = C - c - v = C - (c + v) = C - k$, is the surplus value which belongs to the capitalist and which he spends for the purpose of personal consumption and for the expansion of production (i.e., accumulation). In this way the entire value which is received is divided into a fund for the reproduction of constant capital (c), the subsistence fund of labor or the reproduction of labor power (v), and the fund for the subsistence of the capitalist and for expanded reproduction (m).

Surplus value arises because the labor which is expended by workers in the process of production is larger than the labor necessary for the production of their subsistence fund. This means that surplus value increases to the extent that the labor expended in production increases and the labor necessary for the production of the worker's subsistence fund decreases. Surplus value is determined by the difference between total labor and paid labor, namely by the unpaid or surplus labor. Surplus value is "created" by surplus labor. However, as we explained above, it is erroneous to represent the problem as if the surplus labor, as if the material activity, "created" surplus value as a property of things. Surplus labor "is expressed," "is manifested," "is represented" (sich darstellt) in surplus value. Changes in the magnitude of surplus value depend on changes in the quantity of surplus labor.

The magnitude of surplus labor depends: 1) on its relation to the necessary, paid labor, i.e., on the rate of surplus labor or the rate of surplus value ~; 2) (if we take this rate as given) on the number of workers[244] i.e., on the quantity of living labor which is activated by capital. If the rate of surplus value is given, the total sum of surplus value depends on the total quantity of living labor and, consequently, on the surplus labor. Let us now take two equal capitals, of 100 each, which give equal profit because of the tendency of the profit rate to equalize. If the capitals are spent exclusively to pay for the labor power (v), then they activate equal masses of living labor and, consequently, of surplus labor. Here equal profits correspond to equal capitals and also to equal quantities of surplus labor, so that profit coincides with surplus value. We get the same result if both capitals are allocated in equal proportions to constant and variable capital. The equality of variable capitals means the equality of living labor which this capital activates. But if a capital of 100 in one sphere of production equals 70 c + 30 v, and another capital of 100 in another sphere equals 90 c + 10 v, then the mass of living labor which they activate and consequently the masses of surplus labor are not equal. Nevertheless, these capitals, being equal, yield equal profit, for example 20, because of the competition of

---

[244] The length of the working day and the intensity of labor are considered given.

capitals among different spheres of production. It is obvious that the profits which these capitals yield do not correspond to the masses of living labor which these capitals activate and consequently, to the masses of surplus labor. The profits are not proportional to the masses of labor. In other words, capitalists get sums of profit which differ from those they would get if profits were proportional to surplus labor or surplus value. Only in this context can we understand Marx's statement that capitalists "do not secure the surplus-value, and consequently the profit, created in their own sphere by the production of these commodities" (C., III, p. 158). Some of Marx's critics understood him to mean that the first of the capitals mentioned above seems to "give" the second capital 10 units of labor activated by the first capital; part of the surplus labor and surplus value "overflow," like liquid, from one sphere of production to another, namely from spheres with a low organic composition of capital to spheres which are distinguished by a high organic composition of capital: "Surplus values which are taken from workers in individual branches of production must flow from one sphere to another until the profit rate is equal and all capitals gain an average rate of profit... However, such an assumption is impossible, since surplus value does not represent an original money price, but only crystallized labor-time. In this form it cannot flow from one sphere to another. And, what is even more important, in reality it is not surplus value that flows, but the capitals themselves that flow from one sphere of production to another until the rates of profit are equalized."[245] It is perfectly obvious, and need not be proved here, that according to Marx the process of equalization of rates of profit takes place through the transfer of capitals, and not of surplus values, from one sphere to another (C., III, pp. 195, 158, 179, 236, and

---

[245] Badge, Der Kapitalprofit, 1920, p. 48. E. Heimann constructed his critique on the same basis. Heimann, "Methodologisches zu den Problemen des Wertes," Archiv für Sozialwissenschaft u. Sozialpolitik, 1913, B. 37, H. 3, p. 777.

elsewhere). Since the production prices established in different spheres of production contain equal profit rates, the transfer of capital leads to the fact that the profits received by the capitals are not proportional to the quantities of living labor nor the surplus labor activated by the capitals. But if the relationship between the profits of two capitals engaged in different spheres of production does not correspond to the relationship between the living labors engaged by these capitals, it does not follow that a part of surplus labor or surplus value "is transferred," "overflows," from one sphere of production to another. Such a conception, based on a literal interpretation of some of Marx's statements, sometimes steals into the work of some Marxists; it arises from a view of value as a material object which has the characteristics of a liquid. However, if value is not a substance which flows from one man to another, but a social relation among people, fixed, "expressed," "represented" in things, then the conception of the overflow of value from one sphere of production to another does not result from Marx's theory of value but basically contradicts Marx's theory of value as a social phenomenon.

If, in capitalist society, there is no direct dependence between the profit of the capitalist and the quantity of living and thus surplus labor which is activated by capital, does this mean that we should completely give up the search for laws of the formation of average rates of profit and for causes which influence their level? Why is the average rate of profit in a given country 10%, and not 5% or 25%? We do not look to political economy for an exact formula for the calculation of the average profit rate in each case. However, we do look to political economy not to take a given rate of profit as the starting-point for analysis (a starting-point which does not have to be explained), but rather to try to determine the basic causes of the chain of events responsible for increases or decreases in the average rate of profit, i.e., the changes which determine the level of profit. This was Marx's task in his well known tables in Chapter 9 of Volume III of Capital. Since the second and third of Marx's tables take into account the partial consumption of fixed capital, we will take this as the basis of his first table in order not to complicate the computations. We will complete this table in a consistent manner. Marx takes five different spheres of production, with capitals of different organic compositions invested in them. The rate of surplus value is everywhere equal to 100%.

Capital	Labor Value of Product	Surplus Value	Average Rate of Profit	Production Price of Product	Deviation of Production Price from Value (and of Profit from Surplus Value)
80c+20v	120	20	22%	122	2
70c+30v	130	30	22%	122	-8
60c+40v	140	40	22%	122	-18
85c+15v	115	15	22%	122	7
95c+5v	105	5	22%	122	17
390c+110v	610	110	110	610	0
78c+22v	---	22	---	---	---

The total capital of society consists of 500, of which 390 is c and 110 is v. This capital is distributed among five spheres, with 100 in each. The organic composition of capital shows how much living labor, and thus surplus labor, is in each sphere. The total labor-value of the product is 610, and the total surplus value is 110. If the commodities of each sphere would be sold by their labor values, or, which is the same thing, if the profits in each sphere would correspond to the quantities of living labor and thus the surplus labor engaged in each sphere, then the profit rates of the individual spheres of production would be: 20%, 30%, 40%, 15%, and 5%. The spheres with the lowest organic composition of capital would get higher profit, and the spheres with a higher organic composition would get a lower profit. But, as we know, such different rates of profit are not possible in the capitaUst society, since this would cause a transfer of capitals from spheres with low rates of profit to spheres with high rates, until the same rate of profit is established in all spheres. The profit rate in the given case is 22%. Commodities produced by equal capitals of 100 are sold at equal production prices of 122, even though they are produced by unequal quantities of labor. Every capital of 100 receives a profit of 22%, even though equal capitals activate unequal quantities of surplus labor in the different spheres. "Every 100 of an invested capital, whatever its composition, draws as much profit in a year, or any other period of time, as falls to the share of every 100, the n'th part of the total capital, during the same period. So far as profits are concerned, the various capitalists are just so many stockholders in a stock company in which the shares of profit are uniformly divided per 100, so that profits differ in the case of the individual capitalists only in accordance with the amount of capital invested by each in the aggregate enterprise, i.e., according to his investment in social production as a whole, according to the number of his shares" (C., III, p. 158).

However, at which level is the average rate of profit established? Why is this rate equal precisely to 22%? Let us imagine that all the spheres of production are arranged in a decreasing sequence depending on the amount of living labor activated by each 100 units of capital. The variable parts of the capitals (taken in percentage shares) decrease from the top down (or the organic composition of capital increases from the top down). Parallel with this and in the same relation, the rates of profit decrease from the top down. The rate of profit which falls to each capital depends (in this example) on the quantity of living labor which the capital activates, or on the size of its variable capital. But as we know, such a difference in rates of profit is impossible. Competition among capitals would establish an average profit rate for all spheres of production; this average rate would be situated somewhere near the middle of the falling rates of profit. This average rate of profit corresponds to a capital which activates an average quantity of living labor or an average size of variable capital. In other words, the "average rate of profit ... is the percentage of profit in that sphere of average composition in which profit, therefore, coincides with surplus-value" (C., III, p. 173). In the given case, the entire social capital of 500 consists of 390 c + 110 v, the average composition of each 100 is 78 c + 22 v; if the rate of surplus value is 100%, every 100 of this capital of average composition gets a 22% rate of surplus value. The magnitude of this surplus value determines the size of the average rate of profit. This rate, consequently, is determined by the relation of the total mass of surplus value (m) produced in the society, to the total social capital (K), or $p' = m/k$.

Marx reaches the same conclusion in a different way. He uses the method of comparison which he often uses to explain the characteristic properties of the capitalist economy. In the given problem, the question of the average rate of profit, he compares the developed capitalist economy to 1) a simple commodity economy, and 2) an embryonic or hypothetical capitalist economy, which differs from developed capitalism by the absence of competition among capitals in different spheres of production, i.e., each capital is fixed within a given sphere of production.

Thus we can assume first of all a society of simple commodity producers who possess means of production with the value of 390 labor units; the living labor of its members amounts to 220. The productive forces of the society, which makeup 610 units of living and past labor, are distributed among five spheres of production. The combination of living and past labor is different in each sphere, depending on the technical properties of each sphere. Let us assume that the combinations are as follows (the first number represents past labor, the second living): I 80 + 40, II 70 + 60, III 60 + 80, IV 85 + 30, V 95 + 10. Let us assume that the productivity of labor has reached such a level of development that the petty producer reproduces the value of his subsistence goods with half his labor. Then the total value of the production, 610, breaks down into a fund of reproduction of means of production, 390, a fund for the subsistence of the producers, 110, and surplus value, 110. The surplus value remains in the hands of these same petty producers. They can spend it to expand consumption, to expand production (or partly for one and partly for the other). This surplus value of 110 will be proportionally distributed among the different spheres of production and the individual producers in terms of the labor expended. The distribution among the individual spheres will be: 20, 30, 40, 15, 5. Actually, these masses of surplus value are proportional only to the masses of living labor, and not to the past labor allocated to each sphere. If the masses of surplus value are calculated on the whole quantity of labor in each sphere (living and past) they give unequal rates of profit.[246] But in a simple commodity economy, producers are not aware of the category profit. They do not look at means of production as capital which must yield a given rate of profit, but as conditions for the activation of labor which give each commodity producer the possibility to put his labor on equal terms with that of other commodity producers, i.e., on terms or in

---

[246] It is understood that the categories of surplus value and profit are not known in the simple commodity economy. Here we are dealing with that part of the value of commodities produced by simple commodity producers which would have the form of surplus value or profit in conditions of a capitalist economy.

conditions where equal quantities of living labor yield equal value.

Let us now assume that capitalists, and not petty commodity producers, are dominant in the economy. The other conditions remain unchanged. The value of the entire product, and the value of individual funds into which it breaks down, remain unchanged. The difference is that the fund for expanded consumption and expanded production (or surplus value) of 110 does not remain in the hands of direct producers, but is in the hands of capitalists. The same total social value is distributed in a different way between the social classes. Since the value of the product of individual spheres of production has not changed, the surplus value is distributed in the same proportions as before between individual spheres and individual capitalists. The capitalists in each of the five spheres get: 20, 30, 40, 15, 5. But they calculate these masses of surplus value on the entire invested capital, which is 100 in each sphere. As a result, the rates of profit are different. They can only be different because of the absence of competition between the individual spheres of production.

Finally, let us pass from hypothetical capitalism to actual capitalism, where there is competition of capital between the different spheres of production. Here different rates of profit are impossible, because this would cause a movement of capital from one sphere to another until all spheres had the same rate of profit. In other words, the distribution of the earlier mass of surplus value between different spheres and between individual capitalists will now be different; it will be proportional to the capitals invested in the spheres. The distribution of the surplus value is modified, but the total value of the fund of expanded consumption and expanded reproduction remain unchanged. The earlier mass of surplus value is now distributed among individual capitalists according to the size of their capitals. The average rate of profit is thus derived. It is determined by the relation of the total surplus value to the total social capital.

The comparison of a simple commodity economy, a hypothetical capitalist economy and a developed capitalist economy is not developed by Marx in the form in which we have presented it. Marx speaks of simple commodity production in Chapter 10 of the third volume of Capital. He takes a hypothetical capitalist economy as the basis of his analysis in Chapter 8 and in the tables of Chapter 9, where he assumes the absence of competition among individual spheres, and different profit rates. The comparison of the three different types of economy which we have carried out leads to certain doubts. A simple commodity economy presupposes the dominance of living labor over past labor, and an approximately homogeneous relation between living and past labor in the various branches of production. However, in our schemas this relation is assumed to be different in each sphere. This objection does not have a great deal of significance because different relations between living and past labor (even though they were not characteristic of the simple commodity economy) do not logically contradict that type of economy and may be used as an assumption in a theoretical schema. More serious doubts are aroused by the schema of the embryonic or hypothetical capitalist economy. If the absence of competition among the capitalists of the different spheres of that economy explains why commodities are not sold according to production prices, this absence of competition also makes it impossible to explain the sale of goods according to their labor values. In the simple commodity economy, the sale of goods according to labor-values can be maintained only on the condition that labor can transfer from one sphere to another, i.e., if there is competition among spheres of production. In one passage Marx noted that the sale of goods by their labor values assumes as a necessary condition that no natural or artificial monopoly makes it possible for the contracting sides to sell above value or forces them to sell below value (C., III, p. 178). But if there is no competition among capitals, if each capital is fixed in each sphere, then the state of monopoly results. Sales at prices above labor-values do not bring about a transfer of capital from other spheres. Sales at prices below labor-values do not cause an outflow of capital from the given sphere to others. There is no regularity in the establishment of exchange proportions among commodities in terms of their corresponding labor-values. On what basis does the schema of the embryonic capitalist economy assume that the sale of commodities takes place according to labor values, if competition among capitalists in different spheres is absent?

It is possible to answer this question only if the schema is explained in the form in which we explained it above. Diagram No. 2 is not a picture of an embryonic capitalism which existed in history, but a hypothetical theoretical schema derived from Diagram 1 (simple commodity economy) by means of a methodological procedure which consists of changing only one condition of the schema, all other conditions remaining the same. In schema No. 2, compared to No. 1, only one condition is changed. It is supposed that the economy is not run by petty commodity producers but by capitalists. The other conditions are assumed to be the same as before: the mass of living labor and past labor in each sphere, the value of the total product and the mass of surplus value, and thus the price of products; the selling price of commodities according to labor values is kept at the same level as earlier. The sale of commodities is a theoretical condition transferred to schema 2 from schema 1, and is only possible if there is another, additional theoretical condition, namely if there is no competition among capitalists in different spheres. Therefore, since we change this single condition by moving from schema 2 to schema 3 (developed capitalism), i.e., since we introduce the assumption of competition of capitals, the sale of goods according to their labor-values gives place to the sale of goods according to production prices in which an average rate of profit is realized by capitalists. But in carrying out this transition from schema 2 to schema 3 by the same methodological procedure, by changing one condition, we leave unchanged the other conditions, particularly the earlier mass of surplus value. In this way we reach the conclusion that the formation of a general average rate of profit reflects a redistribution of the earlier total mass of surplus value among capitalists. The share of this surplus value in the total social capital determines the level of the average rate of profit. We repeat that this "redistribution" of surplus value must not, in our view, be understood as a historical process which actually took place and which was preceded by an embryonic capitalist economy with different rates of profit in different spheres.[247] It is a theoretical schema of the distribution of profit in the capitalist economy. This schema is derived from the first schema (simple commodity production) by means of a two-fold change in the conditions. Moving from schema 1 to schema 2 we assumed that the social class which gets the surplus value changed. Moving from schema 2 to schema 3, we assumed that, in the context of the same class of capitalists, a redistribution of capital took place among the different spheres. Both of these transitions in essence represent two logical links of an argument. They are separated for the sake of clarity, even though they do not exist separately. In our opinion, the transformation of the

---

[247] It is to be understood that we do not deny that in a real capitalist economy, different rates of profit in different spheres can be observed constantly. They bring about a tendency toward the transfer of capital and this, in turn, removes the inequality in the rates of profit. We also do not deny that in the period of undeveloped capitalism, inequalities of profit rates were very significant. But we reject the theory which holds that these inequalities of profit rates were caused by the fact that commodities were sold according to labor value on one hand, and that competition among different spheres was absent on the other hand. If we assume that competition among the different spheres was absent, then it becomes unexplainable why commodities were sold according to labor values.

intermediate logical link, schema 2, into a picture of an economy which existed in history as a transition from simple commodity production to developed capitalist production, is erroneous.

Thus, the average rate of profit is quantitatively determined by the relation between the total mass of surplus value and the total social capital. We assume that in Marx's system the magnitude of the average rate of profit is derived from the mass of total surplus value and not from the different profit rates, as it may seem from a first reading of Marx's work. Deriving the average rate of profit from different profit rates provokes objections based on the fact that the existence of different profit rates in different spheres is not logically or historically proved. The existence of different profit rates, according to this view, was brought about by the sale of products of different spheres according to their labor-values. But as we have seen above, different rates of profit in different spheres of production only played the role of a theoretical schema in Marx's work, a schema which explains the formation and magnitude of an average profit rate by means of comparison. Marx himself pointed out that, "The general rate of profit is, therefore, determined by two factors:

"1) The organic composition of the capitals in the different spheres of production, and thus, the different rates of profit in the individual spheres.

"2) The distribution of the total social capital in these different spheres, and thus, the relative magnitude of the capital invested in each particular sphere at the specific rate of profit prevailing in it; i.e., the relative share of the total social capital absorbed by each individual sphere of production" (C., III, p. 163). It is obvious that different rates of profit in individual spheres are used by Marx only as numerical expressions, indicators of the organic composition of capital, i.e., masses of living labor and thus of surplus labor activated by each 100 units of capital in a given sphere. This factor is combined with others; the quantity of surplus labor which belongs to each 100 units of capital in each sphere is multiplied by the size (the number of hundreds) of capital invested in the given sphere. As a result we get the mass of surplus labor and surplus value, first of all in the individual spheres, and then in the whole social economy. Thus the average rate of profit is not determined, in the last analysis, by the different profit rates in different spheres, but rather by the total mass of surplus value and by the relationship of this mass to total social capital,[248] i.e., by magnitudes which are not theoretically suspicious from the standpoint of the labor theory of value. At the same time these magnitudes reflect real facts of the social economy, namely the masses of living social labor and the social capital. The specific character of Marx's theory of production price consists precisely of the fact that the entire question of mutual relations between surplus value and profit is transferred from individual capitals to the total social capital. This is why, in our presentation of Marx's theory, different rates of profit in different spheres do not serve as a necessary intermediate link for a theory of the average rate of profit; this can be briefly summarized in the following way. In the capitalist economy the distribution of capital is not proportional to the distribution of living labor. A different quantity of living labor and thus of surplus labor belongs to each 100 units of capital in the different spheres. (The different

---

[248] If the entire social capital is 1000, and the mass of total surplus value is 100, then the general average profit rate will be 10%, regardless of how the total living labor of society is distributed among the individual spheres, and regardless of what kinds of profit rates would be formed in the individual spheres. Inversely, if the total mass of surplus value increases to 150, and the total capital remains the same (1000), then the general average profit rate rises from 10 to 15%, even though the profit rates would remain unchanged in the individual branches of production (this is possible if the capital is distributed among the different branches in a different way).

rates of profit represent numerical expressions of this mutual relation between surplus labor and capital in each sphere.) This organic composition of capital in the different spheres and the size of the capital in each sphere determine the total mass of surplus labor and surplus value in the individual spheres and in the entire economy. Because of the competition of capitals, equal capitals in different spheres gain equal profits, and thus the profit which the individual capitals gain is not proportional to the quantities of living labor activated by these capitals. Consequently, the profit is not proportional to surplus value but is determined by the average profit rate, i.e., by the relation between the total surplus value and the total social capital.

If a reading of Chapter 8 of the third volume of Capital gives the impression that the differences in profit rates, which arise because of the sale of commodities according to their labor values, play the role of an indispensable link in Marx's constructions, this is explained by the following properties of Marx's exposition. When Marx approaches the decisive places of his system, when he must move from general definitions to more particular explanations, from general concepts to their modifications, from one "determination of form" to another, he resorts to the following method of exposition. With an enormous power of thought, he draws all the logical conclusions from the first definition which he develops, intrepidly developing all the consequences which follow from the concept to their logical end. He shows the reader all the contradictions of these consequences, i.e., their divergence from reality. When the reader's attention has been strained to its limit, when it begins to seem to the reader that the starting definition must be completely rejected because it is contradictory, Marx comes to the reader's help and suggests an exit from the problem, an exit which does not consist of throwing out the first definition, but rather of "modifying," "developing" and completing the first definition. Thus the contradictions are removed. Marx does this in Chapter 4 of the first volume of Capital, when he examines the transition from the value of commodities to the value of labor-power. He draws a conclusion on the impossibility of the formation of surplus value on the basis of an exchange of commodities according to their labor-value, i.e., he reaches a conclusion which openly conflicts with reality. In the further analysis, this conclusion is rejected by the theory of the value of labor power. This is precisely how the eighth chapter of Volume III of Capital is constructed. On the basis of the sale of goods according to labor-values, Marx concludes that different rates of profit exist in different spheres. Developing this conclusion to all its consequences, he ascertains at the end of Chapter 8 that this conclusion conflicts with reality and that this contradiction must be resolved. In Volume I of Capital, Marx had never claimed that the existence of surplus value was impossible; here he does not say that different profit rates are possible. The impossibility of surplus value in Chapter 4 of Volume 1, and the possibility of different profit rates in Chapter 8 of Volume III, do not serve Marx as logically necessary links for his constructions, but as proofs of the opposite. The fact that these conclusions lead to a logical absurdity shows that the analysis is not yet finished and has to be continued further. Marx does not determine the existence of different profit rates, but on the contrary, the inadequacy of any theory which is based on such a premise.

We have reached the conclusion that the average rate of profit is determined by the relation of total surplus value to the total social capital. From this it follows that changes in the average profit rate may result from changes in the rate of surplus value and also from changes in the relation of total surplus value to total social capital. In the first case, the change "can only occur either through a rise, or fall, in the value of labor-power, the one being just as impossible as the other unless there is a change in the productivity of the labor producing means of subsistence, i.e., in the value of commodities consumed by the laborer" (C., III, p. 205). Now we take the second case, when the changes start from capital, namely from an increase or decrease of its constant part. The changed relation of constant capital to labor reflects a change in the productivity of labor. "Thus, there has been a change in the productivity of labor, and there must have occurred a change in the value of certain commodities" (Ibid.). Changes in the average rate of profit, whether they result from the rate of surplus value or from capital, are in both cases brought about, in the last analysis, by changes in the productivity of labor and, consequently, by changes in the value of some goods.

From this it follows that changes in costs of production and changes in average profit rates are caused by changes in the productivity of labor. And since the production price consists of production costs plus average profit, changes in production prices are in the last analysis caused by changes in the productivity of labor and in the labor-value of some goods. If the change in production price is caused by a change in production costs, this means that the productivity of labor in the given sphere of production and the labor-value of the given sphere have changed. "If the price of production of a commodity changes in consequence of a change in the general rate of profit, its own value may have remained unchanged. However, a change must have occurred in the value of other commodities" (Ibid., pp. 205-206), i.e., changes in the productivity of labor in other spheres. In every case, the production price changes in relation to changes in the productivity of labor and corresponding changes in labor-value. Productivity of labor-abstract value-value-costs of production plus average profit-production price: this is the schema of causal relations between production price, on one hand, and the productivity of labor and labor-value, on the other.

IV: Labor-Value and Production Price

Now, finally, we can consider the chain of logical links which complete Marx's theory of production price. The chain consists of the following basic links: productivity of labor-abstract labor-value-production price-distribution of capital-distribution of labor. If we compare this six-element schema to the four-element schema of simple commodity production: productivity of labor-abstract labor-value-distribution of labor, we see that the links of the simple commodity production schema have become components of the schema for the capitalist economy. Consequently, the labor theory of value is a necessary foundation for the theory of production price, and the theory of production price is a necessary development of the labor theory of value.

The publication of the third volume of Capital gave birth to an enormous literature on the so-called "contradictions" between Volume I and Volume III of Capital. Critics held that in Volume III, Marx had in essence repudiated his labor theory of value, and some even assumed that, when he had composed the first volume, he had never dreamed of the difficulties and contradictions into which the labor theory of value would lead him when he had to explain the profit rate. Karl Kautsky's foreword to the third volume of Capital documents that when the first volume of Capital was published, the theory of production price explained in Volume III had already been worked out by Marx in all its details. Already in the first volume, Marx frequently pointed out that in the capitalist society, average market prices deviate from labor-values. The content of the third volume of Theorien liber den Mehrwert also informs us of another important circumstance. All post-Ricardian political economy revolved around the question of the relation between production price and labor-value. The answer to this question was a historical task for economic thought. In Marx's view, the particular merit of his theory of value was that it gave a solution to this problem.

Critics who saw contradictions between the first and third volumes of Capital took as their starting-point a narrow view of the theory of value, seeing it exclusively as a formula of quantitative proportions in the exchange of commodities. From this standpoint the labor theory of value and the theory of production price did not represent two logical stages or degrees of abstraction from the same economic phenomena, but rather two different theories or statements which contradicted each other. The first 'theory holds that commodities are exchanged in proportion to the expenditure of labor necessary for their production. The second theory holds that commodities are not exchanged proportionally to these expenditures. What a strange method of abstraction, said Marx's critics; first it holds one thing, then another which contradicts the first. But these critics did not take into account that the quantitative formula for the exchange of commodities is only the final conclusion of a very complex theory which deals with the social form of the phenomena related to value, the reflection of a determined type of social production relations among people, as well as the content of these phenomena, their role as regulators of the distribution of social labor.

Anarchy in social production; the absence of direct social relations among producers; mutual influence of their working activities through things which are products of their labor; connection between the movement of production relations among people and the movement of things in the process of material production; "reification" of production relations, the transformation of their properties into the properties of "things"-all of these phenomena of commodity fetishism are equally present in every commodity economy, simple as well as capitalist. They characterize labor-value and production price in the same way. But every commodity economy is based on the division of labor, i.e., it represents a system of allocated labor. How is this division of social labor among various spheres of production carried out? It is directed by the mechanism of market prices, which provokes inflows and outflows of labor. Fluctuations of market prices display a certain regularity, oscillating around some average level, around a price "stabilizer," as Oppenheimer appropriately called it.[249]

This price "stabilizer," in turn, changes in relation to the increase of the productivity of labor and serves as a regulator of the distribution of labor. The increase of the productivity of labor influences the distribution of social labor through the mechanism of market price, whose movement is subject to the law of value. This is the simplest abstract mechanism which distributes labor in the commodity economy. This mechanism exists in every commodity economy, including the capitalist economy. There is no mechanism other than the fluctuation of market prices which distributes labor in the capitalist economy. But since the capitalist economy is a complex system of social production relations in which people do not relate to each other only as commodity owners but also as capitalists and wage laborers, the mechanism which distributes labor functions in a more complex manner. Since simple commodity producers spend their own labor in production, the increase of productivity of labor, expressed through the labor-value of products, causes inflows and outflows of labor, i.e., influences the distribution of social labor. In other words, the simple commodity economy is characterized by a direct causal relation between the productivity of labor expressed in the labor-value of products, and the distribution of labor.[250] In the capitalist society this causal relation cannot be direct since the distribution of labor takes place through the distribution of capital. The increase of productivity of labor, expressed in the labor-value of products, cannot influence the distribution of labor any

---

[249] Franz Oppenheimer, Wert und Kapitalprofit, Jena, 1922, p. 23.

[250] More precisely, this causal relation is not direct, since the productivity of labor influences the distribution of labor by changing the labor-value. Thus here we speak of the "productivity of labor which is expressed in the labor-value of products."

other way than through its influence on the distribution of capital. Such influence on the distribution of capital is in turn possible only if changes in the productivity of labor and labor-value cause changes in costs of production or in the average rate of profit, i.e., influence the production price.

Thus the schema: productivity of labor-abstract labor-value-distribution of labor, represents, so to speak, a theoretical model of direct causal relations between the increase of productivity of labor expressed in labor-value, and the distribution of social labor. The schema: productivity of labor-abstract labor-value-production price-distribution of capital-distribution of labor, represents a theoretical model of the same causal chain, where the productivity of labor does not directly affect the distribution of labor, but rather through an "intermediate link" (an expression which Marx often used in this context): through the production price and the distribution of capital. In both schemas, the first and last terms are the same. The mechanism of causal relations between them is also the same. But in the first schema we assume that the causal connection is more immediate and direct. In the second schema we introduce elements which complicate the situation, namely intermediate links. This is the usual path of abstract analysis, a path which Marx resorted to in all his constructions. The first schema represents a more abstract, more simplified model of the events, but a model which is indispensable for an understanding of the more complex forms of events that take place in capitalist society. If we limited the scope of the analysis to the intermediate links which are visible on the surface of phenomena in the capitalist economy, namely production price and distribution of capital, then our analysis would remain incomplete in both directions, at the beginning and at the end. We would take production price (i.e., production costs plus average profit) as a starting-point. But if production price is explained in terms of costs of production, we simply refer the value of the product to the value of its components, i.e., we do not emerge from a vicious circle.

Average profit remains unexplained, as do its volume and its changes. Thus production price can only be explained by changes in productivity of labor or in the labor value of products. On the one hand, we are wrong if we regard the distribution of capital as the final point of our analysis; we have to move on to the distribution of social labor. Thus the theory of production price must without fail be based on the labor theory of value. On the other hand, the labor theory of value must be further developed and completed in the theory of production price. Marx rejected every attempt to construct the theory of the capitalist economy directly from the labor theory of value and to avoid the intermediate links, average profit and production price. He characterized such attempts as "attempts to force and directly fit concrete relations to the elementary relation of value" (Theorien über den Mehrwert, III, p. 145), "attempts which present as existing that which does not exist" (Ibid., p. 97).

Thus the labor theory of value and the theory of production price are not theories of two different types of economy, but theories of one and the same capitalist economy taken on two different levels of scientific abstraction. The labor theory of value is a theory of simple commodity economy, not in the sense that it explains the type of economy that preceded the capitalist economy, but in the sense that it describes only one aspect of the capitalist economy, namely production relations among commodity producers which are characteristic for every commodity economy.

V: Historical Foundations of the Labor Theory of Value

After the publication of the third volume of Capital, opponents of Marx's theory of value, and to some extent its advocates, created the impression that the conclusions of the third volume demonstrated the inapplicability of the law of labor value to the capitalist economy. This is why certain Marxists were prone to construct a so-called "historical" foundation for Marx's theory of value. They held that even though the law of labor value, in the form in which Marx developed it in the first volume of Capital, is not applicable to the capitalist economy, it is nevertheless completely valid for the historical period which precedes the emergence of capitalism and in which petty crafts and peasant economy are dominant. Certain passages which might be interpreted this way can be found in the third volume of Capital. There Marx says that "it is quite appropriate to regard the values of commodities as not only theoretically but also historically prius to the prices of production" (C., III, p. 177). These cursory comments by Marx were developed by Engels in detail in his article published in 1895 in Neue Zeit.[251] Here Engels gave a basis to the idea that Marx's law of value was in force during a historical period which lasted five to seven thousand years, a period which began with the appearance of exchange and ended in the 15th century, when capitalism emerged. Engels' article found ardent supporters, but just as ardent opponents, some of them Marxists. Opponents pointed out that exchange did not encompass the entire social economy before the appearance of capitalism, that it spread first to surpluses which existed after the satisfaction of the requirements of the self-sufficient, natural economic unit, that the mechanism of general equalization of different individual labor expenditures in separate economic units on the market did not exist, and that consequently it was not appropriate to speak of abstract and socially-necessary labor which is the basis of the theory of value. Here we will not be concerned with the historical controversy over whether commodities were exchanged in proportion to the labor expended on their production before the emergence of capitalism. For methodological reasons we are opposed to relating this question to the question of the theoretical significance of the law of labor-value for the explanation of the capitalist economy.

---

[251] Russian translation in Novoe Slovo, September, 1897.

Marx's Labor Theory of Value ▲ 373

First of all, we turn to Marx's work. Some passages in Volume III of Capital can be used by proponents of a historical explanation of labor value. However, now that other works by Marx are available to us, we know with certainty that Marx himself was strongly opposed to the view that the law of value was in force in the period preceding the development of capitalism. Marx objected to the view of the English economist Torrens, a proponent of a view which one can even find in Adam Smith's work. Torrens held that the full development of a commodity economy, and consequently the full development of the laws which exist in that economy, is possible only in capitalism and not before. "This would mean that the law of labor-value exists in production which is not commodity production (or only partly commodity production), but it does not exist in production which is not based on the existence of products in the form of commodities. This law itself, and the commodity as the general form of products, are abstracted from capitalist production, and now supposedly cannot be applied to it" (Theorien über den Mehrwert, III, p. 80). "It now turns out that the law of value abstracted from capitalist production contradicts its phenomena" (Ibid., p. 78). These ironical notes by Marx clearly show his relation to the view of the theory of value as a law which functions in the pre-capitalist economy, but not in the capitalist economy. But how can we reconcile these statements with some observations in Volume III of Capital? The seeming divergence between them disappears if we return to the "Introduction to the Critique of Political Economy," which gives us a valuable explanation of Marx's abstract method of analysis. Marx emphasizes that the method of moving from abstract to concrete concepts is only a method by which thought grasps the concrete, and not the way the concrete phenomenon actually happened.[252] This means that the transition from labor-value or simple commodity

---

[252] "Introduction to the Critique of Political Economy," in A Contribution to the Critique of Political Economy, Chicago: Kerr, 1904, pp. 293-294.

economy to production price or the capitalist economy is a method for grasping the concrete, i.e., the capitalist economy. This is a theoretical abstraction and not a picture of the historical transition from simple commodity economy to capitalist economy. This confirms the view which we formulated earlier that the tables in Chapter 9 of the third volume of Capital, which illustrate the formation of general average rates of profit from different rates of profit, depict a theoretical schema of phenomena, and not the historical development of the phenomena. "The simplest economic category, say exchange value ... can have no other existence except as an abstract one-sided relation of an already given concrete and living aggregate" (Ibid.), i.e., the capitalist economy.

After having explained the theoretical character of abstract categories, Marx asks: "have these simple categories no independent historical or natural existence antedating the more concrete ones?" (Ibid., p. 295). Marx answers that such instances are possible. A simple category (for example value) can exist historically before the concrete category (for example, production price). But in this case the simple category still has a rudimentary, embryonic character which reflects relations of "undeveloped concreteness." "Thus, although the simple category may have existed historically before the more concrete one, it can attain its complete internal and external development only in complex forms of society" (Ibid., p. 297). Applying this conclusion to the question which interests us, we can say: labor-value (or commodity) is a historical "prius" in relation to production price (or capital). It existed in rudimentary form before capitalism, and only the development of the commodity economy prepared the basis for the emergence of the capitalist economy. But labor-value in its developed form exists only in capitalism. The labor theory of value, which develops a logical, complete system of the categories value, abstract labor, socially-necessary labor, etc., expresses the "abstract one-sided relation of an already given concrete and living aggregate," i.e., it expresses the abstraction of the capitalist economy.

The historical question of whether commodities were exchanged in proportion to labor expenditures before the emergence of capitalism must be separated from the question of the theoretical significance of the theory of labor-value. If the first question were answered affirmatively, and if the analysis of the capitalist economy did not require the labor theory of value, we could regard that theory as a historical introduction to political economy, but not in any way as a basic theoretical foundation on which Marx's political economy is built. Inversely, if the historical question were answered negatively, but if the indispensability of the labor theory of value for the theoretical understanding of the complex phenomena of the capitalist economy were proved, this theory would still be the starting-point of economic theory, as it is now. In brief, no matter how the historical question about the influence of the law of labor-value in the period before capitalism were solved, this solution would not in the least free Marxists from their responsibility to accept the challenge of their opponents on the question of the theoretical significance of the law of labor value for an understanding of the capitalist economy. Confusing the theoretical and the historical setting of the theory of value is not only pointless, as we have shown, but also harmful. Such a treatment puts the proportions of exchange into the foreground, and ignores the social form and the social function of value as the regulator of the distribution of labor, a function which value performs to a great extent only in a developed commodity economy, i.e., a capitalist economy. If the analyst finds that primitive tribes, who live in conditions of a natural economy and rarely resort to exchange, are guided by labor expenditures when they establish exchange proportions, he is prone to find here the category of value. Value is transformed into a suprahistorical category, into labor expenditures independent of the social form of the organization of labor.[253] The "historical" setting of the problem thus leads to ignoring the historical character of the category value. Other theorists, assuming that "the emergence of exchange value must be sought in a natural economy which developed into a money economy," finally determine value not in terms of the labor which the producer spends on his production, but by the labor which the producer would have to spend in the absence of exchange and of the necessity to make the product by his own labor.[254]

The labor theory of value and the theory of production price differ from each other, not as different theories which function in different historical periods, but as an abstract theory and a concrete fact, as two degrees of abstraction of the same theory of the capitalist economy. The labor theory of value only presupposes production relations among commodity producers. The theory of production price presupposes, in addition, production relations between capitalists and workers, on one hand, and among various groups of industrial capitalists on the other.

---

[253] See A. Bogdanov and I. Stepanov, Kurs politicheskoi ekonomii (Course in Political Economy), Vol. II, Book 4, pp. 21-22.

[254] P. Maslov, Teoriya razvitiya narodnogo khozyaistva (Theory of Development of the National Economy), 1910, pp. 180-183.

Chapter 19: Productive Labor

To formulate the problem of productive labor accurately, we must first of all perform a preliminary task: we must determine the exact meaning of Marx's theory of productive labor. Unfortunately, no section of the broad critical literature on Marx is as full of disagreement and conceptual confusion as this question, among Marxists as well as between them and their opponents. One of the reasons for this confusion is an unclear idea of Marx's own views of productive labor.

To interpret Marx's views, it is necessary to start with the fourth chapter of Volume I of Theories of Surplus Value, which has the title, "Theories of Productive and Unproductive Labor." Marx gives a brief formulation of the ideas developed in this chapter in Volume I of Capital, in Chapter 16: "Capitalist production is not merely the production of commodities, it is essentially the production of surplus-value. The laborer produces, not for himself, but for capital. It no longer suffices, therefore, that he should simply produce. He must produce surplus-value. That laborer alone is productive, who produces surplus-value for the capitalist, and thus works for the self-expansion of capital. If we may take an example from outside the sphere of production of material objects, a schoolmaster is a productive laborer, when, in addition to belaboring the heads of his scholars, he works like a horse to enrich the school proprietor. That\ the latter has laid out his capital in a teaching factory, instead of in a sausage factory, does not alter the relation. Hence the notion of a productive laborer implies not merely a relation between work and useful effect, between laborer and product of labor, but also a specific, social relation of production, a relation that has sprung up historically and stamps the laborer as the direct means of creating surplus-value" (C., I, p. 509). After saying this, Marx promises to consider this question in detail in "volume four" of Capital, namely in Theories of Surplus Value. Actually, at the end of the first volume of Theories of Surplus Value, we find a digression which, in essence, represents a detailed development of ideas which were already formulated in the first volume of Capital.

First of all, Marx notes that "Only bourgeois narrow-mindedness, which regards the capitalist forms of production as absolute forms-hence as eternal, natural forms of production-can confuse the question of what is productive labor from the standpoint of capital with the question of what labor is productive in general, or what is productive labor in general."[255] Marx throws out as useless the question of what kind of labor is productive in general, in all historical epochs, independently of the given social relations. Every system of production relations, every economic order, has its concept of productive labor. Marx confined his analysis to the question of which labor is productive from the standpoint of capital, or in the capitalist system of economy. He answers this question as follows: "Productive labor is therefore-in the system of capitalist production-labor which produces surplus-value for its employer, or which transforms the objective conditions of labor into capital and their owner into a capitalist; that is to say, labor which produces its own product as capital" (Ibid., p. 384). "Only labor which is directly transformed into capital is productive; that is, only labor which makes variable capital a variable magnitude" (Ibid., p. 381). In other words, productive labor is "labor which is directly exchanged with capital" (Ibid., p. 153), i.e., labor which the capitalist buys as his variable capital for the purpose of using that labor to create exchange values and to create surplus value. Unproductive labor is that labor "which is not exchanged with capital, but directly with revenue, that is, with wages or profit (including of course the various categories of those who share as co-partners in the capitalist's profit, such as interest and rent)" (Ibid., p. 153).

---

[255] Marx, Theories of Surplus Value, Part I, Moscow: Foreign Languages Publishing House, 1956, p. 380. Italics in original.

Two conclusions necessarily follow from Marx's definitions: 1) every labor which a capitalist buys with his variable capital in order to draw from it a surplus value, is productive labor, independently of whether or not this labor is objectified in material objects, and whether or not this labor is objectively necessary or useful for the process of social production (for example, the labor of a clown employed by a circus manager). 2) Every labor which the capitalist does not buy with his variable capital is not productive from the point of view of the capitalist economy, even though this labor might be objectively useful and might be objectified in material consumer goods which satisfy human subsistence needs. At first glance, these two conclusions are paradoxical and contradictory to the conventional understanding of productive labor. However, they follow logically from Marx's definition. And Marx applies it boldly. "An actor, for example, or even a clown, according to this definition, is a productive laborer if he works in the service of a capitalist (an entrepreneur) to whom he returns more labor than he receives from him in the form of wages; while a jobbing tailor who comes to the capitalist's house and patches his trousers for him, producing a mere use-value for him, is an unproductive laborer. The former's labor is exchanged with capital, the latter's with revenue. The former's labor produces a surplus-value; in the latter's, revenue is consumed" (Ibid., p. 153). At first glance this example is strikingly paradoxical. The useless labor of the clown is considered productive labor, and the highly useful labor of the tailor is treated as unproductive. What is the meaning of these definitions given by Marx?

In the majority of textbooks on political economy, productive labor is treated from the standpoint of its objective necessity for social production in general, or for the production of material goods. In these treatments, the decisive factor is the content of the labor, namely its result, which is usually a material object to which the labor is directed and which is created by the labor. Marx's problem has nothing in common with this problem except the title. For Marx productive labor means: labor which is engaged in the given social system of production. Marx is interested in the question of what social production is, how the working activity of people who are engaged in the system of social production differs from the working activity of people who are not engaged in social production (for example, labor which is directed to the satisfaction of personal needs or to the service of a household). By what criterion is the working activity of people included in social production, what makes it "productive" labor?

Marx gave the following answer to this question. Every system of production is distinguished by the totality of production relations which are determined by the social form of organization of labor. In the capitalist society, labor is organized in the form of wage labor, i.e., the economy is organized in the form of capitalist enterprises, where wage laborers work under the command of a capitalist. They create commodities and yield a surplus value for the capitalist. Only the labor which is organized in the form of capitalist enterprises, which has the form of wage labor, hired by capital for the purpose of drawing out of it a surplus value, is included in the system of capitalist production. Such labor is "productive" labor. Every type of labor which is included in the given system of social production can be considered productive, i.e., every type of labor organized in the determined social form characteristic of the given system of production. In other words, labor is considered productive or unproductive not from the standpoint of its content, namely in terms of the character of the concrete working activity, but from the standpoint of the social form of its organization, of its consistency with the production relations which characterize the given economic order of the society. Marx frequently noted this characteristic. This sharply distinguishes his theory from conventional theories of productive labor which assign a decisive role to the content of working activity. "These definitions [of productive labor-I.R.] are therefore not derived from the material characteristics of labor (neither from the nature of its product nor from the particular character of the labor as concrete labor) but from the definite social form, the social relations of production, within which the labor is realized" (Ibid., p. 153). "It is a definition of labor which is derived not from its content or its result, but from its particular social form" (Ibid., p. 154). "The determinate material form of the labor, and therefore, of its product, in itself has nothing to do with this distinction between productive and unproductive labor" (Ibid.). "... the content, the concrete character, the particular utility of the labor, seems at first to make no difference" (Ibid., p. 392). "... this distinction between productive and unproductive labor has nothing to do either with the particular specialty of the labor or with the particular use-value in which this special labor is incorporated" (Ibid., p. 156).

From all this it follows that, from a material standpoint, one and the same labor is productive or unproductive (i.e., is included or not included in the capitaUst system of production) depending on whether or not it is organized in the form of a capitalistic enterprise. "For example, the workman employed by a piano maker is a productive laborer. His labor not only replaces the wages that he consumes, but in the product, the piano, the commodity which the piano maker sells, there is a surplus-value over and above the value of the wages. But assume on the contrary that I buy all the materials required for a piano (or for all it matters the laborer himself may possess them), and that instead of buying the piano in a shop I have it made for me in my house. The workman who makes the piano is now an unproductive laborer, because his labor is exchanged directly against my revenue" (Ibid., p. 156). In the first case, the worker who produces the piano is included in a capitalist enterprise and thus in a system of capitalist production. In the second case he is not. "For example Milton, who wrote Paradise Lost for five pounds, was an unproductive laborer. On the other hand, the writer who turns out stuff for his publisher in factory style, is a productive laborer. Milton produced Paradise Lost for the same reason that a silk worm produces silk. It was an activity of his nature. Later he sold the product for 5 pounds. But the literary proletarian of Leipzig, who fabricates books (for example, Compendia of Economics) under the direction of his publisher, is a productive laborer; for his product is from the outset subsumed under capital, and comes into being only for the purpose of increasing that capital. A singer who sells her song for her own account is an unproductive laborer. But the same singer commissioned by an entrepreneur to sing in order to make money for him is a productive laborer; for she produces capital" (Ibid., p. 389"). The capitalist form of organization of labor includes labor in the system of capitalist production and makes it "productive" labor. All working activities which do not take place in the form of an enterprise organized on capitalist principles are not included in the capitalist system of production and are not considered "productive" labor. This is the character of working activities directed to the satisfaction of personal needs (remnants of natural household economy). Even wage labor, if it is not employed to yield surplus value (for example, the labor of household servants) is not productive in the sense defined above. But the labor of household servants is not unproductive because it is "useless" or because it does not produce material goods. As Marx said, the labor of a cook produces "material use-values" (Ibid., p. 155), but it is nevertheless unproductive if the cook is hired as a personal servant. On the other hand, the labor of a lackey, even though it does not produce material goods and is usually recognized as "useless," may be productive labor if it is organized in the form of a capitalist enterprise. "... the cooks and waiters in a public hotel are productive laborers, in so far as their labor is transformed into capital for the proprietor of the hotel. The same persons are unproductive laborers as menial servants, inasmuch as I do not make capital out of their services, but spend revenue on them."In fact, however, these same persons are also for me, the consumer, unproductive laborers in the hotel" (Ibid., pp. 154-155). "Productive laborers may themselves in relation to me be unproductive laborers. For example, if I have my house re-papered and the paper-hangers are wage workers of a master who sells me the job, it is just the same for me as if I had bought a house already papered; as if I had expended money for a commodity for my consumption. But for the master who gets these laborers to hang the paper, they are productive laborers, for they produce surplus value for him" (Ibid., p. 393). Must we understand Marx to mean that he recognizes only a subjective and relative criterion, but not a social and objective criterion of productiveness of labor? We think not. Marx only states that the labor of an upholsterer, if it is part of the household of the consumer-customer, is not yet included in the system of capitalist production. It becomes productive only when it becomes included in the economy of a capitalist entrepreneur.

Consequently only that labor which is organized on capitalist principles and thus is included in the system of capitalist production is productive labor. Capitalist production must not be understood as the existing, concrete social-economic system, which is not composed exclusively of enterprises of a capitalist character; it also contains remnants of pre-capitalist forms of production (for example, peasant and craft production). The system of capitalist production encompasses only the economic units which are formed on capitalist principles. It is a scientific abstraction derived from concrete economic reality, and in this abstract form it represents the subject of political economy as the science of the capitalist economy. In the capitalist economy, as a theoretical abstraction, the labor of the peasant and the craftsman does not exist. The question of their productiveness is not treated: "they [craftsmen and peasants-I.R.] confront me as sellers of commodities, not as sellers of labor, and this relation therefore has nothing to do with the exchange of capital for labor; therefore also it has nothing to do with the distinction between productive and unproductive labor, which depends entirely on whether the labor is exchanged for money as money or for money as capital. They therefore belong neither to the category of productive or of unproductive laborers, although they are producers of commodities. But their production does not fall under the capitalist mode of production" (Ibid., pp. 394-395).

From the standpoint of Marx's definition of productive labor, the labor of the civil servant, of the police, of soldiers and priests, cannot be related to productive labor. Not because this labor is "useless" or because it is not materialized in "things," but only because it is organized on principles of public law, and not in the form of private capitalist enterprises. A postal employee is not a productive worker, but if the post were organized in the form of a private capitalist enterprise which charges money for the delivery of letters and parcels, wage laborers in these enterprises would be productive laborers. If the job of protecting freight and passengers on roads were not carried out by the state police but rather by private transportation bureaus which maintained armed protection by hired workers, the members of such bureaus would be productive laborers. Their labor would be included in the system of capitalist production, and these private bureaus would be subject to the laws of capitalist production (for example, to the law of equal rates of profit for all branches of production). This cannot be said of the post or the police, which are organized on principles of public law. The labor of postal or police civil servants is not included in the system of capitalist production; it is not productive labor.

As we can see, when Marx defined productive labor, he completely abstracted from its content, from the concrete, useful character and result of the labor. He treated labor only from the standpoint of its social form. Labor which is organized in a capitalist enterprise is productive labor. The concept "productive," as well as the other concepts of Marx's political economy, have a historical and social character. This is why it would be extremely incorrect to ascribe a "materialistic" character to Marx's theory of productive labor. From Marx's point of view, one cannot consider only labor which serves the satisfaction of material needs (and not so-called spiritual needs) as productive labor. On the very first page of Capital, Marx wrote: "The nature of such wants, whether, for instance, they spring from the stomach or from fancy, makes no difference" (C., I, p. 35). The nature of the wants plays no role. In the same way, Marx did not attach any decisive significance to the difference between physical and intellectual labor. Marx spoke of this in a well-known passage in Chapter 14 of the first volume of Capital, and in numerous other places. With reference to the labor of the "overlooker, engineer, manager, clerk, etc.-in a word, the labor of the whole personnel required in a particular sphere of material production," he stated that, "In fact they add their aggregate labor to the constant capital, and increase the value of the product by this amount. (How far is this true of bankers, etc?)" (Theories of Surplus Value, Part I, p. 160).[256] Intellectual laborers are supposed to be "indispensable" for the process of production, and thus they "earn" rewards from products / created by physical workers. According to Marx, however, they create new value. From this value they receive a reward, leaving a part of this value in the hands of the capitalist in the form of unpaid value, surplus value.

Intellectual labor necessary for the process of material production in no way differs from physical labor. It is "productive" if it is organized on capitalist principles. In this case it is completely the same thing whether the intellectual labor is organized together with the physical labor in one enterprise (engineering bureau, chemical laboratory or an accounting bureau in a factory), or separated into an independent enterprise (an independent experimental chemical laboratory which has the task of improving production, and so on).

The following difference between types of labor has major significance for the problem of productive labor: this is a difference between labor which "embodies itself in material use-values" (Ibid., p. 162) and labor or

---

[256] The reservation about bankers will become clearer below.

service "which assume no objective form -which do not receive an existence as things separate from those performing the services" (Ibid.), namely, where "production cannot be separated from the act of producing, as is the case with all performing artists, orators, actors, teachers, physicians, priests, etc." (Ibid., p. 398).[257] Assuming that "the entire world of commodities, all spheres of material production-the production of material wealth-are (formally or really) subordinated to the capitalist mode of production" (Ibid., p. 397), the sphere of material production as a whole is included in the sphere of productive, namely capitalistically organized labor. On the other hand, phenomena related to non-material production "are so insignificant compared with the totality of production that they can be left entirely out of account" (Ibid., p. 398). Thus, on the basis of two assumptions, namely, 1) that material production as a whole is organized on capitalist principles, and 2) that non-material production is excluded from our analysis, productive labor can be defined as labor which produces material wealth. "And so productive labor, along with its determining characteristic- which takes no account whatever of the content of labor and is entirely independent of that content-would be given a second, different and subsidiary definition" (Ibid., p. 397). It is necessary to remember that this is a "secondary" definition which is valid only if the above-listed premises are given, i.e., if capitalistically organized labor is assumed in advance. Actually, as Marx

---

[257] Economists do not always carry through a clear difference between labor which has a material character, labor which is designated to the satisfaction of material needs, and labor which is embodied in material things. For example, on two pages, S. Bulgakov, when he speaks of productive labor, has in mind either "labor directed to making objects useful to man" or "labor directed to the satisfaction of material needs," in "O nekotorykh osnovnykh ponyatyakh politicheskoi ekonomii" (On Some Basic Concepts of Political Economy), Nauchnoe Obozrenie (Scientific Survey), 1898, No. 2, pp. 335 and 336.

himself frequently pointed out, productive labor in the sense defined above, and labor which produces material wealth, do not coincide; they diverge in two ways. Productive labor encompasses labor which is not embodied in material things if it is organized on capitalist principles. On the other hand, labor which produces material wealth but which is not organized in the form of capitalist production is not productive labor from the standpoint of capitalist production (see Theories of Surplus Value, p. 162).[258] If we do not take the "secondary definition" but the "decisive characteristic" of productive labor, which Marx defines as labor which creates surplus value, then we see that all traces of "materialistically" defined labor are eliminated from Marx's definition. This definition takes as its starting-point the social (namely capitalistic) form of organization of labor. This definition has a sociological character.

At first glance, the conception of productive labor which Marx developed in Theories of Surplus Value diverges from Marx's view of the labor of workers and clerks employed in trade and credit (Capital, Vol. II, Chapter 6, and Vol. III, Chapters 16-19). Marx does not consider such labor productive. According to many social scientists, including Marxists, Marx refused to consider this labor productive because it does not bring about changes in material things. According to them, this is a trace of "materialistic" theories of productive labor. Noting the position of the "classical school, that productive labor, or labor which creates value (from a bourgeois point of view, this is a simple tautology), must certainly be embodied in material things," V. Bazarov asked with astonishment: "How could Marx commit such a mistake, after having discovered the fetishistic psychology of the commodity producer with such

---

[258] See B. I. Gorev, Na ideologicheskom fronte (On the Ideological Front), 1923, pp. 24-26.

ingenuity?"[259] A. Bogdanov criticized theories which separate "intellectual" and "material" aspects of labor, and added: "These conceptions of classical political economy were not subjected by Marx to the critique which they deserve: in general, Marx himself supported these conceptions."[260]

Is it actually true that Volumes II and III are imbued with the "materialistic" conception of productive labor which Marx subjected to detailed and destructive criticism in Theories of Surplus Value? Actually, such a glaring contradiction in Marx's views does not exist. Marx does not renounce the concept of productive labor as labor which is organized on capitalistic principles independently of its concrete useful character and its results. But if this is so, why does Marx not consider the labor of salesmen and store clerks, organized in a capitalistic commercial enterprise, productive? To answer this question, we must remember that wherever Marx spoke of productive labor as labor which is hired by capital in Theories of Surplus Value, he had in mind only productive capital. The addendum to the first volume of Theories of Surplus Value,[261] which has the title "The Concept of Productive Labor," begins with the question of productive capital. From here, Marx moves on to productive labor. This addendum ends with the words: "Here we have been dealing only with productive capital, that is, capital employed in the direct process of production. We come later to capital in the process of circulation. And only after that, in considering the special form assumed by capital as merchant's capital, can the

---

[259] V. Bazarov, Trud proizvoditelnyi i trud, obrazuyushchii tsennost' (Productive Labor and Labor which Creates Value), Petersburg: 1899, p. 23.

[260] A. Bogdanov and I. Stepanov, Kurs politicheskoi ekonomii (Course of Political Economy), Vol. II, 4th Edition, p. 12.

[261] Cf. K. Kautsky's edition of Marx's Theories of Surplus Value, New York: International Publishers, 1952.

question be answered as to how far the laborers employed by it are productive or unproductive."[262] Thus the question of productive labor rests on the question of productive capital, i.e., on the well-known theory, in Volume II of Capital, of the "Metamorphoses of Capital." According to this theory, capital goes through three phases in its process of reproduction: money capital, productive capital and commodity capital. The first and third phases represent the "process of circulation of capital," and the second phase, the "process of production of capital." "Productive" capital, in this schema, is not opposed to unproductive capital, but to capital in the "process of circulation." Productive capital directly organizes the process of the creation of consumer goods in the wider sense. This process includes all work which is necessary for the adaptation of goods for the purpose of consumption, for example, preservation, transport, packaging, and so on. Capital in the process of circulation organizes "genuine circulation," purchase and sale, for example the transfer of the right of ownership abstracted from the actual transfer of products. This capital overcomes the friction of the commodity capitalist system, so to speak, friction which is due to the fact that the system is splintered into individual economic units. It precedes and follows the process of creating consumer goods, though it is linked to this process indirectly. The "production of capital" and the "circulation of capital" become independent in Marx's system, and they are treated separately, even though at the same time Marx does not lose sight of the unity of the entire process of reproduction of capital. This is the basis for the distinction between labor employed in production and labor employed in circulation. However, this division has nothing to do with a division of labor into labor which produces changes in material goods and labor which does not possess this property. Marx distinguishes labor hired by "productive" capital, or more precisely by capital in the phase of production, from labor which is hired by

---

[262] Marx, Theories of Surplus Value, Part I, Moscow: FLPH, 1956, p. 400.

commodity or money capital, or more precisely capital in the phase of circulation. Only the first type of labor is "productive," not because it produces material goods, but because it is hired by "productive" capital, i.e., capital in the phase of production. The participation of labor in the production of consumer goods (not necessarily material goods) represents, for Marx, an additional property of the productive character of labor, but not its criterion. The criterion remains the capitalist form of organization of labor. The productive character of labor is an expression of the productive character of capital. The movement of the phases of capital determines the characteristics of the labor which they hire. Here Marx remains true to his view that in the capitalist society the moving force of development is capital: its movements determine the movement of labor, which is subordinate to capital.

Thus, according to Marx, every type of labor organized in forms of the capitalist process of production, or more precisely, labor hired by "productive" capital, i.e., capital in the phase of production, is productive labor. The labor of salesmen is not productive, not because it does not produce changes in material goods, but only because it is hired by capital in the phase of circulation. The labor of the clown in the service of the circus entrepreneur is productive even though it does not produce changes in material goods and, from the standpoint of the requirements of the social economy, it is less useful than the labor of salesmen. The labor of the clown is productive because it is employed by capital in the phase of production. (The result of the production in this case consists of non-material goods, jests, but this does not change the problem. The clown's jests have use-value and exchange-value. Their exchange-value is greater than the value of the reproduction of the clown's labor power, i.e., than his wage and the expenditures for constant capital. Consequently, the entrepreneur draws a surplus value.) On the other hand, the labor of a cashier in a circus, who sells tickets for the clown's performances, is unproductive, because he is hired by capital in the phase of circulation: he only assists in transferring the "right to watch the show," the right to enjoy the jests of the clown, from one person (the entrepreneur) to another (the public).[263]

For an accurate grasp of Marx's idea, it is necessary to grasp clearly that the phase of circulation of capital does not mean an "actual," "real" circulation and distribution of products, i.e., a process of real transfer from the hands of producers to the hands of consumers, which is necessarily accompanied by the processes of transport, preservation, packaging and so on. The function of circulation of capital is only to transfer the right of ownership of a product from one person to another, only a transformation of value from a commodity form to a money form, or inversely, only a realization of produced value. It is an ideal or formal transition, but not a real one. These are "costs of circulation, which originate in a mere change of form of value, in circulation, ideally considered" (C., II, p. 139). "We are concerned here only with the general character of the costs of circulation, which arise out of the metamorphosis of forms alone" (Ibid., p. 138). Marx established the following proposition: "The general law is that all costs of circulation which arise only from changes in the forms of commodities do not add to their value" (Ibid., p. 152).

Marx sharply distinguished this "formal metamorphosis," which is the essence of the phase of circulation, from the "real function" of commodity capital (C., III, p. 268). Among these real functions Marx

---

[263] What has been said does not mean that Marx did not see any difference between material and non-material production. Recognizing as productive every labor employed by productive capital, Marx apparently held that inside of this productive labor it was necessary to distinguish "productive labor in a narrow sense," namely, labor employed in material production and embodied in material things (Theorien über den Mehrwert, 111, p. 496).

included: transport, storage, "distribution of commodities in a distributable form" (Ibid., p. 267), "expressing, transporting, distributing, retailing" (Ibid., p. 282 and p. 288). It is to be understood that the formal realization of value, i.e., the transfer of the right of ownership over products, "acts as middleman in their realization and thereby simultaneously in the actual exchange of commodities, i.e., in their transfer from hand to hand, in the social metabolism" (Ibid., p. 282). But theoretically, the formal realization, the genuine function of capital in circulation, is completely different from the real functions mentioned above, which are in essence foreign to this capital and have a "heterogeneous" character (Ibid., p. 282). In usual commercial enterprises these formal and real functions usually intermingle and intertwine. The labor of a salesman in a store serves for the real function of preservation, unpacking, packing, transport, and so on, and the formal functions of purchase and sale. But these functions can be separated in terms of persons as well as territorially: "purchasable and saleable commodities may be stored in docks or in other public premises" (Ibid., p. 289), for example, in commercial and transportation warehouses. The formal moment of realization, purchase and sale, may take place elsewhere, in a special "sales bureau." The formal and the real aspects of circulation are separate from each other.

Marx viewed all the real functions as "production processes continuing within the process of circulation" (Ibid., pp. 267-268), "processes of production which may continue in the process of circulation" (Ibid., p. 288). They are "processes of production which are only continued in circulation, the productive character of which is hence merely concealed by the circulation form" (C., II, p. 139). Thus labor which is applied in these "processes of production" is productive labor which creates value and surplus value. If the labor of salesmen consists of carrying out real functions: preservation, transport, packaging, etc., it is productive labor, not because it is embodied in material goods (preservation does not produce such changes) but because it is engaged in the "process of production," and is consequently hired by productive capital. The labor of the same commercial clerk is unproductive only if it serves exclusively the "formal metamorphosis" of value, its realization, the ideal transfer of the right of ownership over the product from one person to another. The "formal metamorphosis" which takes place in the "sales bureau" and which is separate from all real functions, also requires certain circulation costs and expenditures of labor, namely for accounting, bookkeeping, correspondence, etc. (C., III, p. 289.) This labor is not productive, but once again not because it does not create material goods, but because it serves the "formal metamorphosis" of value, the phase of "circulation" of capital in pure form.

Accepting Marx's distinction between "formal" and "material" functions (we prefer the term "real," which is found in Marx's work; the term "material" may lead to misunderstanding), V. Bazarov denies that the formal functions can require "the application of a single atom of living human labor."[264] "In reality only the 'material' aspect of the functions of commodity capital absorb living human labor. However, the formal metamorphosis does not require any 'expenditures' from the merchant." We cannot agree with Bazarov's view. Let us assume that all real, "material" functions are separate from the formal functions, and that goods are preserved in special warehouses, docks, etc. Let us assume that in the "sales bureau" only the formal act of purchase and sale takes place, the transfer of the right of ownership over the commodity. The expenditures for the equipment in the bureau, the maintenance of the clerks, sales agents, the keeping of accounts, to the extent that these are caused by the transfer of the right of ownership from one person to another, are all "genuine costs of circulation" related only to the formal metamorphosis of value. As we can see, even the formal metamorphosis of value requires "expenditures" by the merchant and the application of

---

[264] Bazarov, Op. Cit., p. 35.

human labor which, in this case, is unproductive according to Marx.

We turn the attention of the reader to the question of bookkeeping because, as some writers claim, Marx denied the productive character of labor in bookkeeping in all cases.[265] We hold such a view to be erroneous. Actually, Marx's views on "bookkeeping" (C., II, Chapter 6) are distinguished by extreme obscurity and may be interpreted in the above sense. But from the standpoint of Marx's conception of productive labor, the question of the labor of bookkeepers does not raise particular doubts. If bookkeeping is necessary for the performance of real functions of production, even if these functions are carried out in the course of circulation (the labor of the bookkeeper is related to production, preservation, transport of goods), then bookkeeping is related to the process of production. The labor of the bookkeeper is unproductive only when he performs the formal metamorphosis of value-the transfer of the right of ownership over the product, the act of purchase and sale in its ideal form. We again repeat that in this case the labor of the bookkeeper is not unproductive because it does not produce changes in material goods (in this respect it does not differ from the labor of a bookkeeper in the factory), but because it is hired by capital in the phase of circulation (separated from all real functions).

These distinctions between formal and real functions of commodity capital, or between circulation in

---

[265] Such a view can be found in the work of V. Bazarov (Op. Cit., p. 49) and I. Davydov, in his article "K voprosu o proizvoditel'nom i ne-proizvoditel'nom trade" (Contribution to the Problem of Productive and Unproductive Labor), Nauchnoe Obozrenie (Scientific Survey), 1900, No. 1, p. 154; and C. Prokopovich, "K kritike Marksa" (Contribution to the Critique of Marx), 1901, p. 35; Julian Borchardt, Die volkswirtschaftlichen Grundbegriffe nach der Lehre von Karl Marx, Berlin: Buchverlag Ratebund, 1920, p. 72.

its pure form and "the processes of production which are carried out in the process of circulation," are applied by Marx in Volumes II and III of Capital. We cannot agree with the view that Marx applied these distinctions only in Volume III, while Volume II arbitrarily treats all expenditures on exchange, including those expended on the real functions of circulation, as unproductive. V. Bazarov[266] and A. Bogdanov[267] expressed such a view of the major difference between the second and third volumes of Capital. Actually, even in Volume II of Capital, Marx relates only "genuine costs of circulation" and not all costs of circulation, to unconditionally unproductive costs (C., II, p. 132). In Volume II he speaks of "processes of production" which are carried out in exchange and have a productive character (Ibid., p. 139). Without taking into consideration minor differences in shades of thought and formulation, we do not find a basic contradiction between Volumes II and III of Capital. This is not to deny that in Chapter 17 of Volume III, and particularly in Chapter 6 of Volume II, discordant passages, terminological unclarity and individual contradictions are found, but the basic conception of productive labor as labor which is hired by capital (even in supplementary processes of production which are carried out in circulation) and unproductive labor which serves capital in the phase of pure circulation or in the "formal metamorphosis" of value, is very clear.

A. Bogdanov objects to Marx's division of the functions of commodity capital into real (continuation of the productive process) and formal (pure circulation) on the ground that in capitalism the formal functions are just as "objectively necessary" as the real, since their purpose is to satisfy real requirements of the given productive system.[268] However, Marx did not intend to deny the

---

[266] Op. Cit., pp. 39-40.

[267] Kurs politicheskoi ekonomii (Course of Political Economy), Vol. II, Part 4, pp. 12-13.

[268] Op. Cit., p. 13.

necessity of the phase of circulation in the process of reproduction of capital. "He [the buying and selling agent] performs a necessary function, because the process of reproduction itself includes unproductive functions" (C., II, p. 134) i.e., the function of pure circulation. "The labor-time required in these operations [of pure circulation] is devoted to certain necessary operations of the reproduction process of capital, but yields no additional value" (C., III, p. 290). According to Marx, the phases of production and circulation are equally necessary in the process of reproduction of capital. But this does not abolish the distinctive properties of these two phases of the movement of capital. Labor hired by capital in the phase of production and labor hired by capital in the phase of circulation are both necessary, but Marx considered only the first productive. A. Bogdanov takes the objective necessity of the labor for the given economic system as a criterion of productiveness. In this way he not only erases the difference between labor engaged in production and labor engaged in circulation, but he conditionally adds "functions which are related to military activity"[269] to productive functions, even though functions related to military activity are organized on the basis of public law and not on the basis of private capitalist production. As opposed to Marx, A. Bogdanov does not take the social form of organization of labor as the criterion of its productiveness, but rather the "indispensability" of the labor, in its concrete and useful form, for the given economic system.

Thus the conceptions of writers who reduce Marx's theory of productive labor to a difference between labor embodied in material things and labor which does not possess this property, must be recognized as unconditionally erroneous. Hilferding gets closer to this problem in Marx's work. He considers every labor "necessary for the social purpose of production, and thus independent of the determined historical form which the

---

[269] Op. Cit., p. 17.

production takes in the given determined social form," to be productive. "On the other hand, labor which is expended only for the purposes of capitalist circulation, i.e., which originates from the determined historical organization of production, does not create value."[270] Some passages in Marx's work (C., II, p. 138 and p. 142) are similar to Hilferding's definition of unproductive labor. However, Hilferding's definition of productive labor as "independent from the determined social form of production" diverges from Marx's definition. Hilferding's conception that the "criterion of productiveness ... is one and the same in all social formations" (Ibid.,) sharply contradicts Marx's entire system. Marx's distinction between labor hired by capital in the phase of production and labor hired by capital in the phase of circulation was reflected and partly modified in Hilferding's conception.

We do not ask whether or not Marx's definition of productive labor, based on the analysis of the social form of the labor, is correct, or whether the conventional definitions in treatises on political economy, which are based on "indispensability," "usefulness," the "material" character of labor or its role in personal and productive consumption, are correct. We do not say that Marx's distinction, which abstracts from the content of the labor expenditures, is more accurate than the more conventional views. We only hold that Marx's view is different from these conventional views and is not covered by them. Marx's attention was turned to another aspect of phenomena, and we may in fact regret that Marx chose the term "productive" for his treatment of the differences between labor hired by capital in the phase of

---

[270] R. Hilferding, "Postanovka problemy teoreticheskoi ekonomii u Marksa" (Marx's Formulation of the Problems of Theoretical Economics), Osnovnye problemy politicheskoi ekonomii (Basic Problems of Political Economy), 1922, pp. 107-108.

production and labor hired by capital in the phase of circulation. The term "productive" had a different meaning in economic science. (Perhaps a more suitable term would have been "production labor.")

Appendix

Abstract Labor and Marx's System

Lecture Given in 1927

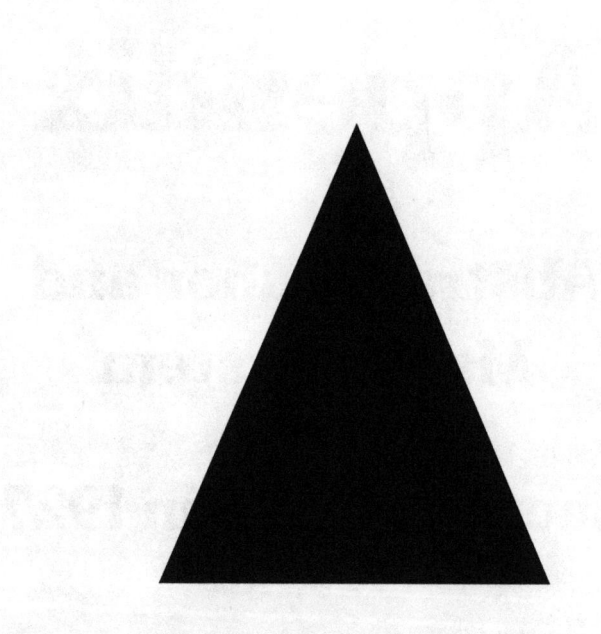

Part 1

Comrades, I have chosen abstract labour and value as the theme of my lecture for two reasons: firstly, I know that the question of abstract labour and the form and content of value has been the subject of heated debate in your seminars. Because of this I decided to organise my lecture in such a way that I may deal with the problem of abstract labour in detail, while covering the question of value, its form and content at the same time.

The second reason which persuaded me to select this theme is that it is the central problem of all Marxist theory. We do not term the theory 'the labour theory of value' for nothing — the name alone indicates that the main problem of the theory is the question of the reciprocal relationship between labour and value. What is the labour which creates or determines value, and what is the value which is created or determined by labour? That is the main problem of Marxist theory, which I hope to illuminate in my lecture.

Before we move to the essential part of the question, I should like to make a few remarks on methodology. By what method do we intend to set about solving this problem? In the Introduction to a Critique of Political Economy (Introduction to the Grundrisse) Marx observed that an economic investigation can be conducted according to two methods: by the transition from the concrete to the abstract, and conversely by movement from the abstract to the concrete.

The former, the analytical method, consists in taking a complex concrete phenomenon as the starting point of the investigation, and selecting a single, or several of the most important, characteristics, disregarding the multiplicity of its features, and so making the transition from the more concrete to the more abstract concept, to the simpler, or thinner concept, as Marx says. By further analysis we move on from this concept to an even simpler one, until we have reached the most abstract concepts in the particular science or the particular complex of questions, which interest us.

To cite just one example as an illustration of the problematic we are dealing with, I may remind you of the reciprocal relation between the following concepts. The Marxian theory of value builds on the concepts: abstract labour, value, exchange value and money. If we take money, the most complex and most concrete aspect of these concepts, and by examining the concept of money make the transition to exchange value, as the more general concept underlying money; if we then move from exchange value to value, and from value to abstract labour, we are moving from the more concrete to the more abstract concept, i.e. we are following the analytical method.

But, Marx says, however necessary the use of the analytical method is in the first stage of scientific enquiry, it cannot satisfy us in itself, and it must be complemented by another method. Once we have traced the complex phenomenon back to its basic elements by means of analysis, we have to take the opposite direction and, starting from the most abstract concepts, show how these develop to lead us on to more concrete forms, more concrete concepts. In our case, this progression from the simpler concepts to richer and more complex ones would be the movement from abstract labour to value, from value to exchange value and from exchange value to money.

Marx calls this method 'genetic', at one point, because it enables us to follow the genesis and development of complex forms. Elsewhere he terms it the dialectical. I hope we can also agree to describe the first method as the analytical, and the second (which includes both the analytical and the synthetic method) as dialectical.

Marx indicates that he considers the dialectical method to be the only one which solves scientific questions satisfactorily. Accordingly, we have to subject the problem which interests us, the question of the relationship between labour and value, to investigation not only by the analytical method, but by the dialectical as well.

Marx gives many examples to show in what respect the analytic method is inadequate. I should like to quote three examples here.

Concerning the theory of value, Marx says "Political economy has indeed analysed, however incompletely, value and its magnitude, and has discovered what lies beneath these forms. But it has never once asked the question why labour is represented by the value of its product and labour time by the magnitude of that value." (Capital I p.80).

In another passage, devoted to the theory of money, Marx says: "In the last decades of the 17th century it had already been shown that money is a commodity, but this step marks only the infancy of the analysis. The difficulty lies, not in comprehending that money is a commodity, but in discovering how, why and by what means a commodity becomes money." (Capital I p.92) Here, as we see, the dialectical method differs once again from the analytical.

Finally, at a further point while discussing religion, Marx repeats the idea which he has stated before, that it is obviously much easier to discover by analysis the core of the curious religious conceptions, than conversely, it is to develop from the actual relations of real life the corresponding forms of those relations. The latter method is the only materialistic and consequently the only scientific one (Capital I p.372 note 3).

Following Marx, we must solve our problem in this way. Our task does not only consist in showing that the value of a product can be attributed to labour. We must also show the converse. We must reveal how people's productive relations find their expression in value.

This is the basic statement of the problem, which must be considered the most methodologically correct from the Marxian standpoint.

If we put the question in this way, we take not the concept of value as the starting point of the investigation, but the concept of labour. We define the concept of labour in such a way that the concept of value also follows from it.

The requirements of the methodology already give us some indications as to the correct definition of the concept of labour.

The concept of labour must be defined in such a way that it comprises all the characteristics of the social organisation of labour, characteristics which give rise to the form of value, which is appropriate to the products of labour. A concept of labour from which the concept of value does not follow, and particularly a concept of labour in the physiological sense, i.e. the concept of labour which lacks all the features which are characteristic of its social organisation in commodity production, cannot lead to the conclusion which we seek from the Marxian standpoint of the dialectical method.

In the following I shall try to show that the difference in conception between the sociological and the physiological understanding of abstract labour can in part be explained precisely by the distinction between the two methods, the dialectical and the analytical. Although the physiological conception of abstract labour can stand its ground more or less successfully from the standpoint of the analytical method, nevertheless it is doomed to failure from the start from the standpoint of the dialectical, since one cannot obtain from the concept of labour in the physiological sense any notion of value as the necessary social form of the product of labour.

So we have to define labour in such a way that from it, from labour and its social organisation, we may understand the necessity of value as the basic social form which the products of labour assume in commodity production and the laws of the movement of value.

Moving on to the analysis of labour, we will start with the most simple concept, with the concept of concrete or useful labour.

Concrete labour is seen by Marx as labour in its useful activity, as labour which creates products which are necessary for the satisfaction of human needs. Labour viewed from this material technical side represents concrete labour.

It is obvious that concrete labour does not interest us in the least, so long as we are speaking of the individual, of Robinson Crusoe overcoming nature, since the object of our science is not the production of a single individual, but social production, the production of a whole group of people which is organised on the basis of a specific social division of labour. The system of the social division of labour is the totality of the various concrete kinds of labour, which are unified in a determined system and complement one another materially.

So we have made the transition from concrete labour in general to the system of the social division of labour, as the totality of the various concrete kinds of labour. We have to inquire more closely into the concept of the social division of labour since it plays a key role in the understanding of the whole of Marx's theory of value.

Marx says that the system of the social division of labour can occur in two-fold form — as he terms it — as a system which is mediated through exchange and as a system which has no need of such mediation, for example the natural economy of a large clan or of a socialist community etc.

We may look first at the system of organised social division of labour which has developed without exchange.

So long as one speaks of an organised system of the social division of labour, we have not only concrete material-technical labour, but social labour as well. In Marx, the concept of the social division of labour is on the border between the concept of concrete useful labour, and social labour in social production. On the one hand, at the beginning of the section on the two-fold character of labour (Capital I p.41 f), Marx examines the social division of labour as the totality of the concrete modes of labour. Elsewhere in Capital, particularly in the chapter on "Manufacture," (Capital I p.350ff), he examines the system of the social division of labour from the standpoint of the human relations of production which characterise this system. In organised production, the relations among people are relatively simple and transparent. Labour assumes a directly social form, i.e. there is a determined social organisation and determined social organs, which distribute the labour among the individual members of the society, whereby the labour of each person enters directly into social production as concrete labour with all its concrete material characteristics. The labour of each person is social, specifically because it differs from the labour of the other members of the society and represents a material complement to them. Labour is directly social in its concrete form. At the same time it is also divided labour. For the social organisation of labour consists in labour being distributed among the individual members of the society, and conversely the division of labour being the act of a social organ. Labour is both social and divided, and possesses these characteristics in its material technical, concrete or useful form also.

Let us now ask this question: is the labour in an organised community also socially equated? Do we find a process which we could describe as a social process of equation of labour in this community?

There are various views on this particular problem. Some economists maintain that this kind of social equation of labour already exists in any production community, which is based on the division of labour, and in a form which does not differ in essence from the equation of labour in commodity production.

Other economists take the opposite view, saying that the process of social equation of labour is a process which is only appropriate to commodity production and occurs in no other form of production. In particular, these economists deny the possibility and necessity for social equation of labour in a socialist economy.

I have suggested a middle road in my book. I pointed out that every production which rests on the division of labour has recourse to social equation of the labour of different kinds and different individuals, to some extent and in one form or another. I also pointed out in connection with this that this equation of labour acquires a very particular social form in commodity production and therefore makes way for the appearance of a completely new category, that of abstract labour. I think that Marx regarded the question in this way, although we have no clear statement by him on the subject. I know of one very explicit observation, which dates already from the first edition of 'Capital'. There he says: "In every social form of labour the labours of the various individuals are related to each other also as human labours but here this relation itself counts as the specifically social form of the labours" (Das Kapital, 1st edition p.238).

We will analyse the end of this sentence at a later point. For the present, I only want to establish that Marx clearly thought that in every social form of labour, the labour of single individuals is related as human labour. It is correct that extreme adherents of the physiological version could maintain that Marx meant here only the physiological equality of the various kinds of labour. But this interpretation seems to me too farfetched. Both the actual sense of the particular sentence, which speaks of the "social form of labour," as well as its relation to many other places in Capital, indicate that Marx meant here the process of social equation of labour.

I think it is necessary to add a certain qualification to the formula that social equation of labour occurs in any social form of production.

I think that in the ancient family, for instance, where the labour was divided between man and woman and was tied to the representative of each sex, where the change from male labour to female did not exist and was even forbidden, the process of social equation of labour could not take place, even in embryonic form. Further, in social organisations which were based on extreme inequality of the various social strata (e.g. slavery), the social equation of labour could only occur for the members of a specific social group (e.g. for slaves or for a specific category of slaves). Even the concept of labour as such, as social function, could not be acquired in this kind of society.

If we then leave aside social organisation which was based on extreme inequality of the sexes or of individual groups, and turn to a large community with division of labour, e.g. the kind found in the large family associations of the Southern Slavs — I think that here the process of social equation of labour was necessary. It becomes all the more necessary in a large socialist community. But this process of the equation of labour in an organised community differs essentially from the process which occurs in commodity production. Let us actually imagine some socialist community where labour is distributed among the members of the society. A determined social organ equates the labour of different kinds and of different individuals, since without this organ there could be no economic planning. But in a community of this kind the process of equation of labour is secondary and only complementary to the process of socialisation and division of labour. Labour is primarily social and divided. The characteristic of socially equalised labour belongs here as derivative or supplementary. The main characteristic of labour is its social and divided aspect and its socially equated aspect is an additional feature.

I may take this opportunity to say that for the sake of clarity I would find it useful to distinguish between three concepts of equal labour:

1) physiologically equal labour

2) socially equated labour

3) abstract labour, as used by Marx, or preferably, abstract universal labour (a term which Marx uses in the 'Critique')

The physiological homogeneity of the various modes of labour existed in all historical epochs, and the possibility that individuals may change over from one occupation to another is the prerequisite for any social division of labour. Socially equated labour is characteristic for all systems with the social division of labour, that is not only for commodity production, but, for instance, for a socialist community. Finally the third concept of labour, as abstract universal, is characteristic only for commodity production. We will come onto this concept. So far we have only discussed the second concept of labour as socially equated and divided.

Let us take a look at the changes which will take place in the organisation of labour in our community, if we imagine it not in the form of an organised whole, but in the form of a combination of individual production units of private commodity producers, that is, in the form of commodity production.

In commodity production we also find the social characteristics of labour, specified above, which we observed earlier in an organised community. Here too we will find social labour, divided labour and socially equated labour; but all these socialisation processes, processes of equation and division of labour, occur in a totally different form. The interrelation between the three characteristics is now completely different, primarily because in commodity production the direct social organisation of labour is missing, and labour is not directly social.

In commodity production, the labour of an individual, a single commodity producer, is not directly regulated by the society, and in itself, in its concrete form, it does not yet belong to social production. Labour only becomes social in commodity production when it assumes the characteristic of socially equated labour; the labour of every commodity producer only becomes social by virtue of the fact that his product is assimilated with the products of all the other commodity producers, and the labour of a specific individual is thus assimilated with the labour of all the other members of the society and all the others kinds of labour. There is no other characteristic for the definition of the social character of labour in commodity production. There is no previously conceived plan for the socialisation of the division of labour, and the only indication that the labour of a particular individual is included within the social system of production is the exchange of the product of a specific labour for any other product.

So in comparison with the socialist community, the characteristics of social labour and of equated labour have exchanged roles in commodity production. Previously, the characteristic labour as equal or equated was the result of the secondary process, of the derived act of a social organ, which socialised and distributed labour.

Now labour only becomes social in the form in which it is equated with all other kinds of labour, and becomes thus socially equated labour.

I should like to quote a few statements by Marx which should confirm this.

The most unequivocal example can be found in the 'Critique' where Marx says that labour only becomes social "by assuming the form of its direct opposite, of abstract universal labour" (p.34), that is, the form of equation with all other kinds of labour. "Abstract and in that form social labour" — Marx frequently characterises the social form of labour in commodity production with these words. I may also call to mind the well known passage from 'Capital' which states that in commodity production "the specific social character of private labour carried on independently, consists in the equality of every kind of that labour by virtue of its being human labour" (Capital I p.74).

And so in commodity production the emphasis of the social characteristic of labour shifts from the attribute of socialised labour to that of equal or socially equated labour, which only becomes socially equalised labour through the equation of the products of labour. The concept of the equality of labour plays an important role in Marxian value theory precisely because in commodity production labour becomes social only in its quality of being equal labour.

Like the characteristic of social labour the characteristic of divided labour also follows from the equality of labour in commodity production. The division of labour in commodity production does not consist in its conscious distribution corresponding to determined, previously expressed needs, but is regulated by the principle of the equal advantage of production. The division of labour between individual branches of production takes place in such a way that in all branches of production, the commodity producers receive an equal sum of value through expenditure of an equal quantity of labour.

We established the three characteristics of labour as being social labour, socially equated labour and divided labour. All these characteristics also appertain to labour in a socialist society, but completely change their character and their interrelationship as compared with commodity production. The three characteristics of labour which we listed here are the basis from which the three aspects of value develop. Marx considers value as the unity of the form of value, the substance of value and the magnitude of value. "The crucially important task however was to discover the inner necessary interrelationship between the form of value, the substance of value and the magnitude of value" (Kapital Ist ed. p.240). The unity of the form, substance and magnitude of value reflects the unity of labour as social, socially equated and quantitatively divided. In commodity production, the relations of labour and of production are "objectified" and the social characteristics of labour assume the form of "objectified" attributes of the product of labour. The "form of value" is the social form of the product of labour, which reflects the particular social character of labour in commodity production. "The substance of value" represents socially equal labour. And finally the "magnitude of value" is the expression of the social division of labour, or more precisely of the quantitative side of the process of division of labour.

The threefold character of labour, which we have suggested, helps us to explain the relationship which exists in the Marxian system between form, substance, and magnitude of value. In particular this division clarifies some problems of the construction of Marx's section on the 'Fetishism of Commodities'.

Allow me to read out this section from the second paragraph: "For, in the first place, however varied the useful kinds of labour or productive activities, may be, it is a physiological fact that they are functions of the human organisation, and each such function, whatever may be its nature or form, is essentially the expenditure of human brain, nerves, muscles etc. Secondly, with regard to that which forms the ground-work for the quantitative determination of value, namely, the duration of that expenditure or the quantity of labour, it is quite clear that there is a palpable difference between its quantity and quality. Lastly, from the moment that men in any way work for one another, their labour assumes a social form" (Capital I p.71).

In the three points quoted, Marx indicates that we can observe the three characteristics of labour, social, equal and quantitatively divided, not only in commodity production, but also in other forms of production.

But, says Marx, "whence, then arises the enigmatical character of the product of labour, so soon as it assumes the form of commodities?" And he answers himself: obviously precisely from the form of commodities, in which the three characteristics of labour are already transformed, "reified," in the value of the products of labour. "The equality of all sorts of human labour is expressed objectively by their products all being equally values; the measure of the expenditure of human labour power by the duration of that expenditure, takes the form of the quantity of value of the products of labour; and finally, the mutual relations of the producers, within which the social character affirms itself, takes the form of a social relation between the products." (Capital I p.72)

In these three points Marx already speaks of the substance, the magnitude and the form of value. His reasoning can be traced particularly clearly in the first edition of 'Capital', where the three sentences quoted are immediately followed by a whole page on the substance, magnitude and form of value. In the second edition the comments referring to the substance, magnitude and form of value are apparently omitted by Marx. In reality they were only deferred. The three paragraphs which precede the analysis of the various forms of production (Robinson's production, medieval production etc.) are devoted to the substance, the magnitude and the form of value[271].

We have now reached the conclusion that equal labour can mean firstly physiologically equal labour, which we have only briefly considered; secondly it can signify socially equated labour, and this kind of labour exists not only in commodity production, but also, let us say in a socialist community or another large community which is based on the social division of labour; and finally there is abstract universal labour, that is, socially equated labour in the specific form appropriate to commodity production, labour which becomes social and divided only by the process of social equation. Only this socially equated labour can be described as abstract or abstract-universal. We should mention here that Marx makes several allusions to the three kinds of equation of labour in the 'Critique of Political Economy', that is to physiological, social equalisation in general and social equalisation in commodity production. Marx does not draw any absolutely clear distinction it is true, but we should point out that he does distinguish three terms: human labour, equal and abstract universal labour. I would not maintain that these three terms coincide with those which we characterised earlier as physiologically equal labour, socially equalised and abstract labour, but there are some points of contact nevertheless.

In dealing with the problem of abstract labour, we cannot therefore stop at the preliminary characteristic of labour as physiologically equal, nor the characteristic of

---

[271] A whole paragraph is devoted to the substance of value, beginning with the words: "Hence, when we bring the products of our labour into relation with each other as values, it is not because we see in these articles the material receptacles of homogenous human labour.". The following paragraph is devoted to the magnitude of value, and the next to the form of value.

labour as socially equated. We have to make the transition from both these characteristics to a third, and investigate that specific form of equated labour which is peculiar to commodity production, that is, the system of the social division of labour based on exchange.

Consequently, not only are the followers of the physiological conception of abstract labour mistaken in our opinion, but also those comrades who understand abstract labour in general to mean socially equated labour independent of the specific social form in which this equation occurs.

We must add, that the two concepts of labour, physiologically equated and socially equated, are frequently confused, and not distinguished from one another sufficiently clearly. The concept of abstract universal labour naturally implies the physiological equality and the social equation of labour, but apart from these it also contains the social equation of labour in the quite specific form which it takes in commodity production.

We could give many quotations from Marx himself to show how he is crudely misconstrued by the followers of the physiological conception of abstract labour. I should like to read just one very characteristic quotation here. In his short sketch of Franklin's views Marx says that Franklin unconsciously reduced all the forms of labour to one aspect, being uninterested in whether the labour was that of a shoemaker, a tailor, etc. Franklin believed that value is determined "by abstract labour, which has no particular quality and can thus be measured only in terms of quantity." Franklin recognised abstract labour. "But," Marx added, "since he does not explain that the labour expressed in exchange value is abstract universal social labour, which is brought about by the universal alienation of individual labour, he is bound to mistake money for the direct embodiment of this alienated labour." (Critique p.56-57).

It is obvious here that Marx is contrasting abstract labour with abstract universal labour. The abstract universal labour which is embodied in value is the labour which is specifically appropriate to commodity production.

We now reach the conclusion: that if we analyse the problem of the relation between labour and value from the standpoint of the dialectical method as well as the analytical, then we must take the concept of labour as the starting point and develop the concept of value from it.

If we follow the analytical method, start out from value and ask ourselves what lies beneath this concept, we can certainly say that physiologically equal labour and socially equated labour are concealed beneath the value of products. But neither answer will be adequate, since there is no way to make the transition from physiologically equal labour or from socially equated labour to value.

In order to arrive at the concept of value dialectically from the concept of labour, we must also include in the concept of labour those features which characterise the social organisation of labour in commodity production and necessitate the appearance of value as the particular social form of the product of labour. Consequently this concept of abstract universal labour must be far richer than both the concept of the physiological equality of labour and the concept of the social equation of labour in general.

Part 2

We moved from physiologically equal labour to socially equated labour, and from socially equated to abstract universal labour. We enriched our definition of labour by new characteristics in the three stages of our investigation and only when we moved on to the third stage and defined labour as abstract universal, from which the category of value must necessarily follow, was it possible for us to move from labour to value.

We could define abstract labour approximately as follows:

Abstract labour is the designation for that part of the total social labour which was equalised in the process of social division of labour through the equation of the products of labour on the market.

In my book 'Essays on Marx's Theory of Value' I gave more or less this definition. I think it is necessary to add that the social nature of abstract labour is not limited by the fact that the concept of value necessarily follows from this concept. As I have already outlined in my book, the concept of abstract labour leads unconditionally to the concept of money also, and from the Marxian standpoint that is entirely consistent. In reality we defined abstract labour as labour which was made equal through the all round equation of all the products of labour, but the equation of all the products of labour is not possible except through the assimilation of each one of them with a universal equivalent. Consequently the product of abstract labour has the ability to be assimilated with all the other products only in the form that it appears as universal equivalent or can potentially be exchanged for a universal equivalent.

One can see particularly clearly in the 'Critique of Political Economy' that the concept of abstract labour is inseparably tied to that of the universal equivalent for Marx.

There Marx approaches the study of abstract labour as follows. As in 'Capital', he starts out from the commodity or value, and uncovers analytically the abstract universal labour which lies beneath value (Studienausgabe p.235). After he has moved by analysis from the equality of values to the equality of labour he goes on to a detailed sociological characterisation of this equal labour, of the "social categories of labour," "social ... in the particular sense" which is appropriate to commodity production. (Critique p.31). In commodity production the social character of labour is expressed by "the labour of the individual assuming the abstract form of universal labour, or his product assuming the form of universal equivalent: (Critique p.33-34). "The universal labour-time finds its expression in a universal product, a universal equivalent." (Critique p.32). "The labour of an individual can produce exchange value only if it produces universal equivalents" (Critique p.32).

As we can see, Marx links the category of abstract labour inseparably with the concept of the universal equivalent, or money. We therefore have to carry the social characterisation of abstract labour still further and deeper, and not confine ourselves to the assimilation of labour through the equation of its products. We must add that labour becomes abstract through being assimilated with a particular form of labour, or through the assimilation of its product with a universal equivalent, which was therefore regarded by Marx as the objectification or materialisation of abstract labour.

From this standpoint, an interesting parallel between Marx and Hegel opens up here. The term 'abstract universal' itself, as we know, is reminiscent of Hegel, who distinguishes the abstract universal from the concrete universal. The distinction between the two can be reduced to the fact that the concrete universal does not exclude the differences between the objects which are included within this universal aspect, while the abstract universal excludes such differences.

In order to understand why Marx describes the equated labour of commodity producers as the abstract universal, we have to compare the process of equation of labour in a socialist community with the process of equation of labour in commodity production. We will notice the following distinction. Let us assume that some organ compares the various kinds of labour one with another in a socialist community. What happens here? This organ takes all these kinds of labour in their concrete useful form, since it links them in precisely this form, but it abstracts one of their aspects and says that these kinds of labour are equal to each other in the given circumstances. In this case the equality appears as a characteristic of these concrete kinds of labour, as a characteristic which was abstracted from these forms; but this universal category of equality does not destroy their concrete difference, which manifests itself as useful labour.

In commodity production comparison of this kind is impossible, since there is no organ which consciously equates all these kinds of labour. The labour of a spinner and that of a weaver cannot be equated, so long as they are concrete useful labour. Their equation results only indirectly through the assimilation of each with the third form of labour, namely 'abstract universal' labour (cf. Critique). This determined kind of labour is 'abstract universal' (and not concrete universal) precisely because it does not include the distinctions between the various concrete kinds of labour but precludes these divergences: this kind poses all the concrete kinds of labour in that it appears as their representative.

The fact that in this case Marx intended the distinction between the abstract universal and the concrete universal, which occurs in Hegel, can be seen clearly in the first edition of 'Capital' where in general the traces of Hegelian concepts and Hegelian terminology stand out far more distinctly than in the second. Here there is a paragraph which reads:

> "Within the value-relation and the value expression included in it, the abstractly general accounts not as a property of the concrete, sensibly real; but on the contrary the sensibly-concrete counts as the mere form of appearance or definite form of realisation of the abstractly general ... This inversion, by which the sensibly-concrete counts only as the form of appearance of the abstractly general and not, on the contrary, the abstractly general as property of the concrete, characterises the expression of value. At the same time, it makes understanding it difficult." (The Value Form, pp.39-140).

At another point Marx says:

> "It is as if together with and besides lions, tigers, hares and all the other real animals, which as a group form the various genuses, species, subspecies, families etc of the animal kingdom, there also existed the Animal, the individual incarnation of the whole animal kingdom." (Kapital 1st ed. p.234).

To decipher this statement by Marx, we must say that in commodity production the abstract universal really appears not as characteristic or attribute of the concrete, the sensuous-real (i.e. of the concrete modes of labour), since in order to abstract the specific universal features from these concrete modes of labour, it would need a unified organ, which does not exist in commodity production. The concrete kinds of labour are therefore not assimilated one with another through abstraction of some universal characteristics, but through comparison and equation of each of these kinds with a particular determined concrete kind which serves as phenomenal form of universal labour. In order that concrete labour becomes universal, universal labour must appear in the form of concrete labour, "if the individual's labour time represents universal labour time, or if universal labour time represents individual labour time" (Critique p.32).

It is only in the light of these comments by Marx, which show clear traces of Hegel's influence, that we can understand the passages from the Critique which we mentioned earlier, in which Marx says that labour only becomes social in commodity production by assuming the form of abstract universality.

This idea is generally related to Marx's views on bourgeois society. In his earlier works, in the 'German Ideology' for example, he expresses the idea that in bourgeois society, where a central social organisation of production is lacking, the representation of the social interest always falls to some single organisation, to a group of people, to a single class. This single social class declares its partial interests to be the interests of the whole society and lends its ideas 'the form of universality'. The particular interest is expressed as the general interest and the general as the dominant (German Ideology, I. Collected Works Vol. V p.60). If we compare these remarks by Marx in the Critique with those statements where he says that social labour assumes "the abstract form of universality" and that the value of a commodity assumes the form of a particular determined commodity, the form of money, then the close ideal relationship of these concepts becomes evident.

To conclude the problem of abstract labour, I must take up two criticisms, which have been made against me, in the article by Daschkowski[272], and by various other comrades.

The first criticism was that I apparently seek to substitute for abstract labour the process of abstraction

---

[272] This refers to an article by I. Daschkowski "Abstraktuy trudi eknomitscheskije kategorii Marksa" ("Abstract Labour and Economic Categories in Marx") in Pod Znamenem Marksizma 6, Moscow 1926.

from the concrete characteristic attributes of labour, that is, that I seek to replace abstract labour with the social form of the organisation of labour.

Admittedly, a substitution of this kind, if it had really occurred, would deviate from Marxist theory. But we maintain that the character of people's relations of production in commodity production unconditionally means that labour, both in its qualitative and its quantitative aspect, finds its expression in value and in the magnitude of value of a commodity. If instead of abstract labour we take only the social form of the organisation of labour, it would only help us to explain the 'form of value', i.e. the social form, which a product of labour assumes. We could also explain why a product of labour assumes the form of a commodity which possesses a value. But we would not know why this product assumes this given quantitatively determined value in particular. In order to explain value as the unity of the form of value, the substance of value and the magnitude of value, we have to start out from abstract labour, which is not only social, and socially equated but also quantitatively divided.

One can find formulations in Marx himself, which, if one chose, would be sufficient reason to say that Marx substituted the social form of labour for labour itself. Since it would be tedious to refer to the various points in Marx, I should just like to mention one passage which, if written by anyone but Marx, would sound heretical. The sentence runs: "The labour which posits exchange value is a specific social form of labour" (Critique p.36). In the same place Marx says in a footnote that value is the social form of wealth. If one combines these two statements, then instead of the thesis that labour creates value, we have the thesis that the social form of labour produces the social form of wealth. Some critic would well say that Marx replaces labour completely with the social form of labour: which Marx obviously did not intend.

I should now like to turn to the second criticism. It has been said that my explanations give rise to the impression that abstract labour is only produced in the act of exchange. One could conclude from this that value also is only created in exchange, whereas from Marx's standpoint, value and consequently abstract labour too must already exist in the process of production. This touches on the profound and critical problem of the relations between production and exchange. How can we resolve this difficulty? On the one hand value and abstract labour must already exist in the process of production, and on the other hand Marx says in dozens of places that the process of exchange is the precondition for abstract labour.

Allow me to quote a few examples. I should like to come back to Franklin. Marx says: "But since he does not explain that the labour contained in exchange value is abstract universal social labour, which is brought about by the universal alienation of individual labour ..." etc. (Critique p.56). Franklin's main mistake consequently was that he disregarded the fact that abstract labour arises from the alienation of individual labour.

This is not a question of an isolated comment by Marx. We will show that in the later editions of 'Capital', Marx increasingly stressed the idea that in commodity production only exchange reduces concrete labour to abstract labour.

To return to our earlier comments: "Hence when we bring the products of our labour into relation with each other as values, it is not because we see in these articles the material receptacles of homogeneous human labour. Quite the contrary: whenever, by an exchange we equate as values our different products, by that very act, we also equate as human labour, the different kinds of labour expended upon them." (Capital I p.74).

In the first edition of 'Capital' this sentence had a completely opposite meaning. Marx wrote: "When we bring our products into relation with each other as values to the extent that we see these articles only as material receptacles of homogenous human labour ..." etc. (p.242).

In the second edition Marx altered the sense of this sentence completely, fearing that he would be understood to mean that we consciously assimilate our labour as abstract labour in advance, and he emphasised the aspect that the equation of labour as abstract labour only occurs through the exchange of the products of labour. This is a significant change between the first edition and the second. As you will know, Marx did not confine himself to the second edition of the first volume of 'Capital'. He corrected the text subsequently for the French edition of 1875, and wrote that he was making corrections which he was not able to make in the second German edition. On this basis he assigned to the French edition of 'Capital', an independent scientific value equal to the German original. (cf. Capital I p.22).

In the second edition of 'Capital', we find the famous phrase:

"The equalisation of the most different kinds of labour can be the result only of an abstraction from their inequalities, or of reducing them to their common denominator viz. expenditure of human labour power or human labour in the abstract" (cf. Kapital p.87).

In the French edition Marx replaces the full stop at the end of this sentence with a comma and adds "... and only exchange produces this reduction, by bringing the products of the most diverse kinds of labour into relation with each other on an equal footing" (Le Capital I p.70).

This insertion is highly indicative and shows clearly how far removed Marx was from the physiological conception of abstract labour. How can we reconcile these observations by Marx, of which there are dozens, with the basic thesis that value is created in production?

This should not be too difficult. The point is that the comrades who discussed the problem of the relationship between exchange and production did not in my view distinguish sufficiently clearly between the two concepts of exchange. We have to distinguish exchange as social form of the reproduction process from exchange as a particular phase of this reproduction process, which alternates with the phase of direct production.

At first glance, exchange seems to be a separate phase in the process of reproduction. We can see that a process first takes place in direct production and is then followed by the phase of exchange. Here, exchange is separate from production, and counterposed to it. But exchange is not only a separate phase in the process of reproduction, it stamps the whole process of reproduction with its specific mark and represents a particular social form of the social process of production. Production based on private exchange: Marx frequently characterised commodity production with these words.

To make this point clearer, I will quote Marx's words from the third volume of the 'Theories of Surplus Value' that "Exchange of products as commodities is a method of exchanging labour, [it demonstrates] the dependence of the labour of each upon the labour of the others, [and corresponds to] a certain mode of social labour or social production" (Theories of Surplus Value vol. 3 p.129). Here too we find a statement which explains why Marx regarded exchange as a social form of labour:

"The whole economic structure of society revolves round the form of labour, in other words, the form in which the worker appropriates his means of subsistence." (Theories of Surplus Value p.414).

Let us ask now in exactly what form the labourer acquires his means of subsistence in commodity production. We repeatedly find the following answer to this question in Marx: In commodity production the only form of appropriation of products is the form of their alienation and, because the form of the appropriation of products is the form of social labour, so alienation, exchange, is a determined form of social labour which characterises commodity production.

If one takes into consideration that exchange is the social form of the production process itself, the form which stamps its mark on the course of the production process itself, then many of Marx's statements become completely clear. When Marx constantly reiterates that abstract labour only results from exchange, he means that it is the result of a given social form of the production process. Labour only takes the form of abstract labour, and the products of labour the form of values, to the extent that the production process assumes the social form of commodity production, i.e. production based on exchange.

Thus exchange is the form of the whole production process, or the form of social labour. As soon as exchange really became dominant form of the production process, it also stamped its mark on the phase of direct production. In other words, since today is not the first day of production, since a person produces after he has entered into the act of exchange, and before it also, the process of direct production also assumes determined social characteristics, which correspond to the organisation of commodity production based on exchange. Even when the commodity producer is still in his workshop and has not yet entered into a relationship of exchange with other members of the society, he already feels the pressure of all those people who enter the market as his customers, competitors or people who buy from his competitors, and ultimately pressure from all the members of the society. This link through production and these production relations, which are directly regulated in exchange, continue to be effective even after the specific concrete acts of exchange have ceased. They stamp a clear social mark both on the individual and on his labour and the product of his labour. Already in the very process of direct production itself the producer appears as producer of commodities, his labour assumes the character of abstract labour and the product assumes the character of value.

Here it is necessary to guard against a mistake which is made by many comrades. Many think that because the process of direct production already has a particular social characteristic, the products of labour, and labour in the phase of direct production, must also possess precisely these social characteristics which they possess in the phase of exchange. Such an assumption is totally false, even though both phases (production and exchange) are closely connected to each other, nevertheless the phase of production does not become the phase of exchange. There is not only a certain similarity between the two phases, there is still a certain distinction too. In other words, on the one hand, we recognise that from the moment when exchange becomes the dominant form of social labour, and people produce specifically for exchange, that is in the phase of direct production, the character of products of labour can already be regarded as values. But the characteristic of the products of labour as values is not yet that which they assume when they are in fact exchanged for money, when, in Marx's terms, the 'ideal' value has been transformed into 'real' value and the social form of the commodity is replaced by the social form of money.

The same is also true of labour. We know that commodity owners in their acts of production take the state of the market and of demand into account during the process of direct production, and from the start produce exclusively in order to transform their product into money and thus also transform their private and concrete labour into social and abstract labour. But this inclusion of the labour of the individual in the labour mechanism of the whole society is only preliminary and tentative. It is still subject to a strict test in the process of exchange which can give positive or negative results for a particular commodity producer. Thus the labour activity of the commodity producers in the phase of production is directly private and concrete labour and only indirectly or latently, as Marx puts it, social labour.

Thus when we read Marx's work, and particularly his descriptions of the way in which exchange influences value and abstract labour, we must always ask what Marx had in mind in a particular case — exchange as a form of the production process itself, or exchange as a separate phase counterposed to the phase of production.

In so far as exchange as a form of the production process is concerned, Marx distinctly says that without exchange there is neither abstract labour nor value, that labour only assumes the character of abstract labour with the development of exchange. Marx's views are quite clear and I have developed them in my book.

Where Marx refers to exchange as a separate phase counterposed to the phase of production, he says that labour and the product of labour possess a determined social character even before the process of exchange, but that this character must yet be realised in the process of exchange. In the process of direct production labour is not yet abstract labour in the full sense of the word, but has still to become abstract labour. Numerous statements to this effect can be found in Marx's work. I should like to quote just two passages from the 'Critique'.

"But the different kinds of individual labour represented in these particular use-values, in fact, become labour in general, and in this way social labour, only by actually being exchanged for one another in quantities which are proportional to the labour-time contained in them" (Critique p.45).

Elsewhere Marx writes:

"Commodities now confront one another in a dual form, really as use-values, and nominally as exchange values. They represent now for one another the dual form of labour contained in them since the particular concrete labour actually exists as their use-value, while universal abstract labour time assumes an imaginary existence in their price..." (Critique p.68).

Marx maintains that commodities and money do not lose their differences because of the fact that every commodity must unconditionally be transformed into money. Each is in reality what the other is ideally, and ideally what the other is in reality. All Marx's writing on this show that we must not approach this problem too linearly. We should not think that because commodity producers are already linked to one another by determined social relations in the process of direct production, therefore their products and their labour already possess a directly social character. The labour of a commodity producer is directly private and concrete labour, but together with this it acquires an additional 'ideal' or 'latent' characteristic as abstract universal and social labour. Marx was always amused by the Utopians who dreamed of the disappearance of money and believed in the dogma that "the private labour of a private individual contained in (a commodity) is immediately social labour" (Critique p.86).

We thus come to these conclusions: Abstract labour and value are created or "come about," "become" in the process of direct production (Marx used the expression "werden" more frequently for this process) and are only realised in the process of exchange.

We have spoken up till now of abstract labour. I should now like to move on to value. Our task is the same in regard to the problem of value as it was with abstract labour. I tried to show that within the concept of abstract labour we must also include the characteristic of the social organisation of labour in commodity production. In the same way I should like to show that within the concept of value we must necessarily include the social form of value, the social form which the products of labour assume in commodity production.

The task which lies before us is to introduce social form into the concept of abstract labour and the concept of value.

How is value usually defined, as distinct from exchange value?

If we take the most popular and widespread conceptions, we can certainly say that value is usually understood as the labour which must necessarily be expended for the production of a particular commodity. The exchange value of a particular commodity is understood as the other product or other sum of money, for which a particular commodity is exchanged. If a particular table was produced in three hours' labour and is exchanged for three chairs, then one usually says that the value of the table is equal to three hours of labour, and finds its expression in another product, which is different from the table itself, that is, in these three chairs. The three chairs represent the exchange value of the table.

In this kind of popular definition it is usually unclear whether the value is determined by the labour or whether the value is the labour itself. Naturally from the standpoint of Marx's theory it is correct to say that value is determined by labour. But then the question arises: What is this value, which is determined by labour? We cannot usually find any adequate answer to this in popular scientific explanations.

Hence the readers form the impression that the value of a product is nothing other than the labour which must be expended in its production. The deceptive impression of the complete identity of labour with value is created.

This idea is very widespread in anti-Marxist literature. One can say that the majority of the misunderstandings and misinterpretations which we came across in anti-Marxist literature rest on the false assumption that for Marx labour is also value.

This false impression frequently arises from the lack of understanding of the terminology and the train of thought in Marx's work; for instance Marx's famous words that value is 'congealed' or 'crystallised' labour is usually construed to mean that labour is also value.

This misconception is fostered by the ambiguity of the Russian verb for 'represent' (darstellen). Value 'represents labour'. But the Russian translation can be read not only as meaning that value is the representative or expression of labour — the only conception which is consistent with Marx's theory, but also as meaning that value 'is' labour: This idea is very widespread in the critical literature directed against Marx, and is obviously wrong.

The critics who interpret Marx's statements that labour constitutes the substance of value to mean the complete identity of the two concepts, do not notice the fact that in this case Marx borrowed Hegel's terminology. Anyone who knows Hegel's 'Logic' with the theory of essence, will remember that Hegel uses various terms when he attempts to clarify the relationship between two objects, one which determines and one which is to be determined. He first says that an object appears as the essence of the other, then he defines it as the ground for the latter object, next he describes it as content as distinct from form, later he regards this same object as substance, as cause and finally he moves on to consider the interrelation between two objects. It is an interesting fact that in Marx's works, the whole scale of expressions which we meet in Hegel can be found, now applied to labour. Labour is also described as the essence of value, and as its ground, its content, its substance and its cause. We have to link all these expressions with the methodological principles on which Hegel's theory is based, and it then becomes clear that Marx's thesis that labour is the substance of value, can in no way be interpreted to mean the complete identity of the two.

In my book I advanced this particular thesis in the chapter on the content and form of value. I was mainly trying to show that labour is only substance of value, but does not yet represent value. In other words, when Marx's critics say: 'In Marx's writings the substance of value is labour, consequently labour is value', it must be emphasised that labour is only substance of value, and that in order to obtain value in the full sense of the word we have to add something to labour as the substance of value, namely the social form of value. Only then do we obtain the concept of value in the sense in which it is found in Marx's work.

What then does value represent as the unity of the content or substance (i.e. labour) and the form of value? What is this value as distinct from exchange for Marx? To find an answer to this problem we have to ask the question: How does Marx move from exchange value to value? Why does he find it necessary to form a new and more abstract concept of value, in conjunction with exchange value which appears in reality in the act of exchange?

You will probably know that Marx had not yet made any clear distinction between exchange value and value in the 'Critique of Political Economy'. In the 'Critique' Marx begins his interpretation with exchange value, and from there passes on to value (which he calls exchange value). This transition is entirely imperceptible, smooth and apparently self evident.

In 'Capital' Marx makes this transition completely differently and it is very interesting to compare the first two pages of the 'Critique' with those of 'Capital'.

The first two pages in both books correspond completely; in both alike the exposition begins with use value and moves on to exchange value. The sentence that exchange value at first sight presents itself as a quantitative relation, as proportion, is found in both books but from then on the texts begin to diverge. While Marx passes imperceptibly from exchange value to value in the 'Critique', in 'Capital' the opposite is the case, as if he intends to linger on this point, foreseeing the objections from his opponents. After the sentence mentioned above, Marx comments: "Hence exchange value appears to be something accidental and purely relative, and consequently an intrinsic value, i.e. an exchange value that is inseparably connected with, inherent in commodities, seems a contradiction in terms" (Capital I p.36). Let us take a closer look. As we can see, Marx had in mind an adversary who wanted to prove that nothing exists beyond relative values, that the concept of value in political economy is utterly superfluous. Who was this adversary to whom Marx was referring?

I would rather not commit myself so precisely, but I assume that this adversary was Bailey, who tried to prove that the concept of value in general is unnecessary in political economy, and that we should confine ourselves to the observation and investigation of particular proportions, in which the various commodities are exchanged. Bailey met with great success with his superficial but witty critique of Ricardo, and attempted to undermine the foundations of the labour theory of value. He maintained that we cannot speak of the value of a table, but that we can only say that the table is exchanged for three chairs on one occasion, for two pounds of coffee on another occasion etc. The magnitude of the value of the table is purely relative and varies in different cases. From this Bailey drew the conclusion which led him to deny the concept of value where the concept of value differs from the relative value of a particular product in a given act of exchange. Let us imagine the following case: the value of a table is equal to three chairs. After a year this table is exchanged for six chairs. We think we can say that although the exchange value of the table has altered, its value has remained unchanged, only the value of the chairs has fallen to half their former value. Bailey finds this assertion meaningless. If the chairs' relation of exchange to the table has changed, then the table's relation of exchange to the chairs has changed, and the value of the table consists only in this.

In order to refute Bailey's theory, Marx thought it necessary to develop the thesis that we cannot understand exchange value unless it is traced back to an underlying unity of value. The first section of the first chapter of 'Capital' is devoted to establishing a basis for this idea, of making the transition from exchange value to value and from value to the unity which lies behind it, to labour. The second section is an extension of the first, in that it simply explains the concept of labour in more detail. We can say that Marx makes the transition from the diversity which is observable in the sphere of exchange values to the underlying unity behind all exchange values, that is to value (and ultimately to labour). Here Marx demonstrates the incorrectness of Bailey's conception of the possibility of confining our investigation to the sphere of exchange value. In the third section Marx retraces the journey and explains how the unity of value of a specific product is expressed in its various exchange values.

Previously Marx had moved from diversity to unity; now he moves from unity to difference. Earlier he refuted Bailey's theory; now he supplements Ricardo's theory, in which the transition from value to exchange value was missing. To refute Bailey's theory Marx had to develop Ricardo's theory further.

In fact, Bailey's intention of proving that no value exists except exchange value was made easier by the one-sidedness of Ricardo, who could not show why value appears in a determined form of value. Marx was therefore confronted with two tasks: 1) to prove that behind exchange value we have to discover value and 2) to prove that value leads necessarily to different forms of its manifestation, to exchange value. In this present lecture I should like to deal only with the former task, as it is my concern to clarify the concept of value. A complete elucidation of the concepts of exchange value and money would take me beyond the confines of my theme.

How then does Marx makes the transition from exchange value to value? Critics and commentators on Marx usually suppose that his main argument consists in the well known comparison of corn and iron, on the third page of the first volume of 'Capital' (Capital I p.37). When one equates corn and iron, Marx concludes, then there exists in equal quantities something common to both, the two things must be equal to a third and this third thing is their value. This is usually thought to constitute Marx's central argument and the critical blows of his adversaries are usually directed against this argumentation. There is no work hostile to Marx which does not make some reference to Marx's attempt to prove the necessity of the concept of value by a purely abstract analysis.

But they completely overlooked this fact: the paragraph which deals with the comparison of corn with iron is no more than a conclusion following on from the previous paragraph, which is usually disregarded, not only by the critics but by commentators on Marx also.

The previous paragraph reads:

"A given commodity, e.g. a quarter of wheat is exchanged for 20 pounds blacking, 1.5m silk or 1/2 oz gold etc; in short for other commodities in the most different proportions. But the exchange value of the quarter of wheat remains unchanged, and is expressed only in the blacking, the silk and the gold. Consequently the exchange-value must contain something distinguishable from these phenomenal forms." (Capital I p.37).

Marx worked on this paragraph with care and gave different variations in various editions. We quoted the passage in the Russian translation of the German edition which was edited by K. Kautsky. We can follow the reasoning even more clearly in the second edition of 'Capital', where the end of this passage reads:

"But since x blacking, y silk or z gold etc. each represent the exchange value of one quarter of wheat, x blacking, y silk, z gold etc. must as exchange values be replaceable by each other or equal to each other. Therefore first: the valid exchange values of a given commodity express something equal." (Capital I p.37)

In other words two commodities which are equal to our given commodity, the wheat, are equal to each other. If we take this conclusion into consideration, as emphasised by Marx in the variations quoted, we can see that the next paragraph follows in logical sequence. If follows from this that one and the same commodity can be expressed in the most different use-values. In the paragraph quoted, Marx comes to the conclusion that two commodities, which are exchanged for one and the same commodity, or are equal to a third, are equal to one another. From this follows also with logical necessity the converse conclusion, which Marx reaches in the next paragraph: if two commodities are equal to one another, then they are equal to a third. It is this thought which Marx expresses in the paragraph where he compares the wheat with the iron. Thus Marx's thesis that two commodities which are equal to one another must also be equal to any third is simply a logical conclusion of the previous thesis, according to which two commodities which are equal to a third, are equal to each other. The true sense of Marx's argumentation consists in the statement of a well known fact about commodity production, the fact that commodities can be equated with each other and that a specific commodity can be assimilated with infinite numbers of other commodities. In other words, it is the concrete structure of commodity production which forms the starting point of all Marx's reflections and in no way the purely logical comparison of two commodities.

Marx thus starts out from the fact of the universal equalisation of all commodities with each other, or from the fact that every commodity can be compared with a vast number of other commodities. Nevertheless this assumption alone is not adequate for all the conclusions Marx draws. There is another tacit assumption underlying these which Marx expressed elsewhere.

The second assumption consists in this: we assume that the exchange of a quarter of wheat for any other commodity, is an exchange which is governed by a known regularity (Gesetzmässigkeit), and the regularity of these acts of exchange is due to their dependence on the process of production. We have to reject the notion that the quarter of wheat can be exchanged for any random quantity of iron, coffee etc. We cannot agree with the assumption that the proportions of exchange are laid down each time in the act of exchange itself, and so have a completely accidental character. We maintain that all these possibilities for the exchange of a specific commodity with another, are governed by a determined regularity which is based in the process of production. In this case Marx's whole argumentation takes the following form:

Marx says: let us take not the accidental exchange of two commodities wheat, and iron, but exchange in the form in which it actually occurs in commodity production, and then we will see that each object can be universally equated with all other objects; in other words, we can observe countless numbers of proportions of exchange of a given product with all others. But the proportions of the exchange are not accidental, they are regular, and their regularity is determined by causes which are grounded in the process of production.

Thus we reach the conclusion, that independently of the fact that the value of a quarter of wheat is expressed on one occasion as two pounds of coffee, on another as three chairs etc., the value of a quarter of wheat remains one and the same in all the different cases. If we were to assume that a quarter of wheat has a different value in each of the infinite number of proportions of exchange — and Bailey's assertions amount to this — then we would be acknowledging that complete chaos reigns in the phenomenon of price formation, in that sublime phenomenon of exchange of products, through and by means of which a universal inter-relation of all modes of labour is established.

We can draw certain conclusions from the train of thought which led Marx from exchange value to value. I came to one conclusion earlier, when I referred to the fact that Marx makes commodity production with its universal equation of all products the starting point of his enquiry, an equation which is closely connected with the course of the production process. Marx does not set out from the contrived example of a random comparison of two commodities, nor from a purely logical analysis of all the characteristics which they may have in common, but from the real form of the exchange of products which is characteristic of commodity production. Our second conclusion comes down to this: when Marx compares wheat with iron, he finds in both something 'common' and in this 'common' factor he recognises the value of the products. In the popular literature, one cannot find a clear answer to the question as to what is the 'common' factor in the exchangeable products to which Marx refers. Sometimes it is correctly seen as value, sometimes though it is identified with labour. If we turn to Marx, we find a clear answer to the question, on the fifth page of 'Capital': "Therefore, the common substance that manifests itself in the exchange value of commodities, whenever they are exchanged, is their value." (Capital I p.38). Marx therefore does not move directly from exchange value to labour. From exchange value he moves to the concept of value and then only by further analysis, from the concept of value to labour. Strictly speaking there are three stages in the chain of reasoning, as it moves from exchange value to value and from value to labour.

The conclusion I should like to draw from this, comes down to the fact which we discussed previously, — that the concept of value must be strictly distinguished from the concept of labour, although there is a tendency, particularly in popular interpretations to explain them as identical.

But what then is this value, which we obtained by abstraction from the concrete proportions of exchange, in which our quarter of wheat is equated with other products. Although we are now abstracting from those concrete products, for which our quarter of wheat is exchanged, nevertheless we do not abstract from the social form of value, which this quarter of wheat possesses, that is, we hold that our quarter of wheat has the capacity to be exchanged in a determined proportion for any other product which exists in the particular society.

Further, we consider the product's capacity for exchange to be its characteristic feature, which is subjected to determined laws, and is in particular closely linked with the conditions of manufacture of a specific product. In other words, no longer does the concept of the social labour necessary for its production alone form part of our concept of the value of wheat. The concept of social labour which assumes 'material form', the form of a particular property of a product, is also included together with the 'content of value' and the 'form of value'. I should like to give one quotation to show that Marx distinguishes value from labour as the content of value.

"Every product of labour is, in all states of society, a use value; but it is only at a definite historical epoch in a society's development that such a product becomes a commodity, viz., at the epoch when the labour spent on the production of a useful article becomes expressed as one of the objective qualities of that articles i.e. as its value." (Capital p.61).

Thus the content of value (i.e. labour) and the social form of value are also included in the concept of value. What then is this 'form of value' which as distinct from exchange value is a part of the concept of value itself?

I should like to give one very clear definition of the form of value from the first edition of 'Capital': "The social form of the commodity and the form of value or form of exchangeability are therefore one and the same" (Studienausgabe p.235). As may be seen, the form of value is the description of the form of exchangeability or the social form of the product of labour which contains the capacity to be exchanged for any other commodities, in so far as this capacity is determined by the quantity of labour necessary for the production of a specific commodity. In this way, we did not depart from the social form of the product of labour when we made the transition from exchange value to value. We have only abstracted from that concrete product, in which the value of the commodity is expressed, but we never lost sight of the social form of the product of labour.

Our conclusion can also be formulated thus: Marx analyses the 'form of value' separately from exchange value. In order to introduce the social form of the product of labour in the concept of value itself, we were forced to split or divide the social form of the product of labour into two forms: into the form of value and into exchange value, the former meaning the social form of the product which has not yet concretised in a specific object, but represents as it were the abstract character of a commodity. I have also explained this distinction between the form of value and exchange value in my book. There I considered them both as qualitative and quantitative aspect of exchange value, it is true. I did this mainly because in some places in Marx's work, the terms form of value and exchange value are scarcely distinguished from one another. A complete identification of the form of value with the qualitative aspects and of exchange value with the quantitative cannot be regarded as correct, since both concepts must be considered both from their qualitative as well as from their quantitative side.

The question does not bear directly on our theme and I will therefore not spend any more time on it. I will simply note that this division of the social form of the product into the form of value and exchange value is extensively dealt with in my book. I had to introduce the characteristics of the social form of the product of labour into the concept of value itself, and thus demonstrate the inadmissability of an identification of the concept of value with the concept of labour, an identification frequently made by popular scientific interpretations of Marx's theory. In other words: I had to demonstrate that value arises not only from the substance of value (i.e. labour) but also from the 'form of value', and in order to introduce the form of value into the concept of value itself, I had to distinguish it from exchange value, which Marx considers separately from value. I had to divide the social form of the product into two parts: into social form, which has not yet acquired a concrete appearance, and into that form which has already acquired a concrete and independent character.

Now that the distinction between the form of value and exchange value has been clarified, I should like to turn to the concept of value and develop the relationship between its various aspects: between the content or substance of value and the form of value.

What relation exists between labour and that social form of value with which we have dealt? The general answer to this question runs: the form of value is the adequate and exact form of the expression of what is contained in value (i.e. labour).

In order to explain this idea, we must come back to an earlier example: a table was exchanged for three chairs. We say that this process of exchange is subject to a determined regularity, and dependent on the development of and the alterations in the productivity of labour. But exchange value is a social form of the product, which not only expresses the alterations in the labour, but also conceals and obscures these very changes. It obscures them for the simple reason that exchange value is the relation between two commodities, between the table and the chairs, and therefore the alteration of the proportions of exchange between these two articles gives us no information about whether the labour expended on the making of the table has actually altered. If the table can be exchanged for six chairs after some time has elapsed, then the exchange value of the table has altered, while the value of the table itself may not have changed one iota. In order to examine the process whereby the change in the social form of the product depends on the quantity of labour expended in its making, in its pure form, Marx had to separate the phenomenon as it exists into two parts. He had to cut it across and say that we must study separately those causes which determine the value of the table, and those which determine the value of the chairs, and that one and the same phenomenon of exchange (the fact that the table can now be exchanged for six chairs instead of for three) can either be caused by reasons connected with the table, or by reasons stemming from the conditions of the production of the chairs. To examine the activity of each of these causal chains separately, Marx had to split the fact of the change in the exchange value of the table into two parts and assume that these changes are exclusively caused by reasons effective on the side of the table, i.e. through a change in the productivity of the labour necessary for the production of the table. In other words he had to assume that all the other commodities for which our table is exchanged maintained their original value. Only on this assumption does the change in the value of the table follow from the change in the quantity of labour necessary for its production, and the social form of labour proves to be a more precise and adequate expression of the content of value or the substance of value (that is of the quantity of labour expended in the process of production.)

The determination of value as unity of content (i.e. labour) and social form of value, carries the following advantages. We can break with the widespread identification of value with labour straight away, and so determine the relation of the concept of value to the concept of labour more correctly. On the other hand we can also determine the relation between value and exchange value more correctly. Formerly, when value was regarded simply as labour and had not yet assumed more precise social characteristics, this value was on the one hand identified with labour, and on the other hand separated from exchange value by an abyss. Economists often saw only labour in the concept of value and could not make the transition from this concept to the concept of exchange value. Now, regarding value as the unity of content and form, we link value through its content with the preceding concept, with labour; on the other hand though, we link the concept of value through the form of value with what follows, with exchange value. In fact when we maintain that value is not labour in general, but labour which has assumed the form of the exchangeability of the product, then we necessarily have to make the transition from value to exchange value. Thus the concept of value is inseparably linked with, on the one hand, the concept of labour, and, on the other, with the concept of exchange value. But the inseparable connection of all these concepts should not lead to their identification with each other. We regard value as social labour which has assumed the form of an 'objectified' property of the product of labour, or as the property of the product to be able to be exchanged for any other product, in so far as this property of the product depends on the quantity of social labour necessary for its production.

In conclusion I should like to point out that the ability to split the social form of the product into two parts (the form of value and exchange value, the former itself belonging to the concept of value, while exchange value is only a phenomenal form of value) possibly recalls an analogous procedure in Hegel's writing. Although Marx does not refer anywhere to a connection between his concept and Hegel's philosophy, one can find an essential similarity between the division of the social form in Marx's work, and Hegel's theory of the 'doubling of the form'. I should like to quote a few lines from the so-called small 'Logic' by Hegel:

> "The essential point to keep in mind about the opposition of form and content is that the content is not formless, but has the form in its own self, quite as much as the form is external to it. There is thus a doubling of form. At one time it is reflected into itself; and then is identical with the content. At another time it is not reflected into itself, and then is the external existence, which does not at all effect the content." (Hegel's Logic, Clarendon Press, Oxford 1975 p.189)

I think the distinction Marx made between the form of value, which is included in value itself, and exchange value, which represents something 'external', 'undetermined' in relation to value, bears some similarity with the doubling of form which we find in Hegel.

I now come to the last part of my lecture which concerns the question of the content or the substance of value. All Marxists agree that labour constitutes the content of value, but the problem lies in determining what kind of labour we are speaking of. The previous part of the lecture should have convinced us as to the variety of different concepts which can be concealed in the word 'labour'. What kind of labour therefore constitutes the content of value? Most readers will have taken me to mean that by the content of value I understand labour in its material technical form. I admit that this interpretation is justified since approximately these formulations may be found in my book 'Essays on the Theory of Value'. Nevertheless I must recall that in my book, in the one chapter on the content and form of value, one can find not one, but three formulations which could show that by the content of value I did not mean labour which is studied exclusively from its material technical aspect (3). There I wrote

"Labour as the substance of value is not seen by Marx as a determined quantity of labour, but as something 'independent and absolute', as something accumulated in the product and materially objectified. This labour is examined from the standpoint of the process of division of social labour among the individual branches of production and taken as part of the total social labour in its relation to the latter, as to the whole."

Elsewhere I quoted Marx's words on value as "form, in which the proportional division of labour is expressed." Lastly, the final conclusion of the chapter reads:

"Considered from the qualitative aspect, the relation between labour as 'substance of value' and 'form of value' signifies the relation between the process of division of labour and its specific social, and exchange form."[273]

These references should justify my conclusion that I did not take the content of value to mean labour considered exclusively from the material technical side. Rather my conception approximated to the concept of socially equated and divided labour discussed earlier. But this concept, which can be found in many places in my book, was not adequately explained, and needed important corrections. In the present lecture I have drawn a sharp distinction between socially equated labour in general (which exists not only in commodity production but also, for example, in socialism) and abstract-universal labour as labour which is equated in the specific form appropriate to commodity production. Let us now ask: does Marx understand the content of value to mean socially equated labour in general or abstract universal labour? In other words, when we refer to labour as the content of value, do we include in the

---

[273] These passages were apparently omitted from the German edition of "Studien zur Marxschen Wertheorie," and cannot be traced in the English edition.

concept of labour all those characteristics which we incorporated above in the concept of abstract labour or do we conceive of labour in the sense of socially equated labour which does not incorporate those characteristics which characterise the social organisation of labour in commodity production? Does the concept of labour as the content of value coincide with the concept of abstract labour which constitutes value, or is the character of the former concept broader than this? At first glance one can find arguments in favour of both interpretations of the 'content of value' in Marx's writings. On the one hand one can find arguments which apparently mean that by labour as the content of value, we should understand something more limited than abstract labour, that is, labour without all those social characteristics, which appertain to it in commodity production.

What arguments can we find to support this solution to the problem?

Marx often meant by content of value something which can not only acquire the social form of value but another social form too. Content is understood as something which is capable of assuming differing social forms. It is precisely this ability which distinguishes socially equated labour but not abstract labour i.e. labour which has already assumed a definite social form. Socially equated labour can assume the form of labour organised in commodity production, and the form of labour organised in, for instance, a socialist economy. In other words in this case we are conceiving of socially equalised labour in its abstract form and disregarding those modifications which are brought about in the content itself (i.e. labour) by one or other of its forms.

Does this concept of the content of value exist in this sense in Marx's work? We can now answer this question positively. Think for example of the passage where Marx says that "exchange value is a definite social manner of expressing the amount of labour bestowed upon an object." (Capital I p.82). Labour is clearly being considered as abstract content here, which can assume either one or another social form. When Marx writes in his well known letter to Kugelmann on 11th July 1868 that the social division of labour manifests itself in commodity production in the form of value, he is again regarding socially divided labour as the content, which can assume this or that social form.

In the second paragraph of the section on the fetishism of commodities Marx explains directly that we can find the "content of the determining factors of value" not only in commodity production but also for example in a patriarchal family or on a medieval estate. Here, as we see, labour represents a content which can assume various social forms.

We may now put forward an argument in favour of the opposing thesis, according to which we have to see abstract labour as the content of value.

Firstly, we find a few statements by Marx confirming this, e.g. "(Commodities) relate to abstract human labour as to their common social substance" (Studienausgabe p.235). This statement leaves no room for doubt that abstract labour is not only a creator of value but also substance of value or content of value. The same conclusion may be reached on the basis of methodological considerations.

I demonstrated earlier that in commodity production, socially equalised labour assumes the form of abstract labour, and value as the social form of the products of labour arises necessarily only from this abstract labour. It follows from this that the concept of abstract labour directly preceded the concept of value in our system, and that would show that we must interpret precisely this concept of abstract labour as the basis, content, or substance of value. But one must also not forget that in the question of the relation between content and form Marx took not Kant's but Hegel's standpoint. Kant regarded form as something external in relation to content and as something which joins on to it from the outside. From the standpoint of Hegelian philosophy, content does not represent something which form attaches to from the outside, rather the content itself in its development gives birth to this form, which was contained within this content in concealed form. The form arises necessarily from the content itself.

This is the main thesis of Hegelian and Marxist methodology, a thesis which stands in contradiction to Kantian methodology. From this standpoint, the form of value also must arise of necessity from the substance of value, and consequently we must view abstract labour as the substance of value, in all the fullness of its social features which are characteristic for commodity production. Finally for our last argument, we will point out that when we take abstract labour as the content of value, an essential simplification of the whole Marxist system is achieved, since in this case labour as content of value is not distinguished from the labour which creates value.

So we have reached the paradoxical conclusion that at one point Marx acknowledges socially equalised labour as the content of value, and at another he acknowledges abstract labour as this content.

How can we resolve this contradiction?

It seems to me that the contradiction disappears if we remember the distinction between the two methods, the analytical and the dialectical, which I discussed at the beginning of my lecture. If we set out from value as a determined social form, and ask ourselves what is the content of this form, it will become apparent that this form only expresses the fact in general that social labour was expended: value proves to be form, which expresses the fact of the social equation of labour, as a fact which not only occurs in commodity production, but can also occur in other kinds of production. By proceeding analytically from the finished form to its content, we have found socially equated labour as the content of value. But we reach another conclusion, when we take not the finished form as starting point, but the content itself (i.e. labour) from which the form (value) must necessarily arise. In order to make the transition from labour, regarded as content to value, as form, we have to include in the concept of labour the social form of its organisation in commodity production, i.e. recognise abstract universal labour as the content of value. It is possible that the apparent contradiction in the definition of the content of value in Marx's work can be explained precisely by the distinction between these two methods.

If we now summarise the interpretation discussed in our lecture, we can say that the following five concepts are the basic concepts on which Marxian theory of value and money rests: (1) the relations of production of the commodity producers, (2) abstract labour, (3) value, (4) exchange value and (5) money.

Engels pointed out in his article on Marx's 'Critique of Political Economy', that Marx's contribution consists in showing us the whole system of the bourgeois economy in its inner interrelations (Critique p.226). Applied to these five categories, Marx's contribution consists in showing the inner inseparable interrelations between all these categories. Unfortunately this interrelation was frequently lost sight of by readers of Marx and these categories were each considered separately. Let us recollect how the relationship between the five categories has usually been envisaged.

Let us begin with the relations of production of the commodity producers. This concept was known to all Marxists. It was generally known that the theory of the production relations between people is the basis of Marxian economic theory. But no one made sufficient attempts to show clearly how these categories arose from people's production relations. There was therefore a complete break between the first and second concepts when we made the transition to abstract labour. Abstract labour was defined as physiologically equal labour, that is, the form of the production relations between people as commodity producers had been completely dismissed. We forgot this form and suddenly found ourselves in the sphere of physiologically equal labour, which is the same in all historical epochs.

Making the transition from the concept of abstract labour to the concept of value, it must be said that these two concepts were always closely connected in Marxist literature. It would actually be very strange, if the adherents to the labour theory of value did not link the concept of labour with the concept of value. But this connection was paid for very dearly in that value was almost identified with labour and it was not clear in what way value is actually distinguished from labour. There was a break again in the next transition, from value to exchange value. Value was identified with labour, and so we did not know how exchange value arises from value either. Lastly, the relation between the concept of exchange and the concept of money was always very consistent in Marxist literature already since Marx emphasised this relation and substantiated it in particular. Thus the five categories we listed were split up into three groups. In the first group were the production relations of commodity producers, in the second, abstract labour and value, and in the third, exchange value and money. The system was only interrupted in two places, at the point where we have to move from the relations of production to abstract labour, and then again from value to exchange value.

These interruptions disappear when we regard abstract labour as labour which possesses a determined social form, and value as the unity of content and form.

Through these two reformulations we now obtain an uninterrupted logical interrelation of all the categories listed. A determined form of the production relations of people as commodity producers gives rise to the concept of abstract labour. From abstract labour in commodity production, viewed not as physiologically equal labour but as socially equated labour in a specific form, the concept of value emerged of necessity. The concept of value, considered as unity of content and form, is linked through its content with the preceding concept of abstract labour and through its form with the following concept of exchange value. Finally, the development of exchange leads of necessity to value.

It would be contrary to my intention, if the interrelation between these categories appeared as some logical self-progression of concepts, which each give rise to one another. The close interrelation of the concepts which follow on from one another logically is explained by the fact that all these concepts are built up from the concept of the relations of production, between people as commodity producers. This concept conceals a multitude of real social relations between people, which consistently conflict and develop uninterruptedly. The economic categories express "forms of existence, determinations of existence, often just individual aspects of this given society" (Grundrisse, p.106). The logical unity of the economic categories is due to the real unity of this society, the actual object of our study.

INDEX

A

abolition
17, 18
abstract
11, 26–28, 35, 39, 43, 45, 47, 48, 86, 104, 107, 132, 135–37, 140–46, 148, 163, 165, 169, 172, 173, 175, 184, 188, 194–200, 202, 205, 206, 211–48, 250–52, 256, 259, 273, 341, 369, 370, 372–74, 376, 383, 399, 401, 402, 404, 407, 409, 411, 414–24, 426–30, 432, 435, 439, 440, 445–51
abstraction
11, 12, 18, 43–46, 54, 86, 141, 161, 214, 231, 232, 234, 238, 245, 368, 371, 374–76, 383, 420, 421, 424, 439
alienation
7–11, 13–19, 24–27, 29, 34, 120–24, 237, 415, 423, 426
anarchy
48, 309, 368, 455
Annenkov
20, 22
Anti-Duhring
174, 259
Aristotle
159, 160
autonomous
16, 34, 62, 63, 109, 113–16, 138, 143, 144, 147, 151, 158, 159, 162, 164, 166, 169, 177, 195, 212, 229
autonomy
73, 160

B

Bailey, Samuel
186, 193, 204, 208, 433, 434
Bazarov, V.
100, 266, 387, 388, 393, 394
Bergson, Abram
3
Bessonova, S.
100
Bilimovich, A.
316
Black, C.
60
Blauner, Robert
7, 14
bourgeois
56, 60, 97, 122, 160, 195, 203, 205, 234, 378, 387, 421, 449
Buddhism
7
Bulgakov, S
194, 282, 386

C

Campbell, Robert
3, 37, 38
capital
8, 9, 19, 21, 24, 25, 27, 28, 30–34, 36, 43–45, 47–49, 55, 59–61, 66, 68, 75–84, 87, 89, 93–109, 111, 113–17, 119, 122–26, 129, 132, 141, 142, 147, 150, 155, 159, 160, 162–64, 166, 168, 172, 175, 182, 183, 185–88, 190, 192, 194, 196, 209, 211, 214–17, 220, 231, 236–38, 264, 266, 271, 281, 291, 294, 296, 310, 319, 325, 326, 332–67, 369–74, 377–80, 382, 383, 385, 387–98, 403, 406–8, 411, 413, 418, 419, 423, 424, 432–36, 438–40, 446
capitalism
3, 6, 13, 14, 17, 26, 31, 39–41, 43, 46, 55, 166, 356, 358, 360, 361,

372–75, 395
  capitalist
    5–9, 12–17, 21–23, 25–31, 33, 35–39, 41, 43, 46–49, 53–56, 65, 70, 76–81, 83, 84, 87, 88, 93–96, 98, 99, 105, 108, 111, 112, 114, 119, 121–24, 126, 132, 144, 161–67, 178, 179, 182, 184, 195, 207, 228, 247, 254, 264, 267–69, 272, 273, 289, 290, 292, 301, 303, 304, 306, 307, 309, 312, 313, 327, 332, 333, 335–40, 342–46, 350, 353, 356, 359–63, 367–87, 389, 390, 396, 397
  commodities
    3, 15, 25–28, 30, 32, 35, 36, 41, 43, 48, 60–63, 65, 67, 68, 74, 75, 88, 96, 101, 110, 111, 114, 119, 125, 126, 134–36, 138, 140, 150, 152, 153, 155–60, 162, 167, 169, 174–77, 179, 182, 186, 188–90, 195, 196, 201, 204, 208, 209, 211, 215–17, 220, 225–28, 231, 232, 235, 236, 239, 241, 242, 250, 254, 255, 257–59, 264–66, 270–75, 277–83, 286–90, 293, 294, 296, 301, 302, 304, 306, 308, 315, 319, 323, 332, 334, 337, 339–44, 346, 348, 349, 352, 354, 355, 357, 359–61, 364–68, 372, 373, 375, 377, 380, 383, 386, 391, 392, 412, 413, 425, 427, 429, 433, 435–38, 440, 442, 447
  commodity
    1, 6–8, 13, 16, 19, 24–29, 34, 35, 41, 43, 44, 46–49, 56, 57, 59–70, 72–74, 76, 77, 79, 80, 82, 87–91, 93–96, 98, 99, 102, 104, 109–16, 118–21, 123–26, 129, 130, 132–44, 146–48, 150–56, 158–62, 164–84, 188–90, 193, 195–200, 204, 205, 207–14, 217, 219, 220, 224–37, 239–43, 245, 246, 248, 249, 252–55, 258, 259, 261, 265, 267, 268,

271, 273, 281, 283, 286–89, 297, 300–303, 326, 330, 332–34, 336, 337, 339–43, 345, 348, 349, 356–62, 366, 368, 369, 371, 373–76, 381, 383, 387, 389–91, 393–95, 403–5, 407–16, 418–23, 425–30, 435–40, 445–51
  commune
    226, 227
  communism
    17, 455
  community
    3, 15, 62, 138, 139, 170–72, 224, 229, 243, 246, 247, 249, 406–10, 414, 419
  competition
    48, 86, 95, 151, 178, 179, 268, 272–74, 287, 301, 303, 320, 322, 330, 332, 338, 340, 351, 356, 358–61, 364
  concrete
    12, 26, 27, 46, 47, 53–56, 81, 84, 92, 104, 118, 123, 135, 136, 140–42, 146, 148, 154, 161, 170, 171, 185, 188, 196, 197, 202, 206, 209–17, 220, 223, 224, 228–37, 240–42, 253, 273, 371, 373, 374, 376, 380, 381, 383, 384, 388, 396, 401, 402, 405, 406, 410, 418–20, 422, 423, 426–29, 436, 439–41
  consciousness
    9, 10, 21, 23, 25, 60, 86, 120, 126, 141, 217, 264
  contradiction
    71, 81, 85, 117, 179, 183, 186, 200, 253, 333, 388, 395, 433, 448, 449
  create
    19, 22, 24, 72, 95, 123, 179, 222, 223, 227, 230, 235, 251, 257, 258, 295, 299, 302, 378, 380, 385, 393

creative
7–10, 12, 16, 18, 26–30, 35
criticism
9, 10, 113, 124, 179, 183, 256, 261, 268, 388, 421, 423
critique
9, 13, 20, 23, 25, 30, 33, 56, 59, 75, 90, 92, 96, 113, 121, 123, 125, 126, 129, 165, 172, 176, 185, 186, 207, 211, 213, 214, 219, 220, 230, 231, 234, 235, 237, 242, 245, 249, 256, 257, 264, 299, 307, 349, 352, 373, 388, 394, 401, 409, 411, 414, 415, 417–19, 421–23, 428, 429, 432, 433, 449

D

Daschkowski, I.
421
dialectical
20, 81, 84, 108, 129, 142, 200, 402–4, 416, 448
Dietzel
160, 183
distribution
35, 42, 43, 47, 48, 90, 91, 109, 115, 133, 134, 136–38, 143–51, 155, 160, 169, 170, 173, 174, 176–79, 182–84, 208, 211, 224, 227, 249, 260, 265–67, 269, 277, 278, 288, 294, 297, 299, 301–3, 309, 311–14, 316, 326, 332–37, 340, 341, 343–47, 357, 358, 361–63, 368–71, 375, 391, 411

E

economic
3–7, 9, 15–18, 24, 27, 29, 31, 34–42, 53–55, 59–61, 70, 73, 75–78, 83, 85, 86, 89, 91–98, 100–102, 104–9, 111–24, 132, 137, 138, 142–44, 148, 149, 151, 155, 156, 158–60, 162–67, 169, 171, 179–83, 207, 208, 212, 214, 216, 217, 222, 223, 229, 231, 233, 240, 245, 267, 268, 271, 272, 281, 283, 285–87, 294, 297, 298, 302–6, 308, 309, 312–14, 319, 323, 340, 347, 367, 368, 372, 374, 375, 378, 380, 383, 389, 396, 398, 401, 409, 421, 425, 449, 451
economics
3–6, 31–34, 38, 39, 42, 44, 87, 88, 120, 121, 161, 245, 292, 382, 397
economy
3–9, 15, 23, 25–30, 33, 35, 36, 39–41, 43, 44, 46–49, 53–56, 59–62, 64, 66, 68–70, 73, 75–77, 80, 84, 86–92, 96–100, 104, 105, 107–9, 111–14, 118, 119, 122–26, 129–44, 146–49, 151–56, 158, 160–62, 165, 167–82, 184–86, 188, 189, 193–95, 197–200, 204, 207–9, 211, 212, 214, 215, 217–20, 222, 223, 225–27, 229, 230, 232–37, 239, 240, 243–45, 247–49, 253–55, 257–60, 263–66, 268, 269, 271, 274, 280, 281, 290, 292, 297, 299, 304, 305, 307, 309, 312, 313, 316, 319, 322, 323, 327, 332–40, 343–46, 353, 356–64, 367–76, 378–80, 382–84, 386, 388, 390, 395, 397, 401, 403, 406, 407, 414, 417, 432, 433, 446, 449
Engels, Friedrich
8, 12, 20, 24, 64, 97, 121, 141, 147, 174, 215, 259, 372, 449, 455
exchange-value
156, 186, 188, 190, 195, 198, 390, 435

exchange-values
188
existentialism
7

F

factory
7, 14, 63, 71, 116, 279, 377, 381, 385, 394
family
18, 121–24, 126, 132, 198, 231, 408, 447, 455
family-community
170
fetishism
1, 6, 8, 13, 16, 19, 24, 25, 27, 29, 32, 34, 35, 41, 49, 56, 57, 59–62, 69, 87, 90, 91, 113, 114, 117–21, 123–26, 129, 130, 142, 143, 168, 198, 220, 246, 368, 412, 447
Feuerbach
10, 11, 120, 121
Fischer, G.
165, 183, 209, 256, 257

G

Galiani
96
Ganilh
205
Gerlach
217
Gottheil
41

H

Hegel, Georg
9, 10, 121, 199, 209, 418, 419, 431, 444
Heidelberg
209
Heimann
183, 352
Hilferding
53, 69, 129, 151, 166, 167, 179, 194, 219, 261, 268, 340, 396
human
4, 7–12, 15–20, 22, 24, 26, 30, 32, 33, 35–37, 39, 40, 42, 44, 53, 59–61, 66, 70, 85, 87, 89, 92, 104, 110, 117, 118, 121–24, 126, 139, 140, 142, 143, 159, 172, 175, 199, 216, 217, 220–26, 228, 231, 232, 235, 236, 238, 245, 270, 379, 393, 394, 405–8, 411, 413, 414, 423, 424, 455
humanism
17

I

Ideology
12, 19, 20, 24, 421
individual
11, 12, 14, 19, 21, 23, 25–27, 31, 35, 37, 39, 45, 46, 62–64, 66, 70, 72, 73, 75, 76, 82, 84, 85, 97, 105, 114, 115, 126, 131–33, 137, 138, 140, 141, 144, 147, 149–55, 158, 170–72, 174, 176–78, 181, 186, 188, 194, 207, 210–14, 220, 223, 225, 230–35, 237, 240–42, 254–56, 263, 264, 270–75, 277, 280, 281, 283, 287, 288, 308–10, 333, 335, 339, 340, 350, 352, 355, 357–59, 362–64, 372, 389, 395, 405, 406, 408–11, 415, 418, 421, 423, 426–29, 445, 451
intellectual
5, 39, 42, 163, 257, 385, 388

K

Kant, Immanuel
199, 447
Kapital
5, 6, 44, 60, 75, 100, 103, 175, 192, 196, 199, 236, 238, 319, 407, 412, 420, 424
Kautsky, Karl
60, 216, 436

L

labor
4, 7–9, 12–17, 25–29, 31, 35–38, 40, 41, 43–49, 53, 62–64, 66, 67, 69, 71, 73, 76–78, 80–83, 87–90, 92, 94, 95, 97, 99, 101–5, 107–11, 114–16, 119, 120, 122–25, 127, 129, 130, 132–55, 157, 159–62, 164–84, 186, 187, 190–288, 290, 291, 293, 294, 297, 299–318, 320–23, 326, 327, 331–37, 339–99
labor-abstract
136, 333, 366, 367, 370
labor-power
26, 28, 30, 78, 93, 99, 216, 220, 232, 236, 238, 254, 258, 259, 335, 344, 365
labor-time
27, 43, 153, 192, 193, 203, 242, 249–51, 253, 256, 258, 259, 270, 271, 276, 281, 284, 319, 352, 396
labor-value
48, 49, 161, 291, 315, 316, 332–34, 339, 343–46, 349, 354, 365–70, 372–75
labour
15, 16, 28, 30–34, 41, 42, 49, 97, 401–34, 438–51
land
31, 32, 43–45, 67, 76–79, 90, 109–11, 177, 314, 317
landlord
30, 77–80, 90
law
45, 77, 90, 136, 145, 148–52, 158, 166, 167, 179, 181, 184, 208, 263, 266, 269, 289, 306, 307, 322, 332, 343, 369, 371–73, 375, 384, 391, 396
Liebknecht
257, 276

M

market
3, 25, 26, 28, 35, 36, 39, 42, 43, 61–67, 73, 95, 109, 125, 130–33, 136, 138, 139, 142, 148, 149, 151–53, 155, 174, 179, 180, 182, 185, 202, 204, 207, 208, 214, 233, 240, 241, 247, 253, 260, 264, 265, 267–69, 271–88, 291–94, 296, 298, 300–312, 314, 315, 317, 319, 321, 325, 326, 328, 334, 336, 339, 342, 344–46, 367–69, 372, 417, 426, 427
Marx, Karl
3, 6–13, 15–25, 27–34, 36–46, 48, 56, 59–61, 63, 64, 66–68, 75, 79–81, 85, 86, 90–93, 96–114, 116, 118–26, 129, 137, 140–44, 147, 149, 150, 152, 153, 155–63, 165–67, 172, 174–77, 179, 183–94, 196–205, 208, 209, 211, 214–17, 220, 221, 225–29, 231–39, 241, 242, 244, 245, 249–51, 256, 258, 259, 261, 264, 268, 270–72, 276, 281–84, 287, 294, 299–301, 307, 308, 313, 317, 319, 320, 332–34, 336, 341, 346, 347, 349, 350, 352, 354, 356, 359, 362, 364, 365, 367, 370–74,

377–80, 382–92, 394–97, 401–3, 405–9, 411–16, 418–26, 428, 429, 431–50, 455
  Marxian
    3, 41–43, 163, 402, 404, 411, 412, 417, 449
  Marxism
    38, 59, 81, 110, 117, 182, 183, 215, 227, 287, 318
  material
    7, 20–23, 27, 29, 30, 35, 49, 54, 66–76, 78, 80–83, 86–90, 92, 96, 98, 99, 103–6, 108–12, 118–20, 123–26, 130, 131, 139, 143, 144, 153, 154, 158–60, 162, 170, 174–76, 193, 194, 202–4, 206, 209, 212, 214, 217, 226, 228, 236, 238, 245, 246, 270, 282, 351, 353, 368, 377, 379–82, 385–94, 396, 397, 405, 406, 414, 423, 424, 439, 444, 445
  materialism
    11, 53, 54, 90, 91, 161, 202
  money
    3, 16, 28, 29, 31, 59, 66–69, 72, 75, 80–82, 87, 93–102, 104, 105, 107, 109–12, 116, 123–26, 131, 138, 141, 163, 207, 208, 210, 213, 229, 230, 233, 234, 241, 242, 265, 336, 352, 376, 382–84, 389–91, 402, 403, 415, 417, 418, 421, 427, 429, 430, 435, 449, 450, 455

N

natural
  28, 60, 67, 68, 87, 88, 94, 107, 147, 159, 160, 177, 209, 218, 225, 230, 231, 295, 298, 299, 359, 372, 374–76, 378, 382, 406
nature
  11, 12, 14, 17, 18, 20, 53, 60, 86, 88–90, 111, 118, 139, 142, 151, 156, 161, 179, 190, 195, 208, 215, 216, 228, 231, 232, 237, 244, 246, 248, 313, 380, 382, 385, 405, 413, 417

O

objective
  5, 6, 12, 13, 38, 44, 61, 62, 68, 88, 89, 103, 113, 116, 117, 126, 138, 157, 178, 216, 264, 267, 336, 340, 378, 379, 383, 386, 396, 439
order
  13, 19, 21, 23, 24, 32, 37, 43, 70, 93, 107, 108, 111, 123, 137, 142, 146, 154, 161, 181, 185, 187, 190, 191, 196, 197, 200, 201, 227, 238, 241, 243, 245, 246, 266, 275, 286, 321, 338, 354, 378–80, 382, 416, 419, 420, 422, 427, 432, 434, 440–42, 449, 454
organisation
  404–6, 408–10, 413, 416, 421, 422, 426, 429, 446, 449
organization
  71, 138, 139, 141, 158, 170, 171, 197, 214, 219, 222, 228, 232, 233, 236, 240, 245, 376, 380, 382, 387, 390, 396
ownership
  30, 45, 78, 111, 114, 151, 157, 167, 389, 391–94

P

phenomena
  33, 49, 61, 85, 86, 89, 91, 100, 109–13, 117, 120, 121, 131, 142, 144, 145, 149, 152, 154, 162, 167, 177, 179, 184, 203, 204, 212, 214, 281, 298, 306, 313, 314, 323, 343, 368,

370, 373–75, 386, 397
philosophy
10–13, 18, 20, 21, 41, 42, 97, 116, 123, 124, 126, 199, 209, 444, 448
Physiocrats
216
poverty
12, 15, 20, 21, 97, 123, 124, 126
power
10, 12, 16, 18, 26–31, 33, 34, 41, 46, 48, 49, 59, 78, 89, 95, 104, 115, 122, 123, 161, 163, 254, 258, 259, 268, 269, 281, 284, 285, 288, 289, 293, 295, 297, 300, 311, 334, 336, 338, 350, 351, 364, 365, 390, 413, 424
price
3, 6, 8, 26–29, 36, 39–43, 46, 48, 49, 63, 67, 101, 109, 110, 113, 131–33, 148, 149, 157, 167, 177, 179, 182–84, 190, 225, 242, 263, 271–74, 277, 282–85, 288–98, 300, 303–8, 310, 314–30, 332, 333, 339–44, 346–49, 352, 354, 360, 363, 366–71, 374, 376, 429, 438
production
4, 5, 7, 8, 12, 13, 20–23, 25, 26, 28–33, 35, 36, 42, 43, 46–49, 53–56, 60–109, 111–20, 124–26, 129–60, 162, 164–67, 169, 172–74, 176–84, 189–91, 193, 195, 196, 201–4, 206, 208–13, 216, 219, 221–24, 226, 228–33, 237, 239–51, 253, 255, 260, 261, 263, 264, 266, 268–74, 276–86, 288, 290–322, 324–63, 366–74, 376–98, 404–16, 418–23, 425–30, 436–40, 442, 443, 445–51
productivity
21, 31, 32, 47, 48, 89, 104–8, 133, 135, 136, 143, 144, 201–4, 208, 209, 252, 260, 272–82, 286, 288, 290, 310, 313–16, 318, 320, 327–29, 331–34, 343, 345, 348, 349, 357, 365–67, 369–71, 441, 442
products
25, 27, 29, 31, 32, 35, 46, 47, 49, 62–64, 66, 67, 69–71, 74, 76, 81–83, 88, 90, 94, 106, 109–11, 123, 125, 126, 132, 136–38, 140, 141, 143, 144, 147, 148, 150–54, 169, 171–78, 180–83, 185, 190, 193, 195, 202, 204, 207, 210, 211, 214, 222, 223, 229, 231–33, 235, 237–40, 242, 246–50, 253–56, 258–63, 265–69, 271, 272, 274–76, 278, 282, 286, 295, 297, 300, 302–8, 311, 314, 318–20, 329, 334, 339, 346, 347, 360, 362, 368, 369, 371, 373, 385, 389, 391, 392, 404, 405, 410, 411, 413, 414, 416–18, 423–27, 429, 430, 438, 439, 447
profit
28, 31, 33, 46, 48, 81, 83, 89, 95, 105, 107, 109, 115, 132, 163, 164, 167, 182, 215, 219, 225, 264, 273, 315, 332, 337–41, 343, 348–67, 370, 371, 374, 378, 384, 454
Proudhon, Pierre
20, 122–24

Q

qualitative
16, 28, 29, 135, 137, 140, 144, 145, 155, 157, 158, 167, 178, 192, 201–4, 209, 233, 246, 248, 250, 253, 270, 281, 422, 440, 441, 445
quantitative
28, 29, 119, 135, 137, 140, 144–46, 148, 155, 157, 158, 167, 184, 185, 192, 193, 201–4, 209, 212, 243,

246–49, 251, 253, 270, 274, 279, 281, 299, 329, 349, 367, 368, 412, 413, 422, 433, 440, 441
  quantity
    28, 30, 47, 62, 69, 130–35, 141, 144, 156, 173, 179, 180, 182, 189, 194, 196, 201–3, 207, 209, 214, 218, 229, 243, 247–50, 256, 258, 259, 265, 270, 271, 275, 278, 281–84, 286–88, 291–94, 296, 300–314, 323–25, 327–32, 334, 337, 344, 347, 348, 351, 353, 356, 357, 363, 412, 413, 415, 437, 440, 442, 443, 445

R

racism
  48
regulation
  25, 35, 37, 43, 44, 47, 48, 63, 67, 125, 278
revolution
  23, 112, 163
Ricardo
  28, 38, 39, 44, 45, 86, 113, 121, 124, 186, 187, 193–95, 203, 205, 208, 316, 317, 319, 433, 434

S

servant
  31, 382, 384
slavery
  159, 408
socialism
  3, 24, 40, 122–24, 173, 445
socialist
  17, 42, 70, 111, 121, 123, 132, 134, 139, 170, 172–74, 198, 226, 227, 229, 243, 244, 246, 247, 249, 303, 406–10, 412, 414, 419, 446
society
  3, 5, 8, 9, 12–15, 17, 18, 21–23, 25–27, 29–31, 33–37, 41, 43, 46–48, 53–56, 62–66, 70–77, 79–84, 90, 92, 93, 95–98, 105, 109, 111, 114, 115, 118, 119, 122–24, 126, 129, 130, 132–35, 138–40, 142, 144, 145, 147, 149–56, 159–62, 164–68, 170, 171, 173, 174, 177, 180–82, 184, 195, 202, 212, 219, 224, 228–31, 234, 235, 240, 241, 250, 254, 258, 261, 264, 267, 268, 271–73, 278, 283, 286, 288–90, 294, 297–99, 301–3, 306, 309, 314, 333, 336, 346, 347, 350, 353–57, 363, 367, 369, 370, 374, 380, 390, 406, 408, 410, 412, 421, 425–27, 439, 451, 455
  state
    10, 18, 54, 105, 117, 132, 134, 137, 144, 147, 148, 157, 177, 178, 195, 234, 241, 242, 248, 260, 268, 277, 278, 282, 284, 291–93, 296, 299, 304, 312, 316, 326, 340, 343, 360, 384, 427
  Stepanov
    100, 266, 376
  Stolzmann
    245
  structure
    6, 8, 14, 17, 25, 55, 56, 59–61, 63, 64, 77, 91, 92, 104, 114, 126, 129, 130, 142, 153, 154, 156, 159, 160, 164, 165, 169, 188, 277, 288, 311, 320, 329, 340, 425, 436
  subjective
    88, 116, 117, 149, 154, 157, 179, 218, 264, 316, 336, 383
  subsistence
    77, 107, 108, 259, 288, 289, 306, 336, 337, 348, 350, 351, 357, 365, 379, 425

surplus
28, 29, 48, 93, 97, 104, 107, 108, 120, 163, 164, 166, 181, 205, 215, 278, 284, 332, 337, 339, 342, 344, 346, 350–66, 377–80, 382, 383, 385, 387–90, 392, 425

surplus-value
89, 272, 338, 352, 356, 377–79, 381

system
4, 35, 37, 38, 41, 42, 45, 47, 53, 55, 59, 60, 62, 66, 67, 70, 71, 73, 75, 79, 83, 93, 96, 100, 101, 113, 115, 116, 119, 121, 123, 129, 132, 133, 135, 150, 156, 162–64, 166, 172, 183, 202, 205, 206, 213, 224, 227, 231, 245, 256, 268, 276, 280, 293, 309, 312, 313, 332, 362, 364, 368, 369, 374, 378, 380–84, 389, 395–97, 399, 405, 406, 410, 412, 415, 447–50

T

theories
3, 6, 24, 39, 86, 101, 105, 120, 154, 166, 205, 216, 284, 320, 368, 371, 376–78, 380, 385, 387–89, 425

theory
6–8, 10, 11, 13, 16–19, 23, 24, 27–29, 31, 34–46, 53–57, 59–61, 88–91, 104–6, 109, 110, 112–14, 117–21, 123, 124, 126, 127, 129–31, 136, 137, 140–48, 153–58, 160–63, 165–68, 172, 176, 177, 179–81, 183, 184, 186–88, 190–92, 194, 195, 202–4, 207–9, 212, 214–17, 219–22, 227, 232, 243, 244, 246, 247, 253–55, 257, 258, 260, 261, 266–68, 281, 282, 297, 306–8, 314, 316–18, 320, 322, 323, 331–33, 343, 344, 347, 349, 350, 353, 361, 363, 365–68, 371–77, 380, 384, 389, 396, 401–3, 405, 411, 417, 422, 430–34, 441, 444, 449, 450, 454, 455

U

underproduction
133, 293, 311

universal
18, 101, 120, 172, 195, 197, 200, 213, 214, 218, 231, 242, 409, 411, 414–21, 423, 429, 437, 438, 445, 449

V

value
6–8, 13, 24, 27–29, 35–48, 53, 59, 60, 62, 65–69, 72, 77, 79–82, 87, 88, 92–94, 96–99, 101, 104–10, 113–17, 119–21, 123–27, 129–69, 173, 175–77, 179–210, 212, 214–23, 225–29, 231–41, 243–46, 250, 253–86, 288, 290–308, 310–22, 324, 326–37, 340–44, 346–54, 356–83, 385, 387–93, 395–97, 401–5, 411–18, 420–25, 427–51

value-form
195, 204, 232

W

wage
29, 76–79, 83, 97, 98, 101, 102, 104, 111, 123, 132, 139, 254, 289, 342, 344, 350, 369, 380, 382, 384, 390

wage-labor

13, 14, 17, 87, 335

wages

31, 107–9, 123, 164, 225, 335, 342, 350, 378, 379, 381

worker

7, 14–16, 26–30, 34, 41, 76, 78, 94, 99, 112, 121–23, 243, 247, 249, 251, 253, 254, 258, 334, 381, 384, 425

working

4–6, 10, 13, 26, 27, 33, 35–37, 39, 40, 43, 46, 49, 53, 60, 62–67, 70, 74, 89, 92, 104, 110, 111, 122–24, 133, 149, 152–55, 158, 174, 183, 193–95, 205, 210, 212, 214, 222–24, 229, 232, 233, 236, 241, 243, 248–51, 271, 283, 289, 334, 347, 351, 368, 380, 382

Other Radical Reprints

1. *Catechism of a Revolutionist - Sergey Nechayev*
2. *Society of the Spectacle - Guy Debord*
3. *The Right To Be Lazy - Paul Lafargue*
4. *Manifestoes of Surrealism - Andre Breton*
5. *Art and Religion - Max Stirner*
6. *Unfixing Authority - Mikhail Bakunin*
7. *Anarchy and the Sex Question - Emma Goldman*
8. *The Feminist Manifesto - He-Yin Zhen*
9. *Marxist Theory and Revolutionary Tactics - Anton Pannekoek*
10. *The Revolutionary Catechism - Mikhail Bakunin*
11. *The Revolt of the Unique - Renzo Novatore*
12. *What Was The USSR? - The Aufheben Collective*
13. *The Human Species and The Earth's Crust - Amadeo Bordiga*
14. *Dialogue With Stalin - Amadeo Bordiga*
15. *The Right To Be Greedy - For Ourselves!*
16. *A World Without Money: Communism - Friends of 4M wrkrs*
17. *The Holy Family - Marx & Engels*
18. *Paris: May 1968 - Maurice Brinton*
19. *What is Communism? - Paul Mattick*
20. *Theories of Surplus Value Vol. 1 - Karl Marx*
21. *Theories of Surplus Value Vol. 2 - Karl Marx*
22. *Theories of Surplus Value Vol. 3 - Karl Marx*

Coming Soon

Capital and Community - Jacques Camatte

The American Communist Reader

A Black Communist Reader

The Chinese Anarchist Reader

The Paris Commune Reader

The He-Yin Zhen Reader

The Max Stirner Reader

Reform and Revolution - Paul Mattick

Lesson of the Counterrevolutions - Amadeo Bordiga

Fundementals for a Marxist Orientation - Amadeo Bordiga

Quotations - Mao Tse Tung

The Ego and Its Own - Max Stirner

The World's First Anarchist Manifesto - Anselme Bellegarrigue

The Destruction of Nature - Anton Pannekoek

Principles of Communism - Friedrich Engels

A Brief Description of Egoist Communism - D.Z. Rowan

Platform - Nestor Makhno

Marx and Keynes - Paul Mattick

Mutual Aid - Peter Kropotkin

Economic and Philosophic Manuscripts of 1844 - Marx

Contribution to the Critique of Political Economy - Marx

The Poverty of Philosophy - Marx

The World's First Anarchist Manifesto - Bellegarrigue

Radical Reprints

The Radical Database

Linktree

The Radical Reprint series is an imprint of Pattern Books and Schizine to make radical theory immediately accessible through cheap books and cheap/free zines, and is a project of translating and recirculating forgotten works.

We deserve to receive free revolutionary theory anywhere. In order to change the world, we deserve the privilege to access awareness of the way the world operates, we deserve immediate access to everything that came before us and everything that currently exists.

The Radical Reprint books, such as this one, are printed to make press-printed books more accessible. These are not printed for profit, they are printed a few cents above the cost to manufacture. All proceeds from the print books go to mutual aid funds -- directly to mutualaidhub.org

To print radical reprint zines and pocket books, the PDF files are available on Internet Archive, Radical Reprint Google Drive (bit.ly/2OYZ3rz), Issuu, and radicalreprint.com or .org or whatever we're using at the time you see this. It is recommended you take over a printing press to print more and disseminate theory to everyone.

For more online theory/strategy/support, please check out the Google Drive folder at bit.ly/3jCEaka, and check theradicaldatabase.com for more resources, mutual aid, and reading lists. For further links, scan the Linktree code.

Everyone is encouraged to make their own Radical Reprint, anyone who wants to have their reprint/comic/zine, etc directly in the series and printed, contact virtualsituation@protonmail.com

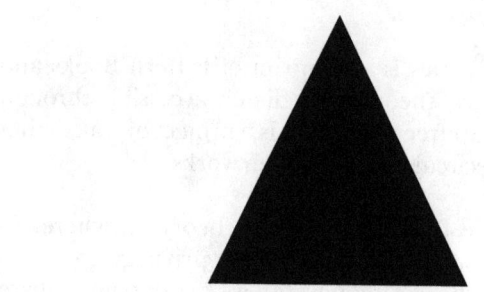